ISBN 978-1-333-60070-9
PIBN 10524908

This book is a reproduction of an important historical work. Forgotten Books uses
state-of-the-art technology to digitally reconstruct the work, preserving the original format
whilst repairing imperfections present in the aged copy. In rare cases, an imperfection in
the original, such as a blemish or missing page, may be replicated in our edition. We do,
however, repair the vast majority of imperfections successfully; any imperfections that
remain are intentionally left to preserve the state of such historical works.

For support please visit www.forgottenbooks.com

1 MONTH OF
FREE
READING

at
www.ForgottenBooks.com

By purchasing this book you are eligible for one month membership to ForgottenBooks.com, giving you unlimited access to our entire collection of over 700,000 titles via our web site and mobile apps.

To claim your free month visit:
www.forgottenbooks.com/free524908

English
Français
Deutsche
Italiano
Español
Português

www.forgottenbooks.com

Mythology Photography **Fiction**
Fishing Christianity **Art** Cooking
Essays Buddhism Freemasonry
Medicine **Biology** Music **Ancient
Egypt** Evolution Carpentry Physics
Dance Geology **Mathematics** Fitness
Shakespeare **Folklore** Yoga Marketing
Confidence Immortality Biographies
Poetry **Psychology** Witchcraft
Electronics Chemistry History **Law**
Accounting **Philosophy** Anthropology
Alchemy Drama Quantum Mechanics
Atheism Sexual Health **Ancient History**
Entrepreneurship Languages Sport
Paleontology Needlework Islam
Metaphysics Investment Archaeology
Parenting Statistics Criminology
Motivational

IVING ONDON

ITS WORK AND ITS PLAY
ITS HUMOUR AND ITS PATHOS
ITS SIGHTS AND ITS SCENES

EDITED BY

EORGE R. SIMS

VOL. II

WITH OVER 500 ILLUSTRATIONS

CASSELL AND COMPANY LIMITED

London, Paris, New York & Melbourne.—MCMII

CONTENTS.

CONTENTS.

LIST OF ILLUSTRATIONS.

LIST OF ILLUSTRATIONS.

The Illustrations are from Drawings by J. H. BACON, GORDON BROWNE, R.I., R.B.A., JAMES DURDEN, J. S. ELAND,
C. H. FINNEMORE, H. H. FLERE, CLEMENT FLOWER, A. H. FULLWOOD, PROFESSOR MAURICE GRÜN, A. P. GARRATT,
W. H. HUMPHRIS, E. LANDER, W. H. MARGETSON, F. PEGRAM, H. PIFFARD, VICTOR PROUT, W. RAINEY, R.I.,
EDWARD READ, A. MONRO SMITH, ISAAC SNOWMAN, ALLEN STEWART, W. R. S. STOTT, L. CAMPBELL TAYLOR,
H. E. TIDMARSH, F. H. TOWNSEND, C. D. WARD, ENOCH WARD, R.B.A.; *and from Photographs, nearly
all of which were specially taken for this work by* MESSRS. CASSELL AND COMPANY, LIMITED.

Photo : Turt & Son, Notting Hill, W.

NEW SCOTLAND YARD.

LIVING LONDON.

NEW SCOTLAND YARD.

By MAJOR ARTHUR GRIFFITHS.

PROTECTION is the keynote of the London police system. To secure the comfort and safety of the people, to shield and safeguard personal liberty, to protect property, to watch over public manners and public health — such are the aims and objects of the vast organisation which has its heart and centre in New Scotland Yard.

The work of a police began, as its name implies, when men gathered together to live in a *polis* or city, and an essential part of good government was to empower a few to shield and defend the many. Despots used the weapon of the police to enslave and oppress ; in these latter days a fussy and too paternal authority, moved by the best intentions, may tend to lessen the self-reliance of law-abiding citizens, but the latter are taught, and they have learnt the lesson, that the policeman, according to our modern methods, is their best friend. His more serious functions, coercion, repression, vindication, are, as a rule, kept in the background ; most people rely upon him rather than fear him. It may be his painful duty to arrest you and lock you up if you offend, but he much prefers to be your guide and champion, to help and stand by you at every turn. His eager and unremitting guardianship is everywhere constantly on view : at the crowded street crossing, when with uplifted finger he stays the multitudinous thunder of the traffic ; in the lonely night watches, when he tries every door and window and, if needs be, rouses the careless householder to look to his fastenings, or, later, risks his valuable life against the murderous burglar. See the trustfulness with which the lost child trots beside him, hand in hand, securely confident of the kindness of this great man, who has babies of his own at home ; see him again amidst the turbulent East-Enders, giving short shrift to the ruffianly wife-beater, or in Hyde Park at a stormy Sunday meeting, or at a fire, or after an accident. With gentle or rough, he is always the same, civil-spoken, well-mannered, long-suffering but sturdy and uncompromising servant of the public.

The constable on his beat, with the law at his back, possessing and exercising power and responsibility, is the outward and visible sign of the ruling authority. He stands at one end. the Chief Commissioner, who only wears uniform on State occasions. at the other The former is in actual contact with people and things; the latter inspires and directs him, acting through him as the unit that distributes the current, so to speak. of concentrated authority through all the ramification of the colossal machine. The Chief Commissioner is subject to the

trusted to him, the muzzling of dogs, the precautions against contagious disease; he has the right to check gambling, and may send his myrmidons into a house to break up any coterie collected to play games of pure hazard. Crime, its prevention, pursuit, and detection, are, of course, primary duties devolving upon the chief of police, and he has at command the *personnel* of the force, a magnificent body of men. a finer *corps d'élite* than any army has ever owned or any general has ever been privileged to handle in the field.

Home Secretary as his superior, and in that sense is not supreme, but within certain limits he is practically an independent autocratic ruler. He has great statutory powers. and it would take pages to give them in any detail. He really holds all London in the hollow of his hand. The streets and thoroughfares, the routes and arteries through the town, are subject to his regulations, so is every driver of any kind of vehicle, from the state coach of an ambassador to the automobile car. The 'busmen and the cabmen come to him for their licences, and to be tested in their skill in driving and knowledge of the streets; and one of the most curious sights is to see the police examiner at work, seated with his pupil on the box of a prehistoric 'bus, or old-fashioned waggonette, starting on the test journey, when practical proof of competence must be given.

The Chief Commissioner rules, too, at all times of rejoicing and equally of disturbance, preventing obstructions and maintaining order both on shore and on the Thames; the abatement of public nuisances is en-

TESTING CAB AND OMNIBUS DRIVERS.

All this and much more appertaining thereto would be beyond the personal ken of a single individual, and the chief has three principal assistants at his elbow to relieve him by a judicious division of the great mass of business that must be transacted day after day. These, the heads of the police hierarchy, are men of mark, having very distinctive qualities and gifts, and all of them public servants of approved value.

There is little at first sight to associate the Chief Commissioner with the police officer and the stern duties he is called upon to discharge. Gentle, unobtrusive in manner, soft-voiced, of polished courtesy, he seems more fitted to shine in society than as the strict disciplinarian, the master of many legions, the great prefect of the greatest city in the world. Yet he is a leader of men, strong and purposeful, ready to take a decided line and never weaken in it under pressure either from above or below. The old saying that the nation is happiest which has no history applies to the Metropolitan police, which, after some periods of discontent and unrest, has long been quietly and peaceably governed. The three Assistant Commissioners for general duties are long-tried officials, constantly engaged; and in addition there are four Chief Constables. India has always been a favourite recruiting-ground for our police officials, and many of the best have been obtained from there.

Even if armed with the best credentials, it is not an easy matter to gain access to these chiefs. Constable-messengers meet all visitors to New Scotland Yard, subjecting them to strict inquiry and detention before ushering them in. Not only must the superior officers be spared interruption in the midst of business, which is incessant—for all matters, those even of minor importance, come before the departmental heads—but there may be danger, certainly inconvenience, in admitting strangers. In the worst days of the dynamite terror a daring ruffian got some way inside with an infernal machine, and irresponsible persons come who may be mischievous as well as importunate. The police are worried to death with callers on all errands, and on none more foolish than the desire to make spurious confession of some notable crime. One day a lady arrived in a cab with several children and a heap of baggage, clamorous to see the Chief Commissioner, and determined to go straight to gaol with all her belongings as the murderess of a soldier whom she declared she had killed, cut up, and buried. It was all nonsense, of course, but she was only got rid of by an ingenious ruse. Her chief terror was lest she should be separated from her children, and she was told this would not happen and she might remain at large if she would sign a paper promising to appear when called upon.

Divide et impera. To parcel out authority and pass it on through various branches is an essential condition of a great public office. Decentralisation is constantly kept in view at police headquarters, and executive business is done for the most part locally at the twenty-two "divisions" or units of administration into which the Metropolis is divided. But the lines all centre, the threads are all held in New Scotland Yard, from which all orders issue, to which all reports are made, to which all difficulties are referred. This gives supreme importance to the telegraph-room department, the great department with its army of operators continually manipulating innumerable machines. Every division is in direct communication with headquarters; every item of news is flashed along the line, and the Chief has his fingers at all times upon every subordinate in every part of London. The unity of direction thus conferred is obviously most valuable: New Scotland Yard knows all that is going on, and can utilise at will and almost instantaneously its whole wide-reaching machinery. On one occasion this was amusingly illustrated when

---

the Frenc police appealed for help in the arrest of a certain fugitive. The emissary came over with a photograph and full description, and the latter was at once disseminated through London. That same afternoon a constable stopped the very individual in Regent Street, and at a second call in the afternoon the prisoner was handed over to the French police officer. There was good luck in this, of course, but some good management, and it serves to show how extensive is police control. It may be added here that our police are by no means despised by their French *confrères*, although our peculiar ideas, by exalting the liberty of the subject, greatly limit the powers of our authorities.

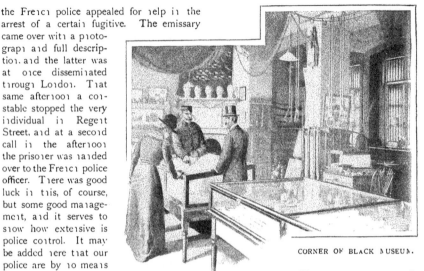

CORNER OF BLACK MUSEUM.

New Scotland Yard is kept constantly informed of the state of crime in the Metropolis. Every morning a full report of all criminal occurrences during the previous twenty-four hours is laid before the third Assistant Commissioner, the Director of Criminal Investigation. He sees at a glance what has happened, and decides at once what should be done.

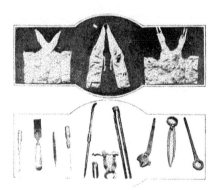

BURGLAR'S POCKETS FOR HOLDING THE TOOLS SHOWN BELOW THEM.

He has many expert subordinates and specialists within reach—men who have handled detective matters for many years with unerring skill. The best advisers are called into council when serious and mysterious crime is afoot, local knowledge also, the divisional detectives being sent for to assist those at headquarters. From the Director's office, after anxious conference, the hunt begins, any clue is seized, and the scent cleverly followed, until, as a rule, the game is run to ground.

Detection and pursuit are greatly aided by other branches at New Scotland Yard. There is first the "convict office," at which all ex-prisoners discharged from penal servitude are obliged to report themselves, and, if sentenced to police supervision, to record their intended place of residence and proposed way of life. The conditions upon which release has been accorded before the expiring of sentence are plainly stated on the "licence" or document which is issued to all as their credentials or permission to be at large, and it must be produced at all times when called for. Often enough, it is to be feared, the perpetrator of a new crime is to be found among these old hands. The predatory habit is strong, and the shrewd detective on the hunt almost always looks first among the

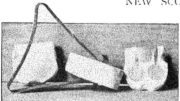

COINER'S MOULDS (SHOWING SPRING TO HOLD THEM TOGETHER).

licence-holders or ticket-of-leave men who are known practitioners in a particular line or "lay." It is no uncommon thing to take a man for a small matter and find he is the very one wanted for a greater. The chance "stop" or pick up of a suspicious - looking character leads to his identification as the author of a big job not yet brought home.

LIFE PRESERVERS.

When an arrest has been made, it is usual to pass the prisoner with as little delay as possible to Holloway Prison ; but now and again a person suspected of mysterious or political crimes is taken to New Scotland Yard for examination of a special kind. There are many aids to identification, to stimulating recollection, at police headquarters. The stored archives, the records and registers and photographic albums are most useful. The search may be long and tedious, for there is a strong family likeness in the dangerous classes, the criminal braid brings features to one dead level, but

PICKLOCKS, VICE, AND CENTRE-BIT.

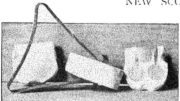

BURGLAR'S FOLDING LADDER.

many a dark horse has been revealed by his portrait in police hands. There are,

however, more prompt and infallible methods of identification coming into force —for instance, the system of measurements after the plan of M. Bertillon for recording unchanging personal characteristics ; and now the record of the "finger prints" is to be more largely applied to all who come within the grip

SKELETON KEYS.

of the law. It was long since discovered in India that every human being carries a distinctive mark in the impression of his five finger tips on a white surface after they have been duly blackened. All we need now is a greater accumulation of these records, the extension of the system to all criminals in custody, and the legal power to enforce the "printing off" on all arrested persons. Comparison can then be instituted between the new and the old as classified in the central office, and certain identification must follow. At present, photographs, tattoo marks, and recognition, the latter carried out at Holloway and applied to all under suspicion, are still the chief guides.

KNUCKLEDUSTER.

The detective police officer, anxious to improve himself professionally, will find much

COINER'S IMPLEMENTS (INCLUDING RACK FOR HOLDING COINS DURING PLATING PROCESS, MELTING POT, LADLE, POLISHING BRUSH, ETC.).

useful information in another branch at New Scotland Yard, the well-known Black Museum. This is more than a collection of grim and ghastly curiosities, the relics of celebrated crimes, such as those pictured on the two preceding pages. It is a school wherein the intelligent student may learn lessons to serve him in the conduct of his business. The methods of criminals are revealed to him here ; he may judge from the implements and tools of the craft how top-sawyers succeeded in it. Here are the " jemmy," the screw-jack, the rope ladder (Peace's), light and easy of carriage under an overcoat, the neat dark lantern made out of a tin matchbox, the melting pot and ladle of the coiners, with mould and other apparatus used by them ; together with relics that reveal the more elaborate processes of the banknote forgers, such as copper plates, burins, lithographic stones, and so on. There are many deeply interesting relics in the Black Museum, such as the chisel, on which the syllable " rock " was scratched, that led to the detection of Orrock, the Dalston murderer ; the rope with which Marguerite Dixblanc dragged the corpse of her murdered mistress into the scullery ; and others.

There is another museum at Scotland Yard of a less gruesome kind, in which the exhibits are constantly changing. The Lost Property Office is an institution which has its humorous side, bearing witness to the carelessness of the public, and at the same time to the general honesty of its servants. Some forty thousand articles are about the average annual crop of things dropped or forgotten in cabs and public carriages, or mislaid, and the harvest is a strange one. All manner of property is passed across the police counter, brought in by cabmen and others, and handed back to its owners on proof and payment of the necessary fees ; and among these are found such diverse articles as bicycles and perambulators, rabbits, cats, jewellery, umbrellas, and sewing-machines.

The Metropolitan Police is a mighty engine worked, happily, for good. It has been so admirably built up, so slowly and completely perfected, exercises such far-reaching and extensive functions, that it is well for the people of London it is ever devoted to their good, and acts primarily in their best interests. An organisation so powerful in the hands of despotic authority would make life a daily burden, and the word " liberty " would be an empty sound. But it is—as we may congratulate ourselves—the servant, not the master, of the public, and we need only blame ourselves if it should ever become the latter.

IN THE LOST PROPERTY OFFICE.

LEAVING THE LONDON THEATRES.

By A. ST. JOHN ADCOCK.

TOWARDS ten o'clock at night a breath of the drowsy quietness that has already settled down in the heart of the City seems to blow out along the West-End thoroughfares, and lull them as with some passing thought of sleep. Office windows are dark; half the shops are closed, and others are closing; 'buses, no longer crowded, are no longer in a hurry, and the conductor is saving up his voice for an hour later, when it can be used to better purpose; traffic generally has dwindled on the pavement and in the roadway until you can walk the one without elbowing your neighbours, and cross the other safely and at leisure.

LEAVING THE PAVILION THEATRE, WHITECHAPEL.

Glance into the refreshment-rooms and hotels, into the fashionable or Bohemian restaurants in the Strand and round by Leicester Square, and you will see only long rows of tables, their snowy cloths neatly set with knives and forks, silver-plated cruets, folded serviettes, and branchy, torch-shaped epergnes flaming atop into many-coloured flowers; and, except for some stray visitor, perhaps, who looks lonely amid the waste of white cloths, none of the tables are occupied. The waiters gather in idle knots to tell each other privately what they think of the manager, or they doze apart as if the business of their day was finished instead of being about to begin again; the young ladies at the confectioners' shops have time to look at their hair in the mirrors; and aproned men behind the oyster bars are yawning over the evening papers.

When half-past ten is turned, you feel the very air becoming tense with expectancy of something that is to happen. Crush-hatted men in evening dress appear in the street, singly or in pairs, or with fair companions who trip beside them, bonnetless and in opera cloaks: the later items in the music hall programme were not attractive enough to keep them; the play bored them, and they have left before the end. Commissionaires or gorgeously-uniformed attendants are bolting back the outer doors of theatres in readiness for departing audiences; and the traffic in road and on pavement is momentarily thickening.

Now, too, if you look up almost any byway of the Strand you will see that it is lined with ransoms and four-wheelers and hired and private carriages waiting to be called. Other cabmen, arriving too late to get front places in these waiting lines, sneak into the Strand by circuitous routes, and, failing to dodge past the policemen, hover as near as they dare to one or other of the theatres, keeping a wary look-out for the playgoers to emerge and a signalling umbrella to be hoisted.

With the advent of broughams and private carriages in the byways, dapper footmen go on sentry duty outside the principal entrances to the theatres, or stand patiently amongst the ferns and huge palms that adorn box-office vestibules. Here they pose, almost as imperturbable as a row of statuary, until the strains of the National Anthem filter out to them from within, then they come to life, and peer eagerly into the passages and up thick-carpeted stairs that converge on the vestibule.

Suddenly, one of them catches a glimpse of the figures he is looking for, and is out in a twinkling, and beckoning in the lamplight at the nearest corner. A carriage detaches itself from the line, sweeps smartly into the Strand, and draws up opposite the theatre. My lady and her guest, in a splendour of diamonds and low-necked dresses half hidden under loose cloaks, trip lightly into it; my lord and his guest, plainer, but no less immaculately garbed, step in after them; the footman slams the door, mounts the box, and they are gone.

In like manner come and go other carriages, and cabs that have answered to the shrill whistling of the commissionaire or have been fetched by some perspiring tout, who will gallantly hold a ragged flap of his coat over the dirty wheel whilst his more finely-garmented patrons are getting in, and trot a few paces alongside to catch the largesse that will be flung to him.

Men and women and a sprinkling of children, aristocrats and plebeians mingling, are now pouring steadily out of the Gaiety, the Lyceum, the Tivoli, Criterion, Her Majesty's, and all the theatres and music halls in the Strand, the Haymarket, Charing Cross Road, and thereabouts, the swelling tide in the main thorough-fares being fed by narrower but more plenteous streams that gush into it out of side channels from pit and gallery doors, till the surge and rush of foot passengers everywhere, of cabs and carriages and 'buses, are denser and swifter than even at mid-day.

It is an orderly crowd, talking for the most part of how to get home, but inclined to a desultory more or less impersonal criticism of the plays and players it has seen. It is an orderly crowd, but in a hurry; it is being whisked up, and whirled off momentarily in cabs and carriages; it mobs the 'buses at the top of the Strand, and swarms on to them till they are crammed full; it billows both ways along Coventry Street, dodging and darting in and out under the noses of cab and carriage horses, and making lightning dashes across the tumultuous road. Everywhere among the well-dressed multitude go opera - cloaks, and shawls, or hooded heads; white cloaks and black cloaks, blues, pinks, scarlets, and shawls as varied in hue, and always beside them the formal black and plenteous white linen of masculine evening dress.

For the most of an hour this pandemonium reigns—but it is a very respectable pandemonium, and very good-tempered. Some of the opera-cloaked ladies, waiting for a 'bus, may grow irritable because it is tardy in coming, and so full when it does come that they have to charter a four-wheeler after all; or a policeman, struggling in the welter of congested traffic, may lose his temper with a cabman, and goad him to such impertinent responses as result in his number being taken and a summons threatened; but, on the whole, the prevailing characteristics of the multitude are careless good-humour and a yearning for supper.

The majority speed straightway home for it; but a large minority prefer to sup in town. Wherefore, in the oyster bars the aproned men yawn no longer over newspapers, but toil behind their counters briskly ministering to the needs of a shopful of appetites that are not easily satisfied. Hebe at the confectioner's has no more time for setting her hair straight, for customers have flocked in from pits and galleries, with a sprinkling from the dress-circles, and, impatient with fears of missing last trains,

LEAVING HER MAJESTY'S THEATRE.

all wait serving at once. Look into the hotels, and fashionable and Bohemian restaurants, and the waiters are all wide awake and running their legs off in attentive zeal; for where half an hour ago scarcely a table was occupied now scarcely one remains vacant.

In some places you shall take your supper to a musical accompaniment played on a piano and stringed instruments, or on strings and brasses; in all, there is a constant effervescence of laughter and cheery voices; bewildering visions of beauty and beautiful hats and dresses; young men fully enjoying the freshness and novelty of their surroundings; testy old men trying hard not to be bored by them; blithe old men enjoying themselves as heartily as any youngster of them all—staid men and women taking their pleasure with the typical British stolidity.

Here, in one of the most fashionable of such resorts, you come upon a famous actor, fresh from his evening's triumphs, sociably supping with a select circle of admirers; or a famous actress similarly entertained, and the centre of furtive glances from every corner of the room. There are cosy, elegant parties of two or four monopolising small tables; there are larger, merrier, and equally elegant parties feasting royally round larger tables, and over all are the brilliance of electric lights and an air of contented affluence, and amid all are the delicate fragrances of flowers and scents, the mingling babble and laughter, and dreamy cadences of the music.

Nor do the humbler public-houses near the theatres lack for patronage. Unfashionable men, average men, and men below the average, several with wives or sweethearts, flock to these hospitable bars for liquid refreshment, supplemented, maybe, by a sandwich or a pork pie. Thither repair straggling units of emancipated orchestras with their instruments in funereal cases; and there, too, smart young City clerks and shop assistants drop in for a last drink, which, in some cases, is a preliminary to so many drinks after the last that, in the end, they come out to learn they have missed the last 'bus, and accept the alternative with boisterous cheerfulness. One faces southwards alone, and has facetious farewells shrieked after him; the others, after much striking of matches and relighting of pipes and cigarettes, set out northwards, and will

SUPPER AT AN EAST-END FRIED FISH SHOP.

by and by be scandalising sober suburban streets with cock-crows and rousing choruses.

The emptying of suburban theatres is a comparatively small matter; for the suburbs have their theatres singly, and not in clusters. There is the same rush and scattering of the audience, but on a reduced scale, and, generally, the proportion of evening dresses is very much smaller. In fact, in many of these theatres evening dress is not the fashion, and anyone wearing it is by way of being a rarity.

Come down East on Saturday night, and see how the people pass out of the Pavilion Theatre in Whitechapel.

Whitechapel Road has scarcely begun to think about sleep yet. Not only do all the provision shops remain wide open, but tailors' and drapers' and toy and furniture shops, with many others, are open as well: costermongers' barrows stand thickly by the kerb; in the middle of them a huge brass weighing machine towers up, flashing dazzlingly in the light of

IN COVENTRY STREET, 11.15 P.M.

naphtha lamps, and near beside it is a hooded whelk stall similarly illuminated. A baked-potato merchant passes and repasses, sowing sparks from the big black can on his barrow. The public-houses are full; the pavement is covered with men and women and children, well-dressed, shabby or disreputable, shopping, or leisurely promenading. The curtain has not fallen in the Pavilion yet, but there is as much life here as there is in the Strand when the theatres are emptying.

It is five minutes to eleven. Two ancient four-wheelers and a single hansom have driven up, and are standing, forlornly hopeful, opposite the theatre. An attendant bolts the doors back, and a moment later a dark mass surges up the long bare passage from the pit, and a second less compact crowd simultaneously flows by the broader exit from the stalls and boxes.

As the earliest to emerge from the gallery door round the corner are batches of rampant, hooting boys, so the first hundred or so to burst into the open air from the front entrances are all men. One, a seedy, melancholy-looking man, breaks out, solitary, stares round as if he were dreaming, and, with his hands in his pockets, pushes through the promenaders, and makes for home, taking his dreams with him. The huge poster that leans against the lamp-post opposite, and represents a scene from the play, has a strange fascination for many; they cross straight to it, and stand regarding

SUPPER AT THE SAVOY HOTEL.

it critically. "We never see that!" objects a lady carrying a sleeping infant. "Yus, we did, silly!" declares her husband, carrying an elder child, who is also asleep. "Ain't that where 'e's a-savin' of 'er from that Russian chap?" "Oh, ar! But they didn't do it like this," she insists, and follows him still protesting.

The general inclination, especially among the fair sex, is to discuss the play as if it had been sheer reality, and to pour scorn and loathing on the villain, a tearful pity on the distressed heroine, and unlimited admiration on the hero, but a select few of the male sex, who are habitual attendants at

the theatre, concern themselves less with the play than with the merits of individual actors, old favourites, to whom they refer in familiar, even affectionate, terms.

So for some ten minutes the crowd streams out from the front and round from the gallery door, and the larger crowd moving up and down Whitechapel Road easily absorbs it. Passing trams or 'buses are besieged; a weedy young man is regaling his much be-feathered sweetheart at the baked-potato can; two men in tall hats and a miscellany of less imposing persons congregate around the whelk stall, and hand the pepper and vinegar about with gusto. There is an influx of trade to the public-houses; the boxes of an adjacent fried fish shop are full of hungry revellers, and faces of men and women peer in increasing numbers over its counter, demanding "middle pieces" well browned. You meet these customers strolling a little later eating fried plaice out of scraps of news-paper, or carrying it wrapped up to be eaten more comfortably at home. Nobody has hired any of the cabs, but the drivers linger still, on the chance of finding a fare among the actors and actresses.

The illuminated arch of coloured glass goes out suddenly over the main entrance to the theatre; lights within are dying out; here, as in the West-End, doors are being closed up with a clanging of bolts and bars; players are filing into the street from the stage exit; while, in the desolate interior, attendants potter about, covering up boxes and dress-circle, and the fireman, swinging his lantern, tramps over the darkened stage, taking a last look round.

RELEASED FROM WORK.

LONDON SWEETHEARTS.

By GEORGE R. SIMS.

WHEN the twilight shadows have veiled the face of the garish day, then London becomes one vast "Lovers' Walk." Lost in the rapture of "Love's Young Dream" are thousands of young couples released from the world of work-a-day. You can see them everywhere with the old sweet story writ large upon their happy faces, and at a glance you know them. In one class of life their arms are linked and their fingers are intertwined; in another class their arms are round each other's necks; in another, *her* hand rests lightly on *his* arm; in still another, they walk demurely side by side; but no one mistakes them for aught but what they are. Young husband and wife never walk together as lovers walk. There is a different step, a different clasp of the arm, and the *al fresco* embrace is no longer in the programme.

Discreetly, modestly, and with the tenderest consideration for the feelings of the inhabitants, let us take a stroll this quiet summer evening through Love-land in London.

The houses of business have just closed in the West, and the main thoroughfares are filled with the lads and lasses released from toil. The girls come out by themselves in

light-bloused, straw-hatted groups, and the young fellows walk up the street in little knots for a time. But gradually the sexes mingle, and in a short time almost every laddie has his lassie, and happy pairs stroll quietly away together.

The custom of raising the hat, once considered Continental, has won its way to-day among all classes, and many a hat is raised by fellow clerks and shopmen as they pass the proud swain walking by the side of his "young lady." Between eight and nine o'clock the shopping streets of the West are filled with sweethearts. So far, there is no pronounced affection displayed. The linked hands and clasped waists are for the less aristocratic streets and for a lowlier class of lovers, the factory girl and the working lad, the young hawker and his "donah," the general servant and her "chap."

You can walk through the streets of London at the evening hour, and read the honest love of lad and lass in a never-ending panorama of happy faces. There is no false shame about these young couples. They are proud of each other, proud of their tender relationship, and if every now and then they give outward and visible signs of the warmth of their affection, it is but the natural reversion of Adam's sons and Eve's daughters to the happy Eden days of the first sweethearts.

In the parks and along the Embankment many a pair of lovers sit side by side and gaze into each other's eyes needless of the passers-by, who are generally sympathetic, and show their sympathy in a practical manner. If only one couple is occupying the seat or bench made to accommodate four, the vacant space is rarely intruded upon by the single man or woman. It is left for the next pair of lovers that may come along. For lovers do not mind other lovers sharing the dreamy silence of the seat beneath the tree. But the presence of any person, male or female, not absorbed in the tender passion would be considered an unwarrantable trespass on Cupid's domain.

London lovers of the class who nestle to each other when the evening zephyrs murmur among the trees have few opportuni-

ties of quiet courtship in their homes. There are too many noisy children and rough neighbours about, and there is no romance in the surroundings. Many a love scene in the London parks is as idyllic, as tender, and as true as any that ever poet sang, and the wooing of the swain is often as loyal and as respectful as that of the young curate who whispers honied words in the ear of the vicar's daughter among the roses of her father's garden beneath the first pale stars of eve.

Love is of no rank and no degree, and so, because the hush of evening is the hour of the heart, we, the wayfarers in Love-land, may see the lordly lover also, as he bends down and speaks softly to the blue-blooded maiden of his choice. Out on to the balcony of the great house they come, and stand against a background of soft lights in the beautiful room that we see through the open windows. What a charming picture they make! His black coat and wide expanse of shirt front throw into relief the soft chiffon of the graceful, willowy girl by his side. The rising breeze tenderly touches her wealth of wavy hair, but it is not that which brings the faint flush to her cheek. The young earl has bent and spoken softly in her ear the trembling words of love. We are too far away to hear the answer that she makes, but we can see her smiling face, and, when the rules and regulations of Society and its marriageable daughters have been observed, we may be sure that there will be an announcement in the *Morning Post*, and all the world will be told the sequel of that little love story of which we have seen the beginning on the Park Lane balcony to-night.

The blinds are down in this dull-looking house in a London square, and we cannot see if love is beneath the roof, but the area gate is open, and on the top

ON THE EMBANKMENT.

step a pretty London housemaid is taking the air. She looks anxiously towards the corner, every now and then throwing a furtive glance at the drawn blinds. Presently a young man comes sauntering along. He saunters until he catches sight of the fluttering strings of a little white cap. Then he quickens his pace, and the young housemaid trips lightly to meet him. In the shadow of the house next door, out of the line of sight of any eyes that may peer from the house in which she is a handmaid, Mary lingers with her lover for a while. He holds her hand in his, and they talk earnestly together. The policeman passes with a nod and a smile. The young man knits his brow a little, but it is only a summer cloud. Presently the clock of a church close by strikes ten. Mary gives a little start. " I must go!" she exclaims. Then there is a long lingering pressure of hands, and then—we discreetly turn our backs, but a familiar sound strikes our ears, and a minute later Mary softly closes the gate, and disappears down the area steps. The young man waits at the corner for a moment, then lights his pipe and strolls past the house along the square. I fancy he is going to have another look at that policeman.

In the fierce glare of the sunny afternoon a familiar pair of sweethearts come holding each other's hands along the outer circle of Regent's Park. How proud the little girl is of the bronzed sailor lover by her side! He has come up from Portsmouth to see her, and she has got a day off from the factory and walks on air. There is a chivalry as well as a heartiness about the love-making of the young Jack Tar. He has not the all-conquering air of the Adonis in scarlet, and he does not occupy himself so much with the twirling of a moustache and the flicking of a cane. The sailor and his lass are on their way to the Zoo, and there with his sweetheart on his arm Jack will gaze at the strange animals, and tell her of the far-off lands to which he has sailed and seen the like, not in iron cages, but in their native lairs. And Jack will be free with his money and treat his sweetheart generously. When the afternoon is over, and she is tired, he will take a hansom for her, and after tea at a little café he will suggest a music hall, and

ON THE BALCONY.

there he will enjoy himself to his heart's content and hold his little girl's hand lovingly all the time, and press it sympathetically when the serio-comic lady sings of sweethearts who are true " though seas divide." And at night he will see her to her mother's door, and kiss her heartily and with a sounding smack that all her folk may hear, before

THE AREA
BELLE.

he rolls off on his way to the other end of the town where his old mother is sitting up waiting for him. And you may be sure that when he went into a shop that afternoon, and bought a little present for his sweetheart, Jack did not forget his mother. He has something in his pocket that he is going to gladden the old lady's eyes with, as he sits down to the bread and cheese and cucumber and the big jug of beer that have been waiting for him since eleven o'clock.

The boy and girl sweetheart of the London streets are in their glory on Bank Holiday. It is the day on which the lad with the first faint signs of a budding moustache arrays himself in a new light suit and pair of yellowish brown boots, and counting the silver or the coppers that remain to him after the outlay on his wardrobe, invites the girl of his heart to accompany him to Hampstead Heath. Hampstead is the general choice of the boy sweetheart, because there is no admission, and the side shows are a penny instead of sixpence. His sweetheart has not spent much on her wardrobe, but she is generally neat, and has made deft use of her

fingers in arranging fresh ribbon on an old hat, and she has probably altered and retrimmed an old dress to make it look like a new one. Boots, as a rule, are the weak point of the little girl sweetheart on a Bank Holiday. Boots are a terrible item to many of us, but when your wages are ten shillings a week you have to make one pair do duty for a very long time indeed.

But the boy sweetheart is not particular about the boots so long as his "gal" looks smart about the hat. He is a good boy to her in his way and as far as his means will allow, and affectionate and considerate as boys go. He thumps her in the way of play with a force which a gently-bred girl would consider a violent assault. But Sally takes it in excellent part, and thumps back again with much top-note exclamation. In the matter of refreshment Tom is as liberal as he can afford to be. He treats his "gal" to a pennyworth of sweets as they come along. On the Heath they share an ice, bite an apple between them, and "drink fair" out of a ginger-beer bottle.

There is not much sentiment about these boy and girl sweethearts. They are practically children, and they play and romp. Towards evening, as they go home to the little side street where they live, their arms may be about each other's necks, but it is more "show off" than anything else. They both want to ape their elders. He tries to let the passing boys see that the girl is not his sister but " his young woman," and she is anxious that all passing females should know that she has attained to the dignity of a young man.

At the front garden gate of the suburban villa, as the clock strikes the hour after which it is not considered correct for the daughters of the house to be abroad, a young couple linger lovingly. The evening stroll through the lane near at hand is over; the hour of parting has come. This young couple are engaged. But the young fellow knows that the brothers and sisters of his adored one do not like the too frequent presence of a " spooiny couple," and, moreover, he has a long way to go to get to his own home, and he has to be off to the City at eight every morning. So ten o'clock sees the parting, as a rule, but the linger at the gate is always sweet, and difficult to bring to an end.

After she has gone inside the front garden she does not go up the little pathway to the door. She leans on the gate for a while, and they stand silently gazing into each other's eyes and enjoy the silence of love.

But at last she breaks the spell. " I *must* go, Frank," she says. Then she puts her pretty little face over the gate, and he stoops down and their lips meet. Then a light dress flutters up the pathway in the semi-darkness. He watches it till it disappears. Then he says " Darling !" aloud to himself, and steps out briskly for his mile and a half walk. And the memory of that parting kiss goes with him and makes the dusty road a path of roses.

The sound of military music crashes on the early morning air, and there is a great rush of womenfolk to the windows. It is too early for the families to be up and about in this aristocratic neighbourhood, so the servants gather at the dining-room window, and some run upstairs to their own bedrooms to get a better view.

The Life Guards are out for an early ride.

WITH JACK AT THE ZOO.

AT " 'APPY 'AMPSTEAD."

The band is with them. Probably it is some special occasion. There is a head from every upper window as they pass, and, as a rule, the head has a little white cap on it.

Most of the troopers glance upwards and smile. Mars is never insensible to the glance of beauty, and is given to nodding pleasantly to ladies to whom he has not been introduced.

At one upper window there is a pretty face wreathed in smiles. Jenny, the parlourmaid, knows that her lover, Trooper Thompson, is with his regiment, and will be looking out for her. And Trooper Thompson knows exactly where Jenny will be; she told him the previous evening when they parted in Wellington Road. Trooper Thompson is a handsome young fellow with a fair moustache that Jenny thinks is absolutely perfect. He is not perhaps quite so much in love with Jenny as she is with him, but he does not make her jealous by smiling and laughing at all the other housemaids in the terrace some of his comrades do. He looks directly in front of him, heedless of the admiring glances cast at him, until he comes to Jenny's house. Then he raises his head

and smiles and nods, and Jenny is in the seventh heaven of rapture.

She is engaged to Trooper Thompson and means to marry him. It will have to be a long courtship. But Jenny does not mind. She has good wages, and she makes her soldier lover pretty presents—pipes, and tobacco pouches, and cigars, and all that sort of thing—and Jenny has been to the ball at the barracks and lived in fairyland, for her handsome lover in scarlet danced every dance with her. And she counts the hours till it is her evening or her Sunday out when she can meet her gallant admirer, and walk about or sit in the park with him, or treat him to the music hall.

When, as they walk along, she sees the young women turn their heads and cast sidelong glances of admiration at her hero, she gives a shy little laugh, and grasps his arm a little more closely to signify absolute possession, and she thinks she is the happiest girl in the world. She is a good girl, and will

THE PRIDE OF THE PARK.

make a hard-working, devoted wife. Let us hope that Trooper Thompson will appreciate the affection he has won, and that Jenny may never regret the love that loved a scarlet coat.

It is a long walk through Love-land, for north and south, and east and west, at every turn we find the old, old story being told again. To the busy tea shop, where neat-handed Phyllises trip from table to table, the patient lover comes now and then, and they exchange a word or two of tender greeting as she hands him his scone or cup of coffee. And all the girls in the establishment know that the young fellow is Phyllis's sweetheart, and after he has gone they talk sympathetically to her about him, and congratulate her on his loyalty in coming to the shop so frequently. The barmaid's sweetheart cannot linger as long by his lady-love in business hours, for the landlord has a keen eye for the engaged barmaid's young man, and discourages the attention that, as a rule, is long and unprofitable, and, moreover, monopolises the fair Hebe's conversation and sometimes keeps her from giving proper attention to the other "paying guests" of mine host.

There are the sweethearts of fashion, who meet in the Row and canter side by side; there are the sweethearts who talk small talk at Society gatherings, and whose courtship is a diary of fashionable events; there are the sweethearts of humble life, the working man who woos and wins some honest hard-working lass, and is as proud of her the day they stand before the clergyman as the elderly duke who wins the beauty of the London season.

And there are the old couples whom we meet arm in arm, with happy, smiling faces beneath their crown of silvered hair—men and women who have shared each other's joys and sorrows from youth to old age, and who, in the evening of their well-spent days, are sweethearts still.

THE LINGER AT THE GATE.

SOME LONDON HOME TRADES.

By ARTHUR B. MOSS.

WE are all familiar with the large trades by which men and women earn their living. The work of the carpenter, the bricklayer, the engineer, the printer, the tailor, and the bootmaker, is brought constantly before us in our daily lives, and most of the trades in which girls and women are employed in factory and workshop are well known. There are, however, a large number of small obscure trades in which men and women are engaged, and which have to serve in many cases as the sole source of income. These trades are conducted in the workers' homes, and to see them we must pay a series of visits and enter the dwellings of the poor without ceremony.

Let us call first at the humble abode of the Hat Box Maker. We find it on the third floor of one of the model dwellings in a thickly populated district in South London. As we have entered uninvited an introduction is necessary. Mrs. P—— is a widow who has one child of her own, and takes care of another that belongs to a friend. She has for many years earned her living by making hat boxes at home for a firm that supplies some of the chief manufacturers of silk hats.

"I only do the stitching," says Mrs. P—— in answer to a question ; " I generally get a young woman to do the pasting for me."

HAT BOX MAKING.

By this she means that the box is supplied with an outside covering of white glazed paper which is stuck together with paste, but the body and the bottom of the box are sewn together with thread. Mrs. P—— knows how to do the pasting as well as her companion, but she finds that it materially assists the speed of putting together a gross of such boxes to have this assistance. " I have to find the paste, and the needle and thread, and when I've finished a gross I get half-a-crown. I don't grumble at the pay, for when I can get the work I'm able to make a very decent living for a poor widow. It's only when we're slack I don't like it, for then I have to go out charing, and such work is a little beyond my strength."

Still sticking to the paste and paper, we enter another room in which we find a young man and a young woman working away industriously at the Paper Bag Making. Paper bags of all sizes are made by this energetic couple, who supply the shops at a very low figure per gross.

"It's like this," says Mr. S—— ; " we make thousands of these bags every week. First we have to cut them to the size we want, then we paste away all round the edges except the top, then fold them over, and when they're properly dry we have to

FIRE-STOVE ORNAMENTS.

tie 'em in packets. I finish the business by taking 'em round to the shops. 'Paper Bag Poets?' Oh, yus, there's some fellers that write poetry, as they calls it, to put on the bags, but the printers engage them, and I expect they're the same chaps as write verses for the rag merchants."

Let us now turn our steps towards Tabard Street (late Kent Street), Borough, for here we shall find many home industries of the kind that people take very little notice of except at the particular time of year at which they are forced upon public attention. Here we see a poor woman making Ornaments for the Fire-stove. The little kitchen table is covered with coloured paper, and here and there are long strips of gold shavings, as well as rosettes of various colours ; these are dexterously pieced together and form a very pretty ornament. A very precarious income is earned, however, by hawking them about the streets of London, and many of these women find it necessary to follow another calling in addition, most of them making artificial flowers for the winter months.

While in Tabard Street we find ourselves in the midst of the Brush Making industry. A great deal of it is done at home. Here we find men and women engaged in making scrubbing brushes, laundry brushes, shoe brushes, etc. It is an interesting sight to watch them at work. First we see them cut the bass, or fibre, with a sort of guillotine knife, or, when they do not possess one of these, with a large pair of shears. Then we see one of the boys preparing the glue. The hairs having been dexterously placed in holes specially made, are again dressed round by the shears until they are of uniform length, and then prepared for sale.

In one of the model dwellings in the Borough we find a young woman who does some of the best sort of work. She is in almost constant employment at home, and she likes the work because it is clean and light and free from danger. "This is real hair I am using," says Mrs. M——, "and this brush when finished will be used in the confectionery business. You see how light it is ; it is a real good article, and they call it an egg brush."

But now let us go in search of the Rag Merchant Poet. We find him in a common lodging-house. He is no doubt a man of fine poetic genius ; at all events he thinks so, and that should suffice. He lays claim to being the author of some of the most moral poems ever written for the rag trade, as well as for the quack medicine man. He gives us a few samples of his work, but we fail to appreciate them. So we make our way to a rag merchant's and take down a few specimens of verse by the poets who are looked upon as the laureates of the trade. Two examples will suffice.

PEACE AND PROSPERITY.

Let's hope that trade will soon revive;
And each and all begin to thrive.
I think that things are on the mend;
So have a little cash to spend
To buy your rags, books, or papers,
Kitchen stuff or cuttings from the draper's,
Old clothes, old books; all that you can find,
Old bottles too of every kind;
Jampots, jars (not family ones I hope),
Blankets, string, or any kind of rope.

From the heights of Parnassus the poet always descends to the plains of the every-day world.

GOOD ADVICE TO ALL.

So, Sally dear, you think it funny
That I should save my rags and turn them into
   money.
Now if you'd like to have a happy home,
Nor wish to see your husband roam,
Remember this, a *Golden Rule*,
And one I learned when young at school,
" A penny saved is a penny earned,"
Which could not be so if my rags I burned.
If you waste such things as these
You lose the bread and want the cheese,
But if you're frugal, think what a treasure you
   will be;
And you'll save rags and bones as well as me.

Another branch of the rag and bone business is carried on by an itinerant vendor of Farthing Windmills, who pushes a barrow through the streets, and, having a number of these windmills and paper flags displayed, soon gets a crowd of children around his vehicle, and tells them that if they can induce their parents to part with their bones and bottles he will supply them with a flag or a windmill gratis. Windmill making is a home industry in London, and in the season the vendors do a brisk trade. But the season is short, and the harvest must be reaped at the proper time.

Since the establishment of large sanitary laundries in almost every industrial community, the amount of washing and mangling done at " small laundries " has been considerably reduced. There are still, however, a large number of poor women, mostly widows, in crowded neighbourhoods, earning a living by washing and mangling for those families who, in the belief that it is better and less expensive, prefer their washing and mangling to be done in a small private house, however humble, rather than in a large factory. And so we may reasonably expect that for many a long day yet small Home Laundries will continue to exist, if not to flourish, among the poor.

At a lodging-house of the better class we find two interesting persons. One of them is a manufacturer of Fly Papers—"Catch 'em alive O!" He sells them at a halfpenny a sheet. The other is the manufacturer and vendor of Penny Opera Glasses.

Let us go into the basement where the first man makes his Fly Papers and see them in the process of manufacture. There is a big basin of size and ochre lying on the table, and on a row of lines hang dozens of papers—old newspapers cut into various sizes, and covered with a thin layer of this solution. When these are dry there is another basin of solution, composed of resin, oil and turpentine, in readiness to be plastered over them, and then, hey presto! the " Catch 'em alive O!" papers are complete. An old Irishman is the hawker of these, and in the warm weather he does a brisk business.

The Penny Opera Glass Manufacturer is a young man, and a skilful workman in his own line of business. With the aid of two small bone ornaments, such as are generally to be found in the tassels of a parasol or sunshade, and a small brass ring similar to those used for hanging up pictures, or in lieu of the ring a little brass wire, he produces something in the shape of miniature opera glasses. Then having covered the top of them with a thin layer of glue, which has the appearance of transparency, they look for all the world like the real article. A remarkable number of these small articles are sold in the market places of the Metropolis every Friday and Saturday evening, and this man carries on a prosperous business for several months during the year.

Having witnessed the manufacture of these interesting articles we turn our steps in the direction of the home of a poor Single-handed Tailor. Only a few yards from the rear of Guy's Hospital, on the first floor of buildings that look from the outside very like

TOY WINDMILLS.

ARTIFICIAL FLOWERS.

52

a huge warehouse, we find our tailor seated on a big wooden table with his legs crossed hard at work. He does all kinds of work, from making a suit right out to repairing trousers or vest. As a rule, he works for a large firm of tailors, but he does not disdain to do an odd job or two for a private customer.

In every poor neighbourhood one of the flourishing "Home Trades" is that of the Boot Repairer, or, as he used to be called, the "cobbler." At various seasons of the year the boot repairer is very busy, especially after a series of wet days. He does his work, for the most part, in the front parlour of his little house, in the window of which is the announcement—"Boots and Shoes Neatly Repaired" at such and such a price. Sometimes the wording is in verse thus:—

"If you think your boots are ended,
Bring 'em here and get 'em mended."

Except that Monday is generally a lazy day with him, the cobbler is an industrious man who, generally, works all hours of the day, and sometimes far into the night, to please his customers.

In another building we find the Cheap Shirt Maker, who stitches away hour after hour for a miserable pittance. Tom Hood's "Song of the Shirt" still exactly describes

her condition. She works every day from early morning till late at night. Mrs. W—— is a widow with a family of four, and if she relied solely on shirt making for a living she and her children would be often on the verge of starvation. Fortunately for her she gets occasional small jobs in the sewing line from neighbours, and thus she manages to subsist.

Wooden and Tin Toys are for the most part made abroad. They come principally from Germany. There is, however, a man in the Borough who makes toy tables and chairs. He does not make these articles for shops, but sells them in the street at a penny each. Judging from his appearance this mode of earning a living is not a profitable one. There is also a young woman who makes tin weights and scales for street sale, and a man who makes wire puzzles. But all these occupations are so ill paid that they are only aids to a living. The "manufacturers" have generally another employment.

But now we come to a real home industry that affords a substantial living to those who are engaged in it, viz., Haddock Smoking. Fifteen years ago there were a large number of "Smoke Holes" in the Borough, in Orange Street, Green Street, and Friar Street, as well as some in Bermondsey. Now most of them are removed to some of the back streets in Camberwell, where they still flourish. There

BRUSH MAKING.

BEETROOT BOILING.

are two or three of them, however, still left just behind the Blackfriars Road, and a large one in Rockingham Street, Newington Causeway, but the chief smoking is done in Camberwell. Jem B—— is an old-established smoker. If you watch him at work you will notice that he puts a lot of haddocks on a long iron skewer, which he places in the smoke hole; he then sets fire to a quantity of oak sawdust and allows this to smoulder for hours, and thus the haddocks get well smoked and browned. Jem's haddocks have an enormous sale among the poor.

Another good trade is that of Beetroot Boiling. Mr. M—— is a general dealer, and when at home lives in Chapel Court, Borough. He is a bit of a philosopher in his way. "I boil hundreds of beets in this boiler, sir, in the season," he says, "and if you come about 'opping time you shall see me doing it, as you used to in Peter Street. But it's no good buying beetroots yet—the ones you get ain't no class; a little later on it'll be all right. Nobody can't teach me my business. In the season I sell hundreds of beets, as you know, in the streets, and in the market place in the Walworth Road on Saturday nights."

Two very interesting small Home Trades we find carried on in Bermondsey. One is that of a Clay Pipe Maker; the other that of a Muffin and Crumpet Maker. The first manufactures thousands of pipes out of white clay, with a small machine, and with a dexterous use of his augers. He then bakes them in a kiln which he has in his back yard. When they are complete he sells them to publicans at about one and sixpence a gross. The second mixes up a quantity of flour and water in a pail, and ladles it into a tin with small circular apertures, puts it on a large tin over a fire, and when it is withdrawn behold muffins and crumpets ready for the Londoners' tea.

The Italian Bronze Figure Maker is found chiefly at Saffron Hill and Leather Lane, but there are a few of them in the Italian quarter in the Peckham Park Road. It is not, however, an extensive business that is carried on there. Italians prefer the Ice Cream trade in the summer and the Baked Chestnut trade in the winter. And neither of these industries requires much capital. On the other hand a fair amount of money is required to carry on the business of a Bronze Figure Maker. The workman has to manipulate his plaster with skill, quite apart from the work that is done with moulds. And English people have so little appreciation of his art: a bust of Lord Salisbury or Mr. Joseph Chamberlain might have a sale among Unionists, but who cares for an art figure that represents somebody whom nobody knows? The Italian boy calls at various houses and asks in bad broken English a high price for his figures. But when he is offered half the price he takes it with only a shrug of the shoulder.

Artificial Flower Making is an industry in which hundreds of girls and women are engaged. But it is a trade that is divided into several branches. The highest branch is that in which girls are engaged in making the flowers that adorn ladies' bonnets. Some of these are made at home, as our illustration on p. 25 shows, by girls who are most dexterous in the use of their fingers, but the best of them are made in factories. The artificial flowers most patronised by the poor are made of coloured paper, and are manufactured in their homes by poor women who, as I have said, divide their time between these articles and ornaments for your fire-stove. There are also men who make artificial flowers—and very real they appear too—out of raw carrots and turnips, and these have a very fair sale among a certain class, who find them last longer, and serve their purpose better, than natural flowers.

The last trade to which we can refer here is one which is not strictly a Home Trade, though all arrangements for carrying it out have to be made from that centre. It is the gentleman who makes a living by calling workmen early in the morning at sixpence per week. At many common lodging-houses an early caller finds constant employment, but I do not purpose to write about persons who wake up the lodgers for a consideration. I refer now to a very different sort of individual—a gentleman who finds his chief source of income in calling at workmen's houses and waking them up very early in the morning, so that they can be at their employment while the bell is ringing or the clock is striking the hour. All over London such men are engaged. There is one who does a large business in North Camberwell.

In the window of his front parlour may be seen the accompanying announcement. When you enquire you find that the price for being "called" is twopence a morning or sixpence a week. The caller finds a good many customers needing his services, though he comes in constant competition with the night policeman, who is as a rule open to accept engagements on the same terms. But the gentleman in blue is liable to be called away just at the time he is required to wake his customer. Remembering this fact, workmen trust themselves to the man who has no other engagements to distract his attention. And so the old gentleman who begs workmen to "enquire within" does a very fair business. The only other business he takes in hand is selling books and newspapers, but these principally occupy his attention on Sundays, when the workman does not ask to be called early, but prefers to remain in bed and dream on undisturbed.

TAILORING.

JEWISH BOY REPLYING TO A TOAST AFTER A "CONFIRMATION" DINNER.

JEWISH LONDON.

By S. GELBERG.

A HUNDRED thousand men, women, and children, some of them fugitives still suffering the punishment of Cain, others just sloughing the Ghetto skin, yet others in whose ears the "*hep, hep*" of the Continent is a long-forgotten cry. A great congregation, the majority still standing (in its faith) with the Law-giver at Sinai, while a few are marching in the vanguard of the sceptics. An eager, restless body, most devout of peoples, yet swiftest of foot in the commercial race; fascinating microcosm of the latter-day world, yet braided with the mark of antiquity; full of the hopefulness of youth, yet seamed and scarred with the martyrdom of ages. Such, in brief, are the Jews of London.

Let us turn aside into the Whitechapel Ghetto, where they most do congregate. Many of its narrow courts and mean slums have fallen before the fiat of the sanitary authority or the advance of the factory owner. Yet enough still remains of its original quaintness, its babel of tongues and chaos of races, to make it stand prominently

out as a unique entity from the dull grey mass of the East-End population. Its denizens are a complicated piece of human patchwork, with the ringleted Pole at one point, the Dutch Jew at another, the English Hebrew in his own corner, and the Gentile coster running like a strange thin thread through the design. The whole is a reproduction in little of the stricken Jewish world. If you would understand the immortal agony of Jewry, go into the East-End colony. Its cosmopolitanism is symbolic of the vagabondage of the race. Its beshawled women with their pinched faces, its long-coated men with two thousand years of persecution stamped in their manner, its chaffering and huckstering, its hunger, its humour, the very Yiddish jargon itself which is scrawled on its walls and shop windows, are part of the grand passion of the chosen people.

But it is its utterly alien aspect which strikes you first and foremost. For the Ghetto is a fragment of Poland torn off from Central Europe and dropped haphazard into the heart of Britain—a re-banished

Jewry weeping beside the waters of "Modern Babylon."

On Sunday Middlesex Street (better known as the "Lane") and its adjoining tho-

KILLING AND PLUCK-
ING POULTRY.

SLAUGHTERHOUSE WHERE POULTRY ARE KILLED.

long and far into the night the factories make dismal music in the Ghetto. From break of day till the going-down of the sun rings the song of the coster through its grimy streets. " Weiber, Weiber ! reimische Beigel ! " * sing out the women, with handkerchief drawn tightly over head. "Customeers, cus-tomeers ! veer are you ? " chime in the men. " Stockings feer poor (pairs) a shilling ! " groans a hapless elder driven in his old age to tempt fortune in a strange land. Often, soon after dawn, the costers are quarrelling with one another for a suitable "pitch," with a sheer, perhaps, at a Gentile sleeping off a public-house debauch on the pavement ; and long after the shadows have lengthened in the Ghetto they are still vouching by their own lives or the kind-ness of the Shem Yisboroch (God) to Israel for the quality of their wares. So spins the toiling Ghetto round its daily orbit.

roughfares are a howling pandemonium of cosmopolitan costerism, a curious tangle of humanity, with the Englishman (Jew and Gentile) in possession and the alien in the background. In these congested streets you can be clothed like an aristocrat for a few shillings, fed *al fresco* like an epicure for sixpence, and cured of all your bodily ills for a copper coin—the chorus of the children in the Hebrew classes often answering the roar of the gutter merchant, like a new and grotesque Church antiphony. The " Lane" on Sunday is, indeed, the last home of the higher costerism. Round its stalls the coster humour reaches its finest fancies, the coster philosophy its profoundest depths, the coster oratory its highest flights. But the most abiding impression it leaves on your mind as you struggle out of its seething, shouting, gesticulating population is of infinite pic-turesqueness, and the life-stream tumbling like a swirling torrent along its course.

On the weekday, however, the scene is transformed. The noise and bustle are gone. The alien with his Yiddish holds the field. You are in a city of endless toil. All day

Why do these Jews labour so? It is because of their passionate yearning for a " place in the sun." Unlike the Gentile, they are in the East-End, not of it—strangers and sojourners in its midst ; alien Dick Whittingtons in side curls and "jupizes" (long coats), who have put down their bundles a while to peer into the promised land beyond, and thereafter rest not till they have retired beaten from the struggle or found social salvation in Maida Vale.

And yet this Ghetto is not all poor. It is really homespun lined with ermine, Dives cheek by jowl with Lazarus. These in-dustrious female costers, for instance, arguing volubly with reluctant customers, have left a husband—working in a factory—who is preparing to blossom into an employer, a son retailing jewellery in a second street, and a daughter selling hosiery in a third.

* " Ladies, ladies ! rolls for sale just like those in our native land."

In a few years a vigorous pull and a pull all together will have hauled the family up to a plane of comparative affluence and the Ghetto have become a distant memory. Quite a crop of Jewish *nouveaux riches*, too, has ripened in the various shops and factories that stud the Ghetto.

And if the Ghetto is not wholly poor neither is it entirely famished. Kosher restaurants abound in it; kosher butcher shops are clustered in thick bunches in its most hopeless parts (seven of them at the junction of Middlesex Street and Wentworth Street), and if the expert handling of the fowls on the stalls by ill-clad Jewesses is not a revelation of epicureanism in humble life, then, most assuredly, things are not what they seem.

Only the superficial think this Jewish colony a mere vale of tears. In the groan of its machinery and the roar of its markets I can distinguish an unmistakable titter—the titter of the Hebrew at his would-be converters, the full-throated laughter of the Ghetto at the Yiddish play, the merriment of the buxom and placid-faced Jewess taking the air by her street-door, the fun of the youth in corduroys who finds a foretaste of Gan Eiden (Paradise) in a game of cricket on the broad spaces of Bell Lane or the green fields of Frying-Pan Alley. On Chometz Battel night[*] the Ghetto even gives itself over to wild carnival till the flaring naphtha jets on the stalls have died to a spluttering flicker and the Christian world is fast asleep. Nay! let no one call the Ghetto melancholy who has not looked in at its dancing clubs and watched an old crony of seventy at a Hebrew wedding foot the furious Kosatzki with a gay old dog of ten winters more.

And there is learning as well as piety in the Ghetto—piety in a dirty face, scholarship behind a mask of rags. How interesting is the spectacle of the bearded elders — peripatetic philosophers of the Ghetto—wending their way slowly from the synagogue, rapt in Talmudic discussion. The coster, too, has sometimes much Rabbinic lore. As he sits, spectacles on nose, behind

[*] The night before Passover Eve, on which all "leaven" is removed from Jewish houses.

his stall absorbed in the political columns of one or other of the new-born Yiddish Press (which, by the way, never prints racing news, and once even boasted a kind of Yiddish *Punch*), I often wonder whether this ill-clad person may not enshrine the brilliancy of a stunted Lassalle, the genius of a Disraeli *manqué*.

The Ghetto's piety is written on nearly every pinched face and across every brick wall. Was ever such a religious slum—a slum with a passion for scattering little synagogues (or chevras) up and down its dark courts—even, so it is said, in garrets and basements? It is artistically religious, this Ghetto, delighting in hymns rendered with the proper trills and anthems delivered in an operatic dress—actually not hesitating to pay £300 for a few services to a truly musical chazan (reader of the services). In its fervour it has brought with it from Poland the melammed (or poverty-stricken pedagogue), who has set up his bare and humble little schoolrooms all over the district, and hammers Hebrew instruction by the hour into the jaded heads of the children of the Ghetto. These little scholars scurrying Chederwards of an evening, clutching the remains of a hurried tea, are one of the most touching and instructive spectacles of this strange colony. Now and then something like a shiver of horror passes over the Ghetto when

A CHEDER (JEWISH SCHOOL) IN WHITECHAPEL.

A "KOSHER" WARNING.

it is discovered that a traitor has been palming off trifah* meat on his customers as kosher. The the Board of Sheceta,† which attends to such matters, pastes a solemn warning on the walls to the faithful, and the offending stall is promptly forsaken. Altogether, indeed, a unique little cosmos, this East-End Hebrew colony—a poverty-stricken, wealthy, hungry, feasting, praying, bargaining fragment of a "nation of priests."

But the Ghetto is not the whole of London Jewry. On its borders stands the famous Houndsditch—one of the world's great toy-lands, whence the Hebrew merchant scatters his playthings and fancy wares over the world, and where our roaring gutter-commerce hunts out its penny wonders. Out in Soho has been planted another vigorous little settlement—mostly of tailors. Across the North of London — Dalston and Canonbury — stretches a third thick Hebrew belt. Here you are in presence of the Jewish bourgeois —the well-groomed, prosperous English Jew (as he loves to call himself), with the keenest of brains and a heart of gold. His ear always to the ground to catch the first distant murmurs of every trade movement, he has made himself prominent in every commercial walk he treads. Go into the Diamond Club in Hatton Garden. It is nothing but a Jewish rendezvous. Speak to the salesmen

in Covent Garden. They will tell you, with a merry twinkle in their eye, of the portion of the market once called "The Synagogue"; and it is almost the same with the fancy, fur, cheap clothing, boot, and furniture trades. But this easily won Hebrew gold circulates freely. For the bourgeois Jews are full of the *joie de vivre*. You see it in their dances, their card parties, their "confirmation" dinners (when the Jewish lad of thirteen, having been called to the reading of the Law in the Synagogue, replies to the toast of his health in a carefully learnt speech), their enthusiastic patronage of the theatre, their great summer migration—like a new Exodus—to the seaside, and the resplendent finery of their handsome women-folk, without whom the North of London would be infinitely duller and the great emporia of Islington poorer indeed. Their religion, however, is in a state of flux. Some of them, like many "upper-class" Jews, have outgrown the spiritual outfit of the East without acquiring a substitute; hence a state of religious nakedness. They are far indeed from Nazareth. But they are equally distant from Jerusalem. They wander on a half-heathenish middle track.

Further afield—in Maida Vale, Hampstead, and Bayswater—are the tents of upper-class Jewry. In them mingle the arts and the sciences, fashion and beauty, Jew and Gentile;

PERIPATETIC PHILOSOPHERS OF THE GHETTO.

---

* Not killed according to the Jewish rites; meat eligible to be eaten is said to be "kosher." The illustrations on p. 30 show a shed in which fowls are killed by the shochetim (slaughterers) at a penny a-piece.

† Literally the Board which looks after the slaughtering of the cattle.

for those who own them are often wealthy, frequently polished, English to the core always. In business they are stock-brokers, merchants, art connoisseurs. As professional men they are giving their fatherland a clever band of authors, artists, and lawyers. Year by year their offspring are found in the ancient English seats of learning in greater numbers—the grandchildren of the Ghetto studying at Jesus' or graduating at Christ's with equal impartiality What's in a name? And everywhere they are, in conjunction with other Jews, endeavouring by a huge effort —by Jewish study circles, literary societies, and the like — to save their people from the Gehinnom of materialism.

Yet let no one think that the Jewry of the East and the Jewry of the West are separate worlds revolving in separate orbits. In essential characteristics they are really one. East-End or West-End, the Jew is still the family man among the nations, delighting keenly in the joys of domesticity. Out of this love of a home and married bliss has sprung that humorous rogue, the Shadchan, or professional matchmaker — a glib fellow of elastic conscience who worries Hebrew bachelors into matrimony in return for a five per cent. levy on the dowry received. Occasionally, when the marriage is a *fait accompli*, the parties snap their fingers at Mr. Shadchan. Upon which he summons them to the Chief Rabbi, who, with two other rabbis, constitute the Beth-Din — a Hebrew judicial bench beset by

BEFORE THE BETH-DIN (JEWISH COURT).

pious men in religious doubt, jilted women, landlords and tenants, and other members of a regrettably contentious race. In many cases the word of the Beth-Din is law.

All these London Jews, too, whether East-End or West-End, are patriots to their fingertips. This patriotism has impressed the physiognomy of the race on at least one East-End Volunteer regiment. It converts the naturalisation returns into catalogues of Biblical (and Polish) names. It has given birth to what a British officer with an unkindly sneer once called the "Houndsditch Highlander." It has resulted in the flower of many a Jewish family being left to die on the African veldt. And it has produced the Jewish Lads' Brigade —an organisation for evolving the Joab and the Judas Maccabæus who lie buried deep down under the Jewish stock-broker or hawker. You can often see the lads of this brigade marching smartly to the beat of the drum through the London streets, like a new Army of the Lord of Hosts —though a juvenile one, to be sure. But while with the upper-class Jew the cry is, "England my Zion, and London my Jerusalem," the aliens' patriotism co-exists with their Zionism. They tumble in their thousands after the music of Zionist oratory as resistlessly as the children of Hamelin city after the ravishing note of the Pied Piper.

London Jewry is a wonderful network of charity. With the aid of his middle-class brother, the West-End Jew has built up a system of philanthropy which follows the poor from cradle to grave—educating their young ones (at the Jews' Free School, the greatest elementary school on earth), rearing their orphans (at the Jews' Hospital and Orphan Asylum), apprenticing their lads to honest trades through the medium of the Jewish Board of Guardians (itself comprising remarkable charities, prophylactic and curative), dowering their brides, tending their sick (in special Jewish wards in the hospitals), nursing their convalescents, feeding their aged, and laying their dead decently in the grave.

But it is on its religious side that the fascination of London Jewry is greatest. The

squalid darkness. Look into the room whence it proceeds. A snow-white cloth covers the table. Two candles are burning with a joyous brightness. Two chalos (or twists) rest pleasantly. one on the other. It is the Jew-pedlar's home on a Sabbath eve! Presently the master of this little paradise returns. "May God make you as Ephraim and Manasseh," he says, laying his hands on the head of his stooping boy. "May God make you as Rachel and Leah," he prays, extending his palms gently over his daughter's head. Then, for the rest of that evening, Psalms and good cheer. On the morrow, the Sabbath peace.

LADS' BRIGADE, JEWS' HOSPITAL AND ORPHAN ASYLUM, WEST NORWOOD.

return of the Jew to earth is devoid of the floral pomp that marks the interment of the Gentile. A plain deal coffin in a sombre black cloth, a few notes of submission to Providence moaned into the echoing air, the cry of the minister, "May he come to his place in peace," the heavy thud of the clay as it is cast on the coffin by the nearest kindred of the dead (oh! bitterest of Jewish practices!), and the Hebrew is at rest with his fathers.

Yet, this natural exception apart, the religion of the observant Jew is a perpetual joy to him, dashing his drab existence with the vividest colouring and ranging like a brilliant rainbow across his sky. The Hebrew wedding, with its many-hued canopy, its crashing of a tumbler under foot, its conjugal pledges in "Babylonish dialect," is like a calculated variant on the monotony of life. Then, the Sabbath! High up in an East-End model dwelling a gleam of brightness pierces the

The Passover, with its unleavened cakes, subjects the Hebrew to a not unpleasant little dietary revolution. The festival of Pentecost, bathing his synagogue in flowers, puts sunshine and springtide into his blood. The Feast of Booths wafts him for nine days into a fruit-and-lamp-hung arcadia*; while the blast of the ram's horn on his New Year's Day transports him in spirit back to the land where the sound of the shofar † proclaimed rest to the soil and liberty to the slave. It is a time of reconciliation and brotherhood and peace; for are not the destinies of all being decided before the judgment seat of God? and so between Jew and Jew pass New Year cards bearing the familiar device in Yiddish, signifying: "May you be inscribed for a good year in the Book of Life." Then,

* That is to say, into the succah or tent in which the Jew is supposed to live during the whole of the festival—a memory of the booths in which Israel dwelt during its journeying in the desert.

† "Shofar" is the Hebrew name for the ram's horn.

that day of days, the great White Fast.* Go on that solemn fast day into the Cathedral Synagogue, down East. There, wealth in the person of Lord Rothschild rubs shoulders with poverty in the form of the alien refugee; and West in the shape of evening-dress meets East in the form of the long white gown (or kittel). The edifice is packed with a great penitent congregation—prominent among them the Yom Kippur Jew making his annual call on Providence. The Cohanim, or priests,† with outstretched palms and praying-shawls on their heads, bless the people, saying: "May the Lord bless thee and guard thee." Through the livelong day rise the plaintive prayers for pardon. Time and again the penitents beat their breast and prostrate themselves humbly in the dust. The morning slowly wears to afternoon, the afternoon fades into night. The air grows close and heavy. Yet not till the "day has turned" and the lights are lit is the atonement ended. Then the congregation draw white praying-shawls over their heads and say after their Reader the prayer for the dying:

"Hear, O Israel, the Lord is our God, the

* So called by Gentiles on account of the many white praying-shawls, white caps, etc., in the synagogue on that day. The Hebrews call it Yom Kippur (Day of Atonement).

† Shown on the right of the picture forming the frontispiece to this volume.

A JEWISH NEW YEAR CARD.

Lord is One." The congregation repeat the words with a shout like a thunder-crash.

"The Lord, He is God," sings the Reader.

"The Lord, He is God," repeat the people seven times, with a roar like the cry of a lost nation. Then, with a shrill note from the ram's horn, the congregation is dismissed—the merchant to his office, the clerk to his desk, and the penitent, perchance, to his crooked ways again.

Such is the London fragment of the Eternal race. It is a growing community, not unmarred by faults, yet not without its ideal side. And it is testing in its own person the combination in one body of the devoted Jew and the English patriot. If it fail, it adds yet another chapter to its people's martyrdom. If it succeed, it knells the end—however remote—of the great Jewish tragedy.

JEWESSES TAKING THE AIR BY THEIR STREET DOORS.

PAWNBROKING LONDON.

By C. A. CUTHBERT KEESON.

PAWN-TICKET.

LONG before the inhabitants of London were blessed with a County Council the at one time universal practice of attracting customers to a shop by means of a sign had fallen into almost complete disuse; but even in this twentieth century no enterprising pawnbroker would think of opening a shop without there hung over it, conspicuous from every point of view, "The Three Brass Balls," "The Swinging Dumplings," "The Sign of the Two to One."

It is the fashion in the trade to speak of these emblems as the insignia of the old Lombard Merchants, and the arms of the Medici. What, however, do those three bright globes mean to thousands of people who walk the streets of London? Some perhaps may pass them unnoticed, but to the poor—the working man who finds it difficult to properly apportion his weekly wage, the clerk out of a berth, the racing man who has had a spell of bad luck, to the small shopkeeper and the costermonger in want of ready money to replenish their stock, to the actor and actress not "in the bill"—they mean a great deal. They mean food for the wife and children when cupboard and pocket are empty—a little money to keep things going till next pay-day; they mean to thousands shelter, warmth, and something to eat; and although many may consider the pawnbroker's shop an encouragement to

improvidence and unthriftiness, every philanthropist who would abolish it admits that he would have to substitute some municipal or charitable pawnshop in its place.

It has been asserted that "to one in every two persons in London the pawnbroker has been in some period of his or her life a stern and unavoidable reality." This estimate may appear to be somewhat exaggerated, but investigations into the amount of business done in the pawnshops of London show that the statement is not very wide of the mark. Within a radius of ten miles from the Royal Exchange are 692 pawnbrokers' shops. From figures obtained from a trustworthy source (the *Pawnbrokers' Gazette*) it appears that the average number of pledges taken in per month at each shop

ARRESTED WHILE PAWNING.

is 5,000, making an aggregate for all the shops of 3,460,000, or 41,520,000 pledges per year, or rather more than six to each head of the population. In these figures pledges of more than £10 in amount are not taken into account, and a very large proportion of the London pawnbrokers do a big business of this kind. Inquiries made at some seventeen shops in different parts of the Metropolis show that out of a million and a-quarter pledges extending over a period of twelve months 66,700 only were for amounts above ten shillings. In the trade these are known as "Auctions," having, if left unredeemed at the end of twelve months and seven days, to be disposed of at public auction. All pledges for sums under ten shillings at a like period become the absolute property of the pawnbroker. In the seventeen shops referred to the average amount lent upon each pledge worked out at four shillings—£250,000 in all. Taking the total number of pledges made annually in London upon the same basis, viz. 41,520,000 at four shillings each, it will be seen that the pawnbrokers supply the "hard-ups" of London annually with the very large sum of £8,304,000.

There are few things in the ordinary way of life more calculated to unnerve a man than a first visit to the pawnshop. Hence most pawnbrokers, to put their customers as much at ease as possible, have their shops divided into separate compartments known as "the boxes," with the entrance up a side street, or rendered as inconspicuous as the character of the house will permit. For the better class customers the modern pawnbroker provides a comfortable "private office."

The nervous pledger, dreading he knows not what, surveys for some minutes the contents of the window, and only after much hesitation and many false starts finds himself within the shop of that mysterious "Uncle" of whom his companions have talked so glibly. What his business was is known only to that "Uncle" and himself, and as he walks triumphantly down the street, relieved in mind and circumstance, he asks himself why he made all that fuss about so simple a matter. Yet it takes a good many visits before he feels quite at his ease. The interview usually lasts less than a couple of minutes, and as a memorandum of it the obliging pawnbroker hands his customer a

STORING BUNDLES IN THE "WEEKLY PLEDGE" ROOM.

neat little square-shaped envelope containing a piece of paste board bearing upon its face a description of the article deposited and on the back an abridged version of the Pawnbrokers' Act.

Very differently does it fare with the pawner of stolen property. Ask a pawnbroker in what way his suspicions are aroused. He will tell you that he does not know. "There is generally something," he says, "about the pawner's manner or in his replies to questions that sets the pawnbroker on his guard." He cannot deny precisely what that "something" is, but he plies the would-be pledger with more pertinent queries, sets a junior hand to run over the "Police List," looks again at the article offered and at the offerer. Experience may not have made him infallible, but his daily dealings have made him wary. If the man

SATURDAY NIGHT AT A PAWNBROKER'S.

is a "wrong 'un" the long delay makes him fidgety, and then "Uncle," confirmed in his suspicions, secretly sends for the man in blue. Sometimes a thief will stay and try to brazen the matter out, at others he makes a dash for liberty, frequently only to run into the arms of an officer waiting at the shop door. If the article be not in the "Police List," or if the pawnbroker be not satisfied in his own mind that the goods have been dishonestly come by, he may decline the goods and let the man depart, for it is a dangerous thing to be too hasty in delivering any one into custody.

Pawnbrokers know that if they take in a stolen article they will have to restore it to the owner, lose the money lent upon it, and attend the courts. That knowledge makes them cautious. Many magistrates and public officials contend that a considerable portion of the property stolen in the Metropolis finds its way into the hands of the pawnbrokers. Every day reports appear in the papers in which stolen goods have been pawned, and there are a still larger number of cases which are not reported. Unquestionably quantities of stolen articles find their way to the pawnbroker, and it is generally a good thing for their owners when they do, for by means of that "automatic detective," the pawn-ticket, they are generally traced and restored. A pawnbroker has to keep a pledge by him for twelve months and give a ticket, which many thieves seem to have a peculiar fondness for preserving. Stolen articles, however, form but an infinitesimal item in the forty-one millions of pledges made yearly. Statistics prepared for the House of Commons show that they fall far short of one per month for each of the 692 pawnbrokers in London.

To redeem a watch or an article of jewellery is an easy matter, and for even the nervous man it has usually no terrors. There are times, however, when the act of redemption is not so easy. Come with me to a busy working neighbourhood like Walworth, where pawnbrokers' shops abound and thousands of homes are dependent upon them. It is Saturday night, and the shop and stall keepers are doing a roaring trade. We turn down a side street, where the lamps do not burn so brightly, and meet a continuous procession of women hurrying away with bundles of all sorts and sizes. Some carry but one, others, assisted by children, have as many as half-a-dozen. They all come from that little door by the side of a pawnbroker's. Standing in the background of the shop, we are confronted by a row of faces peering over the counter. The shop is one that, possibly for the convenience of so large a throng, dispenses with the boxes, and the customers all mingle together. It is a strangely animated scene, with nearly all the characters played by women. It is a rarity to see a man among them, though children are too many for our liking. Girls and even boys are there, all ready with their money, for they may redeem pledges, though the law forbids the pawnbroker to receive a pledge from anyone under the age of sixteen. The women are mostly bare-armed, and look as though they had just come from the wash-tub. They betray no sense of shame if they feel it. They talk and gossip while waiting for their bundles, and are wonderfully polite to the perspiring assistants behind the counter. Though everybody is in a hurry there is little noise or unseemly jostling. An assistant seizes a battered tin bowl, and the front rank of pledgers toss their tickets therein. He then rapidly sorts them out, and gives some to a boy, who darts away to the far end of the counter. The remainder he places in a canvas bag which we have noticed dangling at the end of a string at the back of the shop; he shakes the rope, and immediately the bag is whisked out of sight up the well of the lift used for conveying pledges from the shop to the warehouse above. In a minute it begins to rain bundles until the floor is thickly strewn with them.

In a conspicuous spot on the wall is a notice that no furniture or heavy goods will be delivered after 4 p.m. From that time the rapid delivery of bundles has been proceeding; and so it goes on, hour after hour, Saturday after Saturday, year after year; every pledge produced systematically; no disputes, no haggling about change; unexamined bundles exchanged for money; money swept into a huge till; the whole accompanied with a running fire of bundles from the unseen regions above, hurled down what the pawnbroker calls the "well," but what is more familiarly known as the "spout"

FURNITURE ROOM IN A PAWNBROKER'S WAREHOUSE.

—that spout up which so many things have mysteriously disappeared.

The year round there is an average of 2,000 bundles delivered each Saturday night from this shop, and if we chance that way on the following Monday and Tuesday we shall meet that same procession of women, though this time trooping towards that little side door. Occasionally a man comes on the same errand, shamefacedly trying to conceal his bundle beneath his coat. It is undoubtedly a sad scene for the moralist, but these people know no other way of living, have no place where their Sunday clothes will be safe, have no one but the pawnbroker to apply to when they feel the pinch of hunger. He is their banker and their safe-deposit, and although they know they pay dearly for it in the long run, they are thankful that they have him to turn to in their need. They might easily be worse off, might have no other resource but to sell their sticks and clothes, or, what is as bad, take them to a "Dolly" or "Leaving" shop, so named after the "Black Doll," the conventional sign of the small brokers and rag shops, where articles that a pawnbroker will not receive may be "left" for a short term at high interest. Thanks to the provisions of the

Pawnbrokers' Act, the police, so far as London is concerned, have stamped these latter pests out of existence.

The nature of a pawnbroker's business can, perhaps, be best estimated by a visit to his warehouse and an inspection of the heterogeneous collection of pledged articles. This differs, however, with the character of the shop. There are the chief pawnbrokers of London, who lend only on plate, jewellery, and property of the highest description. By the courtesy of Mr. Henry Arthur Attenborough, we were permitted to inspect the well-known premises of Messrs. George Attenborough and Son, at the junction of Chancery Lane with Fleet Street. As in most pawnbrokers', there are the boxes for the general pledger, and in addition there are two or three small offices for the reception of persons who wish to transact their business privately. All sorts and descriptions of men, and women too, come to Messrs. Attenborough. They have lent £7,000 upon a diamond necklet, a present from a royal personage to a celebrated member of the demi-monde, the said necklet being redeemed and deposited again time after time. The coronet of an Austrian nobleman remained in their custody for several years with a loan of £15,000 upon it. A savant pawned the fore-arm and hand of a mummy wearing a fine turquoise scarabæus ring on one of the fingers. Upon the day of our visit we saw that an advance of 1s. 6d. had been made on a ring, and we were shown an application for a loan of £40,000 upon jewellery.

The seamy side of the picture is presented by the warehouse of the pawnbroker, whose chief business consists of pledges of "soft" goods. The whole house from basement to roof is built up in skeleton frames or "stacks," in which the pledges, each carefully done up in a wrapper, are neatly packed, the tickets to the front. On the first floor the weekly pledges are usually stored, that they may be ready at hand for Saturday night. There is one room devoted to the storage of furniture, in another are rows and rows of pictures, looking-glasses and over-mantels. There are shelves for china and glass, ornaments and clocks; tools of every kind, sufficient to start many workshops. In odd corners we come across odd sights—sea boots and the huge boots of a sewerman; a bundle of sweeps' brooms, apparently not very long retired from active employment, picks, spades, fire-irons, musical instruments, cabmens' whips, umbrellas — yes, even a tiny pair of child's shoes—everything.

Of the thousands of pledges stored in a pawnbroker's warehouse the majority are redeemed, but there are many, variously estimated at from 20 to 33 per cent. of the whole, which remain unredeemed at the expiration of the twelve months and seven days' grace. These are known in the trade as "forfeits," and

HER CHILD'S SHOES.

are disposed of in divers ways. Forfeited pledges, upon which sums of less than 10s. have been advanced, become, as already stated, the pawnbroker's property. Some are placed in the sale stock; occasionally the whole bulk of two or three months' forfeits are sold to a dealer at a discount of 15 or 20 per cent. off the price marked upon the tickets, the pawnbroker being anxious to get rid of them at almost any price. The remainder are sent to public auction.

WITH STEALTHY TREAD.

Of the auctioneers who make a speciality of this business the rooms of Messrs. Debenham, Storr and Sons, King Street, Covent Garden, are, perhaps, best known to the public. On the first floor a sale of "fashionable jewellery," silver plate, watches, plated ware, etc., is proceeding. Suspended upon hooks at the far end of the room near the auctioneer's rostrum are watches too numerous to count. You may buy a bundle of them for little more than a sovereign. An irregular horseshoe of glass-topped cases, in which the more important lots are stored,

AN UNWELCOME PLEDGE.

form the boundary of an inner ring, into which the privileged and well-known buyers are alone allowed to enter; wooden desks or tables form the outer boundary for the smaller dealers and that peculiar class of people who haunt the auction-rooms—people who display an interest in every lot, yet have never been known to buy.

Simultaneously a miscellaneous sale of "sporting goods" is taking place on the ground floor. People of quite a different type attend this sale: men of sporting tendencies and horsey appearance take the place of the Jews, who form a large proportion of the buyers at the jewellery sales. Here are sportsmen's knives and bicycles, guns by the score, walking sticks, shooting boots, billiard cues and fishing rods, boxes of cigars, and bottles of champagne or burgundy; all things which no true sportsman should be without.

Incredible as it may seem to the uninitiated, there are thousands of persons in London alone who are making a comfortable living out of "Uncle" by buying or manufacturing and pledging goods. There are regular manufactories where clothing can be purchased

at a price which the unwary pawnbroker will advance upon, and several pledges in the course of a day will bring a handsome profit. Plate and jewellery are manufactured for the same purpose. Now it is a gold charm for the watch chain; again it is a silver cigarette box, the weight of which has been considerably increased by the insertion of a piece of base metal between the cedar wood lining and the silver exterior. Everything that the pawnbroker will lend money upon—that is to say everything that has any market value whatever—is manufactured for the sole purpose of deceiving him, while sometimes even the natural beauties of goods are artificially enhanced by the aid of scientific knowledge.

To please his clients, to be careful without giving offence, to prevent fraud, and to detain the guilty while trying to make a little for himself, is no light task. If "Uncle" does not give satisfaction all round it is scarcely to be wondered at. He does his best under difficult and often disagreeable circumstances, and those who are too prone to blame him for a mistake are generally quite ignorant of the nature and extent of his business.

A SALE OF UNREDEEMED GOODS (DEBENHAM, STORR AND SONS).

LONDON SCOTTISH : THE ORDERLY ROOM.

VOLUNTEER LONDON.

By CAPTAIN J. E. COOPER.

THE Londoner born and bred is probably no less attracted than his country cousin by the sight of a regiment of Volunteers. The most casual observer could not fail to notice how greatly Volunteering has become an integral part of the life of the Metropolis. Every evening signs of it are to be noticed, and the occasion of a Church Parade on a Sunday morning is a popular event in many suburbs. The regiment will assemble most probably at its headquarters, all the men as smart in appearance as careful attention to uniform and accoutrements can ensure. For this muster the full-dress head dress is worn, and the men carry side-arms. Preceded by the band, as they march to church, they are sure to be keenly watched by the residents. The service will most likely be conducted by the chaplain of the corps, and there are few preachers who cannot so fit the words of their sermon as to make a definite impression on their hearers. In accordance with military usage the service concludes with "God save the King," and, filing out of their seats, the men form up outside. Once more they march through the streets, where doubtless a throng of persons await their return, and on arrival at headquarters they will be dismissed.

But Saturday afternoon is, of course, the grand opportunity for an interested spectator. At the Armoury House, Finsbury, he may see the historic Honourable Artillery Company, a lineal descendant of such a train-band as that in which John Gilpin was a captain. The Honourable Artillery Company takes precedence of all Yeomanry and Volunteers, and is amongst the very few corps which have the right to march through the City of London with fixed bayonets. It will be observed that it has two batteries of Horse Artillery, the men of which are clothed in a somewhat similar manner to the Royal Horse Artillery, and an Infantry Battalion, turned out in scarlet and bearskins, very much like the familiar uniform of the Foot Guards. As a spectacle of pomp and circumstance, let the observer, if possible, be present when the colour is "trooped" by the H.A.C.; and fortunate indeed will he be if he can procure an invitation to one of their dinners, and listen to the traditional cry of "Zaye, Zaye, Zaye!"

As one passes through the Metropolis many men will be seen, in various uniforms, all wending their way to the rendezvous of their several corps. A goodly number of those in dark green will possibly belong to the 2nd London.

In whatever direction a journey be taken Volunteers will be conspicuous. Passing

collective exactitude displayed by the young athletes would form a convincing proof of how erroneous it is for pessimists to declare that the nation's manhood is degenerating.

Let us now go out into the crowded streets again. Surely that sound we hear is the wail of the pipes? Yes; in a few minutes a kilted battalion marches by in grand style, the 7th Middlesex, the famous London Scottish. "Certainly," remarks a critical

Photo Gregory & Co., Strand, W.C.　　　　　　　　THE H.A.C.: A MARCH PAST.

Somerset House may be heard the strains of "God Bless the Prince of Wales," for the 12th Middlesex (Civil Service Rifles), the Prince of Wales's Own, are on parade in the square. We pass on to the School of Arms, a truly fascinating spot for the lover of all kinds of physical exercises. Here take place bouts of fencing—best of training for quickness of hand and eye in combination—and rounds of boxing, an equally exacting test of pluck and good temper. The gymnastic apparatus — parallel bars, horizontal bars, trapeze, rings, vaulting horses, ladders—speak for themselves. The keen activity and

bystander, "the physique of the men from over the Border is not to be surpassed." We enter the orderly room of the regiment to find the colonel seated at the table, and the adjutant giving instructions to staff-sergeants. The adjutant is here responsible for the accuracy of no mean amount of correspondence and "Returns," as on the parade ground he is answerable for the instruction of all ranks, and the correctness of drill.

Turn aside for a moment from the purely official side, and look at another aspect of Volunteer life in London. Near Charing

LONDON IRISH : THE CANTEEN.

the 1st Middlesex Royal Engineers. Here a detachment is
busily at work building a bridge.
Without Engineers the best army
in the world is likely to be useless.
The Engineers render points of
vantage accessible, roads passable,
woods clear, rivers no hindrance.
They extinguish, as it were, time
and space by means of the field
telegraph. Hard would it be to
fix a limit to the extent of their
functions of utility.

We next betake ourselves to
Hyde Park. On the way let
us call at the Guildhall, where
a company of the Volunteer
Medical Staff Corps is drilling.
The name suggests the province
of the Corps, as the particular
duties pertaining to military
ambulance receive most attention.

On reaching Hyde Park a
large mass of troops are to be seen taking
up position. On the right of the line are
over a hundred mounted men, the Mounted
Infantry Company of the 13th Middlesex,
Queen's Westminster. The corps, in neat grey
uniform and
the now al-
most univer-
sal slouch

Cross are the headquarters of the 16th Middlesex, the London Irish. The Emerald Isle
has furnished many gallant soldiers for the
Empire, and its Volunteer representatives on
this side of the water are generally "as smart
as paint." We see some of them here
pleasantly occupied in the canteen.

Imagine the interested observer to be shod
in a pair of the legendary seven-league boots.
He takes one short stride and
stands in the headquarters of

1ST MIDDLESEX ROYAL ENGINEERS : BRIDGE BUILDING.

nat, is deservedly popular. We go to their headquarters, Buckingham Gate, where we see a line of men awaiting their turn to take the oath of allegiance to the Sovereign and to be duly enrolled. Who will wonder that the line is so long? Yet not a few who wished to be numbered in that line have been rejected. The height standard, the chest-measuring tape, the heart and lungs examination, the sight test, all contribute to their exclusion.

Once more returning to Hyde Park, a strong battalion clothed in a serviceable light grey uniform is encountered. An expert explains that they are the 20th Middlesex, widely known as the Artists'; and before the Park is left behind a party of signallers attracts attention. The men are engaged in " flag-wagging "—the slang term for this method of signalling. Any message can be communicated by means of the Morse alphabet, as far as the movement of the flag can be discerned. A powerful telescope enables flag signals to be read at a considerable distance. By night the same effect, the Morse combination of long and short signs — technically " dashes " and " dots "—can be obtained by the use of a flash-lamp. And great results have been exhibited by the heliograph, which, as its name implies, avails itself of the sun's aid to produce the necessary succession of long and short gleams on a. reflector, or the same principle that the naughty boy on a sunny day creates flashes of light on the ceiling of the schoolroom by means of the polished blade of his new pocket-knife. Messages have been directly conveyed a distance of eighty miles by the employment of the heliograph. Ponder these facts and view the signalling party with added respect.

Proceeding to Regent's Park, below the sheen of bayonets a glimpse is caught of scarlet and busbies. A hoarse voice is heard shouting the order " Advance in Column," followed by the voice of a captain giving the command " No. 1, By the Right, Quick March," and the band strikes up " The British Grenadiers." " A Volunteer battalion of the Royal Fusiliers," announces one who knows. In the distance yet another assemblage of citizen soldiers looms in sight. On nearer approach a critic, closely scrutinising, remarks, " All very young — boys in fact."

Quite true. They are the 1st Cadet Battalion of the King's Royal Rifle Corps, but as thorough in drill, and as well equipped with signallers, Maxim gun, and ambulance as the most severe, old-fashioned martinet on the one hand, or the most up-to-date theorist on the other, could desire. Think of what a boy learns in a cadet battalion; and, ye educationalists, forget it not that he *likes* to learn it. He is taught how to stand, how to turn, how to march. He is taught the intricacies of squad drill, with the complications of front and rear forming. Then he is given his carbine, in lieu of the longer rifle, and is instructed in the manual and firing exercises, physical drill with arms, and the bayonet exercise. Judicious attention is paid to aiming drill, and even in the heart of London he can procure a species of target practice and become an accurate marksman by the use of that excellent invention the Morris tube. All the training tends to cause the cadet to acquire habits of discipline, punctuality, and exactitude, which can but stand him in good stead in his journey through life.

Pride of place has been given in this article to the H.A.C.; but the Londoner must not think that he has seen all the Artillery. Let him come to Leonard Street, City Road, and watch the members of the 2nd Middlesex Volunteer Artillery engaged in gun-drill. Truly in these days a gunner has much to learn, but the gunnery and its kindred subjects are most absorbing studies. See, in the hall, the concentrated attention of a batch of recruits while a patient lecturer is giving theoretical instruction. Outside a detachment is seen, all the men with their coats off, evidently prepared for " Repository exercise." They are about to lift and move a heavy gun and mount it on a carriage.

Again we go down into the heart of London and pass within the charming precincts of Lincoln's Inn. On one side of New Square will be seen a small building, bearing a notice that it is the headquarters of the 14th Middlesex Volunteer Rifle Corps. The 14th Middlesex are the Inns of Court Rifles, and, owing to the legal profession of the members, are known to the humorist as the " Devil's Own."

It is meet and right now to journey

CIVIL SERVICE RIFLES : SCHOOL OF ARMS.

VOLUNTEER MEDICAL STAFF CORPS : AT DRILL.

QUEEN'S WESTMINSTERS : ENROLLING RECRUITS.

VICTORIA AND ST. GEORGE'S M.I. :
RIDING DRILL.

regiments afford. As a gradual step from grave to gay, attend a parade of a very "crack" corps in the Volunteer Force, the London Rifle Brigade, on an occasion when a leading feature is the presentation of "The Volunteer Long Service Medal" to those veterans who have completed twenty years' service. In London the recipients are not unlikely to receive it from the hands of the general commanding the Home District ; and the proceedings naturally

to West Brompton, to 69, Lillie Road, the home of the Cyclist Corps. The members of the 26th Middlesex are all cyclists, and are drilled and exercised as such, hence the official title. At present the Corps is attached to the 12th Middlesex (Civil Service) erstwhile seen at Somerset House ; but it is not unlikely that eventually it will have an absolutely separate identity. Particularly worthy of attention is the Maxim gun, most ingeniously mounted on cycles, a weapon with which the special detachment has several times given a striking display. The sight of this mobile corps suggests Infantry differently mounted. The above illustration affords a characteristic scene of some members of the Mounted Infantry Company of the Victoria and St. George's Rifles qualifying themselves in military equitation at the Riding School in the barracks, St. John's Wood.

A view has now been granted of various corps representing all branches of the service, and nearly always occupied in learning or practising in some form their professional duties as soldiers of the King. But many, nay most, of our London Volunteers become more closely knit together, and their *esprit de corps* thereby increased, through the opportunities for social intercourse their

arouse enthusiasm and the spirit of emulation in the breasts of the younger Volunteers present in the ranks. Another somewhat similar *fête* will be the annual distribution of prizes. The greater number of prizes are, of course, generally awarded for success in shooting ; but knowledge of and smartness in drill, attendance at parade, and skill in almost any gymnastic exercise or fencing are not often left unrewarded.

On another evening we attend a smoking concert of some Volunteer regiment, nearly always an agreeable *réunion*. Every corps as a general rule possesses a sufficiency of musical talent, and the songs are usually well-chosen and popular. The good-feeling existing between officers and men is also apparent.

In this article little or nothing has been said about the relative positions of the different ranks. In London especially, it may often happen that home or civilian relationships are completely reversed on donning the King's uniform. Yet a combination of tact, common-sense, and soldierly instincts has rendered unpleasantness from this cause practically unknown. Still, at the military quarters of the corps, rooms and general accommodation are necessarily separate for the officers, sergeants, and men. Particularly well-arranged and commodious are the headquarters of the 17th (North) Middlesex V.R.C., situated in High Street, Camden Town. Entering through an arched gateway, we first get a peep at a good-sized drill hall. Turning to the left we pass the orderly room, and proceed up a number of stone steps distinctly suggestive of barrack life. After having noticed the sergeants' mess we go further down the passage and reach the spacious mess-room of the officers. Here, if we cannot be present on a guest night and drink the health in response to the formula " Mr. Vice, the King," "Gentlemen, the King," we are at least sure to be hospitably entertained.

Acquaintance with the social side of Volunteering in London is not complete without attending a Volunteer ball. Soldiers are proverbially the best of hosts, and as now on the parade ground the Volunteers are in very close touch with the Regulars, so in the ball-room they perform their duties in an equally soldierly manner. How attractive is the scene! The extensive room, the brilliant lights shining on an artistic arrangement of weapons and the regimental crest, the gay uniforms, all contribute to produce a picturesque effect. And how excellently is the music performed by the regimental band!

Do not, however, imagine that Volunteer life in London is all " beer and skittles." Many of the duties that sound quite fascinating when mentioned are wearisome and tedious when the novelty has worn off. It is hard for a man, after a long and harassing day's work, to turn out and drill attentively, perhaps having to journey far from his home to do so. Then those who desire promotion must contrive to study no small amount of technical matter, and will have to face scarcing examinations. It would be easy to multiply drawbacks. But, all said and done, the days spent in Volunteering generally stand out in a man's memory as amongst those he would wish to live again. We have been accused of being "a nation of shopkeepers." But our thousands of citizen soldiers—" the boys who mind the shop,' as *Punch* once so happily put it—prove that the military instinct is far from being dead within us.

26TH MIDDLESEX CYCLIST CORPS : A GUN TEAM

AT PICCADILLY CIRCUS.

LONDON'S FLOWER GIRLS.

By P. F. WiLLIAM RYAN.

PICCADILLY CIRCUS is a brilliant whirl! Vehicles of every size and colour roll hither and thither. Pedestrians, obviously much concerned for the safety of their bones, step briskly from the circumference to the centre, or *vice versâ*, sometimes sacrificing dignity to a comical little trot. The air quivers with a thousand blended sounds, in which nothing is clear but the frequent tinkle of the 'bus conductor's bell. In the centre of the changeful scene, the bevy of flower girls, seated on the steps of the Shaftesbury Fountain, are models of industrious and stolid indifference.

They are fashioning buttonholes. In a small way they are rivals of the great florists in Regent Street or Piccadilly. How artistically their stock is disposed! Delicate roses are perched coquettishly on stakes a foot high, which stand in baskets of dark-green moss. And what colour combinations! Every vagary of taste is anticipated. Business

is brisk. Between attending to customers and preparing for them they seem to have scarcely an idle minute. But as the sun goes down you may sometimes see a flower girl absorbed in her evening paper, while gilded London throbs around her.

The Shaftesbury Fountain is a luxurious position for the flower-sellers compared with some others. At the junction of Charing Cross Road with Oxford Street they have to stand at the kerb hour after hour, their baskets suspended from their necks by a strap. Their busiest time is Saturday night; and on a fine Sunday they do a roaring trade with pedestrians making their way to Hyde Park. The flower girls at Ludgate Hill are in much the same line of business. They too, stand at the kerb. But the fever of the' City has touched them, and they push their wares much more vigorously.

For the flower hawker, Ludgate Hill is one of the best thoroughfares. Profit is light, but the turnover is rapid. During the middle of the day people making their way to and from luncheon or dinner throng the footpaths. Working girls form a large proportion of the crowds; they are frequent purchasers.

A well-defined economic law decides whether a flower girl shall sell bouquets or loose flowers, or both. Where women are the chief purchasers loose flowers or large bunches predominate. Oxford Circus is the headquarters of this trade. But Westbourne Park Road, the great shopping centre of the Bayswater district, runs it very close as a mart for loose flowers. On a smaller scale, one sees the same thing in Euston Road, and in Southampton Row, the favourite resort of the Bloomsbury flower girl.

The buttonhole is a speciality of the Royal Exchange flower girls. Amongst their patrons there are no ladies. The well-to-do City man is a dapper fellow, who feels that his coat fits all the better for being decorated with a smart flower. The women who sit in the shadow of the Duke of Wellington's monument sometimes make seven or eight shillings in a day out of this little foible of his. Outside some railway stations seasonable buttonholes are generally on sale. This is so at Ludgate Hill Station, Cannon Street, King's Cross, and Victoria. But railway stations do not seem to be favourite stands for flower sellers. You seldom see one at such important places as Euston, the Great Central, Paddington, or Waterloo.

One branch of the trade is plied mainly at night. See its representative in an oldish draggled woman, framed in a panel of white light, cast on the pavement by a flaming shop-front. She sells in public-houses. It is a precarious mode of obtaining a livelihood, for the publican often gives the hawker an inhospitable reception, lest she should annoy his customers. Nevertheless, it is a form of the industry that flourishes in almost every quarter of London. The best locality for it is the neighbourhood of Leicester Square. If the public-house hawker carries a basket it is a sign of prosperity. Many flower sellers who visit the public bars at night make a tour of the residential streets by day, calling at likely houses to show their gladiolas and asters, and perhaps huge bunches of sunflowers, or whatever else happen to be the flowers of the season. The coster frequently hawks not only cut flowers but potted plants and stunted shrubs for house decorations. A neat hand-cart, laden with flower-pots artistically decorated, may regularly be seen passing through the streets, in charge of a prosperous-looking couple—the woman perhaps carrying a gaily-dressed flower-pot. The restaurants are their best customers.

Amongst the army of flower girls are skirmishers who "advance to the attack." St. Paul's Churchyard is the skirmishers' paradise. Sir Robert Peel's statue at the western end of Cheapside is their base of operations. They leave their stock around the pedestal while they move about, lynx-eyed, eager, prompt. It requires boundless energy to bring their wares under the eyes of the sprinkling of people in that jostling crowd who are potential purchasers, and need but to be tactfully tempted. There are often as many as nine girls at the statue; but that is only for a minute or two, to replenish their stock from the reserve. They are quickly off again to the kerbstone. The skirmisher in the Strand or Fleet Street has an easier time. But there, trade is far from being so lively. For flower girls of this class Primrose Day is a golden anniversary. Many volunteers, however, divert much of the profit from the pockets of the regular members of the craft. Such interlopers are not welcome. There is also a sort of militia who join the ranks of flower sellers every Saturday night, especially in summer, having bought their rather faded stock for a trifle from the ordinary hawkers.

Covent Garden market in the morning is the place to see the various types. You notice that the prosperous flower "girl" is more often a woman than a girl, and that in the

SHOWY AND CHEAP.

dress of all there is a remarkable similarity. A trio are bargaining over a box of China asters, that look like the face of a finely wrought marble slab. They wear large black knitted shawls, hanging loosely from their shoulders, and wide white aprons with mitred hems. A trifle lends them a slightly un-English air. It is their large earrings. A melancholy-looking woman of middle age bends over a box of sweet pea. Her dark hair is parted in the middle. A rusty bonnet is set far back upon her head. Her apron is also mitred, and her shawl is home-knitted, but its ends are fastened by the

services at their mission hall in Clerkenwell —the headquarters, by the way, of the Flower Girls' Christian Mission, an institution which from its birth attracted many earnest and generous friends, amongst the number the Baroness Burdett-Coutts. On such occasions the girls avail themselves of the resources of their wardrobe with becoming pride. But it is

ROUND SIR ROBERT PEEL'S STATUE (CHEAPSIDE).

OUTSIDE LUDGATE HILL STATION.

at a wedding that a flower girl's delight in warmth of colouring is most palpable. Flowers are not obtrusive; but her hat, her frock, her jewellery are tropical in their contempt for sedate tones.

belt of her apron. Not far away is a girl whose hair is drawn tightly into little knobs with curling-pins. A fat slattern with twinkling eyes is considering the saleable prospects of a box of apple blossom. A beautiful species of speckled lily engages the attention of a young woman with much jet embroidery on her tightly-fitting black silk bodice. She is of the aristocracy; and so too is a scrupulously tidy old lady, with a self-centred air that suggests a snug bank account. A great number of flower girls attend the weekly

Tea and bread and butter at Covent Garden are often the flower girl's breakfast. More usually she has her meal before leaving her home, especially if she is well off. Her husband, if in the trade, sometimes fetches her midday meal. After buying her flowers, she generally proceeds at once to her stand, which may be a couple of miles away. Nowhere is competition keener than in the East-End. On Saturdays particularly, baskets and barrows of flowers make many bright

" VIOLETS."

splashes in High Street, Whitechapel. In Aldgate, principally near the Metropolitan Railway Station, there is a large trade done in buttonholes and loose flowers. The passers-by are mostly Jews. Yet, strangely enough, one rarely, if ever, sees a Jewish flower girl. Working men returning home buy large bunches of loose flowers in Whitechapel to brighten their humble tenements on Sunday. The weary-looking factory girls cannot resist the temptation to take half a dozen roses for a penny. Jewesses dressed in their best for the Hebrew Sabbath are also good customers.

The flower girl tries to avoid bringing home any of her stock save on Saturday night, which must of course be an exception if she purposes to work next day. At Piccadilly and Oxford Circus, and all the principal stands, business goes on much as usual on Sundays. The very prosperous, however, begin the week by taking a rest, while women with families often remain at home a day in mid-week to do their house-work. For the well-to-do a summer holiday out of town is not uncommon. On Sundays many flower girls, with admirable shrewdness, flock to the leading hospitals to dispose of their stock to visitors at somewhat reduced prices. In some quarters the hawkers make Sunday rather depressing with a display of funeral wreaths of doubtful freshness.

Now and then the flower girl stands out vividly from the crowded canvas of the streets. Perhaps she is little more than a child, and holds out a solitary bunch of violets. Observe, too, a mother and daughter —at least you guess that to be the relationship—standing at the kerb opposite a big tobacconist's in Oxford Street. Just for a moment their pose is matchless, as for some reason they search each other's eyes, seriously, questioningly. The girl is a lovely dark-eyed creature, with raven hair brushed back from her forehead, and tied with a ragged crimson ribbon. One bare, earth-stained toe peeps through a worn, misshapen boot. A small basket hangs from her neck by a piece of cord ; and cord to match fastens her boots!

Here is a pretty incident of the pavement. A young exquisite, whose business in life might be the spending of a handsome allowance, pauses to take a lovely flesh-coloured rose nestling in maidenhair from a girl-woman ; a young mother, you feel sure, as you note the melting tenderness in the depths of her eyes and the waxen hue of her fingers. A piece of silver passes between them, and he turns on his heel. He is above small change.

AT OXFORD CIRCUS.

There are flower girls the poorest of the poor. To them winter is pitiless. You have only just turned your back on the glitter of a theatre perhaps. The north-east wind and December sleet sting your face. As you hurry forward, a bloodless hand at the street corner is outstretched with dripping blossoms. From beneath the drenched shawl comes a faint cry—a baby's tiny voice. That is one of the haunting, heart-breaking spectres of the great city!

The flower girl's funeral! It must come. Sometimes it is the last act in a sombre drama. But happily not always. There was one that fell in the opening days of this century. Its memory will live long. She was a white-haired woman of seventy when the Reaper beckoned her away. But even so, her heart was young at the end. For her life was lived in the midst of life where, year in year out, the pace never slackens and one loses count of time. Her sisters of the craft came from far and near to say good-bye. Around the sleeper they strewed lily-of-the-valley, and violets, and snowdrops, and rare blooms their pockets could ill afford, for it was winter, when choice flowers were scarce.

The last journey to Kensal Green was taken with a funeral car and four horses; two mourning coaches, and six cabs! The number will never be forgotten, will not at all events ever grow less. They ranged themselves round the graveside, silent, puzzled, solemn, their eyes fixed curiously on the gaping bed. Sharp contrasts they presented: some quite young, some more than middle-aged. One worn and haggard, another bronzed and vigorous. Here a flabby matron, there a refined-looking girl. None prim—a few rakish. Not a tear was shed. They had no tears. From infancy they had been out in the storm, hardening in the stern school! But over all was the glamour of simplicity, the poetry of rugged truth. When the first horrid rattle of earth on timber changed to the muffled thud of earth on earth the spell was broken, their tongues were loosened. It sounded strange to hear the young ones, mere slips of girlhood, speaking of her glibly by name as though she was the flower girl still. . . .

The men rested upon the handles of their shovels while lovely wreaths and crosses were heaped on the freshly-turned clay. It was her last stock, left there to yield up all their sweetness for her—just as though she were a fine lady for whom flowers were grown, only to die at her breast!

A FLOWER GIRL'S GRAVE.

MUSEUM-LAND IN LONDON.

By JAMES BARR.

IN the heart of London there is a land where speech is hushed and the soul of silence reigns; a land where dwell the people of sibilant tongue, and to which doors are closed and when night spreads its black mantle over grinning idol and dried human head, the silence is denser indeed, but only a little denser than it has been all

BRITISH MUSEUM : THE READING ROOM.

haster those of the soft tread; a region of silence and of drift — Museum-land. Thrown up by the waves of time and caught in shelves and cases, as flotsam caught in the crannies of the cliffs, is the quaint drift-wood of the world; and to view this come the people, who stare and pass on. And those that dwell in the land, they hear nothing of the roar that fills the outside world, but their ears catch the sounds of silting feet and the sibilant whisper. All day long the people drift, drift, drift, through the highways and byways of the dim land; but even when

day. The policeman's foot sets up a more hollow sound, but a not much louder din than it did during the hours when Museum-land was a land for the people.

To the English-speaking world "The Museum" means one Museum, and that is the British. Secure a permit and slip into the Reading Room! At once the similarity to a mighty hive is evident : the lofty dome, the busy workers, the hum and buzz, the little hole-like door at the far point where in and out crawl the bee-like workers, as it were, bringing in the honey in the shape of books, to be consumed by the human bees inside, who grow big through much eating. Every visitor sees this startling likeness to a hive. But how few know that the likeness is carried even farther? Round this hive, behind unseen doors, are miles and miles of honeycomb cells, narrow, dim passages, one on top of the other, divided by gratings through which an uncertain amount of light from the glass

BRITISH MUSEUM : A LECTURE IN THE ASSYRIAN GALLERY.

roof slides down; and against the walls of each passage is stored the honey of ages, the books of all lands and all times; and here are many workers in semi-gloom and still air. These store back the particles when those in the hive have finished, or produce fresh sweets as they are called for. This honeycomb in itself is one of the most wonderful curiosities of the Museum, and to be ushered in and led through a section will give one a better idea of the enormous resources of the Museum than any amount of listless gazing at the show cases.

Directly opposite the door by which one enters the great Reading Room is the passage which leads to the home of all the most precious books the library contains. Before one can gain permission to visit this—the Holy of Holies—one must first have secured entrance to the Reading Room, and there obtained specific permission to be shown into the inner room.

But this British Museum is a region of many unseen or seldom seen books, to enter which one must either get written leave or at least ring a bell. The jangle of a bell usually betokens the waking up of an expert in some out-of-the-way path in knowledge, old coins and medals, china, flint nuds, ancient prints and paintings from India, and such-like curiosities. From every quarter of the world come strangers with things precious and things they think precious carefully lugged to their heart, and no matter what its class, or where it comes from, there is a cool-brained, cold-eyed expert who takes the thing, turns it one critical turn, and tells the anxious owner exactly what it is, where it came from, and what it is worth.

However, the majority of people shun bells and stick to the "open road," and this road leads quickly through strange lands and distant ages. If you are so favoured by fortune as to come upon a lecturer surrounded by his little knot of listeners industriously going through, we'll say, the Assyrian Gallery, attach yourself to the party and listen to the strange things he tells. For a few minutes it will strike you as almost unholy to hear a man speaking loudly in a museum, more especially among those mammoth personifications of silence the stone bulls; but this feeling will wear away, and you will enjoy an experience typical of the educational side of this many-sided institution.

In museums everyone employed, whatever

his position, is in a way a detective. This is a necessity. Museum treasures are in danger from almost every description of the unregenerate, ranging from the maniac who smashes into smithereens the Portland Vase to the cowardly sneak who surreptitiously tears a rare engraving out of a book. Not one visitor in a thousand is able to recognise the Museum detectives. For instance, if you slip in to see the Portland Vase, you are sure to find a gentleman gazing with mighty admiration at the treasure. He looks for all the world like an ordinary spectator; but drop in again next day or next month, and you will still find him there. His eggs are all in one basket, and he watches that basket. The thief who steals for mercenary profit, although he is found at museums, is nothing like so dangerous a character as the dishonest man with a mania for collecting, or the savage who loves destruction for its own sake. Thus to their ordinary duties is added that of keeping a sharp eye on all who enter the place, and especially those who have in their possession for a time precious books and specimens. Therefore it is that in the British Museum there are many bells to ring and doors to be knocked at before a glance at the choicest treasures can be had.

Staring across Lincoln's Inn Fields at each other are two

BRITISH MUSEUM: LOOKING AT THE PORTLAND VASE.

museums so totally dissimilar that their juxtaposition is one of the grim humours of London. Facing towards the south is that sleepy little Soane Museum, so like an ordinary solicitor's office of the usual Inn type that the unknowing hundreds who daily pass, if they learn the nature of the building at all, learn only by chance. A century ago this dwelling-house belonged to Sir John Soane, an architect famous in his generation, and when he died he left the house with all its treasures—the collection of a busy life-time—to the public. Few Londoners consult a guide-book dealing with London, therefore few know of this Museum, the names on its visitors' book being mostly foreign and provincial. To enter the place is to step into a section of the sleepy mediæval. Somewhere in the loft of the building one knows there is a curator,

SOUTH KENSINGTON MUSEUM: "PUFFING BILLY."

INDIAN MUSEUM : FAÇADE OF A NATIVE SHOP.

UNITED SERVICE INSTITUTION MUSEUM : MODEL OF TRAFALGAR.

and a silent-voiced man shows one through
the rooms full of strange inanimate things,
but empty of all animate. Of all the denizens of Museum-land not one is so lonely,
so sleepy, so empty of human life: the din
and stress of Hogarth's "Election" and his
"Rake's Progress" almost seem out of place
on its walls. Soane's Museum, too, hibernates
during the winter, going to sleep at the
end of August and waking again in March.

Across the "Fields" and facing the north
is the other museum, wide awake and full of
horrors. The entrance to the Museum of
the Royal College of Surgeons is as noble
as the Soane is unpretentious, and those who
flock to its doors are of the bustling, breezy
stamp of character, for few except surgeons
and medical students care to visit this place
of skulls and bones, and of bottles filled with
"specimens" in spirits. Inside, the light
falls strong and glaring on the exhibits,
and before cases sit the medical students,
book in hand, alternately reading a paragraph
and gazing upon the bottled object to
which the paragraph refers. In this section
of Museum-land no children wander, and few
womenkind visit it. Indeed, it is not a
place for those that do not care for ghastly
sights and the glint of steel lances and
cruelly-shaped instruments.

It is strange that people should hate the
surgeon's knife, yet love the bayonet and the
sabre. The change from the Surgeons'
Museum to that of the Sailors and Soldiers—
the United Service Institution Museum—is a
striking one. Our country's defenders were
fortunate in obtaining possession of the
historic Banquetting Hall in Whitehall, from
one of the windows of which King Charles
stepped to the place of his execution. In
this ancient and majestic room the Services
have stored their curiosities, relics of many
a fierce fight and fruitful adventure, and
among these sailors and soldiers stride in
numbers, for all who wear the uniform of
his Majesty are made welcome without price.
The blue jacket and the red or khaki coat
are the predominating garb to be seen, and
the comments heard smack of the salt sea
and the tented field. The centre of popularity in this place is the mighty model of
the Battle of Trafalgar, little white battered
motionless ships, friends and enemies ap-

parently in a hopeless mix, upon an equally
motionless sea of glass. The attendants—
some of whom are shown in our photographic
illustration on the opposite page, and who
are all retired sailors and soldiers—are taught
to explain the fight to visitors. There is a
breezy air of jollity abroad in this Museum,
for even the civilians who pay their sixpences
at the door are for the most part of the
healthy, lusty sort, as should be when strife
and struggle are the themes brought to mind
by the objects all about.

South Kensington, the home of museums,
has not one so popular as that of the alive-
seeming dead, the Natural History Museum.
All people love contrasts, and those who take
care of this Museum and guard its treasures
live in an atmosphere of contrasts. Exhibit
contrasts strongly with exhibit, visitor with
visitor. Here flock the little children;
hither hobble the aged. Like takes to like.
The daintily-caparisoned children cluster
round the glass cases of exquisitely-plumaged
birds and soft-furred animals; the aged and
dried, spectacles on forehead, peer search-
ingly at the bones of beasts that disappeared
as living things from this earth ages ago.
Each of the staff that guards over the alive-
seeming dead is deeply learned in Nature's
lore, and, as part of their recompense, they
see treasures which the drifting public are
not privileged to behold. For the exhibits
that so proudly display plumage and fur to
the casual sightseer are by no means the
best specimens of their time and tribe in this
bit of Museum-land.

The truth is that light kills colour; brightness of plumage is dimmed, blackness of
fur is blurred, by the light that floods in
through museum windows. So it comes to
pass that not in the public halls, but in dark
basements, are the true treasures of this
Museum, and there they may be seen by those
who can gain entrance. Down in the gloom
student and custodian turn over and study
the skins of birds and beasts in all their
pristine glory, for those pelts and hides
and skins that are the choicest specimens
of their kind are all hidden away from the
garish light, so that only the people who
have a serious interest in the exhibits are
allowed to handle and hold them. Under
this roof in South Kensington the staff is

small, but the real roof of the Natural History Museum is the blue sky, and under it, in all impossible places of the world, scurry men, gun or net or trap or hook in hand, surprising the unwary, circumventing the cunning of Nature to add to the shelves or dark rooms of this building, which, like the Nature it represents, has an appetite that is insatiable. The "Living" Natural History Museum, therefore, is not to be found at South Kensington, but is scattered over the face of the globe, wherever insect crawls, beast runs, or bird flies.

Near to the home of Natural History stands that amorphous bit of Museum-land familiarly known to the public as the "South Kensington." This Museum sprawls over a vast extent of ground, and its exact shape is not easily grasped, while, as to its moods and its personalities, they are many, ranging from the dreamy, Eastern, mystic show of gaudy things in the Indian Section to the harsh practical pulsations of the Western machinist's constructive genius. And with the visitors who stream in at its many doors the practical is easily the most enthralling of its moods. Stand and glance at the great vista of working models of engines. The wheels turn silently, the little pistons dodge forward and back, everything working mysteriously silent. But clustered about each indolently industrious machine see the big-eyed, excited knot of boys, watching every motion, skipping about and straining for a better view of the polished model. And then the joy of actually feasting eyes and surreptitiously laying fingers on "Puffing Billy"! The unattached urchin raises a "whoop" when he first sights the ancient locomotive, and the schoolboy shepherded by his master, although less demonstrative, is quite as gleeful. To see a crowd

of schoolboys examining this old engine makes one wonder what boys admired before engines were invented. This section of the "South Kensington" is the happy hunting ground of the lads of London; lads by themselves, school lads with a master trying his best to keep some sort of order among his bevy, and to tear the atoms of his class away from the mechanical toys. In this portion of the Museum is certainly to be seen one of the heart-warming sights of Living London.

Contrast makes London what she is, a city of more lights and shadows than any other place in the world. And here in South Kensington the contrast is great. From the Engineering Section of the Museum one should skip across to the Indian Museum, which nestles by the impressive Imperial Institute. Once inside, the visitor finds himself transported to the Orient. All the indolence of the East is in the air, the atmosphere is heavy and the light subdued, and the attendants who stand among the cases filled with things barbaric in their splendour of colour, seem to dream the hours away. There is no bustle, no sense of unrest, and the visitors are few. In at the door occasionally drift groups of picturesque natives of the great empire of India, and these loitering through, looking at things familiar to their eyes, seem part of the Museum itself.

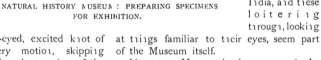

NATURAL HISTORY MUSEUM : PREPARING SPECIMENS FOR EXHIBITION.

Altogether Museum-land can scarcely be called a part of Living London; it would be nearer the truth to name it dreaming London, sleeping London. Living seems to infer bustle and noise and strife, but in Museum-land all these are far away; are swallowed up in an all-encompassing silence and subdued lights.

" MONKEY BOATS " WAITING AT ENTRANCE TO ISLINGTON TUNNEL.

ON LONDON'S CANALS.

By DESMOND YOUNG.

A STAGNANT waterway, on which slides a narrow, slender "monkey boat" drawn by a horse that occasionally gets his head down at so much collar work. In front of the animal a budding bargee (he ranks as fourth mate—or fifth, or sixth), with a fine display of shirt sleeve and a gift of repartee never allowed to lie dormant when the tow line gets crossed. Now and again he makes a flick at a fly on the horse's "near" ear, thereby hurting his charge considerably more than the insect. In the stern of the boat, behind the entrance to the cabin, on top of which a caged throstle pours out a ceaseless song, and partly hidden from view by the dog kennel—perhaps a soap box or an old caustic soda tin—a buxom female whose russet face is framed in a print sun-bonnet of the "truly rural" pattern, her hand on the tiller, her eyes generally looking ahead, as a good steerswoman's should.

The picture is familiar to bridge loungers in many parts of London, though it is much more frequently to be seen north of the Thames than south. Not very often is it to be witnessed on the Surrey Canal, because

that "cut" leads nowhere, running as it does only from Rotherhithe to Camberwell Road and on the way throwing out an arm to Peckham. But on the Grand Junction and the Regent's it is common. While the craft that frequent the one are mostly wide, mastless boats for local traffic and brown-winged barges which bring chalk, flints, and the like from Kentish and Essex ports and take away in exchange coke and other products, the majority of the tiny argosies on the northern canals carry everything and go everywhere. They are "monkey boats," or, as they are called in the country, "fly boats." The origin of that term is plain. "Fly boats" are the greyhounds of inland waterways. Given anything like "good luck," they can reel off on an average about four miles an hour.

Flat barges (never to be classed with "monkey boats," any more than you can lump together dirty ocean "tramps" and crack liners) there are, of course, on the Grand Junction and the Regent's also; but it is on them only that you see many "monkey boats." Life on these arteries, indeed, is really canal life; and a trip along the Regent's, moreover, is an epitome of canal navigation in general.

Leaving Paddington on the right, a boat bound for the City Road Basin or Limehouse is drawn as far as Maida Vale. There the towing path ends at a tunnel, which has to be passed through by "legging." Meanwhile, the captain, having come on in advance, has hunted up a man, or, if he is not in the humour for much exertion—

the two men pushing their feet against the wall—which is worn away from end to end by contact with hob-nails—till the day dawns again.

After leaving this bore the horse takes up his burden anew, and there is a stretch of sylvan scenery, succeeded by miles of houses relieved by an occasional wharf. Presently another arch, on the left of which is fixed a signal that seems to have strayed from the iron road, stretches over the

READY TO START " LEGGING."

and "legging" *is* work—two men. The canal company allows for only one assistant, and if the skipper engages an extra help the shilling he has to give him comes out of his own pocket. By the time the boat reaches the tunnel nearly everything is in readiness for the subterranean journey. Two "wings" are fixed to the sides of the boat so that they project at right angles to the keel, on these the men throw themselves at full length, having previously tucked up a coat, or anything else that is handy, for a pillow, and then away into the pitchy darkness—absolute darkness, save for the light from a single lamp. Under villas and roads and gardens the little craft goes, propelled by

waterway. This is Caledonian Bridge— the western entrance to the longest tunnel on the canal.

Again does the little "flyer" glide under London, this time drawn, in the wake of other boats and barges which have been waiting, by an engine suggesting an impossible compromise between a locomotive and a raft: under thousands of toiling citizens, under busy Chapel Street, under the Agricultural Hall, under the New River, the presence of which is unpleasantly manifested by water dropping from the roof, to emerge at last at Colebrooke Row, three-quarters of a mile, by tunnel, from Caledonian Bridge.

The rest of the journey is easy. To drop down to the City Road Basin or to Limehouse is plain sailing, everyday work, the work which the idler sees and which seems neither hard nor disagreeable.

Ah! that picture! The eye, taking in merely the broad details, does not see that the principal figure—the woman at the helm—is often steering, suckling her last born, watching her older children on the cabin floor, lest they come to harm, and paying attention to the pot on the top bar simultaneously. And the little inhabitants of the floating home need to be carefully watched. Be sure of that. You will have to take a long walk on the towing path before you find a boy or girl of fifteen who has not had at least one narrow escape from drowning. In fact, your journey would extend from London to Liverpool, if not farther. To understand canal life aright, moreover, other pictures need to be viewed. You want to be in Mark Lane sometimes, and see the good wife, when her boat is tethered to a wharf, and when she is supposed to be resting, turn up, alert and businesslike, ready to receive orders for the return journey to Birmingham, Nottingham, Stoke, Wolverhampton, Derby, or elsewhere. Not that the titular skipper always, or even generally, casts this burden on the broad shoulders of his spouse. She does his work a great deal oftener than she should—that is all.

A HALT FOR REFRESHMENT.

"My dear woman," said a staid City merchant, looking hard over his spectacles at a buxom figure in petticoats who had come straight from the canal bank, "where—*where* is your husband?" "My man?" quoth the feminine skipper. "Oh, I can't trust he!" In that remark there is a whole volume. The "cut," too, should be seen at early morn and late at night. Long before London is awake—at half-past four or five o'clock—the boat-woman is astir, and it is asleep when she lies down to rest.

And that cosy-looking little cabin, is that what it seems? Drop into it, and you find yourself in a home with rather less elbow room than a railway compartment—to be exact, about 250 cubic feet. On your right is a locker forming a seat, on your left a small stove, or, if the boat is new, perhaps a range, polished a beautiful glossy black and the brass rods above it, as well as the ornaments at the side nearest the bow, glistening like burnished gold, for the women, as a rule, keep their domiciles spotless. Beyond the fireplace knobs of cupboards and more lockers, and that is all, with the exception of a clock and a few household articles here and there. The eye has completed its survey of a narrow boat cabin.

You wonder how people live in such a miniature

AT TEA IN A "MONKEY BOAT" CABIN.

domicile. They don't; they live outside it, at all
events in the summer. Take a walk along the
canal, and you get endless glimpses of boat
folk's domestic life. Here a meal is in progress on the cabin top, there the family wash
is likewise being done in public, and presently you nap on youngsters engaged in
the delicate operations of the toilet in full
view of all the world that cares to look.
Canal people are veritable children of the
open air.

other youngsters would be on the cabin floor,
underneath their parents' bed.

This is home as canal folk know it, the
only home in very many cases. Sometimes
a family works a pair of boats tied side
by side, and in that case the older children
have the cabin of one to themselves; but
this arrangement does not alter matters very
much, for, although there is more room, the
environment is the same always. Here the
typical boatman is born. Here he spends

MORNING TOILET.

Beds there are none visible in the cabin,
though in some cases one can be seen at
the end. And yet this dwelling, small
as are its dimensions, is registered for
four people — a man and his wife and
two children. Where, then, shall we discover the beds? If we could take an
Asmodeus glimpse of the cabin, we could
see them—and, possibly, the lack of them.
The captain and his helpmeet would be
revealed asleep at the far end of the cabin,
resting on a cupboard door (kept closed
during the day-time) let down and extending
from side to side, and the children would be
curled up on a locker near the door—some of
them, at all events. If the boat should carry
more than her regulation complement, the

his boyhood and early manhood. Here, or
just above, he does most of his courting. Here
he brings his bride, having used the address
of a friendly ratepaying bargee or of a
shopkeeper for the publication of the banns.
Here he rears and brings up his family
with all the worries incidental thereto, only
accentuated enormously. Imagine, for instance, washing-day on board a canal boat in
mid-winter, with the little home reeking of
soapsuds and the air laden with steam from
the drying clothes suspended on lines from
the roof. Ugh! Not even use can make
that aught but a misery. Here he lies in
his last illness. And here, amid the old
familiar surroundings, he probably closes
his eyes on the world for ever, though only

very rarely does his body remain afloat to the last.

Many a mournful procession has actually started from a boat lying at a wharf, but the funeral has been that of an infant, not of an adult. When the long, weary struggle is at an end, and the tired spirit has fled, the corpse is taken ashore and deposited either in the home of a charitable canal-side dweller or in a towing-path public-house, where it lies till it is committed to the dust. Thus it happens that even in London, of all places under the sun, a

cause it's in a book," claimed in the youngest, a bright-eyed urchin of fourteen.

As for the ability to read, that is a rare accomplishment among canal children. Nothing else can be expected considering their upbringing. Few boatmen are in the position of a well-known "character" of the Surrey Canal, who is wont to declare that he has never seen all his olive branches together. Able to dispense with their services in navigating his boat, he has

WASHING-DAY.

man often rests longer under a roof in death than ever he did in life.

The children of the canal, again : what is their lot ? As a class, they are as wild as gipsies, and as ignorant. Of this the energetic and earnest agents of the London City Mission could give many proofs. Not long since a gentleman attached to that organisation discovered three boys seated in a cabin. As a means of introduction, he asked one of the lads, aged about fifteen, his name. "Jonah," promptly replied the youth, adding, "Jonah and the fish." The oldest of the trio— he was about seventeen—then remarked, " It is strange that they always talk about the fish when they talk about Jonah." "It's be-

scattered them among his relations, who are attending to their education. In general a man has to carry his children with him, and, as he is nearly always on the move, he can only send them to school for a day or two occasionally. If he choose to set the law at defiance—and sometimes he does, partly because he is indifferent to the future, and partly because his offspring, when they grow big, complain tearfully of being put among the "babies" in a Board school and of being laughed at as dunces—it is very difficult to prevent him. To track one of his youngsters a "kidcatcher" has to display the tireless persistence of a bailiff laying siege to the domicile of a suburban debt dodger and the agility and fleet-footedness of a 120 yards' runner.

OUTSIDE MAIDA VALE TUNNEL.

Out at Brentford, where the long-distance boats stop, a highly praiseworthy attempt is being made to teach the little ones to read and write at least without any of the usual restrictions. Here a school was opened specially for them by the daughter of Mr. R. Bamber, of the West London Canal Boat Mission (London City Mission). And a curious little school it is. Over its well worn desks on most mornings are bent a number of children, most of them engaged in laboriously forming pothooks and hangers. Some of the older girls are accompanied by the youngest born of the family, and they can learn nothing till, after infinite sh—sh—sh—ing, they get their charges to sleep. The boys are, with few exceptions, without collars, and some, bargee-like, have neither coat nor waistcoat. One or two, moreover, want a wash—want it badly. These an ordinary teacher would punish or send home; but the tutor here adopts neither course, because if she did the youngsters would not come again. No; when a scholar is shockingly begrimed he is gently taken out and introduced to soap and water.

It is equally impossible, of course, to insist upon punctuality, and its twin sister, regular attendance, is beyond hope of realisation.

You might visit the school at ten o'clock—when work should be in full swing—and find it empty, and yet at eleven there might be a dozen scholars present, and at three in the afternoon as many as fifteen or twenty. Everything depends on the number of boats which arrive. Never, too, are the same faces seen on more than two or three days in succession. Children depart into the country, and do not return for weeks. Of the 500 on the register only about a score are present at any one time.

That they make much progress in these circumstances is not claimed; but for all that some of the little wanderers fill their parents with boundless wonder and pride. They can read, they know a little geography, and occasionally they have mastered the intricacies of long division. Great achievements are these to people who cannot themselves read the same on their own boat and who use words in a sense which would surprise even Mrs. Malaprop herself. One woman, in describing the death of a poor fellow who had been killed in an accident, assured her friend that they "held a portmanteau on him," and another said that a certain child had "happy collection fits."

No less admirable than the school, let

me say in passing, is another department recently added to the Boatmen's Mission—a maternity room. Such a provision for the needs of our canal population had long been wanted, and there can be no question that it will be the means of saving many valuable lives. A minor, but still important, consideration is that it will tend to lessen the number of irregularities in connection with births. A case in point—one out of many —that came to light may be mentioned. For certain reasons the exact age of a child about three years old was wanted. When the mother was appealed to she could give no definite information. She had neglected to register the birth of the child, and she could not remember where it took place. All that she knew was that the weather was cold at the time. On her suggestion, recourse was had to a medical man at Birmingham, but without success, and to this day the mystery remains unsolved.

Apart from education, however, the little ones of the towing path will bear comparison with any class of youth. They lack nothing physically. Fed on plenty of good plain food, kept of necessity in the open air, initiated into work as soon as possible by being taught to look after the horse and run ahead and open locks, they grow up strong, robust, and self-reliant, able to fight their way in their own world.

On the whole, canal life is not exactly what it seems to the chance observer. But if it is not idyllic, neither is it so vile as some have delighted to paint it. They have seen only the drunkenness, the fighting, the immorality —which, after all, are dying out, or, at least, are not nearly so common as they were only twenty years ago—among boat people. They have shut their eyes to the noble charity, the sturdy independence, the self-sacrifice, the toil and stress—in a word, the poetry of canal life.

LOVE'S YOUNG DREAM.

DISSENTING LONDON.

By HOWARD ANGUS KENNEDY, M.L.S.B.

DO you remember Mr. Stiggins? Does not a vivid portrait appear in your mind's eye when you hear the name of Chadband? They were among the unloveliest of Dickens' creations, scarcely less repulsive than Bill Sikes or the monster Quilp. Yet in the novelist's pages, and in the minds of a multitude who knew no better, the hypocritical "Shepherd" and the oily expounder of "terewth" appeared as types of the Nonconforming ministry.

There are some keen-eyed folk who profess that they can always tell a Nonconforming from a Conforming parson by the cut of his clothes, and even, by some miraculous insight, distinguish a Wesleyan from a Congregationalist. But these clever people are often mistaken, especially when they are most positive. As a rule we do not pay our ministers very well, so they cannot indulge in much elegance of apparel—to which, indeed, they are somewhat indifferent; but then there are many of their Anglican brethren who are no better paid, and scarcely more punctilious about the cut of their clerical uniform. On the other hand, some of our preachers habitually appear in the clerical collar which more than any other week-day sign is believed to betoken the minister of the Established Church.

On Sundays—well, even then you might go into one of our places of worship and imagine you were in an Anglican Church. For instance, at the magnificent edifice in the Westminster Bridge Road, notable for the ministries of Dr. Newman Hall and the Rev. F. B. Meyer, the liturgy is in constant use. So it is in quite a number of the Wesleyan Methodist churches, at least at the morning service. Indeed, there are other points in which the public worship of the Wesleyans resembles that of the Established Church. If you are in the neighbourhood of the City Road on the first Sunday evening of the month, drop into the chapel where John Wesley himself used to hold forth. You will find the congregation joining in the communion service very largely in the words and forms prescribed by the Prayer Book. "The table at the communion time"—so opens the form of service prescribed by the Wesleyan governing Conference —"having a fair white linen cloth upon it, shall stand in some convenient place"; that is, generally, on the platform in front of the pulpit, at the edge of which the people come and kneel, several at a time, in order to receive the bread and wine. In at least one church of this denomination you will see the choir, of men and boys, all clad in black gowns; but it is only, so far as I can discover, at the church of the Countess of Huntingdon's Connexion in Spa Fields that you can see a choir in full-blown surplices, and there the minister himself wears a surplice till sermon time comes, when he puts on the black gown. In most of our Nonconformist places of worship the people take the communion sitting in their pews, the bread and wine—almost always unfermented wine, by the way—being carried round by those who have been ordained as elders, deacons, or stewards. A recent innovation, inspired by modern sanitary ideas about the spread of infection, is the provision of a separate cup for each communicant. The Presbyterians prepare for the sacred ordinance by spreading white cloths over the book-boards in front of each pew.

Practically the whole Nonconformist community—that is, the people who call themselves Christians but do not belong to the Roman or Anglican communion—are comprised in the Congregational, Baptist, Presbyterian, and Wesleyan churches, with two or three minor branches of the Methodist stock, and the Salvation Army—which is so much more and also so much less than a church or denomination that it can hardly be dealt with in this article. Even

A COMMUNION SERVICE (WESLEY'S CHAPEL, CITY ROAD).

A BAPTISM (METROPOLITAN TABERNACLE).

A NIGHT SERVICE (GREAT ASSEMBLY HALL TENT, MILE END ROAD).

bow, as the County Councils bow to the national Legislature, yet they have in the last few years become federated in a Free Church Council, at which the plans are laid for all sorts of united campaigns against the common enemy—the forces of evil. The union of all Nonconformists, and even of Dissenters with Church folk, for certain forms of philanthropic and religious work is, happily, no new thing; and at many a society's May meeting in Exeter Hall you may see rectors and vicars and Free Church pastors co-operating in the most brotherly and effective fashion.

Londoners like to go where there is a crowd. Where for one reason or another a congregation has begun to decrease—by the migration of the old members to a more pleasant locality in the suburbs, or through the displacement of dwellings by warehouses and factories—it is very hard to get new people to come in; the vacant places they might fill only frighten them away. So in the older and more central parts of the town you will find great buildings which once were crowded by hundreds of eager worshippers now drearily frequented by a few score. But even in these central regions there are churches to which vast congregations flock. There is the City Temple, on Holborn Viaduct—so long identified with the name of Dr. Joseph Parker—crowded twice every Sunday by worshippers from every part of London, and even by country cousins, as well as the young men who live in the City's wholesale drapery stores, all singing triumphantly to the accompaniment of trumpets and organ. There, too, amid the whirling life of "The Elephant," in South London, stands the Metropolitan Tabernacle, equally identified with a great name—the name of

the few churches I have named are united in so many points and divided in so few that you might worship with them all, going from one to another, Sunday after Sunday, without finding out the difference. To tell the truth, the only important difference is in the way they govern themselves; and methods of church government are of too little importance to be often mentioned when the people have come together in public to worship God. Just as Kent and Essex have their County Councils for local administration, without one being a jot more or less English than the other, so the Methodists have their Conferences, the Presbyterians their Synods, the Baptists and Congregationalists their Unions and Church Meetings, without one being a jot more or less Christian than the other. Though it would not be quite correct to say that the Dissenting churches have a supreme church parliament to which they all

Spurgeon. The original "Charles H." has departed, but the Tabernacle is still a shrine to which thousands of pilgrims weekly wend their way. Another Baptist chapel which has been made famous by the name of a great preacher, the name of Clifford, is situate at Westbourne Park. On certain occasions if you happen to be at the Tabernacle—or, indeed, at any Baptist chapel—you will see a chasm open in front of the platform, into which the candidates for church membership descend one by one to be baptised by immersion at the hands of the minister. You will see no musical instrument at the Tabernacle, by the way: the only organ you will hear is

are Scots and the children of Scots, but they no longer insist on the ways of their Caledonian kirks, nor grumble at the minister for giving them short measure if he preaches for twenty-five minutes instead of an hour.

When you have joined in the hymns—generally the same hymns, wherever you go; when you have bowed in prayer and heard the Bible read; when you have listened

A DINNER-HOUR CONCERT (CITY TEMPLE HALL).

to the sermon—you naturally ask yourself the question, "Who are these people in the pews around me?"

They are just your neighbours; ordinary men and women like

that which God has built in every human throat.

This is very exceptional. Even the Presbyterians have outgrown their prejudice against the "kist o' whistles"—the Presbyterians in London, that is. Yes, and they sing hymns, three or four of them to perhaps one of those "metrical psalms of David" which used to afford the congregation its only vocal exercise during the "diet of worship." Only the minister's gown and bands remain, and perhaps his northern accent, to remind you that you are "sitting under" a successor of John Knox. To a large extent these London Presbyterians

yourself, and of almost every class. Happy is the church where the rich and the poor meet together, remembering that the Lord is the Maker of them all; and happier still the church where the minister can be at the same time simple and profound, so that he "breaks the Bread of Life" in a manner that suits every kind of mental digestion. In the dumb hearts of the common men and women you meet in business or in the street there is more self-examination and striving after the highest life than you would imagine. And the minister, as a rule, tries hard to help them with preaching of the most practical kind.

Photo: Russell & Sons, Baker St., W.

A MAY MEETING (EXETER HALL).

Even in the highly respectable suburban congregations there is always a sprinkling of "working men," though they are disguised in black coats and sometimes in high hats. Nearer the centre of the town you will find churches practically made up and controlled by members of the industrial classes. They certainly prefer services of their own, and the "Pleasant Sunday Afternoon" gatherings contain hundreds of artisans, labourers, and other frankly plebeian persons of the male persuasion, singing with stentorian lungs to the accompaniment of a cornet or even a full brass band, and echoing the strong points of a colloquial address with cheers instead of "amens" and "hallelujahs." And it must be further confessed that in the present stage of their religious experience the ordinary working man and woman feel a certain shyness about entering a "regular church" of any kind, with its ecclesiastical architecture and its cushioned pews. They will flock in their thousands to Mr. Charrington's Great Assembly Hall and Tent in the Mile End Road, or the "Edinburgh

Castle" taken over from the liquor trade by Dr. Barnardo at Limehouse, or the Great Central Hall managed by Wesleyans in the Bermondsey New Road.

Anyone who listens to the long string of "notices" given out from the pulpit or platform on a Sunday must get the idea that the whole of the Dissenters' week is crowded with church activities; and that is the fact. There is always an evening service in the middle of the week; there are prayer meetings, and mothers' meetings, and Christian Endeavour or Guild meetings, and social gatherings — even entertainments, concerts, and lectures. The mid-day concerts held in the hall underneath the City Temple cater particularly for men and women at a distance from home who have no pleasant place to spend the dinner-hour in. There is the Boys' Brigade drill, too—one of the most effective antidotes to Hooliganism yet discovered. And in connection with some churches, if there is room to spare, there are club rooms where the working men can chat or read the papers, and even engage in a friendly game of billiards without the stimulus of either alcohol or betting.

Among the Methodists there are two regular events which you will find rather out of the ordinary, if you have never been to them before. One of these is the "class meeting." The rule is that every member of the church must come regularly to one or other of the weekly "classes" unless unavoidably prevented; and in a large church there may be as many as twenty classes, held at different times, to suit the working hours of all sorts of people. In the old days the class leader, who is generally a layman, used to ask every member in turn to give his or her "experience"; but this is not generally insisted on nowadays. And then there is the "love-feast," generally held after a Sunday service, when the stewards hand round plates of biscuits and mugs or glasses of water, and anyone whom the Spirit moves to relate some striking passage of individual heart-history does so.

The operations of these Christian brotherhoods that we call churches are by no means confined to their own premises. It is not often that you see them marching through the streets with banner and drum, after the fashion of the Salvation Army; yet this does sometimes happen, and open-air preaching is carried on at many points of the Metropolis Sunday by Sunday. There is, for instance, the Wesleyan West London Mission, which gathers great crowds into St. James's Hall, and on a summer Sunday afternoon makes itself heard in Hyde Park. But if you want to see the churches at work in unchurchy surroundings, go with a little band of devoted workers into the wards of our workhouses; or, better still, dive with them into the kitchen of a common lodging-house, where the Gospel is preached and sung while the inmates cook their suppers and dry their clothes at the common fire.

I have given you scarcely a glimpse of many of the ways in which the army of Christian workers forming the backbone of Nonconformity are toiling from week's end to week's end to lighten the spiritual and moral darkness of the modern Babylon. I have not even mentioned the Sunday Schools, in which every church without exception is supplementing and filling out the religious instruction given in the Board schools, though rarely, if ever, teaching any doctrine that could be called sectarian. Nor have I touched on the numberless charities by which the churches collectively and church members individually are constantly trying to relieve the physical necessities of the poor. But I have said, perhaps, enough to make it plain that in the best way they know the "Dissenters" are taking an active and important part in the great fight against evil, and are contributing largely and unselfishly to the sum of those influences which will one day lift the life of London to a level of health and purity it has never yet reached.

LEAVING WESTBOURNE PARK CHAPEL AFTER A SERVICE.

COSTER TYPES.

COSTER-LAND IN LONDON.

By C. DUNCAN LUCAS.

HE may like his pot of ale, and in times of stress his language may be a trifle lurid, but there is not much that is harmful in the London costermonger. When Big Ben tolls the hour of four in the morning sixty thousand costers are getting out of their beds and wondering where the next meal is to come from. Men whose fathers and grandfathers have been barrow-pushers before them, raw recruits, ex-shopkeepers, solicitors who have been struck off the rolls, artists, actors: young and old, female as well as male, nearly every class is represented.

The annual turnover of these people is several million pounds sterling, yet a very large number of them cannot afford to rent more than a single room. For all that the coster's home is his castle. It is the only place in the whole world where he rests his feet; and let us not forget that he is on them for sixteen hours a day. Besides, he is a family man, and proud of the fact. With his missis and the baby he shares his bed; in each corner, buried in a mound of miscellaneous wrappings, is another offspring; before the grate stands the inevitable orange-box on which his

clothes are spread out to dry; a table, a couple of chairs, and washing utensils complete the outfit.

To maintain this home, the London coster labours incessantly. Watch him as he starts out of a morning to fetch his barrow, the stabling of which costs him a shilling a week. He may be fat, he may be lean, but the tired eyes and the tightly-drawn cheeks show that there is not much joy in his life. He has had, perhaps, three hours' sleep. It was wet the night before, and you can wring the water from his clothes. Even his billycock hat and

SELLING A PONY AND BARROW (ISLINGTON CATTLE MARKET).

the faded neckerchief that does duty as a collar are soaking. No matter; he has but one suit, and the terrors of rheumatism are nothing to him as long as he can bring "somefink 'ome for the kids," and put a lump of beef on the Sunday dinner table. To provide that lump of beef with regularity is the one ambition of his weary life. And so he goes to market.

He is a cautious man, this coster. On him the flowery and persuasive eloquence of the auctioneer of fruit is lost. He gazes at the sample boxes behind the rostrum and reflects.

markets, the biggest of which is in Lloyd's Row, Clerkenwell.

The coster is now ready to earn his Sunday beef. If he is a Hoxtonian he may sally forth to Hoxton Street or Pitfield Street; if a South Londoner he may go to Walworth Road, the New Cut, or Lambeth Walk; or he may make for Farringdon Road, or Goodge Street, or Whitechapel. He may go on the tramp. Ten to one he is a "little punter" with few friends—one who has only enough capital to buy a day's stock. No man fights more fiercely for bread

GROOMING COSTERS' DONKEYS.

He wonders whether the contents of those boxes are not a good deal better than the stuff that is to be sold.

"Blessed if I don't go down into the slaughter-house!" he exclaims; and making his way forthwith to the "slaughter-house," which is the warehouse basement, he rummages the stock. If he is satisfied, he returns and buys; and, his purchases over, he proceeds to dress his barrow, a task requiring no little ingenuity. For not only must the coster so arrange his fruit that it will appeal to the eye, but he must balance his barrow. A tyro will often so load his barrow that he cannot move it; the bred-and-born coster, on the other hand, distributes his wares so cunningly that he can push a load of twelve hundred-weight with comparative ease. The barrows can be hired from one of the various barrow

than the "little punter," for if trade is slack and his goods perish he has no money to replenish his barrow. With the old and respected coster it is otherwise. He may be "down on the knuckle" once a month, yet he need never be hungry. Such is the loyalty of these men to a comrade in distress, they will literally strip their barrows, one here giving a bushel of apples, one there a box of grapes, to save him from standing idle.

The tragedy of the coster's existence is best realised on a wet Saturday night, but to understand it one must have been behind the scenes. The line of barrows stretches for perhaps half a mile. Butchers, bakers, fruiterers, fishmongers, booksellers, sweetstuff vendors, dealers in winkles and mussels, crockery merchants; sellers of plants, bulbs, and seeds of all descriptions: half a thousand

I. BASKET RACE (COSTERMONGERS' SPORTS). II. MID-DAY IN COSTER-
LAND (HOXTON STREET). III. A COSTER'S FRUIT STALL.

are engaged in one continuous roar for custom. Apparently there is not much sadness here. But study the faces of these toilers by the light of the flaring lamps. There is not one that is not careworn. For the truth is that a wet Saturday brings ruin to the coster. The poor decline to come out and buy, and this means in many cases that the stock, a perishable commodity, will have become uneatable by Monday. A succession of wet Saturdays drives hundreds to bankruptcy. There are few more melancholy spectacles than that of a coster running up his pony on the stones at the Islington Cattle Market. Barrow as well as pony he must sell, for the weather has hit him hard. Saturday after Saturday it has poured, and he has not the heart to begin life over again. We laugh at the "pearlies," but there is little laughter in the coster's life. Nor are there any "pearlies," for the true London coster never dreams of sporting such buttons.

What stories one could tell of the patient heroism of these men! Once upon a time a little "punter" lost his all, and his barrow stood empty. On a Wednesday he met his sister, who took him home and lent him her husband's Sunday clothes to pawn. He was to return them on the Saturday, so that the husband should not know to what use his suit had been put. With the money he received from the pawnbroker the "punter" bought some fruit, but it rained on the Thursday, and the weather was even worse on the Friday, and there was no money to redeem the garments. On the Saturday this man tramped for sixteen hours, first north, then south, then east, then west, trying to get enough to buy back the suit. It was a battle against time. The pawnbroker closed at midnight, and if the money was not forthcoming by then the owner would have no Sunday clothes to wear, and there would be strife between husband and wife. At eleven o'clock he was still half-a-crown short, and it was raining, and trade was slackening fast. Five minutes before twelve he was still in want of sixpence. He wondered if he should put an end to his life. Providence decided for him. As the clock of Marylebone Church was striking midnight the "punter" sold sixpennyworth of grapes. Leaving his barrow

to the mercy of any passing thief, he ran to the sign of the three brass balls as he had never run before. The shutters were going up; a moment later and the brave little "punter" would have been too late. During the night the suit was smuggled into the house of the owner, and all was well.

This is no exceptional instance of the perseverance of the coster. At four o'clock one Saturday morning a coster left Edgware Road with a barrow on which was heaped ten hundredweight of fruit. He pushed that barrow to Woolwich, and stood by the gates of the dockyard till ten at night. And he pushed it back again.

What of the coster's love story? It is a very brief and unromantic one. The coster does all his courting in the gutter, with one eye on his "filly" and the other on his stall. The wedding is generally a "walking" one, the principal parties proceeding to the church by different routes and meeting at the door. When the clergyman has done his work, the bridegroom returns to his barrow, and his wife celebrates the occasion with her friends as best she can.

There is a certain costermonger whom we will call George. He is one of the leaders of the fraternity. George's description of his nuptial day applies to the average coster wedding. Says George : "When I got married I come out of church and give my ole woman two shillin's, and went to work and didn't see her till 12.30 at night. I hadn't a pound in the world."

But there is high society in Coster-land as there is elsewhere. If the bride's parents possess a few shillings, and if the bridegroom has a sovereign in his pocket, the usual thing when the weather is propitious is to have an outing. The friends bring their donkey chariots, and, the ceremony over, off the party goes — it doesn't much matter where, provided there are a few refreshment-houses on the road. On wet days the parents of the bride invite the company to partake of a chunk of beef, potatoes, and greens, and a bucket of beer. A peculiarity of these feasts is that they last all day.

The best points of the coster are seen

BARROWS FOR HIRE.

when the days of a comrade are numbered. Peep reverentially into the chamber of death. Day is breaking, and the grey old fellow on the bed has but a few hours to live. By the ragged bedside are two men, rough-looking perhaps, yet each is as gentle as the gentlest lady in the land. Listen! The dying coster's mind is taking him back to Covent Garden. He asks the price of grapes, whether oranges will sell. The watchers humour him and wipe his brow. These costers were pushing their barrows at one o'clock in the morning, and they have been here since two. They will work for another sixteen hours before they sleep. Presently there is a tap at the door, and another coster enters. He will sit with the patient through the day. He may not have a penny to bless himself with, and there may be naught in the larder for the children. What of that? A neighbour will tend and feed the youngsters, "and the missis will look arter the barrer." These men are heroes. When a coster lies sick, there is not a barrow-pusher in London who will not help him.

But to return to our little punter. He

has drawn his last breath, and his comrades have arranged a "brick" or "friendly lead" in his behalf. The "brick" is held in the parlour of a public-house. On a table near the door is a plate into which every visitor drops a coin. The most valuable coin is usually contributed by the man who was the deceased's greatest enemy, for on these occasions it is the custom for those who have not been on speaking terms with the departed to do their best for him. At the far end of the room are seated the chairman and the vice-chairman. Pots of beer figure somewhat conspicuously; the ladies criticise each other's feathers rather loudly; and the young bucks relieve the tedium of the wait with a little hat-bashing. Regarded as a whole, the "brick," got up though it is to bury a dead man, is remarkably free from any trace of melancholy. Not that the chairman is forgetful of his responsibilities. If you remain long enough you will hear a great hammering.

"If you don't shut up I'll sling you down!" roars the president, fixing a fierce eye on a young and frolicsome lady coster. "I will, straight. Now then, Mary, 'The 'At my Farver Wore.' Quiet!"

Another bang with the hammer, and up rises Mary. The artistes follow each other in quick succession, and the "sing-song" is kept up till near closing time.

A big affair is the funeral. No London coster goes to his grave without twenty or thirty vehicles "behind him," and no widow leaves the graveside without receiving many pressing invitations to drown her sorrows at the nearest hostelry. The poorer

"ALL A-GROWIN'."

a coster is, the greater is the attempt made to provide him with a brilliant send-off to the other world. Some months ago a young coster was fighting with death in a London infirmary. He had neither father nor mother, and his brother was in prison. Two comrades were sitting by his side, and to them he observed as his life was fast ebbing away: "I'd like to see my brother come 'ome afore I kick, but it's no good a-wishin'. Get me a bit of paper. I want to nominate my old pal George to receive anyfink as may be due to me."

they contribute to their society—the Costermongers' Federation—has to be spent in upholding their rights in the courts of law.

With the exception of a few hours snatched for the annual parade of donkeys, the London costers enjoy but one holiday in the year, and this they devote to attending what is called "The Costers' Derby," but which is in reality the Costermongers' Athletic Sports, one of the most amusing events in the programme of which is a basket-carrying contest. To Kensal Rise, where the events are decided, they go in their thousands,

A COSTER'S FUNERAL
(WALWORTH).

PART OF THE PROCESSION.

Only a shilling or two was due, but George saw that the man had four horses to draw him to the grave, five pounds' worth of flowers on his coffin, and a band costing fifty shillings to play him to his last resting-place.

These, then, are the men who are buffeted about from pillar to post—men who help their fellows as no other class does, and who, although they labour for sixteen hours out of the twenty-four, live literally from hand to mouth. Perpetually at war with the local authorities, who are determined to clear them notwithstanding that they are indispensable to the poor, the word peace is not contained in their vocabulary. Nearly every man's hand, save that of the policeman, is against them, and almost every penny which

and every man who boasts a "moke" drives his missis up in style. Not one coster in a hundred, by-the-bye, possesses a donkey. If a barrow-pusher wants a four-legged assistant he goes to a stable where these animals are kept for hire, and on presenting the owner with half-a-crown gets a "moke" and a barrow for a week. The photographic illustration on p. 75 shows a stable yard at Notting Hill where three donkeys are being groomed preparatory to a day's work.

The costers have their foibles like other men. When they find themselves with a spare sovereign they worry themselves until they get rid of it; but let us always remember that the coster never thinks he can go too far in serving a friend.

MAIL VAN LEAVING MOUNT PLEASANT.

THE GENERAL POST OFFICE.

By BECKLES WILLSON.

TELEGRAPH MESSENGER.

IF you were to tramp through all broad London, and penetrate its most occult official recesses, you would probably not find a nearer human similitude to a bee-hive than those three great stone buildings which comprise St. Martin's-le-Grand.

We cannot enter the General Post Office at the front—the old public corridor has been utilised for official purposes. Let us, then, ascend a flight of stairs at the back, and, presenting our order of admittance to the Circulation Office (as this department is officially styled), be conducted at once to a gallery overlooking the appropriated entrance corridor.

Standing here, from our position in the gallery we are able to command a bird's-eye view of the central room in the Circulation Office—that is to say, the Receiving and

Stamping Room—with the two great Sorting Rooms to our right and left. The middle room, which was formerly the public entrance-hall, until, as I have said, the exigencies of the service demanded its utility, is crammed with some two hundred employés, who, seated at long, plain tables, are engaged in what one of them described to me (professionally, no doubt) as "breaking the back" of the correspondence. For this great room lies just behind the letter-boxes, through whose apertures descends an unceasing and heterogeneous rain of letters, packets, newspapers, and post-cards destined for London—its heart and suburbs—and for each of the four quarters of the whole earth besides. London and the Universe—these are served here—the United Kingdom is another matter. A regulation provides that that class of matter known as "Country" correspondence must be sent to and dealt with at Mount Pleasant, another large establishment half a mile away. To this we will revert later. London and the Universe ought, surely, to suffice to fix our present attention upon St. Martin's-le-Grand.

In a narrow cubicle just behind the letter-boxes are two employés, attired in grey blouses, busily heaping the letters into baskets. As fast as they are filled they are seized by the waiting carrier boys and borne to the long, flat "facing table," as it is called, where newspapers, circulars, pamphlets, and letters proper are severally disengaged with quick fingers, after which they are hurried to the stampers, whose brief, brisk, official thud at one blow defaces the stamp, and indicates the time and place of posting. To illustrate how everything in the Post Office is regulated, how every act can be traced to the individual cog or wheel in the great instrument, we may mention that when each of these stampers arrives for his day's work he is obliged to enter his name under the particular stamp or postmark he intends using that day, so that the device on any letter out of a million can, if necessary, be brought home to its perpetrator.

A row of desks, marked off into compartments three feet wide, occupies the entire space of the south room, that is, the room looking towards Cheapside. It is at these desks that all the City or East-Central letters are sorted, and by the ingenious moveable index strips, upon whose surface are inscribed all sorts of Metropolitan localities, the desk is made to serve for as wide an area as the necessity of the occasion demands. Thus, at one moment the strips at the desk would seem to indicate a series of pigeon-holes—as Fenchurch Street, Minories, Eastcheap, Ludgate Hill, Mile End, and Moorgate, while, if a paucity of correspondence for these localities occurs, a twist of the sorter's thumb and forefinger and the index strip presents an entirely new set of names to guide him in the process of sorting. As a matter of fact, an expert operator often manages to dispense with the pigeon-hole indexes altogether, and, much to the perplexity of the visitor, goes arbitrarily piling up epistles addressed to places in the neighbourhood of St. Paul's in a compartment distinctly labelled "Bethnal Green."

As he works, the carriers are piling up unsorted correspondence at his left hand, while postmen are striding the length of the tables, pausing at every sorter's com-

LETTER SORTING (ST. MARTIN'S-LE-GRAND).

partment to snatch up bundles of letters concerned with their own itinerary. In the case of packets and newspapers, large baskets are substituted for the pigeon-holes on the sorters' desks. And while we speak of newspapers, we must by no means overlook the newspaper "detective," whose peculiar function it is to lay hold of newspapers at hazard on the supposition that they may contain letters, money, or articles which should, if sent in another class, render his Majesty a greater pecuniary profit on their transmission. Yet, absurd as the hypothesis appears, it is sad to have to state that this particular official is astonished several times a day by the discovery of this illicit device for cheating the Post Office.

At this building in St. Martin's-le-Grand alone there are nearly two thousand employés engaged on inside and outside

I. WIRE REPAIRERS AT WORK. II. A REEL OF WIRE.

service. Of course, prior to the removal of the Country Mails Department to Mount Pleasant in 1901, the strain was tremendous, and the exciting scene known as the "Six o'clock Rush" was one of the features of the establishment. The pressure having thus been lightened, matters assume, as evening draws on, a less nervous tension; but there is yet throughout the building and without it greater life and animation than in any other department under the Government.

We have glanced at the sorting, which is the same in the two great halls at either end of the building. Before noting other and, though minor, yet more curious departments on the ground floor, the eye of the visitor will have fallen on the legend "Blind"

at regular intervals throughout the desks. This is a technical expression for letters whose address is either illegible or insufficient, or perhaps is absent altogether. If the former, the "blind" correspondence is carried in bundles to the "Blind" Department, where it passes into the hands of several clerks whose function it is to ascertain by means of directories, gazetteers, and other aids to knowledge, the more precise whereabouts of the addressee. "Mr. Wite, J., Lead Gate, Senpoll's, V.C.," is, it will be admitted, a superscription not remarkable for its perspicuity; but it took an official of the "Blind" Department just two minutes to discover its signification to be, "Mr. J. White, Ludgate House, St. Paul's Churchyard, E.C." Similarly mystifying were those familiar examples: "Santling's, Hilewita," and "Obanvidock," for "St. Helen's, Isle of Wight," and "Holborn Viaduct," which are inscribed amongst the archives of St. Martin's-le-Grand.

"That is the hospital yonder," murmurs our guide, as we thread our way between the tables. We peer through the intervening space, while visions of maimed and crippled postmen and van-drivers, martyrs to duty, flash across our senses. But we may spare our sympathy: the hospital is for maimed letters, packages, and newspapers, whose outer vestments have so suffered in their journeyings as no longer to hide their nakedness or preserve them from fatal loss. Such are "Found Open and Officially Sealed," either by gummed paper or by twine. Senders of wedding cake, fragments of which are strewn over the desk, are the chief offenders, and it is a standing joke amongst the other officials that the surgeons of this letter hospital largely subsist upon "blind" wedding cakes, an insinuation which, being indignantly resented, has, of course, no foundation.

The presence of one or two registered

LOADING MAIL VANS (ST. MARTIN'S-LE-GRAND).

Again descending the stairs, we came across several openings to the street through which bags are being flung — bags in all stages of rotundity hailing from, or destined for, all parts of the globe, *via* Waterloo, Paddington, or Charing Cross and other railway stations. Several fully-loaded crimson mail coaches are now leaving the Post Office, driven by picturesque drivers in picturesque costumes, a species of apparel descended to them from the days of the stage-coach, when it drew up in spanking style, after a hundred miles' journey, at these very portals seventy or eighty years ago. The royal van-drivers, notwithstanding their uniforms and gold lace, are not employés of the Government, inasmuch as all cartage of the mails is performed nowadays by private individuals under contract.

letter packets in the hospital reminds us that these are, as they should be, the aristocrats of the mails; that practically, unless they happen to be damaged, they pass through only two men's hands from the time they arrive until they are sent away from the building. As a registered letter is taken out of bag or basket it is handed to a separate clerk who gives a voucher for it and does not part with it unless and until he receives a similar receipt from another clerk. ·

The department in which letters from and for abroad are received, sorted, and despatched is on the upper floor. · The process, although the same, demands a different degree of ability, for it must be borne in mind that the superscriptions are executed in every known language (and occasionally a dead one), and therefore actually involve somewhat greater knowledge and possibly more alert faculties. "Examination in Foreign and Colonial Sorting" is the title of a placard I noticed as we passed into the room, and hints at a special kind of ability and special remuneration.

A G.P.O. INTERPRETER.

As to the volume of the business done here, statistics give little idea when they tell us that a billion letters and postcards and four hundred millions of newspapers are annually handled at the General Post Office. A City firm has posted 132,000 letters at one time; while as many as 167,000 postcards have been received in a single batch. Parcels are taken in here, but are immediately despatched to Mount Pleasant, where the Returned (or Dead) Letter Office is.

The chief Money Order Office of the kingdom is situated a few streets away in Fore Street. Here the business of posting up and checking off the vast aggregate sum (nearly £100,000,000) which millions of people send annually through the post is attended to by a numerous staff. Again, although the Government has acquired a huge telephone business—worked in connection with the Post Office—it is carried on at some little distance from St. Martin's-le-Grand, which has nothing to do with telephones. "Telephone London" is treated separately in another part of this work; and the Post Office Savings Bank is referred to under the heading of "Thrift London."

Mount Pleasant is not, as its name would lead a stranger to suppose, a venal eminence crowned by an Ionic fane. Its name suggests less the Ionic than the ironic, inasmuch as it was formerly the Coldbath Fields Prison, now converted into a Government building and christened with the title of an adjacent street or lane. It is in Farringdon Road, and now vies with St. Martin's-le-Grand in importance as a receiving and distributing centre. Our illustration on p. 80 shows one of the mail vans, laden with parcels, about to start from there on a night journey to the country.

For a more important and fascinating department under the control of the Postmaster General we need not travel so far as Farringdon Road. Immediately opposite the leading Post Office of the kingdom is the headquarters of the telegraph system of these islands, and by far the greatest telegraph office in the world. A reminder of its vast ramifications is furnished to us in the small pictures on p. 82, showing, first, a couple of men repairing a wire just below a street pavement; and,

next, several lusty employés rolling along a huge reel of wire, eight feet in diameter, for use by the department.

To those who have never before visited a telegraph headquarters the sight of these vast galleries packed with their hundreds of operators, male and female, together with their throbbing instruments, at first suggests a factory. But the simile in the mind's eye is gone in a moment. The machines click-click eternally, but there is no fabric woven. There is a restrained intensity about the place; it is reflected in the keen eyes of the operators; a vivid intelligence seems to float in the very atmosphere; there is no running to and fro, no movement of bodies as at the Post Office; there is nothing needed to simulate excitement; you feel as if you were in the presence of a mighty brain. And it is so: you are not deceived. In each of these four or five huge rooms, each with its two hundred or so operators, are the concentrated intelligence, the action, the movement, the aspirations of the world. Everything is passing here—from the death of a nation's ruler to the result of a horse-race. Three hundred thousand messages a day pass through these galleries.

Living London—what could be more alive, more vital than this? These operators are a nervous race—ever busy with their instruments—even when there is no necessity for being so. Meanwhile let us glance very briefly at some of the features of this great department, whose very existence would have been an incomparable puzzle to our grand-fathers.

First in our itinerary is the room or, as the authorities prefer to denominate it, "Instrument Gallery," from which and through which messages are sent to the Press of these islands. By means of a wonderful invention (*not* of transatlantic origin) known as the Hughes' Perforator, a long telegram is instantly duplicated on eight narrow ribbons of paper, each of which is put into a separate instrument and its purport automatically delivered to eight provincial cities. So that a description of a tragedy, a boat-race, or a new drama, while speeding into the office, perforates eight strips of paper in such a fashion as to make each equivalent in verbal value to the

THE PNEUMATIC TUBE ROOM (ST. MARTIN'S-LE-GRAND).

THE SUBMARINE CABLE ROOM (ST. MARTIN'S-LE-GRAND).

cylinder of a phonograph, and these being immediately transmitted in turn, Liverpool, Glasgow, Manchester, and Birmingham almost simultaneously receive the account, not in perforated paper, but in dots and dashes.

In another gallery is the headquarters of the London telegraph system, in another the Provinces, in another the Foreign. The last-named is the Submarine Cable Room, the wires of whose specially - constructed instruments are laid beneath the English Channel. All the Atlantic cables are, of course, worked by private companies.

A feature of the galleries soon after half-past four in the afternoon is the appearance of tea-cups and bread-and-butter. It was figured out by a former Postmaster-General that if the two thousand employés were to be granted a short interval for tea outside the establishment it would cost, in round figures, £8,000 a year. It would also cost the employés themselves about £8,000. By serving them tea *gratis* at their desks, therefore, a saving of £4,000 to the Department would be effected, to say nothing of the economy to the purses of the operators. Tea in the Telegraphs costs the Government just £4,000 per annum. Indeed, the Government may be said to look after the physical welfare of its assistants with some benevolence.

It contributed to the acquisition of the enclosure popularly known as the "Postmen's Park," close to St. Martin's-le-Grand, and it has even constructed a spacious tennis-court on the roof of the great new building known as G.P.O. North.

There is another department which has not been mentioned. It is in connection with the Pneumatic Tube system—by means of which cylinders propelled by air travel with the speed of lightning underground to and from some of the principal branch offices in London, as far west as the Strand. The tubes are served by boys; and our picture on p. 85 shows the room in which their contents are dealt with. The engines in the basement, which primarily accomplish the work, are four in number, of 50-horse power each.

But the greater engines—the real engines, after all—are the brains that devised and that now maintain the whole system which I have attempted to describe: the marvellous accuracy, the amazing promptitude, the ease and quietness with which the whole correspondence, posted or telegraphed, of over forty millions of Britons at home and many millions abroad is conducted, and which must, in spite of occasional disparagement, ever remain one of the proudest monuments of Living London.

IN THE POSTMEN'S PARK.

KING'S CROSS CORNER.

LONDON STREET CORNERS.

By GEORGE R. SIMS.

IF you would watch the great panoramas of London life unfold themselves, there is no better standpoint than a busy street corner. There you may study the ever-changing crowd. There you may watch the wondrous traffic converging from the four points of the compass, mix itself together for a moment, then separate and widen out into broad distinct streams, each stream flowing towards a different quarter of the Metropolis. Stand, for instance, at the Elephant and Castle on a sunny afternoon. You see on one side the trees and green gardens of St. George's Road, on the other the crowded pavements of Newington Causeway. You gaze in one direction and Walworth Road, with its typical scenes of South London bustle, lies before you; you turn your head and the New Kent Road gives you a totally different picture. Another turn of the head and the London Road opens up to your wondering eyes. In every direction heavily-laden trams and buses are passing each other. By you on

the pavement is a line of 'bus and tram timekeepers, every one of them busily making notes in a bulgy pocket-book with a stumpy lead pencil.

The folk who pass you are of all sorts, but mostly of the humbler class. The shopping ladies who come from Newington Causeway are some of them smartly dressed and suggest villadom, but the female note of the district is the useful little basket in one hand, and the purse and latch-key in the other. The brown paper parcel that is carried past you is generally loosely tied. It suggests some manufacture. The factory girl and the coster girl mingle with the crowd, the male loafer leans against corner-posts, the Irish lady with a faded shawl and a top-knot order of *coiffure* comes and goes at intervals, and the halfpenny evening papers are eagerly purchased by horsey-looking men and youths who turn instantly to the racing results. Just across the road in a little shop there is a picture of the Elephant a hundred years ago. Let us look at it, for it is in-

ELEPHANT AND CASTLE CORNER.

teresting. In the vast open space now filled
with trams and 'buses, and carts and cabs,
there are four-horse coaches, horsemen,
and porters carrying heavy packs. There
is a postchaise with a young gentleman and
a young lady in it. It looks like an elope-
ment. A pretty girlish face is pressed to
the window while we are looking, and a
man's voice exclaims, "Look, 'Lizer, that's
the old Elephant a 'underd years ago!"
We turn and see the bride of to-day leaning
on her young husband's arm. She is in
bright blue satin, and wears a big white
hat and feathers. The newly-wedded couple
attract little attention. Brides and bride-
grooms threading the crowd arm in arm are
by no means novelties at the Elephant,
where the honeymoon is the afternoon walk
and an evening at the music hall, and both
parties to the contract go to their work the
next morning.

Hyde Park Corner! On one side the
great Hospital abutting on the street; opposite it the stately archway through which the
tide of fashion flows into the famous Park.
This is surely the corner of pleasure and
of pain. Through the windows of the wards

the patients of St. George's can see
Buckingham Palace and the broad avenue
up which many a time and oft come the
glittering Life Guards escorting Royalty.
This is the most picturesque, the most
inspiriting, corner of London. Past it
roll daily the equipages of the noblest
and the wealthiest of the King's subjects.
Everywhere the eye rests on splendid
architecture and vast expanses of turf
and tree. But the Hospital is always
there. In the great building facing the
Park of Pleasure and the Palace of the
King the maimed and suffering lie in
agony.

Ludgate Circus. What a change of
scene! Here all is crowded and noisy,
and men and women hustle each other
without apology. Trains rattle and
scream across the bridge that spans Ludgate Hill, heavy waggons clatter along
Farringdon Street, 'buses and vans
and cabs are mixed up in apparently
hopeless confusion in Bridge Street.
Country folk coming from St. Paul's
stand nervously on the kerb waiting to
cross the road. At the office of Messrs.
Cook & Sons intending tourists are studying
the attractive window bills, and forgetting in
their admiration of the Italian lakes that
they are blocking the footway in one of
London's narrowest busy thoroughfares. One
young fellow, who is evidently off for a Continental holiday for the first time, calmly
reads a book until he is run into by a
newspaper boy rushing off towards the City
with the four o'clock edition of an evening
paper on his shoulders. The young fellow
drops his book. It is "French Conversation
for Travellers."

Down Fleet Street and round the corner
from Bride Street the newspaper carts are
dashing. Journalists and Fleet Street celebrities, printers and press messengers, pass you
at every moment. Down Ludgate Hill come
carriers' carts from the Old Bailey. The
name of the places they serve are painted
on many of them. They bring a breath of
country air into the fumes of the tar— for, of
course, the wood pavement of Fleet Street is
"up."

King's Cross. Stand at the corner opposite the Great Northern Railway side

entrance, and if the proper study of mankind is man, you will have a great opportunity of pursuing a profitable course of education. Down Gray's Inn Road, Pentonville, Euston Road, and York Road flow endless streams of humanity, and the noise of the traffic is deafening, for here three great railway centres contribute their carrying trade to the general confusion. Travellers, especially provincial travellers, abound on the pavements, and the dialects and accents of all the counties of the United Kingdom mingle with the cockney hubbub. It is here that the provincial newly arrived by rail is first faced with the problem of London's vastness. He wants to take a 'bus, but he doesn't know which 'bus to take. The policemen at the corner are directing provincial inquirers in the matter of 'buses for the better part of their time. I should say that the policemen on duty at King's Cross are the best authorities on 'bus routes to be found in the whole of the Metropolis. The cabs that pass you here are mostly luggage-laden. The people that pass you carry hand luggage oftener than not. The brown paper parcel fastened with a leather strap is a common feature of the corner, so is the hot, perplexed, buxom young woman with several parcels, a handbag, a baby, and an umbrella. Family parties are frequent.

From dawn to midnight you will see a knot of loafers hanging about the King's Cross corner. If you are poetical and blessed with a strong imagination you may picture them as men who have been waiting year after year for friends from the provinces —friends who have never come. If you are matter-of-fact you will guess that the loafer loafs here because there are many opportunities of an odd copper, or a proffered drink. Outside the public-house there is frequently a four-footed traveller waiting for a friend. It is the drover's dog from Islington Cattle Market. His master is inside. The dog waits patiently, apparently unobservant. Sometimes he stretches himself close to the wall and slumbers. But the moment the drover comes out wiping his mouth with the back of his hand the dog springs up, and, close at his master's heels, disappears in the traffic.

Right in the full tide of East-End life is the corner of Leman Street. Standing there one can see the ever-changing multitudes that throng Whitechapel High Street, the Commercial Road East, and Commercial Street. Type is writ large in the crowds that eddy round you, and the alien Jew is the most pronounced of all. The joyless,

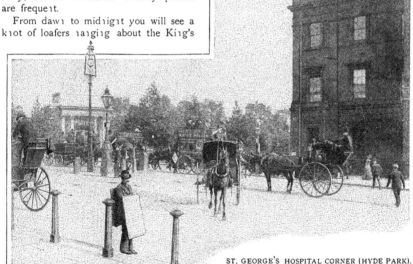

ST. GEORGE'S HOSPITAL CORNER (HYDE PARK).

pensive features of a persecuted race contrast strongly with the careless good-humour of the native population. The work for which the district has a reputation "jumps to your eyes," as the French say, in the barrow-loads of slop clothing that are pushed past you by stunted youths. The rapid rise of many of these aliens from serfdom to comparative

melancholy-eyed men are conversing. Presently you catch sight of a poster or two, and a theatrical announcement printed in cabalistic characters, and then you understand that the conversation around you is being carried on largely in Yiddish and Lettish. But there is plenty of English "as she is spoke" at this corner, for sailors and

FLEET STREET CORNER (LUDGATE CIRCUS).

comfort is shown in the gay dresses and snowy hats with which young Russian, Polish, and Roumanian Jewesses of the second generation brighten the thoroughfares on the Jewish Sabbath. Even the babies make strong splashes of colour among the dark-coated men : for baby's hat is often a deep orange or a flaming red, and his little coat of plush is of a brilliant hue. There are not any perambulators at this corner. Most of the babies on the Saturday afternoon are carried by father, for the reason, probably, that mother is engaged at home.

You have not been standing long at the corner of Leman Street before you wonder what language it is in which the dark-haired,

ships' hands, and carmen, and English working folk abound. Here there is no quiet hour for the 'buses and the trams that pass continually ; they are generally full. But you notice that the hansom cab, which in the West is such a feature of the traffic, is very little in evidence here. After you have passed Aldgate Station the hansom becomes rarer and rarer. A little way beyond Leman Street it is practically extinct.

It is in Leman Street that the first note of Oriental London is struck. The Asiatics who make their temporary home in West India Dock Road and in Limehouse stray occasionally as far as this in little parties. But they rarely loiter. Timidly, almost apologetically, they thread their way through the crowd and disappear in the light mist that has wandered from the Thames and apparently lost its way in the Commercial Road.

Liverpool Street! Here it is no question of flowing tides of humanity. If we are to remain faithful to the simile of the sea, whirlpool is the only word to use. Take your place—you will have some trouble to keep it—any Saturday afternoon about three o'clock on the kerb opposite the Great Eastern and North London termini. There it is a perpetual swirl and eddy of human beings amid a vehicular traffic that appears chaos—that is, in fact, chaos constantly being reduced to order by the most matchless traffic manager in the world, the London policeman. Across the road you see never-ending processions of people mounting the steps to Broad Street, and in another direction a broad stream of human and vehicular traffic pouring into the Great Eastern Company's station. Between the two great termini lies the Goods Station of the London and North Western Railway, so that the two streams of passenger traffic are perpetually divided by a line of heavily-laden railway vans.

The great crowd that throngs the pavements is sharply divided. From Broad Street, the Stock Exchange, the banks and insurance offices, and the great City warehouses, comes a high-hatted, well groomed and tailored mob of business men. From the other direction comes a surging mass of men in billycocks and caps. Mixed up with both streams are the ransoms, and the excursionists arriving from or departing to the provincial towns and the seaside resorts served by the Great Eastern Railway.

The transfer of luggage from Broad Street to Liverpool Street is a feature of this "corner." Porters come and go with luggage-laden barrows. They wheel these dexterously among the cabs and omnibuses, and are followed with much anxiety by the owners. Nervous females grasping a country nosegay in one hand and a bundle of wraps in the other vainly endeavour to keep one eye on their luggage and the other on the cab that is bearing down upon them and is already in perilous proximity. The hardiest cyclists dismount at this corner and carry their machines instead of allowing their machines to carry them. And every minute, if you have an amiable countenance and look like a Londoner, anxious inquirers will test your knowledge of the 'bus and railway system. You have no sooner informed a stout, square-built gentleman with a small portmanteau which is the way to Rotterdam than two young ladies carrying a little box between them will ask you which is the station for Yarmouth. You are fortunate if you are not expected to point out in rapid succession the 'bus that goes to Clapham, the nearest way to Waterloo, the staircase one must mount to find a train for Ball's Pond Road, and the point at which the trams start for the Nag's Head, Holloway. And even after you have answered these questions satisfactorily your knowledge

LIVERPOOL STREET CORNER.

TOTTENHAM COURT ROAD CORNER.

of London may be further tested by an inquiry as to the nearest pier at which a steamboat may be boarded for Blackwall.

In direct contrast to the Liverpool Street corner is the corner where the Holborn district and Oxford Street meet Tottenham Court Road and Charing Cross Road. Busy the scene always is, but the sectne and swirl are absent. There are no train catchers, and the loitering, shop-seeing element leavens the work-a-day portion of the movement. The stage, the music hall, and the British Museum contribute their special features to the crowd. Business men will come up from Holborn at the swing, but the ladies of the suburbs loiter from shop window to shop window, and when they have finished, and wait for the 'bus that is to take them to their homes in Camden or Kentish Town or distant Hampstead, they betray no undue anxiety or haste. The pretty, neatly-dressed chorus or small-part lady may be seen at this corner constantly, for there is a theatrical colony in the streets that run from Tottenham Court Road to Gower Street, and in

those around Bloomsbury Square. The sportsman—or rather sporting man—is not unknown here, for near to this corner was for many years a spot where the odds could be obtained in ready money in spite of the law, and the corner has never quite lost its sporting character. The Twopenny Tube station just across the road receives a rivulet of passengers all day long, and ejects a stream at frequent intervals. The foreign element from Fitzroy Square comes by Tottenham Court Road, and leads dark hair and flashing eyes and comic opera hats to the corner occasionally. But it rarely loiters. It crosses the road and works its way towards the maze of streets that make up Soho.

But the main characteristic of this corner is the "domestic English." The shopping lady, the tradesman, the commercial traveller, the occupiers of furnished apartments, and the inhabitants of North London villadom are more largely represented than any other element; for the nursemaid and the perambulator, and the working population that make High Street, Camden Town, and Hampstead

Road impassable on Saturday night, stop short about Euston Road, and rarely come as far as this corner, where the roadway runs direct into the City in one direction and direct to the West-End in another. The carriages that pass are more of the family vehicle than the smart order, and their presence is mainly due to the fact that in Tottenham Court Road are half a dozen of the most celebrated house furnishers and drapers in the Metropolis.

I have enumerated but a few out of the famous street corners of London, but they are fairly typical ones. The Angel at Islington, the Nag's Head at Holloway, the corner of Piccadilly Circus, the corner by Camberwell Green, the Royal Exchange, and certain corners in the Borough, Hoxton, Kennington, Shoreditch, and Charing Cross have each a special feature, but in general character they fall into line with those dealt with in this article.

I have taken the London Street Corners from the point of view of their characteristic crowds, but they afford plenty of opportunities for the student of manners from the individual point of view also. The street corner character is an interesting personality. The loafer is to be found there in all his glory night and day. For the lovers of London it is at once a meeting and a parting place. The provincial sightseer is never absent from certain corners—notably the Baker Street corner near Madame Tussaud's—and there are some corners which are at night time meeting places for the local youth, and occasionally for the local rough. The street corner is a favourite pitch of the pickpocket and the confidence dodger, and the policeman lingers longer there than at any other part of his beat. The corner of the street is a place for good-byes, not only for lovers, but for friends and relations who live at opposite ends of the town. " I will walk as far as the corner with you" is a phrase that is on the lips of thousands of Londoners every night in the year. And "just round the corner" is a meeting place hallowed by centuries of poetry and song. To many an Englishman and Englishwoman there are " corners" in London streets which are fraught with hallowed memories — and they are not the *busiest* corners either.

LEMAN STREET CORNER (WHITECHAPEL).

TRAM, 'BUS, AND CAB LONDON.

By HENRY CHARLES MOORE.

CABMAN WITH ROSETTE (ROTHS-CHILD COLOURS).

DURING the hours which elapse between the arrival of the first tram at Aldgate, crowded with working men, and the departure suburbwards of the last 'bus, loaded with cheerful folk fresh from an after-theatre supper, cabs, 'buses, and trams carry between them all classes of his Majesty's subjects, from the peer and the millionaire to the coster and the workhouse woman.

Let us begin by seeing the trams at work. It is eight a.m., and at the entrance to a big North London tramyard stand some eight or nine smartly-uniformed for them in a big many-columned book. A car comes slowly from the back of the yard, and the men at the gate stand aside to let it pass. A conductor jumps on it, does his bell-punch, and prepares for work. In less than a minute the car is at the starting-point, where clerks, shop assistants, office boys, and tea-shop girls have been anxiously awaiting its arrival. Several youths and one girl jump on the car before it stops; the others wait until it is at a standstill. Then ten of them attempt to step on the platform at the same time, and not a little pushing ensues, followed probably by some hot words. In a few moments all the seats are occupied; the conductor rings his bell, and the car starts.

At the Finsbury Pavement terminus of the North Metropolitan Tramways we find cars, nearly all carrying their maximum number of passengers, arriving in rapid suc-

WASHING L.C.C. TRAMCARS.

conductors and leather-aproned drivers dis-cussing the latest news. Close by, in the yard inspector's office, are three conductors receiving their boxes of tickets, and signing cession from various northern suburbs. At the Hampstead Road and other termini north of the Thames they are arriving and departing every minute. Passing to South

OMNIBUS DRIVER.

London we see further proofs of the great popularity of trams. The London County Council's cars, filled with almost every type of the great city's male and female workers, are following each other closely on their way to Blackfriars, Waterloo, or Westminster Bridge.

During the afternoon the trams carry comparatively few passengers, but at six p.m. they begin to fill up rapidly at every town-end terminus, including those of the electric cars at Hammersmith and Shepherd's Bush, and struggles to get on them are fierce and frequent. At ten o'clock the trams begin to pass into the yards; at long intervals at first, but after eleven o'clock every two or three minutes. Here is a late one entering the South London Tramway Company's big yard at Clapham Junction. A stableman is awaiting it, and the moment it stops he promptly takes out the horses, and leads them upstairs to unharness, feed, and make them secure for the night. As the horses are being led away, the driver and the conductor put their shoulders to the car and push it along the lines until it is close against the one in front of it. The driver then marches off home, with his rug on his arm and his whip in his hand. The conductor, however, is not quite ready to depart; for two or three minutes he sits inside the car checking his last journey's takings. Having made his money

agree with his way bill, he enters the little yard-office and hands it in, together with his unused tickets, to the night inspector.

The last tram has entered one of the London County Council's yards, the gates are shut, and the washers and stablemen are left to themselves. The washers vigorously sweep the dirt and the "dead" tickets from the roofs and insides of the cars, and not until this task is ended is the washing begun. It is nearly five o'clock before the last car is washed, but the washers' work is not yet finished—the windows have to be cleaned, the brass work polished, and the panels rubbed with chamois leather.

Now let us watch the 'buses. It is a quarter past seven, and the driver of the first 'bus to leave one of the London General Omnibus Company's many extensive yards is already up, standing with his legs astride the brake pedal, and wrapping his rug around his body. A stout, grey-whiskered, red-faced old man, with his rug already strapped around him, is climbing laboriously to the box seat of the second 'bus. He is a conservative old fellow, and wears a tall hat, in spite of the fact that such headgear is going out of fashion among 'busmen. Drivers, ranging in age from twenty-one to seventy, and conductors, mostly under forty, hurry into the yard, greeting and

OMNIBUS CONDUCTOR.

LONDON BRIDGE STATION YARD.

chaffing each other in vigorous language. The only man who appears at all depressed is an "odd" driver who has been three days without a job; but soon his spirits revive, for a bustling little woman enters the yard, and informs the foreman that her husband is "that bad with rheumatism he can't raise a hand, let alone drive a pair of young horses like he had third journey yesterday." The "odd" driver takes out the sick man's 'bus, and the "odd" conductors regard his luck as a good omen.

By half-past eight 'buses of almost every colour, except black, are arriving in rapid succession from all quarters of the Metropolis, and setting down the last of their passengers at the Bank, rumble onwards to join the queue outside Broad Street Station, or to add to the busy scene in London Bridge Station yard. An hour later the London General's Kilburn express, "sixpence any distance," is rattling Citywards along Maida Vale; and at Oxford Circus 'buses are passing north, south, east,

and west. Here are some, each flying a miniature Union Jack, belonging to the London Road Car Company—the first of the two great companies, by the way, to introduce a motor 'bus; and from Edgware Road comes a Metropolitan Railway 'bus, with a big umbrella fixed above the driver's head. Proceeding down Regent Street or an Atlas and Waterloo Association's 'bus we meet, among others, Balls Brothers' "Brixtons," Tilling's old-established "Times," drawn by four excellent horses, and at Piccadilly Circus catch a glimpse of the little eight-seated, conductorless, waggonette-shaped motor-omnibus from Putney.

Near by, crossing Trafalgar Square, we see the yellow 'buses (dubbed by 'busmen

"mustard-pots") of the Camden Town Association, the oldest omnibus body in London. To this and other associations belong the majority of the leading proprietors, including several very old-established firms and such comparatively youthful limited liability companies as the Star Omnibus Company and the Associated Omnibus Company. Proceeding to Peckham, we find 'bus after 'bus starting from Tilling's stables, some bound for the City or West-End, but the majority for various southern suburbs.

MOTOR OMNIBUS.

General Omnibus Company. It is painted and lettered to give the public that impression, but the company's name is not on the panels, and the horses, instead of being strong, well-fed animals, are lean "cabbers."

Later on, an almost empty 'bus, which belongs to one of the great companies, is coming along Fleet Street from Ludgate Circus. The driver glances up at the Law Courts clock, and calculates that by driving somewhat slowly he will arrive at the earliest closing theatre just as the people are coming out. But the Strand policemen's duty clashes with his, and they hurry him on, with the result that, instead of leaving Charing Cross with a full 'bus, he has only five passengers. The 'buses following him are, however, more fortunate. Each gets filled up quickly, and having made its way slowly out of the Strand hurries homewards.

Now it is early in the afternoon—a slack time for 'busmen. Here comes a Road Car with every seat vacant, but the silk-hatted driver is keeping a sharp look-out, and soon picks up three ladies bound for Westbourne Grove. Not far away an empty London General is standing at a "point." The conductor has his hand on the bell-cord, but he is anxious to obtain passengers and does not start the 'bus until the time-keeper signals him to move on.

Here is the conductor of a "pirate," shouting with monotonous reiteration, "Sloane Street, Hyde Park Corner, Piccadilly, Strand." Two ladies enter his 'bus, believing it to belong to the London

The day cabmen, their hansoms and four-wheelers clean and bright from the washers' hands, begin to appear in numbers about nine a.m., some hurrying Citywards with fares, and others

IN A CAB YARD.

proceeding slowly to various stands, where they find a few unfortunate and somewhat despondent night cabmen waiting in the hope of obtaining at least one good job before taking their cabs back to the yard.

Soon we find cabs everywhere, for there are 7,500 hansoms and 3,700

HANSOM.

FOUR-WHEELER.

four-wheelers licensed to ply in the streets. A long line of cabs, each with luggage on its roof, is just quitting Euston Station. Several of the fares have arrived *viâ* Liverpool from distant parts of the world, and can scarcely conceal the pleasure they feel at finding themselves, after many years of exile, once more in a London cab. Down Grosvenor Place hansoms and four-wheelers are hastening to Victoria Station. On a summer day Middlesex and Surrey are perhaps playing at Lord's, and outside the ground the line of empty hansoms, awaiting the close of the day's play, extends to the station end of St. John's Wood Road. Now the theatres have closed, and hansoms and four-wheelers are following close upon each other in all directions. Some are bound for the suburbs; others, the majority, are hurrying to the various railway termini. Even Gower Street, peaceful from morning until night, is noisy with the tinkling of cab bells and the clattering of hoofs.

Here is a smart young cabman ready to mount his dickey. He is, perhaps, the lucky recipient of one of the Rothschild Christmas-boxes—a brace of pheasants—which are given annually to the majority of 'busmen and to some cabmen. In acknowledgment of this generous gift he has adorned his whip with a rosette composed of the donor's colours.

At the West-End we notice an old cabman seated on the box-seat of his four-wheeler. There is an air of contentment about him, for he is on a good stand and knows that it will not be long before he is hailed by a "fare." Near by, waiting outside a club, is a hansom in summer array. Cabby looks very cool in his white hat and light coat, and we see that he has also done his best to make his patrons comfortable; for a white awning is spread over the roof of his cab, and inside the hansom is a palm-leaf fan.

On a certain summer afternoon we may find the pensioners of that excellent society the Cabdrivers' Benevolent Association mustering at Westminster Bridge for their annual summer treat—a river trip to Hampton Court. Many of these weather-beaten old fellows (some are very feeble) have their wives with them, and a happy day is always spent.

The cabmen's shelters are filled with drivers enjoying their midday meal. The accommodation is small, and the men have little elbow-room, but the good quality and cheapness of the food more than alone, in the cabmen's opinion, for limited space. It is while having a meal in a shelter that cabmen discuss matters of interest to themselves. One describes the personal appearance of a well-dressed man who "bilked" him on the previous day, and another distributes cards announcing that a "friendly lead"—or, as it is sometimes termed, "a select harmonic meeting"—is to be held for the widow and children of a deceased comrade. "Friendly lead" cards are usually drawn up by cabmen, and, as the chairman and other officials are generally advertised by their nicknames, they afford amusement to outsiders.

Between the hours of two and five in the afternoon hundreds of cabbies drive to some of the big yards, such as that of the London Improved Cab Company, where they change horses and have their cabs "spotted," that is, the splashes of mud removed. It is a busy scene, and no sooner is it ended than the horsekeepers bring out the horses, which have cooled down, and groom them. The illustration on p. 97 is from a photograph of Mr. Patrick Hearn's well-known yard in Gray's Inn Road.

About 9.30 p.m. the first hansom to finish its day's work of twelve hours returns, and soon the washers begin their long night's work, dipping their pails into the tanks and throwing the water over the wheels and bodies of the muddy cabs. One man quickly finishes his first cab, and getting between the shafts pulls it out into the main yard, where some hours later it will be polished.

Standing at the corner of a street, nearly opposite one of the chief theatres, is a thin, shabbily-dressed, dejected-looking cab tout. His eyes are fixed on the stalls and dress-circle entrance, and the moment the earliest of the homeward-bound playgoers appear he hurries across to them. "Four-wheeler, sir?" he calls out to an elderly man, who is accompanied by his three pretty daughters. A four-wheeler *is* required, and the cab tout dashes off to a side street to fetch one. Soon he returns with it, and is rewarded with sixpence. Seeing that there is no chance of another job at this theatre, for his fellow touts are many, he hurries off to a later-closing one, where he earns eightpence—a sixpenny tip and a twopenny one. His night's earnings are only fourteenpence, but he is quite satisfied. The previous night he spent, supperless, on the Embankment; to-night he will have a fish-supper, a pot of beer, and a bed.

The day cabs continue to pass into the various yards until two o'clock in the morning, and by that time the Metropolis, with the exception of its night workers, is asleep. But hansoms and four-wheelers are waiting on the stands, and before the city awakes many a Londoner will have cause to be thankful that, though trams and 'buses disappear from the streets for a few hours, a cab is always to be found.

IN A CABMEN'S SHELTER.

IN A LONDON WORKHOUSE.

By J. W. WILKINSON.

PAUPER'S ADMISSION ORDER.

To pass in a north-westerly direction through the squares and by the towering flats lying between Langham Place and Northumberland Street, and to enter "York Palace"—no royal palace in fact, but the St. Marylebone Workhouse, and so called because of its palatial appearance and its proximity to York Gate, Regent's Park—is to step from the front door of Dives into the home of Lazarus. Plenty and poverty exist side by side. My lady's boudoir is on the one hand; the pauper's dormitory on the other. Extremes meet in London as they meet nowhere else.

Further contrasts await us at the entrance to this last refuge of civilisation's superfluities and failures, which we may take as a type of the many workhouses scattered over the Metropolis. Tarry awhile at the porter's lodge, and watch the incomers before they lose some of their individuality. Here, with slow, unwilling steps and lack-lustre eyes, comes a man who, worn out with life's struggle, has reluctantly obtained a relieving officer's order for admission. Enter next his antithesis—a London wastrel to the very marrow, shiftlessness stamped on his stubbled face, and with the air of one going through an oft-repeated performance. Who art thou, O unsavoury one, that callest thyself a painter? Let him be put down as a painter, but the officials know him as something more—a confirmed "in and out," a man who discharges himself in the morning and is back at night or the next day. A mere neophyte this, however; he has not yet achieved distinction in the professional pauper army. The gap which separates him from the champion "in and out," a supremely gifted genius of the East-End who has been discharged and admitted about two thousand times, is that which separates lance-corporal from colonel.

Another contrast. In through the doorway of signs comes a typical working man who palpably shrinks from the future, because he knows nothing of the life on which he is entering. When he goes before the Visiting Committee, may good fortune be his! Everybody admitted appears before that body, which is brought into closer contact with the inmates than are the Guardians who, as a board, meet fortnightly; and he is one of those cases which it helps

RECEIVING AN INFIRM PAUPER.

by giving money or finding employment or both. It thus saves men, and does untold good quietly and unostentatiously. He passes; and here is his successor—a man for whom the poor-house has no secrets and no terrors. He was born in the workhouse; all his life—and his hair is white as driven snow—he has lived in the workhouse; and he will die in the workhouse.

Could we wait here for twenty-four hours the iron chain of circumstances would show us still stranger juxtapositions. Picture a common scene. It is night. From the person of a man who has kept want at bay for sixty years or more, and who rolls up easily and comfortably in the official carriage kept for those who cannot walk. Rubber-tyred are the wheels of this vehicle, and it contains every necessary convenience known to medical science.

Leaving the lodge, all these and other types are conducted to the receiving ward, and then they are scattered over the buildings according to age, sex, and other circumstances. To get glimpses of them when they are settled involves some walking.

IN THE AIRING YARD.

Marylebone Road comes to sound save that of a cab bearing a belated roisterer homeward. Tap! tap! from the knocker, loudly, imperiously. The door is opened to admit a policeman carrying in his arms the familiar bundle. No need to ask what he has got. Another little mite has been found on a doorstep, nestled, perhaps, in an improvised cradle, and with a note from its despairing mother pinned to its clothing—a note that adds to the poignancy of the tragedy. "Oh, pray," wrote one poor creature from the depths of a sorrow-laden heart—"oh, pray somebody be kind to my little darling. I have to work very hard for six shillings a week, or I would look after her myself."

This is how tender, budding youth often comes to the workhouse gate. Age is represented not many hours afterwards in the Where shall we begin? In an institution known to one section of the community as "the grubber," one thinks first of the kitchen. Let that, then, be our starting point.

A large, lofty room, lined with white glazed bricks, and with a score of steam-jacketed coppers, tea coppers, roasting ovens, and the like, it seems to have been designed and fitted for a regiment of Brobdingnagians. Here they make sixty-gallon milk puddings, have three teapots of eighty gallons capacity each, cook a quarter of a ton of bacon and a ton of cabbage at an operation, and steam potatoes by the ton. Fixed in the middle of the kitchen is a mincing machine, one of the uses of which is artificially masticating the meat supplied to old and toothless paupers. On a large cutting-up table to the left the joints (always of good quality) are carved, and then, with other food, passed through two trapdoors into the great hall.

What was the menu to-day, Tuesday? Roast mutton and potatoes, with bread. The young men and women each had four-and-a-half ounces of meat, twelve ounces of potatoes, and four ounces of bread. For breakfast the ration was four ounces of bread, one-pint-and-a-half of porridge or one pint of cocoa; and for supper it will be six

measured out in doses at stated times. Adjoining is one of the four special day wards, which introduces us to the classification system. Formerly paupers were lumped together, as " casuals " are, outrageously enough, to this day ; now the best of them are isolated and made comparatively comfortable. As the superior men are discovered they are drafted into one or other of these rooms, which are much more bright and attractive

THE KITCHEN.

ounces of bread and one-pint-and-a-half of broth.

Through the great hall—a fine building capable of seating twelve hundred, and affording an infinitely suggestive scene at dinner-time—out into the airing yard again, past the beds of flowers that fringe it and make it bright and cheerful, by seat after seat occupied by paupers reading in the sun, and presently we reach one of the general males' day wards, of which there are four, all exactly alike. It is full of men, some standing in groups talking, some sleeping, some reading, some playing dominoes on the long table. On another table to the right stand huge bottles of medicine—stock mixtures for coughs, indigestion, and other common ailments of the race—ready to be

than those for the lower grade. The one we have just left is bare, rather noisy, and full of movement; this is hung with steel engravings, the table is strewn with books and adorned with plants, and all is still and quiet. In the other room the men, of a rougher class, wear their hats and like to sleep and play dominoes ; here the inmates are barricaded, and spend much of their spare time in reading. Separate dormitories are also provided for these select paupers, and they enjoy, therefore, a degree of privacy which used to be quite unattainable in a workhouse. In addition there are, of course, rooms exclusively for infirm males, who spend hours sitting apart in silence, as if listening for Time's oncoming footsteps.

More tacking and turning bring us to a

doorway from which proceeds a monotonous "ger—er—er—er." Inside are a number of men, each bent over a crank, which communicates with a huge, overgrown coffee-mill. Able-bodied unskilled paupers, they are literally fulfilling the primeval curse, and earning, as well as making, their bread by the sweat of their brow, since they are converting wheat into whole meal, which, mixed with a proportion of white flour, they will eat later

AN OLD COUPLE'S QUARTERS.

on in the great hall. Two bushels of grain form the daily task.

Crop! crop! crop! with the buzz of a saw, from another shop. It is, of course, the firewood manufactory. The eye takes it all in at a glance. At the far end four men are turning a crank that supplies the motive power to a circular saw, which is fed by a fifth inmate. Scattered about the room other paupers are chopping and bundling the wood. They are all old—mostly too old and too unskilled to do heavier or more profitable work. No fixed output is

IN A WOMEN'S WARD.

exacted. The men, in fact, are here more that they may kill time than anything else.

In other shops pauper "tradesmen" are variously employed. Piled up yonder, awaiting the attention of the cobblers, is a heap of boots about the size of a hayrick. These seats in the corridor, fit for any gentleman's lawn, are home-made, and are for the garden. And now the odour of methylated spirit reaches the nose. We have arrived at the French-polishing shop, concerning which the indefatigable Master of the workhouse could tell a story. Once it had an inmate who too freely supped the potent but nauseous spirit used for polishing. To make the stuff still more horrible, the officials dosed his supplies with asafœtida, and there is every reason to believe that that eloquently noisome drug proved too much for even his palate. But the experiment was only a qualified success, because the offensive product spoiled the spirit for the purposes for which it is generally employed. Over the remaining shops we need not linger. Enough

AT DINNER.

that employment is found for all except the physically unfit, and that all the work of the house is done by its inmates. There are only two salaried artisans in the place.

Now let us pass to the female side, which differs little, except in obvious details, from the male side. One feature, however, has a pathetic interest, and that is the number of aged inmates. Included in the population of this microcosm—two thousand, the full roll of many a country town with a mayor and corporation—are no fewer than two hundred octogenarians, of whom the majority are women. Veritable dear old creatures many of them are! The feeling they produce must needs be one of sadness, and yet there is something pleasing in the spectacle they present when hob-nobbing over their tea in the afternoon. Many of them have their own teapots—presents, in some cases, from the kindly matron—and they get the delicious leaf from visitors and in other ways. Sometimes one of the less infirm women, having no proprietary rights whatever in such a utensil, puts a screw into a pot belonging to a more fortunate companion, and in virtue of that contribution is entitled to a cup of the brew. So there you shall find them all at their accustomed hour, drinking tea as of old, and perfectly contented with things as they are, judging from the nodding of caps and the smiles and the whispered confidences. If they are not happy, appearances belie them. It is certain, at all events, that most of them will gradually rust out, and die at last of the workhouse complaint, old age.

And now we reach the aged married couples' quarters. Consisting of ten little tenements for as many Darbies and Joans — one room, one couple — and a general room at the end for meals, the "private apartments" form a sort of miniature model dwelling that overlooks the Paddington Street Recreation Ground. Admirable is the only word for this division. The brightly-painted walls, the pictures, the official furniture, including a chest of drawers and a table, the photographs and knick-knacks belonging to the inmates, who are allowed to bring in such property and arrange it as they choose—all this makes a "private apartment" home-like and a

62

delight to the eye. If an old couple must spend their last days in the workhouse, one could wish them no brighter or more healthy quarters.

A final pause at the nursery, and then to another gate—that of the casual ward. The infants' room is, perhaps, the saddest side of any workhouse, though everything possible is done for the helpless little mortals in "York Palace." Some little sufferers are in bed; the rest seated together at the end of the room, close to a table where food—milk, bread-and-milk, bread and butter—is always kept in readiness. They are always eating, but they cannot exhaust the supply, for that is illimitable. Though they have not been cradled in the purple, they bear no trace of hardship. A chubby-cheeked girl, who never takes her eyes off your face, came from a doorstep in a neighbouring street, and some of her companions have identically the same history. Where are their mothers—alive or dead? Others are known orphans, and two or three are the children of women in the house. But they all look well and robust.

Five o'clock. The casual ward opens at six, and already there is outside it a mass of the human wreckage that the irresistible tide of London life is ever casting up. Nearly two-score pitiable figures—broken-down professional men, artisans out of work (some of them "too old at fifty"), women with innocent children clinging to their skirts, whole families even, from the head to the suckling at its mother's breast—are waiting for admission. One of the women is eyed curiously by her fellow "casuals." She is decently dressed and—here is the cause for special wonder—wearing kid gloves. What strange decree of fate has brought her here?

At six o'clock prompt the door opens, and the tramps enter the refuge in single file. Listen to the answers they give to the usual questions. One is repeated again and again till it sears itself on the brain. It is "Nowhere." "Where did you sleep last night?" asks the porter. "Nowhere." Nowhere! The key of the street; dropping asleep on a doorstep, or, worse still, while still walking, and being rudely wakened by the shock of stepping on a paving-stone that was not there—dropping, that is to say, off the kerb—or running into a lamp-post or a brilliantly-lighted window; dodging about in the cold, grey dawn to get a wash at a street fountain when a policeman is not looking—these and a score of other miseries are summed up in the pregnant word.

Beyond the office the stream of destitute humanity divides, the women and children going one way, and the men another. The males are next searched to see whether they possess more money than is allowed (the limit here is 4d.), and also whether they have pipes, tobacco, or matches concealed about their persons. All pass muster, and, having had a compulsory bath, sit down to supper, which consists of one pint of gruel and six ounces of bread. The meal ended—and be sure that it does not last long—they retire one by one to their separate cells, each of which contains the unusual luxury of an ordinary bed.

To-morrow morning, after breakfast—which is a mere repetition of supper—the inmates will be set to work, the women at cleaning and washing, the men at cleaning and oakum picking. All day, with only a break for dinner—bread and cheese—will they be thus kept employed. Then will come supper again, then bed; and on the following morning, about thirty-six hours after entrance, they will be discharged, turned on the streets once more.

This is the life of those who by the vicissitudes of things are undermost, temporarily or permanently. It is practically the same all over Pauper London, for, as already stated, "York Palace" is a typical Metropolitan workhouse. Vastly as it has been improved of late years, it can be still further bettered without putting a premium on laziness, and it lies with us who are now on top to see that this is done.

CASUALS WAITING FOR ADMISSION.

READING ROOM, AMERICAN EXPRESS COMPANY.

AMERICAN LONDON.

By ELIZABETH L. BANKS.

THERE was a time when American tourists who came to London returned to their native land and informed their compatriots that there was "nothing fit to eat over there," meaning that all the food was cooked and served in English style, and that benighted Britishers knew nothing of the delights of the products of American culinary skill. That Great Britain could exist, and even wax strong and fat, under such adverse conditions was an ever-increasing puzzle to the visiting American who went from restaurant to restaurant, and boarding-house to boarding-house, with his eyes full of tears and his pockets full of money, seeking, always seeking, for what his appetite craved, yet never finding it.

But those melancholy times are past—it was before the Americanising of London that such tragedies were enacted; and now there are few special American dishes which one cannot find at various eating-places in London if one will but inquire for them. Here is a case in point. I was one of a little American party at a restaurant in the neighbourhood of Charing Cross, where pork and beans, Boston style, and salted cod-fish

"picked-up" (i.e. shredded into fine bits and prepared with thick cream gravy) were served to us as the merest matter of course when asked for—and, I may add, to the astonishment of a certain facetious member of our party, who had ordered these "specialities" of Yankeeland with no other purpose than that of dumbfounding the waiter.

That individual, however, only answered, "Yes, sir; certainly sir!" and straightway brought us our cod-fish; after which we had such a beautifully browned bean feast, with crinkled roast pork in the middle and all, that we could proceed with little effort to fancy ourselves in Boston.

But it was London!

It was London, too, into which we penetrated when we left the restaurant to make our way towards Piccadilly Circus; and the semi-circular street down which we looked, to see dozens of star-spangled banners floating from the tops of the business houses, was Regent Street. It was difficult to believe that we were not in New York or Chicago, walking along a street decorated with flags for some extra-special gala occasion. What did it mean? Nothing, except that the month was July, and the shopkeepers, knowing that the "American Invaders" had descended upon London to the number of many thousands, paid them the pretty compliment of hoisting the Stars and Stripes instead of the Union Jack. To be sure, one could not positively affirm that the shopkeepers were wholly sentimental, and gave no thought to the probable increase of trade that the hoisting of the flag might bring! London shopkeepers are human. Nevertheless this Americanising of Regent Street has always seemed to me an exceedingly graceful thing.

And speaking of shops and shopping, let us hasten along Regent Street, past the Circus, into Oxford Street to see another device in the way of American baiting. A very kindly, clever bait it is, that sign in the window of a large Oxford Street draper's establishment—"To our American Lady Customers : Messrs. Blank, having noticed that their American customers seem often to have difficulty in determining the exact value of English coinage, have prepared a table of money equivalents, by which ladies may see at a glance the American value of the articles exposed for sale. Messrs. Blank will also be pleased to receive payment for their goods in American currency, if more convenient to their customers. They also present, with their compliments, a Guide Book of London, which they are sure will interest and assist American ladies visiting the Metropolis."

"American Rocking Chairs for Sale Here!" "American Shoes!" "American Desks!" "American Pickles and Catsup!" "American Cut Glass!" "American Soda Water and Other Iced Drinks!" "American Bar—Gentlemen, Try our 'Whiskey Sour' and 'Manhattan Cock-tail!'" "American Candies — Made Fresh Every Day!"

Everywhere and hundreds of times a day our eyes are greeted with these and other signs of American London.

Having eaten our American luncheon, and shopped in American fashion with American money with which we have bought American things, let us to Victoria Street to pay our respects at the American Embassy, which has the distinction of being unique in its unpretentiousness and inconveniences among the various embassies of London. We find the Ambassador, who is at the head of American London, receiving numbers of his countrymen and countrywomen, assisted by the different

IN THE COURTYARD, HOTEL CECIL.

tian at the Embassy, and the inconveniences arising from lack of space are proportionately greater. Into the Consulate, to pour all their troubles into the ears of the sympathetic and genial Consul-General, go hundreds of Americans daily during

secretaries. During the "Invasion Season" it is computed that about one hundred Americans daily apply at the American Embassy for the two tickets which the Ambassador has the privilege of giving away each day for entrance to the House of Lords. This means that ninety-eight Americans daily leave the Embassy disconsolate and disappointed, declaring that the only fault they have to find with London is the fact that the chamber of the House of Lords is not so convenient of access as is their own Senate chamber at Washington.

If it happens to be a Fourth of July, the Ambassador is found at his private residence, shaking hands, shaking hands, always shaking hands, with thousands of his countrymen and countrywomen who are resident in or passing through London; and after the hand-shaking, in which the Ambassador is, of course, assisted by his wife, there is a descent to the dining-room for the strawberries— which every honest American will admit to be better than any strawberries eaten in his native land—ice-cream, cake, and punch. There was a time in years gone by when only Americans attended these receptions, given to celebrate the breaking of the chain which bound the American Colonies to England; but in these later years a great many Englishmen and Englishwomen go to the American Ambassador's house every Independence Day. Great Englishmen of title bring their American wives to shake hands with the Ambassador, and jestingly refer to the "Anglo-American Alliance."

At the American Consulate, in St. Helen's Place, the scene is sometimes even busier

OFF FOR THE DAY: I. BY COACH. II. BY CHAR-A-BANC.

the "Invasion Season"; and to the American tourist unaccustomed to the people and manners and ways of English life the Consul-General is expected to act the part of guide, philosopher, and friend. Among these callers are not a few ladies who seek his advice in connection with matters of all kinds.

Also into the Consulate go the "stranded" Americans in London, asking for help to "get back to God's country"; and then the Consul-General and his assistants must kindly but firmly point to a framed legend on the wall, which runs: "This office is not provided by the United States Government with any fund for the assistance of needy Americans in London."

The Consulate is besieged by English as well as American visitors. It is to the Consulate, in the private office of the Deputy-Consul-General, that hundreds of British merchants and others go to make what is known as their "declarations" before shipping goods to America, that is, they "declare" the value of the goods they are exporting.

To the Deputy-Consul-General also go the Americans to get advice upon notarial, legal,

A FOURTH OF JULY RECEPTION AT THE AMERICAN AMBASSADOR'S RESIDENCE.

and other matters of various kinds. There, too, go the many Yankee inventors, who, arriving in London with what they term a "mighty handy device," yet knowing not what to do with it, proceed to St. Helen's Place to seek information from the always good-natured Deputy-Consul-General concerning where to "place" their inventions on exhibition to attract the attention of Londoners.

But the Embassy and the Consulate are only two of the places where Americans in London foregather. Go to the Reading Room of the British Museum, and watch them hunting up their ancestors, diving deep into the records of the Harleian Society, turning page after page of peerage books and works on county families. Observe the smiles when they discover that there was a live lord in the family away back in the centuries agone; see how they chuckle if they can discover connection, however distant, with a dukedom. They like the British Museum for other reasons than that it enables them to discover the secrets of their ancestry. They particularly like the place, because in the summer it is cool and in the winter it is warm, heated after the American manner and sometimes to the American temperature. Thus is the British Museum one of their favourite haunts.

Round the bust of Longfellow, too, in Westminster Abbey, frequently gathers American London, with kindly thoughts of the England that has thus honoured America's poet. Then from the Abbey, on the top of a 'bus, talking with the driver and giving him such tips as are calculated to turn him into the most voluble and interesting of encyclopædias, go the Invaders to the Tower, to St. Paul's, and other resorts which any American after a visit to London of even two days would blush to say he had not seen. In the afternoon at tea-time, or later in the cool of the day, again comes the foregathering, this time in the courtyard of the Cecil, the Palm Court of the Carlton, and the lounges of the other hotels that welcome Americans to the neighbourhood of Trafalgar or Russell Square. Notes are compared while teaspoons click against cup and saucer. There are calls for ice, ice;

and there is such a volume of American accent, American vivacity, and American dressing as would be apt to convince a foreigner dropping suddenly into the scene that London was the chief city of America.

The two classes that go to make up American London are the Settlers and the Invaders. I have so far been writing of the Invaders. It is they who spend their days in sight-seeing, who fill the coaches and char-a-bancs going to Hampton Court and other places of interest. They gather in the shipping offices to purchase tickets to their native land. They haunt the bureaus of information, they go in their dozens to the office and reading-room of the American Express Company in Waterloo Place to see the American papers and inquire if there are any "express packages." Those who cannot afford the high-priced hotels betake themselves to boarding and lodging houses, with a preference for those over Bloomsbury way, and a particular and especial liking for such as are diplomatic enough to display the American flag or the American Eagle shield over the fanlight.

For the benefit of the Invaders, to make them pass their time profitably and pleasantly, the Settlers, assisted in many instances by Englishmen and Englishwomen, have started clubs, societies and unions, and leagues. The first of these societies was probably the American Society in London, which gives American dinners and receptions on such holidays as the Fourth of July, Thanksgiving Day, and Washington's Birthday. Then comes the Society of American Women in London, with its beautiful rooms and its wonderful luncheon parties at Prince's. The Atlantic Union, though it numbers among its members many Colonials, makes a specialty of American members and devising means of entertaining American visitors and bringing them into contact with British subjects; while the Anglo-American League is, as its name indicates, a combination of inhabitants of both countries in the interests of peace, good-will, sympathy, and for the strengthening of the international ties. The fact that membership in this society is open to all British subjects and American citizens, on the payment of a subscription of not less than a shilling or more than a pound, will

in itself show how broad
are its aims and how
wide-reaching should be
its influence.

The American Set-
tlers in London number
about twenty thousand.
Those who make up this
twenty thousand belong
to all sorts and conditions,
from the American society
woman entertaining not
only her own countrymen
and countrywomen, but
members of the English
royalty and nobility, to
the humble American
negro, who elects to reside
in London because of what

MAKING " DECLARATIONS "
AT THE AMERICAN
CONSULATE.

he thinks is the greater degree of " liberty,
equality, and fraternity."

There was a time when to hear the
American accent on the English stage
caused smiles and comments. Now upon
the boards the " American language" is heard
almost as frequently as the English tongue,
while theatrical companies made up entirely
of Americans come to London with the
expectation of remaining the whole year
round.

American journalism, too, with its good
points and its bad ones, has come to London

to stay, not for a year, but probably for the
century. Some papers being " run " on the
American plan, it, of course, follows that the
importation of American journalists has
become a necessity, so all along Fleet Street
American journalists can be seen at any hour
of the day, and almost any hour of the night
as well, flying hither and thither. I myself
have a keen recollection of the time, only a
few years back, when, calling at the office of
a London newspaper, I would feel and express surprise at finding one of my own
countrymen in the editorial chair, ready to discuss with me plans for my
work. Now my journalistic
work constantly brings me
into contact with my own
countrymen as editors of
London papers.

So thoroughly, indeed,
has London become
Americanised, so great is
the influx, both by pre-
ference or by marriage, of
American women into
London society, that it is
really dangerous for the
unsophisticated to discuss
in public American people,
American customs, or
American manners, unless
they are named for the
purpose of praising them.
It was not so very long ago

IN THE DEPUTY-CONSUL-GENERAL'S OFFICE : A MATTER OF BUSINESS.

that a Frenchman, being entertained in the home of a certain Duchess, was discussing at an evening reception the characteristics of American women as compared with those of Englishwomen and Frenchwomen. The Frenchman did not like or approve of American women, and made bold to express his opinion in no flattering terms of certain of their faults and failings. He also ventured to suggest that in point of beauty, charm, intelligence, and morality they were, as a class, far inferior to English and Continental women.

" Do you not agree with me, your Grace? " asked the Frenchman, gallantly bowing to the Duchess.

" That is a somewhat embarrassing question for you to have put to me," answered the Duchess coldly, "since I am an American woman myself, though, of course, I am now a British subject!"

Day by day and year by year this Americanising of London goes on. New " schemes," new enterprises, new inventions —even new customs and manners and new words for the English language—are ever making their appearance in London ; and, inquiring whence they come, one is usually informed "From America, of course!" Then down come some of London's old buildings to make room for steam-heated American office-blocks, which their architects would rear to the thirty-fourth storey were it not for the interference of London's building laws.

Through the streets of London roam the German bands and Italian organ-grinders, playing "The Star-Spangled Banner" and " Hail! Columbia," and little English girls follow, keeping time to the music, dancing as only London children can dance.

All this is American London.

IN THE CONSUL-GENERAL'S OFFICE : AN AMERICAN CALLER.

BOUND FOR SOUTHEND (FENCHURCH STREET STATION)

BANK HOLIDAY LONDON.

By A. ST. JOHN ADCOCK.

IF you happen to live near any of the great open spaces that fringe the outskirts of London, you know what it is to be wakened before sunrise on three mornings of the year by weird, unwonted noises passing without—clattering of hoofs, rattling of wheels, cracking of whips, occasionals shouts, occasional bursts of laughter.

Getting out of bed to peer round the edge of the blind, you see a shadowy, intermittent procession flitting through the ghostly twilight—a donkey-cart laden with sticks and a sack or two of cocoa-nuts, a man perched in front driving, a woman nodding drowsily behind; a slow van top-heavy with painted poles and boat-shaped swings; a sleepy alien pushing an ice-cream barrow; another donkey-cart presently, and another; costers with barrows full of fruit, of nuts, of winkles—all passing dimly like phantoms in a nightmare; but, remembering it is a Bank Holiday, you know you are not dreaming, and that these are enterprising tradesmen racing early for the best places on the adjacent pleasure ground.

By and by you take a stroll out over that ground before breakfast, and find those shadows of the dawn looking solid enough in the daylight. They have lined the roads and paths with their stalls and barrows; the cocoa-nut shies have been prepared, and, pending the arrival of sportsmen, the proprietors are squatting on the grass enjoying an interlude of repose, or sipping at cups of coffee from the nearest refreshment-stand, and assimilating thick slices of bread and butter.

Already, however, the revellers are coming. Here are small boys, bent on missing none of the day and impatient to begin enjoying themselves, tramping in out of the streets clutching newspaper packets of provender. And, supposing the ground of your choice to be Hampstead Heath, and the weather fair, here come other boys, and here, too, come older citizens, who are used to being bleached in City offices on ordinary days of the year, each adventuring forth now with his rod, and a tin can, and a pocketful of worms. Down by the ponds on the Heath, or in Highgate Fields, you shall see them bait their hooks and cast their lines, and settle down to the placid enjoyment of watching their floats.

But they have an hour or more of comparatively peaceful fishing before them yet, for the great mass of holiday-makers are only just getting dressed, or sitting down to breakfast. A small minority are approaching in trains and 'buses and trams, or afoot, but, generally speaking, those who are up so early as this have promised themselves a day at the seaside, and are hurrying to the big railway stations, such as London Bridge or Fenchurch Street, to catch excursion trains to Brighton, Southend, or elsewhere, or—especially on the August Bank Holiday —are pouring down the stone steps on to the Old Swan Pier, and fighting a passage through the increasing throng on to the excursion steamers for Clacton, Margate, and other resorts.

Many who could afford it went away by rail or river on Saturday afternoon, and will not return until to-morrow morning, but the multitudes scurrying now to the railway termini or seething and struggling on the pier will come back to-night weary with too much happiness, with the sea-voices lingering in their ears, and in their eyes a memory of lovelier horizons, to make the jaded city seem, by contrast, dingier than it really is.

Except for such as these, and for the ardent cyclists who are setting forth at this same hour on a long spin into the country, the average Londoner is not inclined to get up unusually early, even to make holiday; in fact, he more often allows himself the luxury of an extra hour's sleep, as if it were a Sunday, and does not emerge into the open till noon, after a premature dinner.

Nevertheless, by nine o'clock Hampstead Heath is alive and growing livelier every minute; after noon the ceaseless flow of new arrivals quickens and swells and spreads itself out over the landscape, until you can scarcely see the grass for the people on it. Up the road from the railway station and the tram terminus the crowd sweeps, closely packed, and as if there would never be an end to it—a jovial, motley crowd, in which very gorgeously arrayed young ladies and dapper young gentlemen mingle with artisans and navvies in working habiliments, and dowdy, draggled women, who are equally happy in the dresses they wear at the wash-tub; and decent, impecunious shopmen and master

mechanics and their trim wives and daughters rub shoulders with embryo Hooligans and pallid, grubby urchins fresh from the slums and alleys they rarely care to escape from except on such a day as this.

Up the road tramps a party of callow youths, singing and

TWO SCENES IN WHITECHAPEL.

A CHILDREN'S PICNIC (WENTWORTH STREET, E.).

marching to a tune one of them is playing on a mouth-organ. Up the road come half a dozen similar youths, with half a dozen maidens in dresses of bewildering brilliance: each pair have changed hats, as a token of affection, and walk droning a plaintive ballad, with their arms round one another's necks.

Up the road comes a small middle-aged father of a large family, wheeling the youngest but one in the perambulator, while his wife carries the youngest, and the five elder children straggle after them eating sweets or apples; the smallest boy creating excitement at intervals by loitering and getting lost, when they have to go back, calling wildly, to look for him, and, having found him, to cuff him in a paroxysm of affectionate thankfulness, and dare him to do it again.

Up the road, in a word, come boys and girls, men and women, old and young, in rags and in finery, married and single, with babies and without; and all the way by the roadside vendors of "ladies' tormentors," long feathers known as "ticklers," penny bagpipes and tin trumpets, stand contributing to the general uproar. In a side street, opposite a public-house, a piano-organ is rattling out a lively waltz, and a bevy of girls are setting to each other, bowing and swaying, or catching each other by the waist and whirling round ecstatically; while their male escorts wait for them, doing impromptu breakdowns, or looking on and grinning, with their hands in their pockets.

But all this is almost Arcadian peacefulness beside the hubbub and riot now in full blast on the Heath itself. Every man at the stalls and the cocoa-nut shies is bellowing his loudest; and as you make what progress you can along the uproarious, congested roadway you are startled by sudden crisp reports from a shooting-gallery on your right or the blunt thud of the hammer being vigorously brought down on the try-your-strength machine to your left. At every step you are embarrassed by invitations to try your weight, to have a swing, to undergo shocks at galvanic batteries, and bewildered by the allurements of stalls that offer you ices, jewellery, tarts, fruit, whelks, pigs' trotters, and inexpensive toys; and suddenly the crowd scatters, laughing and shrieking, to make way for two soldiers and their sweethearts, who are jolting downhill in the heat of a donkey race.

Here and there among the stalls is a side-show. You pay a penny at the door of a

ON BOARD A RIVER STEAMER: PASSING THE BOX FOR THE BAND.

canvas castle, and within view through a series of holes a pictorial representation of the career of a celebrated criminal. For other pennies you witness an unsensational boxing-match in one tent, and in another contemplate waxwork models of the very latest murderer and his victim. In a small open space amidst the dense throng, beyond the stalls, a troupe of acrobats is performing to a packed and appreciative audience. And near by, in a smaller space, the proprietors

head in bandages. There has been an accident; the man has been knocked down by a swing, and he is preceded and followed by men, women, and children who have quitted less exciting games to see him conveyed to the ambulance tent. In like manner there are groups who spend hours in the immediate neighbourhood of the police-tent for lost children, keeping count of the number of the lost, and ready to place their information and their philosophical deductions

A STREET FAIR (BATTERSEA).

of a skipping-rope, who have placed a board on the earth for the use of customers, and are turning the rope for an imaginary skipper shout, "Now, then, lydies! Skip as long as yer like for a penny!" And while they are calling an answer comes from the surrounding thousands, and the imaginary skipper materialises in the shape of a buxom factory girl, who skips with such agility, quickening her pace as the rope goes faster and faster, that it is looking as if the men's arms must tire before her feet, when an interruption abruptly ends the competition.

The crowd warps and splits and bursts in, right across the skipping board, and marching smoothly and swiftly through come two ambulance officers carrying a pale-looking man on a stretcher with his

at the service of any unsophisticated straggler who will lend an ear to them. "Here's another of 'em!" observes a bleary, ruminant man, who leans on the railing drawing hard at a short pipe. "This makes the sixth what's been brought in since I've been 'ere. They ain't all lost, don't you believe it! Their people nips off an' leaves 'em, an' watches till they sees 'em brought in 'ere safe, an' then goes an' enjoys theirselves, an' just calls for 'em on their way 'ome." It does happen now and then, however, that a distracted man and woman rush up and disappear into the tent, and presently emerge with one of the lost infants, masking their agitation from the onlookers under an affectation of wrath or flippant laughter.

But the centre of all the gaiety and noise

ON HAMPSTEAD HEATH.

I. SKIPPING.   II. ACROBATS.   III. THE VALE OF HEALTH.   IV. LOST CHILDREN'S TENT.   V. AMBULANCE TENT.

on Hampstead Heath is in the Vale of Health. There the roundabout calls and calls all day, siren like, and lures the mob down into its tumultuous whirlpool, and will not easily let them go again. Round and round giddily go its wooden horses, each with its rider, man or woman, boy or girl, with such a shrieking of the whistle and rolling of the organ, and singing and giggling and screaming, as no words can give any idea of.

Right and left of the roundabouts boat-swings are rising and falling, full of passengers; across the road, on the green under the trees, young parties are playing at kiss-in-the-ring, and old parties are picnicking sedately. Here, too, are the famous tea gardens where so many generations of holiday Cockneys have refreshed themselves; and within the primitive enclosure, at the primitive bare tables, representatives of the present generation are refreshing themselves now.

Whether it is Easter or Whit Monday or the first Monday in August makes little difference, except in the state of the weather. There may be a cold snap at Easter, or on any of the three days a rain that will drive the merrymakers home depressed, or send them early to whatever entertainments may be had under cover. On Boxing Day, of course, there is practically no provision for out-of-door amusements, unless the ice is strong enough for skating; moreover, most of us who remain in town are occupied with Christmas festivities at our own firesides or, in the evening, swarming to the pantomimes. But on the other three Bank Holidays of the year the joys of Hampstead Heath unfailingly repeat themselves and are simultaneously reproduced, with modifications, along the approaches to Battersea Park; in Wembley and Victoria Parks, in Greenwich Park, on Blackheath, in fact, in and around every park and common and open space to which working London resorts when the time has come for it to play.

They are reproduced at Epping Forest without any modification at all. When you struggle from the overloaded train at Chingford you see and hear the jolly revellers before you get your first view of the forest. Organs are clattering and rippling universally: three are playing different tunes simultaneously

on the grassy patch skirting the forest opposite a big and busy hotel; and behind and before each organ boisterous couples are dancing, light-footed and light-hearted, as if, like Sidney's shepherd-boy, they "would never grow old." While you pause for a moment in the road your limbs are suddenly imperilled by the passing of ladies and gentlemen on unruly donkeys, of children in erratic goat-chaises, of select parties arriving in their own donkey-barrows; in the thick of the hubbub a group of evangelists hold an inaudible meeting; and the inevitable photographer is in evidence with a wheedling insinuation of appeal that a young man with a sweetheart finds difficult to resist.

Meanwhile London's great waterway is almost as lively as its dustier highways. There are gay boating parties putting out from Richmond; and up to Kew, and down to Greenwich, or, further still, to Gravesend, steamers are gliding through the river, with laughter aboard, and music, and even dancing when there is room enough on deck for such diversion.

In a word, everywhere to-day where there is any entertainment to be found a crowd is there to find it. The parks that tolerate no stalls or roundabouts have extra allowances of select and strictly orderly visitors placidly taking the air. Wherever there is a green space sufficiently uninvaded boys and men are playing at cricket; while on the Serpentine, on the lakes at the Welsh Harp, "which is Hendon way," and on every other suburban sheet of water available for the purpose, there is boating as long as the light lasts.

Not one of the public-houses in any district is deserted; most of them are continuously bubbling and boiling over with customers—good-humoured folk in the main, though you may look for a rumpus here and there before the day is over. There are few, if any, vacant seats at this afternoon's matinées, and to-night the theatres and music-halls will be full to suffocation, and turning hundreds away from their doors.

But it is too early to be talking of night yet awhile. The fact that thousands have gone out of town for the day is fully compensated for by the other fact that thousands have come into it for the day from easily accessible provincial towns—strangers and pilgrims who help to swell the hosts that flock to see great cricket matches at Lord's or the Oval, or cycle and foot races and miscellaneous sports and shows at the Crystal and Alexandra Palaces, and the hosts that are attracted to the Zoological Gardens or, during the season, to the latest exhibition at Earl's Court. They mingle also with homelier Cockneys who are turning their leisure to account by making the acquaintance of the Museums, the Art Galleries, the Tower, and the Monument.

Judging by the myriads that have gone out and are still going by road and rail and river, you might expect to find practically all London disporting itself away from home. But, apart from the well-to-do or the sedate, who are superior to Bank Holidays, and prefer to avoid their tumult by remaining within doors, even the poorer quarters of the town are far from being depopulated.

South and east, in Walworth, in Whitechapel, and elsewhere, though most of the shops are shut and the air is strangely peaceful, children are swarming in many of the streets playing every-day games in quite their every-day manner. There are maturer people who like a stroll through their native streets better than the fun of the fair, or who

find all the recreation they desire no further away than the public-house at the corner. There are elderly people, glad of the quiet their more rollicking neighbours have left behind them, seated in the sun outside their doors, sewing, smoking, gossiping, dreaming maybe of earlier years, when they were more disposed to exert themselves and found less pleasure in rest. Some of the children in the streets are the offspring of roistering parents, who have bribed them to contentment with certain pence, and gone off, leaving them in charge of their grandmothers, who thankfully give them liberty to wander off with small companions to invest their unwonted wealth at a suitable shop and hold informal banquets on the pavement outside.

They have a quiet, uneventful time, these and their stay-at-home elders, all day; all day until evening. Then the returning tide of pleasure seekers begins to come in, and goes on coming in till midnight and after, with sounds of discordant singing, groanings and whimperings of concertinas, and buzzings of mouth-organs. And everyone is tired, and nearly everyone is satisfied to be home at last; and to-morrow, for the most part, the workaday world will turn from playing to its old humdrum workaday ways again.

" LOOK PLEASANT, PLEASE ! "

OUTSIDE THE ROYAL EXCHANGE.

THE CITY AT HIGH NOON.

By CHARLES C. TURNER.

OVER our heads the traffic of the City rolls on, the roar of it coming down to us in the subway at the Bank of England, whither we have travelled by rail, in a bewildering confusion of deep, discordant tones. Let us ascend, choosing for our exit the steps leading to Princes Street. As we mount the steps the noise presses round us, the horses' hoofs ring on the asphalt close by our heads. On the top step we secure a foothold on the eagerly contested pavement space. We set our backs to the wall, and regard a scene which in many respects has no parallel in the wide world.

It is midday, and London's business is at high tide. Those whose working hours commence at eight o'clock, nine o'clock, and ten o'clock have all by this time got into the swing of the day's work. Shoppers and leisurely sightseers add to the throng. At innumerable stages, up to four, five, and six miles away, towards every point of the compass, omnibuses have filled at their cor-

ductors' cry, "Bank! Bank!" Through great stress of traffic have they come, and hither in long, uninterrupted processions do they continue to come. Of all colours are they, and so closely ranged together that they blot out of view all but the upper portions of the buildings. At the will of traffic-managing policemen, now this stream of vehicles, now that, holds the field.

The hubbub of it! Underlying all is the incessant rumble of wheels; but high above that rings the clatter, clatter of hundreds of horses' hoofs on the smooth, hard road. The rustling footsteps of thousands of men and women make a light accompaniment. And this babel of sounds goes on incessantly —a continual hum, and roar, and clatter; till you wonder that the hardest pavement does not wear through in a day, that the toughest human nerve can sustain it for a couple of hours. Venture into the stream of people. If you are in a dreamy mood, inclined to philosophise as to the meaning of this tumult of seething life, you will soon be rudely awakened, you will be jostled by a crowd which has not time for day-dreaming. You will find it best to have an object in view. On your left hand is the Bank; opposite the loftier but less impressive Mansion House. Between the two, but set far back, stands the handsome pillared front of the Royal Exchange, sur-

coats, nearly every one of which supports a gold watchchain, the generally well-groomed look about most of the people, may impress you. Cornhill and Lombard Street, its neighbour, are both thronged with streams of hurrying men. Both ways are narrow, absurdly so, a contrast to stately Queen Victoria Street which, close by, makes so busy and impressive a junction in

QUEEN VICTORIA STREET (JUNCTION WITH CANNON STREET).

mounted by the campanile with its gleam-ing gilt grasshopper, which strange device indicates the direction of the wind. Let the Royal Exchange be your objective, and proceed to cross the roads which separate you from it.

You are now in the money region, the land of stocks and shares. Close by are the Stock Exchange, the Royal Exchange, and a remarkable gathering together of banks. Here the throng, representative of the dis-trict, contains a big proportion of men who deal on exchanges or are employed in the banks. The glossy hats, the well-conditioned dark coats and trousers, the expensive waist-

Cannon Street. Both are fed by and connected by an astonishing number of narrow alleys, bearing the oddest names, and lined with banks and offices. At every few yards one of these busy lanes leads off in the most ramified and unexpected fashion, and if you leave the main route and explore them it is like entering another world. The superficial observer sees only the great, im-posing rivers of traffic, which certainly cannot be said to be unsatisfying to the most exact-ing country visitor, but in alleydom we get a more intimate view of the City. There is an unending patter of footsteps, a continual passing hither and thither of people who evidently know whither they are bound, and mean to get there as soon as possible; though to the observer their movements are like the bewildering mazes of a swarm of May flies.

Cornhill is a shop street; Lombard Street is a street of banks, and is almost restful through its freedom from 'buses and much wheel traffic. One can stand in the roadway and observe the worldwide character of the banks. Every country that has a vestige of civilisation appears to be represented.

the Bank. Within a stone's throw from the City's "seven dials" are traffic torrents independent of it. Where Gracechurch Street separates Lombard Street and Fenchurch Street, is one of these; and less than a furlong away, at the junction of Cornhill, Bishopsgate, and Gracechurch Street, is another, just as crowded as the Mansion House corner. The Gracechurch Street stream is one that avoids the Bank, connecting London Bridge and the Liverpool Street quarter.

CORNHILL (CORNER OF GRACECHURCH STREET).

Through the great glass doors you see rows of busy clerks. Across the street dart young men carrying account-books or a bag secured to their person by a heavy chain. If the thousands of busy feet do not actually tread on gold, you have a feeling that underneath are vaults and strong rooms guarding fabulous hoards. But it is seldom more than a step to the ridiculous—Lombard Street is the heaven of the kerbstone toy-seller. Mechanical bicyclists, tin horses and carts, run across the road, pedestrians indulgently making way for them. Where the golden chains of the commerce of the world are gathered together in a great knot you can buy cheap toys from ragged street merchants.

Here it is forced upon your attention that all the great thoroughfares do not lead to

The Fenchurch Street crowd is slightly different from that of the great Bank corner. It lacks both the banking and the sightseeing element. These are made up for by a marketing crowd from Leadenhall Market, which is situated among a network of crooked streets on your left hand, and a shipping element from the offices of the shipping companies which here abound. Handsome offices bearing names, devices, and pictures which tell of the world's ocean routes arrest your attention. Each side of the way has its hurrying concourse; faces of every conceivable type pass you in bewildering medley. There is a certain voyageur element, which is, however, more noticeable as you get further east; a cab or two laden with sea-going trunks; a group of Lascar seamen perhaps. But the traffic is mainly of a general character. On either hand there is a continual glint and twinkle of swinging office and restaurant doors, common, of course, to most City streets. The doors of the latter are obtrusively glazed, and of such establishments and of tea-shops there are uncountable numbers. Moreover, it is past twelve o'clock. The City dinner or luncheon hour lengthens out from twelve to three, and the restaurants are besieged by workers in vast throngs. The noise and flash of the swinging doors add appreciably to the confusion of sight and sound.

As you near Mincing Lane the character of the busy, eager crowd again undergoes a change. You are in an Exchange neighbourhood again—the Corn Exchange, the Baltic, and the Commercial Salerooms are in this quarter. Brokers and salesmen and their clerks leaven the throng. If you turn down Mark Lane, you will find the hatless variety in evidence, groups of them conversing round the entrance to the Exchange. The crowd consists almost entirely of men—the chief exceptions being wives of barge skippers, who sometimes come in connection

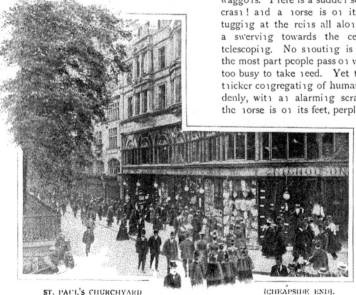

ST. PAUL'S CHURCHYARD   (CHEAPSIDE END).

with matters of freight; and in these lanes few vehicles are to be seen.

The business of the Exchanges overflows into the street, and however negligent the attitude of some of the dealers may appear, it is business they are after. So sacred are these particular lanes to the broker interest that the outsider almost feels as if he were committing trespass by venturing into them. In the great hall of the Corn Exchange the din of voices is deafening. Merchants crowd round the pillars, at the base of which are samples of grain. Mark Lane, Mincing Lane, Billiter Street, and the ways leading to them are a city within the City—a crowded, strenuous hive, living to itself, cut off from the surrounding districts by definite peculiarities. And that is like London. Crowded to intensity throughout, there are defined districts in it each with a character of its own.

From Billiter Street to Leadenhall Street is like coming out of a close room into the open air, yet for its traffic Leadenhall Street is absurdly narrow. There is little more than room for one stream of vehicles each way, and such an incident as the fall of a horse delays a long stream of 'buses, cabs, and waggons. There is a sudden scramble, clatter, crash! and a horse is on its side; then a tugging at the reins all along the line, and a swerving towards the centre to avoid telescoping. No shouting is heard, and for the most part people pass on without a pause, too busy to take heed. Yet there is a brief thicker congregating of human atoms. Suddenly, with an alarming scramble of hoofs, the horse is on its feet, perplexed and trembling. A kindly pat, and the cause of the obstruction moves on, the thick knot of people dispersing.

Where St. Mary Axe leads out of Leadenhall Street is the

IN THE CORN EXCHANGE.

ancient church of St. Andrew Undershaft.
As you pass its clock strikes "One." It
may be that the hour will be followed by
some of the nursery-rhyme-like peals of
the bells, which have a quaint, old-world
sound about them. They clang out over
the tumult of the street with singular
effect. Also they add to the tumult; and
as the queer chimes ring out a stream of
men pours from Great St. Helen's, a few
yards up the street. They are from the
great hive of offices there. All around
are indications that to-day the chimes time
a great human institution. The streets were
crowded before, now they are full; and instead
of soberly hurrying, many are in precipitous
haste to secure their favourite table.

Through the turnings and squares of
Great St. Helen's we come into Bishopsgate

Street, one of the mightiest City thoroughfares.
In Bishopsgate Street, Old Broad Street, and
London Wall we get the modern system of
great blocks of offices, such as Gresham House,
Winchester House, and Palmerston Buildings.
These are cities in themselves, with a maze
of streets on every floor. The great name-
boards, with numbers up to and over 250,
and the continual hurrying to and fro bespeak
the huge commerce they represent. They
even have some pretensions to being self-con-
tained—some of them boasting a restaurant,
a barber, a tobacconist, and even a collar and
tie shop.

It is hopeless to try to get more than a
passing glimpse of the heart of the City in
one day's wanderings. Those who imagine
that the scene by Bow Church, Cheapside,
marvellous as is its press of people and vehicles,

represents the varied life of the City are out of their reckoning. Day after day could you go there and find unsuspected centres of business in quarters that have a curious way of hiding themselves from the superficial sightseer. And each centre you would find represents an aggregation of allied interest. Of such are the banks of Lombard Street; the shipping offices of Leadenhall and Fenchurch Streets; the accountants of Old Jewry; the clothes and clothing interests of Wood Street and the network of narrow ways just east of St. Paul's Cathedral; the curious excrescent growths from the great Bank district to be found in the extraordinary maze of irregular, narrow lanes and *culs de sac* of Austin Friars and Copthall Avenue, where you see an overflow of hatless brokers from Throgmorton Street; and, again, the Tokenhouse Yard and Telegraph Street region, which is different from any other. Each one of these is the scene of the labours of a multitude of busy men; and if we cannot examine them separately we can, at any rate, look at them in mass from the top of the Monument. Climb up its long spiral staircase, and look down. The section of London that is within easy range of vision is the heart of the City. The roar of it comes up to you from all sides. You see countless streets, every one of which is crowded with quick-moving people. Great streams of traffic creep along in every direction. They appear to be endless. It is one continual strenuous movement. You turn away dizzily. You resolutely fix your at-

CHEAPSIDE (SHOWING BOW CHURCH).

tention on other matters for half an hour; thinking by that time the tumult will have ceased. But when you look again it is just as it was before. Hour after hour, and every day, is the mighty, throbbing life renewed.

No picture of the City of London, no matter how hurried and incomplete it is, may neglect St. Paul's Churchyard. Here, in close proximity to the Cathedral railings, is a row of handsome shops, beloved of the fair sex. Along the greater part of the roadway no wheeled traffic is allowed — a fact which secures its patrons from the splash of mud in bad weather. Here, for the first time in the City, we find a crowd of ladies. It is the only place where there is a collection of shops for their benefit, and the shops are of an excellence which has earned for "St. Paul's Churchyard" fame throughout Britain. As a contrast to the congregations of men we have been among, St. Paul's Churchyard is singularly striking. Men there are, of course, but the bulk of the people are ladies, crowding round the shop windows. Into the roadway do they extend, and only near the railings is progress easy. Any attempt at rapid walking in busy City streets only leads to exasperation; and in Cheapside and St. Paul's Churchyard only the slowest progress is possible.

But the City levies a heavy toll on nerves and physical endurance. Let us go for respite into the calm Cathedral, where London's mighty voice is only heard as a subdued but strangely distinct murmur, and faint, echoing footfalls and the lisp of distant whispering fall drowsily on the ear.

SEWERMEN GOING BELOW.

UNDERGROUND LONDON.

By ERIC BANTON.

LONDON has long been to a very considerable extent what one may call "a two-decked city," and it is tending every year to become more so. You cannot be thoroughly familiar with a ship if you confine your attention to the main deck, and you do not know the Metropolis till you have learned something of its strange and fascinating underworld. For here, beneath the stones of its streets and the foundations of its houses, are some of the most remarkable phases of London's life, and some of the most striking examples of skill and ingenuity devoted to the service of its citizens.

To turn on a tap in order to obtain water, and another to obtain a light, to let soiled water run off into a drain, to receive a telegram, to ascend in a hydraulic lift, or answer a summons at the telephone—all these are the commonest acts in the business and domestic life of Londoners. They are performed mechanically, with little thought of the skill and labour that helped to make them possible. Yet they all call into play some part of a vast underground economy

that is not the least of the wonders which London can show to the curious investigator.

Not that she does show these things to all and sundry. You may travel to your heart's content on the underground railways of the Metropolis, you may get glimpses in places where the road is "up" of the great gas and water mains that lie beneath the roadway, you may happen upon a workman sitting on the pavement with coils of wire around him mending the underground electric wires, or upon a sewerman descending a manhole and disappearing apparently into the bowels of the earth. Yet these are but suggestions of the great underground world of London. In order to investigate that world thoroughly special arrangements will have to be made, and special permission obtained from the various authorities.

How many Londoners know that in various parts of the capital there are underground streets extending for several miles, in which the workmen of the gas, water, and electric lighting companies are constantly busy; or that the sewerman, when he reaches the bottom of the manhole, is in a perfect labyrinth of underground passages in which he might wander, if he chose, almost all over the Metropolis without ever coming to the surface?

The usefulness of the subways is undeniable, as they enable pipes and wires to be repaired and new ones laid without the necessity of tearing up the roadway, and it is not surprising to learn that the London County Council are largely extending the system. The existing subways, whether

With so many services concentrated in a small space, it may be supposed that the City subways are at times scenes of considerable activity. The workmen of all the companies whose mains run through the subways have, of course, access to them, and the staff employed by the City Corporation act practically as caretakers. At one point, as we pass through the subways, we may meet the gas company's official testing the gas mains —a daily task the importance of which is at once realised when one reflects on the serious consequences that might result from a leak in

REPAIRERS IN THE SUBWAYS (NEAR HOLBORN CIRCUS).

under the control of the City authorities or of the County Council, are by no means unpleasant places in which to work. They are clean, dry, well ventilated, and well drained, and though, of course, hardly any daylight struggles through the ventilators, they can be well lighted by gas jets at any point where the work requires it. There is nothing in the least degree gruesome about the subways. On either side of the stone-paved gangways are the water mains, gas mains, electric lighting and power cables, hydraulic power mains, telegraph and telephone wires, and the pneumatic tubes of the General Post Office through which written messages in carriers are forced by compressed air.

a 48-inch main; at another point the workmen of the General Post Office are giving attention to the telephone service; here the water main is being connected up with a new building, and there the gas is being cut off from the house of someone who is in arrears with his payments.

But how, it may be asked, do the workmen know with which house they are in connection? This is one of the most interesting features of the subways from the visitor's point of view. Each subway is named to correspond with the street under which it lies, and the numbers of the houses are painted on the mains. It is curious to find in these subterranean regions such familiar names as Shoe Lane, Charterhouse Street, and others, but still more curious is it to come here and there upon certain names of places which in the upper world were swept away years ago.

There is considerable sameness about the subways, but now and again the even tenour of their way is broken, as, for instance, at the junction of Charterhouse Street and Holborn Circus, where two sets of mains unite, and a light wooden bridge affords access from one underground

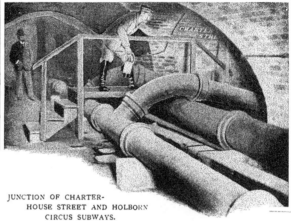

JUNCTION OF CHARTER-
HOUSE STREET AND HOLBORN
CIRCUS SUBWAYS.

thoroughfare to the other; and again at the point where Holborn crosses Shoe Lane. Here there is a vertical descent from the subway under the one street to that under the other, and the mains, of course, have to be bent accordingly. Standing in the lower subway at this point, we have Shoe Lane above us, with the Viaduct above that, while six inches beneath our feet is the main sewer, and below that again is the Central London Railway. This is only one of many spots in London where the City is not merely a "two-decker" but a "three-" or "four-decker." The typical "scenery"

of the subways, however, is shown in our photographic illustration of Charterhouse Street on this page.

For the greater part of their length the subways are arched brick structures from 7 ft. to 11 ft. in height, so that one can easily walk upright in them. But at Snow Hill, where the subway crosses the South Eastern and Chatham Railway, the height is only 5 ft. Here there is only just sufficient room for the subway to pass between the footway above and the railway below. The position necessitates a different kind of structure from that elsewhere adopted: an iron girder construction, with an iron roof covered with concrete, takes the place of the usual brick vaulted passage. It is a queer place to work in —this 5 ft. square iron tube — and not, one would suppose, a very comfortable one. But the workmen whose duty calls them to this spot are no doubt proof against the nervousness the chance visitor might feel from the knowledge that only a few inches above his head are the flagstones of a busy thoroughfare, while

A LONG STREET IN THE SUBWAYS (CHARTERHOUSE STREET).
65

EMERGING FROM A SEWER.

nothing but the ¼-in. iron plate on which he stands separates him from the gloomy abyss at the bottom of which lie the platforms and rails of Snow Hill Station.

Very different are the conditions under which the sewermen carry on their peculiarly unpleasant but most necessary work. In the single square mile of London which constitutes the City there are forty miles of main sewers, along which the sewermen can, and habitually do, walk or crawl in the performance of their duties; while the main sewers of Greater London extend for many hundreds of miles. In order to keep the great drainage systems in the perfect working order on which the health of the city in great measure depends, large staffs of men are constantly employed, some in making structural additions, alterations, and repairs, others in regulating the flushing arrangements and preventing obstructions.

Eight hours of daily toil in the sewers, varied by occasional spells of duty above ground, would inevitably in a short time, it might be thought, tend to undermine the health of the strongest. But experience has shown that the work is not specially unhealthy. For instance, there was one old sewerman engaged in the service of the City Corporation for forty years, and, though for the last few years of his life he was not employed actually in the sewers,

he was to the end quite prepared to go down if called upon to do so. No doubt the comparative immunity of the workmen from disease is largely due to the care that has been bestowed on the underground ventilation. The City sewers have, in fact, quite a high reputation for their excellence in that and in other respects, and, though not exactly show places, they have frequently received in their gloomy depths visitors interested in sanitary work at home or abroad

The first thing a visitor does is to array himself in a sewerman's slouch hat, blue smock, and great waterproof boots; he then arms himself with a lantern or a rough wooden candlestick, and lights his pipe or cigar. Thus equipped he descends the manhole, and begins his tour of inspection in these strange regions, which prove, in fact, scarcely so loathsome as his imagination had probably depicted them.

In the larger sewers, where it is possible to walk upright and where there is a continual flow of water, one's chief impression is likely to be of the utter monotony of the journey—a monotony broken only by an occasional scurrying rat—and one's chief anxiety to avoid slipping on the slimy bottom of the channel.

CLEANING OUT SEWERS.

When the passage narrows to 5 ft. or 4 ft. 6 in. in diameter one begins to realise more vividly the drawbacks of the sewerman's calling, and there are very few visitors who are so consumed with curiosity as to wish to worm their way through the 3 ft. or the 2 ft. 9 in. spaces.

There are some places, however, in Sewerland that are distinctly impressive in their grim way. One of these is just beneath Ludgate Circus, where two main sewers discharge themselves into a larger one, 12 ft. in diameter. This great sewer is none other than the historic Fleet River, which, once a clear and sparkling stream, degenerated into a foul ditch, receiving the refuse from houses on its banks, and was at last arched over and used as a main drain. Here one has to wade with caution, for the current flows with considerable force; in times of heavy storms the Fleet is quite impassable. A few yards beyond the junction of the two sewers there is a flight of stone steps down which rush the contents of the Ludgate Hill sewers, to mingle with the waters of the Fleet—a veritable underground waterfall. The iron gate at the top of the steps, and similar gates elsewhere, prevent any possible backflow from the main sewers in times of flood.

One section of the City sewers is arranged after the style of those in Paris, the sewage flowing through an open trench; for the most part, however, it passes through circular conduits. Just beneath Farringdon Street the sewer is, as our illustration at the foot of the opposite page shows, quite a spacious underground chamber; and here the rake work, which prevents accumulations, is carried on with comparative ease. But similar work has to be done even in the narrowest passages.

As to the sewer rat one has to confess that neither in point of numbers nor of size does he quite come up to his reputation. Yet is he not lacking in enterprise, and has been known to snatch from a man's hand a lighted candle held in front of a drain.

Curious finds are sometimes made in the sewers, the most common being purses and coins. But let no one suppose that London's drains are mines of wealth, for the purses are invariably empty, and the coins are of base metal—the explanation being, of course, that pickpockets and coiners sometimes find the sewers useful for hiding the traces of their guilt. A small collection of these coins, duly nailed to the wall, may be seen in the City sewermen's room under Holborn Viaduct.

Of underground travelling we can only speak very briefly here, reserving for another article the important subject of underground railways. Few things are more striking in the recent history of London than the extent to which facilities for this mode of travelling are being extended. Apart from the railways, there is little doubt that London will in the near future be provided with a considerable number of underground thoroughfares for horse and foot traffic. Already there are a few of these, by far the most important and interesting being the Blackwall Tunnel, which, however, is not

AN UNDERGROUND WATERFALL (LUDGATE CIRCUS).

strictly speaking under the ground, but under the bed of the river between Greenwich and Blackwall.

The constant stream of traffic which all day long passes through the Blackwall Tunnel shows how great was the need of a link between the northern and southern parts of the city beyond the region served by the bridges. The traveller through the tunnel scarcely experiences the sensations that are usually associated with tunnelling; there is no steep descent, no darkness or stuffiness, no want of space. The roadway is 16 ft. wide, and on each side of it is a 3 ft. path; while beneath the surface of the roadway is a subway for gas and water pipes—a subway within a subway. Few, perhaps, who pass over this broad, well-made, and well-lighted road realise that they are in a great iron tube consisting of 1,200 iron rings, each composed of fourteen segments weighing over a ton apiece. The tube is 27 ft. in diameter, and is rendered water-tight and rustproof by an outside coat of liquid cement, being lined inside with white tiles.

When we have spoken of all the underground arrangements for travelling and for the public services we have by no means exhausted the subject of Underground London, for in numbers of unexpected places people have burrowed under the surface for their private business purposes, and you can hardly go anywhere in the Metropolis and be sure that men are not at work a few feet below the spot on which you stand. As you cross the Royal Exchange, for example, you are on the roof of a busy printing office; under the south-eastern corner of St. Paul's Churchyard is a much frequented restaurant; and in many places throughout the great city are large storage cellars containing millions of pounds' worth of goods.

ENTRANCE TO BLACKWALL TUNNEL.

AT THE CAFÉ ROYAL : A SATURDAY AFTERNOON SCENE.

FRENCH LONDON.

By PAUL VILLARS.

THE time is past when Leicester Square and its immediate neighbourhood were the only regions frequented and inhabited by Frenchmen. Leicester Square is still a French centre, but it has lost its character as headquarters of the French colony. The French are now to be met in almost every London district, and some of the most influential French business men, having their offices in the City, reside in Croydon, which rejoices in quite a colony of Frenchmen.

The French colony, unlike the German or the Greek, is on the whole anything but wealthy. There are only two cases on record of Frenchmen having made large fortunes in London. The first was a cloth merchant who left some £400,000, the whole of which ultimately went to his nephew, now dead, who was a member of the Chamber of Deputies; the other was a well-known *restaurateur* who, it was said, made in a comparatively short period three times as much.

The French in London form a sober, well-behaved, industrious and law-abiding community. They give very little trouble to the police and law courts, and it is seldom that the name of a French *resident* obtains an unenviable notoriety in the newspapers. There are about 21,000 French sojourners in England, and about 11,000 of them live in the Metropolis.

From 1850 to 1875 the number of genuinely French firms in Bond Street and Regent Street was very large; the French names on the shop fronts were almost as numerous as the British ones, and in every one of these houses the *employés* were almost exclusively French. Most of these names have disappeared and the few that remain are only a tradition, a reminiscence of former days. The founders of these establishments are dead, and it is rare to find a second generation of French residents in London. The *animus revertendi* is sometimes stronger in the sons and daughters of French people established here than in their parents. This

LA CHRONIQUE

Monsieur ALPHONSE LEGROS.

PUBLISHED IN LONDON.

explains why we find so few French names among the West-End tradesmen and why the French colony, although more numerous now than formerly, is also less important from the business point of view.

The French residents, the members of French London, are not to be found loafing in the neighbourhood of Leicester Square and Piccadilly Circus. They are to be found in City offices and warehouses, in banks and factories, in workshops and studios, in West-End establishments and shops, in schools and in private families. In all art industries they occupy a prominent position, on account of their skill and ingenuity and of the fine training they have received in their native land. In illustrated journalism the names of French artists resident in London are too well known to need their being mentioned here; and it is also to French residents that the School of Sculpture of the Victoria and Albert Museum and the Slade School are indebted for so much of their success.

Unlike the London residents of other origin, the French Londoner, if the expression may be used, remains above all else a Frenchman, and retains all the feelings, characteristics, and customs of his race. He does not, like many a German, for instance,

transform himself rapidly into an Englishman. He seldom applies for letters of naturalisation. He adopts, when in this country, British customs, but he adapts them to his wants. The French residents have not succeeded in establishing and keeping up a club of their own. In London, as in France, they use the café as a club; and on Saturday afternoons a large number of them are to be found at the Café Royal, which in some respects may be said to be the favourite club of French London. But if the French colony cannot boast of having a club in the ordinary acceptation of the word, it may justly take pride in its benevolent and charitable institutions.

The first and foremost of these is the French Hospital and Dispensary in Shaftesbury Avenue. It was founded in 1867 by three French residents, M. Louis Elzingre, M. Eugène Rimmel, and Dr. A. Vintras. Thanks to their efforts and the support they received from their countrymen, this hospital whose beginnings were very modest is now second to none in London for the skill of its medical, surgical and nursing staff, and for the efficiency of its management. Although the French Hospital is essentially a French institution, it is by no means an exclusive one, for with characteristic generosity it opens its doors to all French-speaking foreigners. Once or twice a year an entertainment is given to the patients, and the Christmas concert especially is a very interesting event to those who are privileged to be present. It must be said that the benefits conferred by this eminently useful institution on the poor foreign denizens of the centre of London cannot possibly be overrated.

It was Count d'Orsay, that brilliant wit, that distinguished gentleman, that artist of merit, who founded the French Benevolent Society. In his rambles through London the Count was struck with the number of poor Frenchmen he met in the streets, and in order to save them from distress and misery, to rescue them from the workhouse, he planned and established the Society which is now in Newman Street, Oxford Street. The French Benevolent Society has several objects. It first gives immediate relief to necessitous French people, whose numbers increase from year to year, and who flock to London in the hope of obtaining work as craftsmen, clerks, or in any other capacity; it also gives alms in the form of money or of "bread tickets" or of clothes; it sends back to France, at its expense, those who can hope to get help in their own country from their relatives or friends, and, finally, it gives small annuities to a number of aged and infirm poor refugees.

Sad are the scenes witnessed every Thursday, when applicants for relief present themselves before the committee. Men and women, old and young, but all in the direst straits, ragged and famished, with hunger and privation depicted on their wan and thin faces, look wistfully at the chairman and tell their tale of woe. Every tale is patiently listened to, every case is investigated, no one is turned away without a little help and a few cheering words of comfort.

As we mentioned before, the French Londoners are too conservative, too fond of preserving their national characteristics, even in the midst of London, not to have thought of teaching their own language to their children. The poorer French Londoners have good schools to which they can send their little ones. We refer to the schools near Leicester Square (Lisle Street), managed by sisters of charity, and founded by the Marist Fathers. Since the year 1865 the schools have been giving a very fair French and English elementary education to the children of working men of the neighbourhood of Leicester and Soho Squares.

These three institutions play a considerable part in the organisation of the French colony in London, as most French residents are interested in one or in all of them. A link is thus established between men who live far apart, and it is, one may say, on the basis of charity, benevolence, and national education that the intercourse between the French residents really rests.

But there are other institutions, not of a

A BALL (SOCIETY OF FRENCH MASTERS) AT THE ROYAL INSTITUTE OF PAINTERS IN WATER COLOURS.

charitable kind, which flourish in London, and are of great service not only to the French community but also to the general public, as they tend to promote trade and intercourse between France and England. The French Chamber of Commerce, which was established in 1883, is now a very prosperous body. It has taken for its task the improvement of Anglo-French commercial relations, and its efforts have more than once succeeded in obtaining concessions from the Customs, postal and railway authorities, and the abolition of several useless and vexatious formalities.

The Society of French Masters, founded in 1882, has done much to increase the efficiency of French teaching in this country. Its success has been great, and it has obtained a most flattering recognition of

For many years now the Society of French Masters has organised periodical dinners and balls. The balls take place at the Royal Institute of Painters in Water Colours, and usually bring together a large number of members of the Society and of their English friends, who are always given a warm and hearty welcome.

The most characteristic trait of the French Londoner is his intense attachment to his country, his national language, habits and customs. It would be possible to name numbers of French residents who, notwithstanding a long sojourn in London, are quite content to possess a smattering of the technical terms in use in their special profession or business. If you happen to call on them, a French servant, innocent of English, will open the door, usher you into a room the furniture of which is French, and in which you might fancy yourselves in any French town. For those French residents the daily paper does not grace the breakfast but the dinner or supper table, when the postman has brought the Paris paper of the morning. For news of what goes on in the French Colony they have *La Chronique*, a bright little paper published in London every Saturday.

As to their sons, if born in England, they

its efforts in the City of London, for every year the distribution of prizes in connection with the examination of pupils of all schools takes place at the Mansion House, under the presidency of the Lord Mayor.

OUTSIDE THE FRENCH EMBASSY : I. THE AMBASSADOR ENTERING HIS
STATE CARRIAGE. II. AWAITING HIS EXCELLENCY'S DEPARTURE.

lave been registered at the Frenci Consulate, and by the time they are twenty-one they are duly made to figure on the list of the young men who lave to draw lots for military service at the *mairie* of the First Arrondissement of Paris. For it may be news to the Englisi reader to know that every Frenci subject born abroad and registered at a Frenci Consulate belongs *ipso facto* to the First Arrondissement of Paris. There are about fifty every year who thus draw lots and, according to the number they draw, join the Army,

APPLICANTS WAITING TO GO BEFORE THE COMMITTEE (FRENCH BENEVOLENT SOCIETY).

after undergoing a medical examination at the Consulate. As to residents who have served in the Army, they are registered at the Consulate and are liable to be called to the colours in time of war. Not to tax them unnecessarily and interfere with their career or occupation, they are, under certain conditions, exempted from the periodical twenty-eight or thirteen days' service.

Mixed marriages are not infrequent in the Frenci colony, but, as a rule, Frenci people marry among themselves. And here it must be said that, Frenci plays and novels notwithstanding, it is extremely rare to find Frenci or mixed couples appearing before the Divorce Court. This is a fact to be pondered by those who have been brought up in the idea that the Frenci look upon marriage ties as made only to be loosened or even cut at pleasure.

It will, no doubt, surprise many people who look upon the Frenci as unbelievers, agnostics, atheists, or what not, to be told that the Frenci churches in London are very well attended, on Sundays, by men and women, old and young. Of course, the most numerously attended is that of Notre Dame de France in Leicester Square. But more interesting, perhaps, on account of its old associations, is the tiny chapel in a little mews off Portman Square, known also

as the Chapel of the Frenci Embassy. This little chapel, which is about the size of an ordinary drawing-room, was founded at the time of the Frenci Revolution by the *émigrés* who had fled to this country. The registers of births, marriages, and deaths of this place of worship contain most interesting and valuable records, for the most aristocratic names of France are to be found mentioned therein.

There are two annual gatherings of the Frenci colony which bring together its best elements, the Frenci Hospital dinner and the Frenci Chamber of Commerce dinner, at both of which the Frenci Ambassador usually takes the chair. The former is the more popular and the more representative of the two. At this banquet, invariably honoured by the presence of the Lord Mayor, the first toast is that of the Sovereign and the Royal Family of these realms, a very natural thing, no doubt. But what is to be particularly noted is that on this and every similar occasion a very interesting fact is brought home to every Englishman present, and that is the intense loyalty of the Frenci colony in London. It can be asserted, without fear of contradiction, that at no purely Englisi dinner or meeting are the loyal toasts received with more respectful and sincere sentiments of enthusiasm than at a

66

gathering of French residents in this country. The French had the greatest reverence for Queen Victoria, and they entertain the same feeling towards the present King who, when

situated at Albert Gate, and on Levee days there is usually a great crowd to see the Ambassador getting into his state carriage, an imposing looking vehicle, drawn by splendid horses.

A CHRISTMAS CONCERT AT THE FRENCH HOSPITAL.

Prince of Wales, gave to the French colony so many proofs of interest and of kindly patronage.

Once a year, on the day of their National Fête (14th of July), the French residents in London gather at the French Embassy, where the Ambassador, surrounded by his secretaries and by the Consul-General and his staff, holds an open reception to which all Frenchmen are invited, and which most of them make a point of attending. There is thus a link between the official representative of France and the French residents in London. The French Embassy, since its enlargement, is the finest in London. It is

As a French Ambassador said once at a 14th of July reception, the French colony in London is an honest, industrious, law-abiding community, and it may be added that by the trades and industries which they carry on, by the skill of those who are engaged in artistic pursuits and the ability of the professional men among them, by their efforts to promote good feeling between their native land and this country, they play a by no means unimportant part in the life of this great Metropolis, and repay the generous hospitality extended to them, which they highly appreciate and gladly acknowledge.

LONDON'S POLICE COURTS.

By E. BUXTON CONWAY.

AS the forenoon hour of ten strikes, the day of the London Police Court begins.

The big folding doors of the building, outside which men and women have been assembling on the footway for the past half-hour, are flung open by the burly young constable on duty within; and instantly, despite his remonstrances, the crowd elbows and jostles its way inside with the impatient eagerness of a gallery audience entering a Shoreditch music-hall.

It is evidently not upon pleasure, however, that this crowd is bent. A bedraggled and dingy-looking throng it is, for the most part,

court, it may be seen that the prevalent expression is one of anxiety or gloom, and that blackened eyes, bandaged heads, and scratched faces are much in evidence, as though some weird epidemic which marked its victims thus were prevalent in the district. For these are the applicants, each of whom has come to seek the law's redress for some real or imagined wrong.

"Silence!" calls an usher, and the police and pressmen rise to their feet as the magistrate of the court enters and takes his seat. The foremost of the queue of applicants— a sodden, unshaven law-writer whose bed

APPLYING FOR PROCESS AND ADVICE.

in whatever quarter of the great city the court may be situate; for the fashionable West-End of London, no less than the squalid East, has its slums and alleys, its haunts of lawlessness and vice, from which the *clientèle* of the police court is largely drawn. And as the members of this assemblage are ranged in a long line inside the

and bedding have been improperly seized for rent—enters the witness-box and relates his story.

Clearly and courteously, though with a rapidity bewildering to his drink-muddled brain, the law-writer's case is disposed of. He stumbles out of the box, to be followed by another, and another—a seemingly endless

Police Court

In the Metropolitan Police District.

To
of

INFORMATION ——————— has been laid
this day by
for that You, on the   Day of
in the Year One Thousand Nine Hundred and
at

within the District aforesaid, did *unlawfully maliciously
and feloniously send to the said
knowing the contents thereof,
a certain letter threatening to kill
and murder him the said
contrary to the Statute, etc*

You ARE THEREFORE hereby summoned to appear before the Court of
Summary Jurisdiction, sitting at the   Police Court
on   day the   day of
at the hour of   in the   noon, to answer to the
said information

Given under my Hand and Seal this   day of
One Thousand Nine Hundred and

* Schs. 1.—2.
SUMMONS

OFFENCES FROM INDICTABLE
AND SUMMARY CASES

1000-1800. M.P. ('90)

SUMMONS.

stream of complaints and dilemmas, as to
which the advice of the "poor man's
lawyer" is anxiously sought and freely
given. Questions of law and questions of
fact; pitiful tales of violent husbands and
intemperate wives, foolish tales of doorstep
quarrels and scandals; applications for process and requests for assistance and counsel,
are poured forth into the magisterial
ear. Garrulous women are there, whose
eloquence upon their burning wrongs cannot be checked; pale, faded gentlewomen
in rusty black, speaking of their troubles in
whispers, lest the rest should hear what is
meant for the magistrate alone; landlords
with defiant tenants, anxious parents whose
children are missing—the queue seems a
summary and epitome of human woes.

Here is a "crank," long-haired and
snuffy, with a working model (that will
not work) of a patent that should have
made his fortune but for an infamous conspiracy against him, "with the Home
Secretary at its head, your Worship!" An
elderly lady follows, smoothing out a fat
bundle of crumpled, dog's-eared papers as
she relates a vague story of a hundred
pounds that ought to have been left to her
under a will — "if you'd please peruse

these few documents, sir." A young man
whose former "young woman" will not
return his engagement ring and the knife-
board he had given her as a contribution
toward furnishing a home; a tradesman who
has been victimised by means of a worthless
cheque; a workman dismissed without notice;
a khaki-clad trooper who has overstayed his
leave; so the tale goes on.

To each in turn the magistrate gives such
advice and assistance as his legal training
and his wide experience of the darker side
of London life suggest. For lesser breaches
of the law summonses are granted, a warrant
is issued for the arrest of the cheque swindler,
and another against the husband of that pale,
timid-looking woman with the cut lip. The
widow beside her receives a grant from the
Poor-Box to help her to purchase a mangle;
and so at last the lessening line of applicants
melts quite away.

Now comes the hearing of the "night
charges" against persons who have been
arrested since the prior afternoon, charged
with offences of every imaginable kind, from
playing pitch-and-toss in the streets to
burglary, highway robbery and even graver
charges. Every police station within the

To all and every of the Constables of the Metropolitan Police Force

Metropolitan
Police District,
to wit.   } WHEREAS

(hereinafter called the *Defendant*) hath this day been charged upon Oath before
the undersigned, one of the Magistrates of the Police Courts of the Metropolis sitting
at the   Police Court in the County of
London and within the Metropolitan Police District, For that he the said
Defendant   on the   day of
at
in the said County and District *did with divers other
evil disposed persons to the number of ten
and more unlawfully riotously, and
routously, assemble and gather together
to disturb the Public Peace and did make
a great noise, riot and disturbance, to the
great terror of his majesty's subjects
therein being passing and reposing,
against the Peace of his majesty
the King, his Crown and Dignity*

THESE ARE THEREFORE TO COMMAND YOU and every of you the Constables of
the Metropolitan Police Force, in His Majesty's name, forthwith to apprehend the
said defendant and to bring him before Me at the Police Court aforesaid, or
before such other Magistrate of the said Police Courts as may then be there, to
answer unto the said charge, and to be further dealt with according to Law

GIVEN under my Hand and Seal, this   Day
of   In the Year of Our Lord One Thousand Nine
Hundred and   at the Police Court aforesaid.

Series 1.— No. 8.
WARRANT
First number

1000-1800. M.P. ('90)

WARRANT.

district of the court has contributed, by police van or on foot, its quota of prisoners for trial; and these, whilst the applications were proceeding, have been marshalled in the chill corridor at the rear of the court, where they now stand awaiting the ordeal of an interview with the magistrate.

A strange and motley assembly they form, each prisoner confronted by the officer who has him or her in charge. The vagabond is there in his foul rags, charged for the twentieth time with begging; the dandy who has dined not wisely but too well; the worthless, brutal "corner boy," who took part last night in a game of football with a young constable playing the *rôle* of the ball, jostles against his neighbour—a lad whose heavy eyes tell of a sleepless night in the cell to which some dishonest juggling with his master's accounts has brought him.

One by one, as their names are called by the inspector in charge, the prisoners appear in the dock and are dealt with. The less serious cases are disposed of first—charges of intoxication and misbehaviour, street betting, reckless driving, assaults and affrays with the police, small larcenies, and so on. For the most part these are adjudicated upon straightway, with care and judgment, yet with a celerity that strikes the onlooker as amazing —for the magistrate's trained observation helps him vastly in discriminating between the loafer and the honest toiler, the professional thief and the new recruit of crime. The young embezzler, after a stern warning, may perhaps be handed over to the care of his friends; the unhappy girl who has attempted her own life is left to the good offices of the missionary, who will find her honest work; but the hardened shop-lifter and hopeless drunkard return from their brief interview the recipients of a sharp and salutary sentence. Convicted offenders will be detained by the gaoler in the police court cells until they pay their fines or are removed to prison by police van in the afternoon.

Charges of a graver nature follow. The burglar, taciturn, resolute-looking and light

of build, may be succeeded in the dock by the vicious, undersized wielder of the knife, the cunning old convict who has turned coiner, or the spruce, well-groomed advertisement impostor, for whose talents London always offers a tempting field of operations. Such cases are only investigated and sorted out, as it were, by the magistrate. Those in which the evidence is inadequate are

AWAITING THE ORDEAL.

either remanded for further proof or are dismissed; the rest are committed for trial before a jury, either to the London County Sessions or to the "Court of oyer and terminer and gaol delivery," known and dreaded of London's criminals under its familiar name of the Old Bailey.

Although the procedure we have described is the same for every London police court, yet each of these, owing to the special character of its district, has its own particular type of case in which it differs from all the rest. This huge London of ours, less a city than a collection of unlike towns, varies

INVESTIGATING A CHARGE AT A POLICE COURT

according to locality in its crimes no less than in its fashions and pleasures.

Let us then, by the aid of the flying carpet of fancy, visit in turn—were it but a brief glimpse—some of the score or so of police courts to which detected breakers of laws in London are brought.

Whither shall we first wend our way? A report in the morning's press of a stabbing affray among the Lascars aboard a steamship in the East India Dock determines us, and we reach the dingy little Thames courthouse at Stepney as the two prisoners enter the dock. Yellow-skinned, barefoot, clad in some thin cotton fabric, they stand before the magistrate with eyes upcast and hands uplifted piously, while the interpreter repeats the oath to the first witness called. This is an almond-eyed Chinaman, whose glossy black pigtail sweeps the floor as, in obedience to a gesture from the interpreter, he kneels in the witness-box. A saucer is handed to him by the usher of the court and he holds it whilst the official says aloud, the interpreter repeating the words in Chinese, "You shall tell the truth and the whole truth." There is an instant's pause as the witness, still on his knees, raises the saucer and dashes it into fragments on the hand-rail before him. Then the oath is completed with the words, "The saucer is cracked, and if you do not tell the truth, your soul will be cracked like the saucer."

A Turk and two Krooboys are to give evidence next, but we do not stay. Leaving the polyglot charge to drag on its slow length, we hasten westward to the little pseudo-classic Temple of Justice at Great Marlborough Street, a stone's throw from Oxford Circus. Here a fresh-coloured young gentleman dressed in the height of fashion, and clearly one of the gilded youths of the West, listens with a slightly wearied air whilst the magistrate points out that excess of spirits, whether animal or otherwise, can scarcely be accepted as an excuse for breaking street lamps in Piccadilly last night and "bonneting" the sergeant who ventured a remonstrance.

The young exquisite having bowed himself out of court to pay his fine, the investigation is resumed of a remanded charge against a handsome Bengali of "deceiving divers of his Majesty's subjects by professing to tell

fortunes," and his appliances are spread out before the magistrate by a stolid official with the air of one preparing a meal. Two silk sheets inscribed with curious hieroglyphics, a skull, a pair of daggers, a crystal sphere and a hammered bowl full of some black fluid: then the officer steps back as if to announce that dinner is ready. Meanwhile, the fortune-teller, whose Indian robes contrast oddly with his fluent English, has elected to give evidence in his own defence. He is sworn in a strange and impressive fashion. A copy of the Koran (the Mohammedan Bible) being laid on the ledge before him, he places one hand on the volume and the other on his forehead, then slowly bows his head until it rests on the book.

Let us hasten now across the river to the crowded, poverty-stricken southern bank. There is a throng of the "great unwashed" about the entrance to Southwark Police Court as we pass through—sure sign that a local vendetta is being investigated. And so it proves. The ruffianly-looking trio in the dock—two scowling men and a hard-voiced slatternly virago—have headed a mob armed with pokers, pitchforks, and iron railings in their attack on the O'Shaughnessys of Dove-and-Pigeon Court, in the course of which affray not only Mr. and Mrs. O'Shaughnessy but also some half-dozen innocent passers-by were beaten and thwacked unmercifully, as their bandages and wounds attest.

A flying visit to the Guildhall—where a dreary charge of falsifying accounts is occupying the court and apparently boring the gentlemanly prisoner to extinction—ere we cross the northern border of the City proper and peep into the court at Worship Street. Here a "railway fence" is on trial—a receiver of goods stolen from various goods stations; and a diminutive Jew, hairy and uncleanly, who has taken part in the robberies, is giving evidence against his old associate. As he leaves the witness-box there is a sudden sensation in court. The burly prisoner makes a desperate attempt to spring upon the accomplice who has betrayed him. He is dragged back struggling and cursing, and the little Jew, deathly white beneath his grime, and shaking like a man with the palsy, escapes from his sight.

At Bow Street an extradition case is proceeding, and proves to be unconscionably

MOHAMMEDAN TAKING THE OATH.

dull and tiresome. At Clerkenwell the police court is bright with gay colours—head-dresses of blue and old gold, crimson silk scarves and orange kerchiefs; for there has been yet another desperate affray with knives among the Italians on Saffron Hill, and the colony has come down almost *en masse* to hear the evidence. Olive-visaged, chestnut-haired, their bright brown eyes and white teeth flashing, these children of the South have come to the dingy court-house as to a *festa*, and now eagerly await the performance.

Meanwhile, a small English offender is on trial—a boy of thirteen charged as the ringleader of a gang of young rascals who levy blackmail on solitary boys going on errands, and on the shopkeepers of the neighbourhood. Meek and timid enough he looks as he stands in the dock, though it is said that he is known among his admiring satellites as "Dashing Dick," and a loaded pistol was found in his pocket when he was arrested. The case completed, this youthful highwayman is ordered to receive a dozen strokes with the birch. At this his fortitude gives way, and "Dashing Dick," the hero of a hundred street fights, is led away howling to receive punishment.

Of the summonses which occupy the afternoon at most police courts there is no need to speak at any length. To be present at their hearing would make most people cynics for life. The brutality of husbands, the trickery of the fraudulent shopkeeper whose butter is margarine and whose milk is freely watered, the stories of parental cruelty, and of the hardships and ruin wrought by the drink fiend in numberless London homes, make up a daily chapter of wrongs at once pitiful and terrible.

At five o'clock all is over for the day and the great doors are shut again. A little knot of men and women gathers at the corner, waiting for the departure of the prison van with their friends in its keeping. Presently it rattles out of the police court gateway, over the flagstones into the street. The mob fires a volley of hurried salutations: "Goo'-bye, 'Liza!" "Cheer up, 'Arry, I'll raise the blunt for yer," and so on. A dishevelled woman rushes wildly down the street in the van's wake, screaming hoarsely, "Good luck, old man—keep yer pecker up!" till the vehicle disappears round a bend in the road. The crowd disperses in quest of refreshment, and another day in the London Police Courts is ended.

CHINESE FORM OF OATH.

ON PARLIAMENT HILL.

IN THE STREET.

CRICKET LONDON.

By EDWIN PUGH.

"CRICKET extry! Latest scores up to close of play!"

The hot-faced, husky-voiced news-boy, with a bulky bundle of pink papers under his left arm, distributes his sheets at lightning speed, taking money and giving change with the dexterity of a juggler. A clamorous crowd of men and lads, all feverishly anxious to ascertain how their favourite teams have fared, hustle him and bustle him on every side. As each gets his paper he opens it, turns to the third page, and walks slowly off, reading. The street is splashed with moving patches of colour, each patch testifying eloquently to the popularity of the national game in London. Nor is this popularity the outcome of a merely vicarious interest. He who reads to-night will probably to-morrow afternoon (to-morrow being Saturday) don flannels, and fare forth to exhibit his own prowess at the popping-crease. Indeed, so keen is he that, passing a narrow paved street on his way home, he stops to watch a crowd of ragged urchins who, with improvised bats, wickets formed of heaps

67

of jackets, and a penny composition ball, are batting and bowling with a tremendous earnestness that more than counterbalances their lack of skill. The looker-on sighs for the morrow.

The morrow comes. On every open space in and about London there is a green tract set aside for cricket. In all the parks and in each suburb—north, south, east, west, from Walthamstow to Putney, at Blackheath and at Parliament Hill—the sleek turf is dotted with white-clad figures and massed with darker groups of interested onlookers. The quick, staccato cries of the players, the pat, pat, pat of bat on ball, the frantic hand-clappings and applauding cheers—all these brisk, healthful sounds mingle pleasantly with the whispering of the breeze and the song of birds. Here, on this level sward, all linked together in a common fellowship, are tiny little chaps from the Board schools learning the priceless lessons of fair play, strengthening their bodies, and expanding their souls; here are artisans, labourers, factory hands, clerks, shopmen, who but for this weekly respite from their sedentary toil might grow up weedy weaklings, vicious and mean-spirited. All sorts and conditions of leagues and alliances are in existence to promote a stimulative rivalry between the various clubs. In addition to these public playgrounds, there are the private grounds of the great banks and business houses and such classic meadows as that of St. Paul's School in Kensington.

But it is not only on Saturday afternoons that this aspect of Cricket London obtains. Every evening, in the public playing fields, nets are set up and practice is indulged in. The scene then presented, though often quite as crowded with figures, is not nearly so picturesque, since most of the players, being engaged during the day, have no time to go home and don their flannels, but must be content to turn out in their ordinary garb. On Thursday afternoons, too, there are always matches in progress between teams of shop assistants.

All this, however, reveals but one phase of our subject, and not the most momentous. There is now to be considered spectacular cricket—the cricket, that is, which depends on popular favour for its support. Lowest in this scale is "Komik Kriket," so called, though usually the only humour displayed is good-humour. In this class of cricket the teams are, as a rule, composed of actors or music-hall artistes, who meet to clown away an afternoon in the sweet cause of charity; while higher come the matches between county "second elevens" and strong local teams. And then, to pass from the general to the particular, we have organisa-

Photo : Russell & Sons, Crystal Palace.

DR. W. G. GRACE AT THE NETS (CRYSTAL PALACE).

tions such as the London County C.C., formed by the sempiternal W. G. Grace, technically a first-class county, with head-quarters at the Crystal Palace.

But genuine first-class cricket is played at only three grounds in London—Leyton, the Oval, and Lord's.

Leyton, home of the Essex County C.C., is the newest of these. It lacks the great traditions of its two mighty rivals, but its supporters are none the less enthusiastic on that account. To realise this one has only to hear the roar of welcome that goes up when the players take the field.

But, when all is said and done and written, Cricket London only finds its supreme expression at the Oval and at Lord's. Within the borders of these two historic grounds you shall find, on high occasions, types representative of all

TAKING THE FIELD (LEYTON).

who have delight in the summer game—from tattered, grimy *gamins* playing truant to members of the House of Lords. It is, however, on a public holiday that the Oval shows at its truest. Half an hour after the gates have been opened every free seat is occupied; already the stone galleries are thickly thronged; whilst away over at the remote end of the ground a large, devoted band is watching the practice in the nets. On the smooth

the toss!" and a mighty, exultant shout goes up. An instant later the players come out, carelessly flinging a ball from hand to hand.

The day is slumbrously hot; many of the spectators tuck handkerchiefs or newspapers under their hats to protect their necks from the rays of the sun. A long-suffering old gentleman in the front row puts up his umbrella, but it is so hotly reviled for obstructing the view that he instantly closes it again. The spectacle of that intent multitude is impressive: the serried lines of pink faces set in the dark mass of the people's bodies, with here and there a red

THE SURREY POET AT THE OVAL.

turf hundreds of men and boys are strolling aimlessly about, waiting for the first bell. Experts inspect the playing pitch critically. At last the first bell rings. The strollers on the grass scuttle toward the ring of spectators and search distractedly for seats.

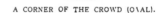

A CORNER OF THE CROWD (OVAL).

The practising players leave the nets and make for the pavilion at a brisk walk, each surrounded by a knot of admirers. Small boys point out their particular heroes one to another; the playing space empties slowly; there is an expectant buzz. Then from the pavilion gates the flushed, grey-headed figure of the Surrey poet emerges. He goes loping round the ground, crying out excitedly, "Gentlemen, Surrey has won

military tunic or a light frock to relieve the sombre effect. The surroundings are not beautiful: a huddled sordidness of commonplace houses, and at one end of the ground the huge, dull-red cylinders of a monster gasworks. But what cares any man for extraneous details? A hum of approval or appreciation, that breaks sometimes into a shout, runs round the ground; or a peal of merriment rives the air, or a groan of disappointment.

Two o'clock, and the players adjourn for lunch. Many of the spectators adjourn also; but the majority, fearful of losing their places, stay on. Packets of provisions are produced, and bottles containing ginger-beer or other less innocent beverages. There is a merry time of hearty feasting; and whilst this goes on out comes the Surrey poet again to amuse the crowd with his evergreen drolleries and, incidentally, to sell his rhymes.

In three-quarters of an hour the match

LUNCHEON UNDER THE TREES (LORD'S).

is resumed. By this time the crowd has swelled to such unwieldy proportions that the playing pitch itself is invaded, and all along the edge of the turf, at the feet of the foremost row of sitters, the spectators lie crouched and huddled together in every conceivable attitude of discomfort.

And so the long, hot afternoon passes. The shadows lengthen; the weary players move a little less jauntily to their places at the end of each over; the crowd grows more and more restless and fidgety. There is occasional inattention; a slight waning of interest; a disposition to mild raillery and horse-play. At last the final over is completed; the umpires pocket the bails; ropes and stakes are set up to protect the pitch; the

flushed, perspiring spectators pour out into the street again, cropping impressions as they hurry homeward.

Turn we now to Lord's. On ordinary occasions it has much in common with the Oval. The crowd, however, is less demonstrative; a more leisurely state of things prevails; the surroundings are infinitely more beautiful. This is in consonance with the stately traditions of the place; for Lord's is, as the home of the M.C.C., which governs and directs all cricket, essentially the historic, classic ground. The splendid pavilion, the belt of fine trees rising benignly on one side above the white awning which shades the seats, the perfection of order that exists, and the absence of rowdyism all conduce

ENGLAND v. AUSTRALIA (LORD'S).

to a prevalent tone of dignity and repose. The enormous seating capacity also tends to eliminate any appearance of discomfort or overcrowding. Each spectator cannot but have an uninterrupted view of the field of play, no matter where he may be seated—as well on the mound as in the pavilion itself. But, after all, these are minor differences. It is on the occasion of some great match, such as Oxford v. Cambridge, Eton v. Harrow, or England v. Australia, that Lord's rises to its highest point of glory. Then the crowd of onlookers is a vastly different one from

beginning to end by the actual participants themselves, is followed by the majority of the more aristocratic visitors with only a feeble interest. Here and there excited groups of boys dance up and down, cheer madly, frantically clap their hands, and call their indifferent elders' languid attention to the splendid doings of a favourite chum. Old Boys—bald-headed and eminent Old Boys some of them—follow the game with glistening eyes, recalling their own youth, and clap their gloved hands softly, murmuring, "Played, sir! Played, indeed!" But, for

LUNCHEON INTERVAL AT ETON v. HARROW MATCH (LORD'S).

that which fills the benches when Middlesex or the M.C.C. are in possession of the field. Demos is in a minority for once. The plebeian billycock or cap shows itself infrequently amid bobbing rows of silken headgear and bewildering millinery confections. The umbrella and gay parasol, that the hardiest of mortals scarcely dares to raise on ordinary occasions, flaunt themselves everywhere now, innocent of any solecism. There are almost as many women as men. Wherever a vacant space is available, commanding a glimpse of the pitch, there you will find carriages ranged in rows, with liveried flunkeys in attendance. The match, played keenly and thoroughly enough from

the most part, the whole affair partakes of the nature of a society gathering. This is apparent when the luncheon interval arrives. The meal under the trees at an end, the lawn is invaded by a brilliant throng of promenaders. The first and the second bell ring. Still they remain in possession. In vain the policemen endeavour urbanely to herd them back to their seats. They complacently ignore these blandishments; and it is not until the teams are actually on the field, and the re-start has been delayed, perhaps, a quarter of an hour, that they consent to let the match go on. It is only on the last day, when the issue hangs in the balance, that there is any general pervasion of enthusiasm. Then, sometimes, all dalliance will suddenly cease. The most frivolous cannot escape the infection of the universal excitement. There is a busn as each ball is bowled; and finally, when the result is beyond question, a tumultuous outburst of pent-up feeling, in which treble and bass mingle harmoniously.

All this, however, is as nothing compared with the heats and chills, the qualms and fervours, that prevail among the spectators at Lord's when England and Australia meet there in a test match. Early in the morning, before even the screever outside the walls has finished his pavement studies of cricket celebrities, the crowd has begun to assemble; by noon there is not a vacant seat to be had. There is nothing lukewarm in the temper of this crowd; there is nothing slack or careless in the play of the rival elevens. As the fortunes of the game fluctuate a sympathetic ripple seems to run through the watching multitude. A catch is muffed, and a mighty roar batters on the welkin. A hero is dismissed, and a murmur goes up like the growl of a disappointed beast. The ball is hit to the boundary

thrice in succession to a crescendo of ecstatic cheering. Now one of the batsmen approaches his century. He has made many centuries during his career; but, veteran though he be, the fatefulness of his position overbears him a little. He plays with a caution that is infinitely trying to our overwrought nerves. Once he scrapes forward at a ball ... misses it. There is an appeal. " Not out! "

A minute later, and our hats are in the air. The scoring-board labours, and up goes " 100." Strangers shake hands with one another; even the Australians themselves applaud; and the din of our voices must surely set the wild beasts roaring half a mile away.

At the cessation of play the crowd rushes on to the field. The heroes of the day walk to the pavilion through a lane of frenzied worshippers, salvo on salvo of applause thundering in their ears.

And, as we turn away from that scene of rapturous excitement we realise for the first time fully, perhaps, how large a part cricket has come to play in the daily life of London.

HEROES OF THE DAY.

KITCHEN IN THE FARM HOUSE, SOUTHWARK.

"DOSSER"-LAND IN LONDON.

By T. W. WILKINSON.

WHEREVER there are particularly mean streets in London the signs of hotels for the poor hang high over the causeway—by day mere "busies," by night beacons for the guidance of wrecked humanity. Boys' lodging houses, men's lodging houses, single women's lodging houses, "couples'" lodging houses, lodging houses of the rural type, open to all comers, irrespective of age, sex, or condition, are scattered all over the Great City to the number of about 1,000, sometimes alone, sometimes in twos and threes, sometimes in groups of a dozen, but in general, whether solitary or clustered together, off the beaten track, in the heart of seething, sordid slums.

The "doss"-houses for men only are most numerous and, perhaps, most varied, ranging as they do from the dwelling which is registered for only about half a dozen to the barrack-like building in which some 600 weary heads are laid down nightly, and from the den reserved for thieves and other "game

'uns" to the admirably conducted hostels of the Salvation Army, Father Jay's institution in Shoreditch, the Farm House in Southwark, and the many homes for particular sections of the "dosser" army.

For a typical lodging house for men we cannot do better than go to the district of which Spitalfields Church is the centre. Dorset Street, with its squalid air, its groups of "dossers" scattered over the pavement, as well as Flower and Dean Street—of little better repute, and having the same characteristics in a minor degree—are almost under the shadow of that edifice.

And as to the time of our visit, let it be eight o'clock in the evening. Here we are, then. There is no need to knock: the door is open. At four a.m. it swings back to let out the market porters and a whole posse of lodgers who carry under their arm the mark of their calling—a roll of newspapers, yesterday's "returns." It closes about one in the morning, though belated "dossers" straggle in afterwards.

Through the ever-open door, along the passage, a sharp turn to the right, and—phew! Never mind; it is only oil of "sea rover," which adheres to the "doss"-house as the rose to the broken vase. You may scrub, you may whitewash, the place as you will, but the odour of bloater will cling to it still.

This is the kitchen, the common room of the house, the loafing place of the idle,

A COUNTY COUNCIL INSPECTOR'S VISIT.

and the workshop of the industrious. Opposite us as we enter, taking up nearly one-half the length of the wall, and framed in dull, dead black, a huge coke fire glows and crackles, diffusing to the remotest corner an oppressive warmth. It burns like a sepulchral lamp, continuously, from year's end to year's end. Above, a serried line of tin teapots, battered and stained with long use, and above that, again, the "Rules of the House," one of which stands out in aggressive capitals: "No Washing on Sunday"—meaning that laundry work is for purely social reasons prohibited on the Sabbath.

In the corner beyond the fireplace a buxom female figure is eyeing the depleted collection of cracked crockery ranged on the shelves, her sleeves upturned over massive biceps. She is the "deputy," the domestic ruler of about 200 men. Her office is, even in hotels of this class, open to both sexes, each of which has qualifications for it denied to the other. Woman's strong point is the celerity and dispatch she displays in carrying out certain very necessary operations connected with bed-making. Hence the comfort of a house where females are entrusted with that work—which is axiomatic. Man's superiority lies in quelling disturbances and "chucking." Generally the male deputy is more or less of a bruiser, though it is a mistake for him to be an expert pugilist, else his whole time will be divided, in unequal proportions, between fighting and lying in hospital. All the Maces in "Dosser"-land will flock to vanquish or be vanquished.

Distributed over the kitchen three or four score men are having tea, or, as they would call the meal, supper. And a grim, picturesque assemblage they make. Yonder a seedy, frock-coated failure, on whose black, glossy curls Time's hand has not yet been laid, is sopping some bits of bread — manifestly leavings begged from a tea-shop—in a decoction made from a "halfpenny tea and sugar mixed," his eyes wandering now and again to a pair of kippers which a market porter tossed from a frying pan on to a plate a few minutes since. At his elbow an old man, whose snowy beard is plainly, when viewed sideways, his shirt front, mouths a greasy ham bone like a decrepit dog. In front of the fire is another figure that arrests the roving eye. A pallid youth has his meal spread before him on an evening newspaper, which is his tablecloth. It consists of tea, bread and margarine, and that delicacy of which the "dosser" never tires, the humble bloater. The cup which the youthful lodger has before him is an old jam pot, his only article of cutlery is his pocket knife, and he conveys the food to his mouth with Nature's forks. Artificial ones are not provided, nor is it customary to supply either knives or spoons. Too portable—that is the explanation.

And now mark the men with tea only before them—tea which represents the waste of the "doss"-house table, since it has come from the abandoned pots of other and more fortunate lodgers. All have that haunting expression—that dull, despairing look in the eyes—which hunger and buffeting engender. Judged by even the low standard of the fourpenny hotel, they are wretched in the extreme, and in comparison with them most of the other inmates of the kitchen are prosperous. Half their nights are spent in the street, considerably more than half their days in this common room, where they doze by the fire, "bull" or "milk" teapots, pick up odds and ends from the table, and, if happy chance serve, share the meals of acquaintances who may themselves, for aught they know, have to postpone the next morning's breakfast indefinitely. They live, in fact, largely on the charity of their own class. "Dossers'" dependents are certainly an un-

CUBICLES IN A "COUPLES'" HOUSE
(SPITALFIELDS).

scheduled section of the community; but they exist in hundreds, and constitute one of the many mysteries of London.

Endless other phases of the underworld can be studied in the kitchen of the fourpenny hotel. The vagrant industries alone afford an unlimited field for investigation. Paper flowers, sand bags, toasting forks, miraculous corn cures, "novelties" of all kinds—such as the walnut thimble case—are made before your eyes. Old, worthless seeds are converted in a twinkling into the "sweet-scented lavender" of commerce. A penny-worth of scent from the chemist's effects the transformation. You can watch the pavement artist doing "all my own work" by deputy, the begging-letter writer studying his private directory and drafting a condensed tragedy on the back of a music-hall handbill, the broken-down journalist racking his brain for ideas that obstinately refuse to come at his bidding, the old soldier—'rejuiced,' as Mulvaney used to say in another sense, "but a corporal waist"—coaching a comrade in the art of cadging from officers of his former regiment. Occasionally even a singing lesson may be witnessed in a kitchen. Not that "griddlers" practise their hymns in a "doss"-house; they learn them at the "ragged churches" on

OUTSIDE A LODGING HOUSE
(FLOWER AND DEAN STREET, SPITALFIELDS).

68

Sunday. It is the waits who sometimes rehearse at home.

Next, the sleeping chambers. It is midnight. The door at the foot of the stairs is locked, but for all that many men are in bed. At intervals the "deputy" has opened it, and taken from each lodger as he passed the numbered metal check given to him by the proprietor earlier in the evening as a voucher for his fourpence. Until the "dosser" is going to bed he is not required to show if he has paid his lodging money.

About a couple of yards up the staircase, and we reach the first landing, from which there are openings to the right and left leading into small bedrooms, and those into other rooms, and so on till the stranger thinks he is rambling half way up the street. Here a number of small, domestic-like chambers occupy the upper part of the house. In others the system is different, there being only two or three rooms, in which beds stretch away in a long line on each side of the door. This associated arrangement is in force at some houses where sixpence per night is charged.

But here is the first room. Bareness is its key-note: no curtains or blind to the window, no covering of any kind on the well-scrubbed floor, no pictures on the walls, which are unrelieved whitewash except for a County Council notice and a number at the head of each bed corresponding to that of a room in an hotel. That notice sets forth for how many beds (six) the apartment is registered, and exactly so many does it contain. One more, if discovered—and the inspector drops in occasionally about half-past two in the morning—would subject the owner to a heavy penalty.

On going higher, and seeing room after room of exactly the same character as the

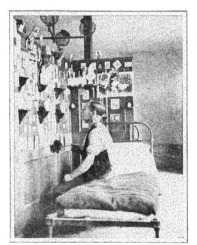

AT FATHER JAY'S LODGING HOUSE (SHORE-DITCH): A PRETTY CORNER.

first, you discover that most beds in the house are occupied. From the foot of one a dark mass protrudes. A man has turned in without undressing—that is all. If the rule of the American hotel keeper, "Guests found in bed with their boots on will die that way," was suddenly enforced in common lodging houses, the rate of mortality among "dossers" would be appalling.

Blacker still is an object under another bed. It is a saucepan containing the remains of a stew, the property of him who sleeps above it. The reason it is stored here is not obscure. Look at the waistcoats peeping out from under pillows, or turn down the coverlets on that empty bed and read the legend stamped boldly on the lower sheet: "Stolen from ——." There is the clue. The prevalence of theft in these places — mean, paltry, contemptible theft—accounts for the presence of the saucepan under the bed. Many a man has woke up to find his boots gone, and occasionally a lodger is robbed of all his clothing — coat, waistcoat, trousers, shirt, everything—while he is asleep.

Now there is a rush of feet on the stairs; a babel of voices rising higher and higher. The "last train" is coming up; the laggards who are always loth to leave the kitchen have been turned out. Soon the whole house will be silent save for the chattering of two cronies who have tarried overlong at the "Pig and Penwiper." Then there will be a bowl from somebody whom they have wakened, and then, perhaps, a fight.

Of exceptional "doss"-houses for men there are many. A hurried survey of two or three will modify the impression that the typical fourpenny hotel has produced. First, Father Jay's hospice in Shoreditch. Here we are in a different atmosphere. A light, well-appointed kitchen, cubicles above, some of them very

KITCHEN IN A SINGLE WOMEN'S LODGING HOUSE (SPITALFIELDS).

KITCHEN IN A COMMON LODGING HOUSE (SPITALFIELDS).

WASHING AND COOKING AT THE
FARM HOUSE, SOUTHWARK.

Let us now visit a typical women's lodging house. Upstairs, it differs in no way from one for men. Downstairs, the kitchen, with its ruddy coke fire, its overpowering aroma of bloater, its heated atmosphere, as before. Never does it vary very much. Though it is between three and four in the afternoon—a time when a house for men is almost deserted—the room is full of females young and old, some eating, some talking, some at work. One is making paper flowers, another knitting, and a third mending a rent in her skirt.

At the outset the mixed and motley group stirs the imagination profoundly, and still more so when one comes to analyse it. How many of the women bear marks of brutality—swollen lips, cut cheeks, black eyes! And what tragedies has outraged Nature written on some faces which have not been "bashed"—lately! You can see faint traces of the finer feelings and aspirations in a mass of male wreckage, but here, if they survive at all, the dim light fails to reveal them.

Study, for a moment, that group near the fire. A young woman with dishevelled hair and open bodice (she has apparently yet to make her toilet) is frying steak and onions. By her side a companion equally untidy is also preparing a meal, breakfast maybe, despite the hour. She drops her "halfpenny tea and sugar mixed" into a pot, cautiously lets two eggs sink on the heap, and then pours boiling water on the lot. This is a wrinkle in "doss"-house cookery. The process saves time and trouble always, and in some establishments is compulsory, by reason of the absence of small saucepans. Behind these lodgers a wrinkled old crone is hutched up over her pipe and basking in the heat. Like many of her class, she is intolerant of

tastefully decorated by their occupants, and still higher the ordinary rooms, split up to a certain extent by fixed wooden screens, one of which is covered with brackets, busts, looking-glasses, pictures, and odds and ends innumerable, the property of the man whose bed is beneath—such are the memories one carries away from the place. All is in striking contrast to the bareness and gloom of the typical East-End "doss"-house.

Secondly, the Salvation Army's institution at Paddington, mainly remarkable for its sleeping side. At night one of its rooms is an eye-opener. To right, to left, in front, beds, beds, beds, in seemingly endless number. There is a whole acre of them, all tenanted as far as can be seen. Two hundred sleepers are contained in this one huge chamber, most of them men in fairly regular work—bricklayers' labourers, navvies, and the like. Ask such a man why he stops here rather than in private lodgings, and his reply is prompt and emphatic. "Oh, give me company," he says. And, indeed, that is the principal reason. It strikes some people as strange; but the same thing is met with in higher strata of life.

Finally, there is the Farm House, in Southwark, another very good specimen of the better class of "doss"-houses. It is one of the few establishments of its class where cooking by gas is practicable.

cold, because she cannot feed her bodily fire and produce natural warmth.

If you fill in the details it is not a pleasing picture. Look back. Long, long ago— twenty years, thirty, forty in some cases —numbers of these women came here or to a neighbouring house as girls. And now look forward. You can see them all going to the workhouse or the hospital gate. That is their well-nigh inevitable end, unless they meet a worse fate. They will not, they cannot, rise to a higher level.

One other kind of lodging house looms large in some parts of London, and that is the establishment for "couples." The difference between a place of this class and one for men or women only lies solely in the sleeping accommodation. There is more privacy in the former, though not much in some cases, for the cubicles are like stable stalls. In general, however, they are similar, only smaller, to those boxed-off spaces which the coffee-shop keeper dignifies with the name of bedrooms.

In these places, as in most other "doss"-houses, no questions are asked and no names taken. A man or woman may live in a four-penny hotel for years, and yet be known to the "deputy" by the number of his or her bed. The majority of the lodgers in hotels for the poor, too, are casuals, not regulars. While one man has had the same "kip" for forty years, and thousands have not changed their quarters for five or ten years or longer, numbers of men and women do not stop many days anywhere. One week a "dosser" may be in the Borough, the next in Spitalfields, the next in St. Clement's, Notting Hill. So that some phases of life in cubicle houses are not so exceptional as the circumstances surrounding certain murders which have been committed in them have led many to assume.

On the whole, "Dosser"-land is a squalid, depressing region. Tragedy, then comedy fitfully, then tragedy again—such is life in it. Yet, if its people make the social reformer despair, who shall say that their environment is not better now than ever it was? Of a truth, since the County Council obtained control of lodging houses the improvement in them has been remarkable. The inspectors not only prevent overcrowding, but insist on cleanliness (no more sheet-changing once a month), ventilation, and other sanitary requirements; and as a result the "dosser" now enjoys a degree of comfort of which formerly he had only heard.

SCENE IN DORSET STREET, SPITALFIELDS.

ON THE STONES, ISLINGTON CATTLE MARKET.

EQUINE LONDON.

By CHARLES DUDLEY

TILL Lon-
don is
conquered
by the motor
car it will re-
main both the
Purgatory and
the Paradise of
horses. It is
the Purgatory
because the
work thrown
on the heavy
brigade knocks up the strongest in a few
years; the Paradise because the aristocrats
of the equine race live in unwonted luxury,
and the aged and the ailing nowhere else
meet with such kind and skilful treatment.

Let us ramble through the horse world of
London, and we shall see both sides of it.
And, first, we will visit Rotten Row this
bright, lovely morning. Half-past ten. We
are rather too late to catch the "liver
brigade." But stay, here is a belated member,
mounted on a fine chestnut, which he keeps
at a steady gallop; he is pounding up and
down in a fashion that will make him go to
his club a new man by and by. Near the
rails a sleek pony, led by a groom, is taking
Master Reginald round for an airing, and eye-

ing his bigger brethren as who should say,
"Ah! you'd see what I would do if they
would only give me a chance." Two fair
maidens with their escorts pass by; and then
three sisters come cantering down the middle
of the Row abreast, their cheeks glowing with
robust health, their long hair flowing behind—
fine types of Britain's daughters. Still more
in the background a mounted policeman,
whose like you may meet at night in far-off
suburban solitudes, keeps watch over this
world-famed stretch.

And now a flash of scarlet catches and
holds the eye. In the road bordering the
park a string of Guards, their white plumes
nodding gently with the steady motion of their
horses, whose backs are hidden from saddle
to crupper under the voluminous top-coats of
their riders, pass along at a walk. They are
on their way to Whitehall, there to take turn
in standing statuesquely in the sentry-boxes
at the Horse Guards—the admiration of
nursemaids and the wondering delight of
children.

Later in the day the Row is empty, but, on
the other hand, the pleasure horse monopolises
the circle, now comparatively deserted.
Singly, in pairs, tandems, and fours, he draws
the family carriage with a lozenge on the
panels, the brougham of the fashionable

SHUNTING RAILWAY
TRUCKS.

sessions in the Royal Mews in Buckingham Palace Road—we stroll to Albert Gate, and pass Tattersall's — now, like Aldridge's and the repositories in the Barbican and elsewhere, given up to the sale of horses and carriages. To one class of purchasers it is what the Cattle Market is to another. Small traders mostly look for their horseflesh on the stones at Islington— where there is a scene as much like a horse fair of the rural type as London can show—while gentlemen to whom expense is no consideration betake them in like circumstances to Tattersall's, whose reputation for straight dealing gives them an enormous business. There is no Flying Fox to be sold to-day for 37,000 guineas, or it would be worth while to step inside and witness the event. Smart "steppers" for the Park usually represent the class of business done at the weekly sales nowadays.

A short walk farther brings us to one of the numerous

doctor, the coupé of the popular actress, the man about town's smart dog-cart.

If we want a contrast to the picture in the Park, the East-End will supply it. High Street, Whitechapel. Gone the high steppers ; gone the glossy carriages ; gone the splendidly impassive footmen. Down the road comes the "general utility" of the equine world and the nearest approach extant to perpetual motion. A shopkeeper's horse more used to the markets and main streets than any other part of London, he is, for the time being, in the service of Pleasure. He is bringing along with a rush a neat little trap, on the front seat of which is the owner, proudly conscious that he can "do it" when he likes, his hat at a knowing angle, a cigar tilted heavenwards between his teeth. Behind an elderly lady lolls in a self-conscious pose; and the rear is brought up, so to speak, by the end of the parlour hearthrug, which dangles behind. Most obviously, the radiant driver is taking the "missus" out for the afternoon. Well, let us hope that they will enjoy their drive.

Returning westwards — not forgetting his Majesty's equine pos-

IN ROTTEN ROW.

jobbing establishments that are scattered over London. Enter the yard. A number of carriages with a festive look are in readiness to go out, and we arrive just in time to see a procession of greys led from the stables. "Wedding greys" are they. And what a strange lot in life is theirs—to be the despised of cabby, the rejected of the omnibus owner and the carrier, and the delight of marrying London! The livery master must have them, because they are indispensable for a wedding. Yet their use is almost, if not quite, as restricted as that of the sensitive Flemish blacks, which are reserved for taking us our last drive.

But it creates no exceptional stir in the place, this preparation for a wedding. The firm gets about twenty or thirty of such orders every day. In addition it will,

A BIG STABLE AT WALWORTH (SOUTHWARK BOROUGH COUNCIL).

and does, furnish horses and carriages for every conceivable purpose. Some of its stud have as many different jobs in a day as a boy messenger. They trot placidly with a gigantic boiler behind them in the morning, a lady's bonnet box in the afternoon, and a set of theatrical scenery at night. And it is only one of many firms doing a similar business. Even Messrs. Pickford—who keep more than four thousand horses and frequently engage other three or four hundred by the day—are job masters on a large scale as well as carriers.

A considerable proportion of the horses one sees in the street are, in fact, hired. The hairy-legged members of the heavy brigade that sluggishly drag along the vans

belonging to a certain firm which moves everybody, from the Marquess of Gaunt, of Berkeley Square, to Mr. Thos. Tittlemouse, of Acacia Villa, Peckham; the dashing "tits" of innumerable butchers, bakers, and other tradesmen; the smart equipages which take many doctors on their rounds, ladies to Bond Street or the theatre, music-hall artistes to their engagements, and are met at every turn in Central London; the superb "goers" in the service of the Metropolitan Fire Brigade, on which every eye is turned as they dash through the streets to a constant accompaniment of "Hi-hi-hi!" —all are jobbed at rates varying according to their value and other factors.

Perhaps the only kind of horse which is not hired, except the stolid animal which acts as a shunting engine on the iron road, is the plunging beauty of the Hippodrome, that intelligent creature which can be trusted to look dashing and full of fire and at the same time to work with the regularity of a steam-engine. Every other variety is jobbed. One firm will horse any business for a fixed sum per year, while another is able to supply a horse, brougham, and man at a total inclusive cost of about £225 or £250 a year. At this rate it is cheaper and more convenient to hire a carriage than to keep one; and consequently private stables are becoming fewer and fewer.

Cross the Thames now to the stable of the Southwark Borough Council in Walworth. Here we are at a typical home of the

municipal horse, than which there is no better animal of its class in the equine world. Well-lighted, adequately ventilated, provided with every necessary convenience, it presents an animated spectacle by reason of a number of men being engaged in polishing the brasses on the harness, the suppleness of which attests the attention it receives. About the fine animals in the stalls there is nothing remarkable except their capacity for backing. At that the

municipal horse is easily first and the rest nowhere. He will push a dust cart into any opening, and, what is more, run no risk of having his legs injured, for he will keep them well under him the while.

The apotheosis of the cart horse! Not the May-Day procession, though in that he has the whole stage and all the limelight to himself, but his principal festival, the show in Regent's Park on Whit-Monday. It is ten o'clock, and right round the inner

AT THE CART HORSE SHOW AND PARADE, REGENT'S PARK.

I. JUDGING.   II. DRAYMAN (FORTY-ONE YEARS' SERVICE) WITH PRIZE HORSE.   III. A FAMILY PARTY.

circle are extended more than one thousand fine specimens of the heavy brigade, attached to nearly every kind of business vehicle, some singly, some in pairs, and some in teams.

Here is a typical turn-out. A sleek, well-groomed horse, no rib or pin bone visible, newly-shod, with blacked hoofs, and gaily decked with flowers and ribbons, stands in the shafts of a coal dealer's van, in which a family party has been brought from a distant suburb. In front is the driver,

all quarters of London, and it will be late when some of them reach home.

Before we leave the park let us learn the result of the long-service competition. The winner on this occasion—the man who takes the money bequeathed by Miss Isabel Constable—is a veteran who has held the same situation for over 41 years, and the four drivers who have been awarded the premiums of one guinea offered by the Cart Horse Society have severally been in the employ of

TATTERSALL'S.

temporarily oblivious — under the subtle excitement of the moment—that he has been working all night on his horse. Behind him is his wife, beaming and happy, and in the rear are grouped the children, and others all in their Sunday best.

Meanwhile, the judging has been going on. It lasts some time, for not only have the horses to be passed under review, but prizes awarded for length of service. It is over now, and a queue is formed, the winners taking the lead, and all the horses parade once right round the outer circle. Then the procession breaks up. For hours hence its component parts will be returning to

one master for nearly as long a period. And yet cynics say that the race of faithful Adams is extinct!

With a rapid survey of two unique institutions our tour round Equine London may end. Much — very much — must for one reason or another be ignored. 'Bus, tram, and cab horses receive attention in another article in this work, while the "knacker's" industry, important though it may be, smacks too much of the shambles to be pleasant.

The first of the two institutions is the Royal Veterinary College in Camden Town. It is three o'clock in the afternoon, and the free clinic is taking place.

Drawn up outside one part of the buildings are the out-patients—a scofe of sorry-looking hacks—attended to by their owners, who mostly belong to the costermonger class and are all too poor to pay for the doctoring of their ailing workers. Through the opening, and we are in the out-patients' ward. It is a covered yard. In the middle is a thick bed of clean straw, on and round which are scattered groups of surgeons and students.

"Look out!" To the right is a horse, which is about to be cast—to be thrown on its side like another patient which lies on our left. "Capped elbow; the largest I ever saw," says the surgeon, pointing to a huge excrescence on the inner side of one of this poor brute's forelegs. Presently somebody comes up with a leather bucket, fixes it over the captive's nose, and tucks a cloth round the top to keep in the fumes. Chloroform! The unfortunate owner, who is holding down the horse's head, looks as if he himself were about to be operated on, since he is ghastly, with restless eyes quick to see every movement. A moment, and the prostrate brute struggles convulsively; but the anæsthetic quickly overpowers him. Then a student drags a bucket of disinfecting fluid nearer the patient, makes a selection from a number of pretty little instruments, and—but we will not stay longer.

What a boon is this free clinic to the indigent horse-keeper! Any afternoon he can bring an ailing steed to it and have it attended to gratuitously.

The other institution at which we will make a call is Friar's Place Farm—otherwise known as the Home of Rest for Horses—at Acton. This is the most pleasing feature of the equine world of London, for it is a sort of combined hydro and retreat for man's faithful friend. Some of the inmates are resting temporarily or undergoing treatment at the hands of skilled surgeons; but many are pensioners, and have been in retirement for years. They are maintained either by ladies and gentlemen for whom they have worked hard and well or by the supporters of the institution.

The farm consists largely of row after row of stables, from one line of which a dozen heads and necks are craned out as we approach. The inmates heard us coming. They are all great pets. Each has a house of his own, and in it he lives comfortably, even luxuriously, with nothing to do but eat and enjoy life. Every New Year's Day the pensioners are specially favoured, for, by the kindness of a benevolent lady, they are provided with a special dinner of apples, carrots, brown and white bread, and sugar.

Vast and many-sided is the horse world of London; and yet it is all to disappear —stables, institutions, pretty customs, everything—before the noisy, ugly, but decidedly convenient and economical motor car! Perhaps—and perhaps not.

A ROW OF PENSIONERS (HOME OF REST, ACTON).

HOSPITAL LONDON.

By R. AUSTIN FREEMAN.

NURSE (WEST LONDON HOSPITAL).

AMONG the multitudes of way-farers that through the streets of the Metropolis there are probably few who, as they pass one of the great hospitals, do not glance up at the massive building with some curiosity, and with, perhaps, a passing thought as to the strange scenes that are being enacted within. Yet by few of these are the significance and importance of these institutions fully appreciated, or the scope of their relations with humanity at large understood.

For the great hospitals of London are not only the refuges of the sick and suffering poor; the agents through which the benevolent minister to the necessities of the indigent; the retreats to which the struggling worker can retire in seasons of adversity, to receive relief in his own person and in the removal from his family of the burden of his helplessness. They are all this, indeed; but, in addition, they are the battle-grounds upon which is fought that never-ending contest in which the intelligence of man is arrayed against those invading forces that ever tend to shorten the period of individual life and to augment the sum of sorrow and suffering for mankind at large.

With a view to getting some insight into the inner life of a hospital, let us present ourselves at the out-patient entrance about nine o'clock in the morning. A considerable crowd has collected, and, as the doors are just opened, the earlier arrivals are beginning to pass through. The crowd is at present a very miscellaneous one, for its constituent units have not yet been sorted out and classified. The pale consumptive jostles a sturdy labourer whose bandaged head furnishes an illustration of the momentum of falling bodies; patients with rasping coughs and panting breath; patients on crutches; patients in splints, with limbs swathed in bandages; men and women, old and young, strong and feeble, are here mingled into an

OUT-PATIENTS WAITING ROOM (MIDDLESEX HOSPITAL).

BOTTLE - SELLING OUTSIDE ST.
BARTHOLOMEW'S HOSPITAL.

indiscriminate assembly. On the outskirts of the crowd an itinerant bottle merchant has set up a little stall (for the hospital does not supply bottles gratis); but most of the frugal patients have furnished themselves from home, and we may see marmalade jars converted into ointment pots, while the jovial whiskey bottle is degraded into a mere receptacle for cod-liver oil.

Inside the doorway a porter and a nurse are engaged in sorting out the patients by means of their cards or letters; and very soon the lobbies outside the various out-patient rooms become filled with groups of patients who, as they sit on the benches awaiting their turn, inspect with an expert and critical eye the new-comers who continue to pass in.

From time to time the door of a consulting room is opened, and an attendant admits the patients in parties of about a dozen, while those who have seen the doctors emerge with their prescription cards in their hands, and go to swell the little crowd that is gathered round the dispensary.

As a batch of patients is admitted we enter a spacious room, round the sides of which are a number of electric lamps fitted with bull's-eyes. At one of these a clinical assistant is examining, with the aid of a reflector fastened to his forehead, a patient's throat, while at another a student is exploring an obstructed ear. The surgeon sits near the window, with a semi-circle of chairs occupied by students behind him, and the patient seated in a good light before him; and as he examines the latter he directs the attention of the students to the salient points of the case, and explains the train of reasoning by which he arrives at his diagnosis.

Of course, the different departments have their own special characters. In the medical,

PORTER (WEST LONDON
HOSPITAL).

AN OPERATION AT CHARING CROSS HOSPITAL.

stethoscopes abound and coughs prevail; in the surgical, bandages, dressings, and antiseptics are in evidence. In the eye department the air is filled with a droning sound of "E, T, B, D, L, N," as the patients read aloud the letters of the test types through the trial glasses, and students, working out "refractions," are seen in dark closets, throwing from their ophthalmoscopes bright, dancing spots of light on to the eyes of their patients. But we must not linger among the out-patients. We have just seen from the window a couple of policemen wheeling a covered ambulance up to the entrance, and thither we now hurry.

Each of the policemen has embroidered on his sleeve a Maltese cross within a circle, a device which indicates that he has gone through a course of instruction in "First Aid to the Injured," and received the certificate of the St. John's Ambulance. This useful Association not only gives instruction, but furnishes stretchers and ambulances for use in street accidents, and, moreover, owns a number of admirable covered waggons or horse ambulances, which may be hired for the conveyance of invalids or helpless persons.

The stretcher is detached from its carriage and placed upon a cushioned trolley, which s wheeled noiselessly along a corridor to a small room where the house-surgeon with his dressers are waiting. The patient, a respectable working man, has been knocked down by a van which has run over one of his legs; and to the injured limb the policemen have attached a temporary splint. This being now removed, and the patient's trousers slit up, a jagged wound is revealed, through which a sharp splinter of bone protrudes. The leg has sustained a compound fracture.

The wound is now carefully cleansed by the house-surgeon, who covers it with a dressing of gauze or tissue that has been subjected to heat in a closed chamber to destroy any germs that might lurk in it. Well-padded splints are next applied to the limb, and the patient is then wheeled off on the trolley to a large lift, which carries him and two porters to an upper floor; where, after traversing a long corridor, the trolley at length brings up alongside an empty bed in one of the great surgical wards. Trolley and bed are now surrounded by screens, and the patient, being lifted on to the bed by the two stalwart porters, is by them undressed with surprising care and gentleness and covered with a blanket. Finally, the screens are removed, and a nurse proceeds to trim up the bed with sheets and counterpane to the required standard of neatness.

Let us glance round the ward into which we have followed our patient. It is a lofty apartment of great length and relatively narrow—somewhat like a very large corridor. The spaces of painted wall between the large windows are hung with pictures and framed

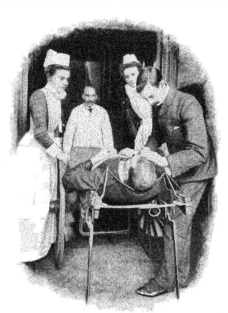

RECEIVING AN ACCIDENT CASE (POPLAR HOSPITAL).

texts, and the floor is of polished oak, elegant in appearance and easy to keep clean, but very slippery. Down the middle of the ward is a range of long tables, supporting flowers, ferns, and palms, as well as basins, ewers, and other appliances.

Each side is occupied by a row of beds extending the whole length of the ward, most of them occupied by patients, whose red flannel bed-jackets contrasting with the white counterpanes impart a very bright and cheerful aspect to the place. Indeed, a general air of cheerfulness and comfort is the most noticeable feature, even of a surgical ward. In most of the beds the patients are placidly engaged in the perusal of newspapers and books; convalescents with crutches or arm-slings are playing draughts at the tables or doing such odd jobs as their condition allows, amid much animated conversation and many lively sallies of cockney wit from the occupants of the beds; while the busy nurses flit from patient to patient, making the building resound with the clatter of their so-called "silent ward shoes."

But the graver side of hospital life is in evidence too. The patients are not all convalescent, nor are they all cheerful and happy. Here, for instance, is a silent, motionless figure, the pallid face surmounted by an ice-cap, and the half-closed eyes singularly ghastly and death-like — a bad case of concussion of the brain. In the bed hard by, the clothes of which are raised by a "cradle," like the tilt of a waggon, a man lies staring fixedly at the ceiling; and when the sister has told us that "23 had his leg amputated above the knee yesterday" we can read in the sad, dejected face the sorrowful thoughts that are passing through the sufferer's mind. We know that he is thinking of the wooden pin on which he is to stump through life, of the struggle for existence made tenfold more bitter, of the sports and pleasures that he enjoyed in the past and will enjoy no more!

While we are looking round the ward one of the house-surgeons, with an attendant squad of dressers, makes his appearance, and forthwith a glass table running on rubber-tyred wheels is brought out to accompany him on his round. The glass shelves of the table are filled with air-tight cases of sterilised gauze, tissue, cotton wool, and bandages, sealed glass tubes of sterilised silk and cat-

solutions of carbolic acid or corrosive sublimate, and the dressings would have been impregnated with iodoform or other germicide substances; but the "antiseptic" surgery which wrought such marvels in the past is disappearing in favour of the still more perfect "aseptic" system of the present day.

The introduction of this new aseptic system —by which it is sought to exclude all microbes from the neighbourhood of wounds, instead of applying to them "antiseptics," or microbe poisons, as was formerly done—has not only produced a great change in the materials and processes used in the dressing of wounds, but has rendered the daily round of the dressers a much less important proceeding. For under the older system a considerable portion of the surgical cases required to have

SINGING TO PATIENTS (LONDON HOSPITAL).

gut for closing wounds, and porringers or little basins for the sterilised water from the Pasteur filter with which the wounds are cleansed if necessary. A few years since these porringers would have contained

the dressings renewed daily; whereas nowadays wounds are commonly sealed up immediately after an operation with germ-proof dressings, which are left undisturbed until the wounds are completely healed. Should some mischief-

VISITING DAY AT A
CHILDREN'S HOSPITAL
(GREAT ORMOND STREET).

working microbe find its way in through the dressings, despite all precautions, and set up suppuration in the wound, there is not a little grumbling on the part of the surgeon, and a strict inquiry is made into the history of the faulty materials with which the wound has been covered.

But, although the daily dressings are now much reduced in number, there is still in a large hospital ward plenty of occupation for the house-surgeons and dressers, and their morning's work will hardly have been completed before the appearance upon the ward tables of mounds of bread, neatly cut into symmetrical "doorsteps," announces the dinner-hour, and as they leave the ward they are met in the corridor by a waggon or large trolley piled high with the smoking materials for the meal, and diffusing a savoury aroma as it passes. Drawn up alongside the table, it disgorges its freight, and volcanic mounds of potatoes, verdant stacks of cabbage, ribs of beef, fried soles, plump chickens, and seething mutton chops attract the expectant regards of the patients and receive the attention of the sister and nurses. Then comes the rather unequal distribution of the delicacies. No. 4, who is recovering from the effects of a blow on the head, is on a

very restricted diet, and, as he wolfishly devours a diminutive sole, glances avariciously at his right-hand neighbour, an emaciated "hip joint" case, who is demolishing half a chicken with the gusto of a South Sea Islander. No. 8 is taking light refreshment through an india-rubber tube with the aid of a funnel, while the street arab in the corner bed assaults a mutton chop literally with tooth and nail, gnawing at the bone with chuckles of cannibalistic glee.

The meal concluded and the ward tidied up, an air of restlessness and expectancy becomes evident in the demeanour of the patients, which is presently explained when we discover that this is a visitors' day. Soon the patients' friends make their appearance, the men holding their hats gingerly and stepping on tiptoe, with immense strides (by which means it has been shown that the maximum amount of sound can be extracted from a pair of creaky shoes), and the women particularly attentive to the conduct of their offspring. Sometimes a visitor goes down with a thump on the slippery floor, to his own unspeakable confusion and the undissembled joy of the regular inmates. The bedside greetings run the whole gamut, from the half-sheepish

70

"Wot-O! Bill! How goes it?" of the male visitor, to the passionate embrace of the anxious wife or mother.

The unconscious "concussion" is visited

her blinding tears or hear her sobs as she hurries away through the echoing corridor.

In the Children's Hospital visitors' day

THE LUPUS LIGHT CURE (LONDON HOSPITAL).

by a pale, frightened-looking woman, who sits by the bed and gazes disconsolately at the silent figure. No. 23 brightens up somewhat as a quiet, trim-looking little woman, leading a sturdy boy of six or seven, approaches up the ward; and when she has seated herself by his side and holds his hand in hers as she chats of the doings outside he grows quite cheerful, although when his boy breaks out into joyous anticipations of the fun they will have "when father comes home" he has to turn away hastily and fumble in the locker by his bedside. The street arab has no friends to visit him, and consoles himself for the fact by putting out his tongue at a juvenile stranger and watching malignantly the little parties round the other beds. The allotted time quickly runs out, and the warning bell rings all too soon. Amidst a clatter of chairs the visitors rise to take leave of their friends, and they slowly troop out of the ward. No 23's wife is the last to go, and she turns at the door to wave her handkerchief and throw him a kiss; and he, poor fellow, greatly comforted by her pluck and cheerfulness, turns over with a sigh of contentment, for he cannot see

is especially a season of rejoicing; for the anxious mothers, who have, perhaps, gone away heart-broken at having to leave their little ones alone among strangers, experience the delight of seeing them again, bright, happy, tenderly cared for, and in the enjoyment of luxuries undreamed of in their own homes.

On days other than visiting days the wards are enlivened by the visits of the physicians or surgeons and the students, who, here at the bedside, receive the practical part of their professional education. Frequently a popular surgeon will be accompanied by twenty or thirty students, who form a semi-circle round the bed while the case is discussed in all its bearings and a *vivâ voce* examination is held upon the points involved in its history, diagnosis, and pathology, and any anatomical or physiological questions arising out of it.

From the wards we may proceed to the operating theatre, where one of the surgeons is already at work. The building is roughly horseshoe-shaped, and consists of a central area surrounded by tiers of platforms, rising one above the other in the manner of a Roman amphitheatre, for the accommodation of students who have come to watch the operation. In the area precautions against the ubiquitous microbe are everywhere in evidence. The group of surgeons, dressers, and nurses around the table on which lies the unconscious patient, all dressed in white sterilised over-garments, and in some cases even guarded by sterilised gloves; the seething trays in which the instruments are boiling, and the air filters that supply the ventilators: all testify to the importance of the great principle underlying modern surgical methods—the exclusion of micro-organisms. But that when the micro-organism has actually effected an entrance into the body he is not at all times secure against the warfare waged by means of modern appliances is made evident in the lupus cure department. For here the bacilli that give rise to this intractable and disfiguring disease are killed by the application of light from an arc electric lamp, the rays being brought to focus upon the diseased tissues, which are rendered more translucent by pressure made upon them with a water lens.

We might continue our ramble through the immense building of a London hospital indefinitely. We might explore the spacious garden where convalescents are taking the air, and where in summer time open-air entertainments are given to the patients; we might examine the dispensary with its multitudes of great bottles and Brobdingnagian jars; we might look in at the kitchen and marvel at the huge gas ovens like bankers' safes, the frying stoves as large as billiard tables, and the rows of cauldrons for cooking vegetables or making soup, each balanced on trunnions and inverted by means of a windlass; or inspect the incubators in which tiny, doll-like, prematurely born infants are reared in an artificially warmed atmosphere. But our time has run out, and, with a final glance at a bright-looking ward where, to the cheerful strains of a musical-box, a number of children are revelling in the enjoyment of toys that will make their recollections of hospital life a dream of bliss, we pass out of the building and mingle with the crowd that surges at its gates.

WAITING FOR MEDICINE (WEST LONDON HOSPITAL).

THE ROYAL MINT.

By CHARLES OLIVER.

BY a singular irony of Fate the building in which the nation's money is made is situated in one of the poorest districts of London. Close by the Mint the hungry docker passes rich on a few pence an hour, while from the wharves adjacent there pours a stream of ragged immigrants, which, percolating into every hovel of the east, sweeps on and on northward to Whitechapel, westward to Saffron Hill and Soho, emptying itself finally into the outlying districts.

There is little in the external appearance of the Royal Mint to attract attention; nothing to indicate the stupendous wealth that reposes within its walls. But as we stand outside there is evidence that something of special interest is about to take place. There are several burly-looking policemen on the spot, and, if we judge them correctly, they are watching for suspicious characters. The fact is we are in luck's way, for the great gates of the Mint are suddenly thrown open, and a van is driven in at a sharp pace. It is a very ordinary looking van—for aught a stranger could say to the contrary it might belong to a caterer—nevertheless its contents are worth a king's ransom. We could not have arrived at a more opportune moment.

RECEIVING SILVER INGOTS.

Having received permission of the Deputy-Master to visit the Mint we are admitted into the courtyard, and, on reaching the lobby, are severally requested to register our names and addresses in a book provided for the purpose. At the door are a number of officials—a representative of the Mint, a clerk from the Bank of England, together with a constable and a couple of porters. They are going to unload the van, and as our presence is not objected to we notice that its precious freight consists of several large chests securely padlocked. A trolley is wheeled forward, and presently one of the clerks produces a bunch of keys, and a case is opened. It is full of silver ingots. Many a hard-working man has to toil for a whole year to earn one of those ingots, while before he can become possessed of a trolley-load the clerk in charge of them has to labour possibly for a lifetime, and be a favourite of fortune as well; but there is no envy in the clerk's breast. His face is as expressionless as the stone flags on which he stands. Out they come one by one until a hundred ingots have been counted—£13,000 worth of solid silver. The metal is the property of the Bank of England, and will soon be converted into money.

MELTING AND POURING GOLD.

The van having disgorged its wealth to the last ounce, we follow the ingots far into the interior of the Mint, first into the Weighing-room, where they are weighed in the presence of the Bank officials, who remain until each ingot has been placed upon the scale, and then into the Strong-rooms. At every turn a dazzling hoard of gold confronts us. We brush against three trolleys on which are stacked a hundred small bags, and our guide observes with characteristic nonchalance that £40,000 would not purchase them. They are full of worn sovereigns—old stagers *en route* for the melting pot.

And now to the bullion stronghold to realise the magnitude of the work performed at the Mint, for there is not a coin bearing the King's head that has not come out of this chamber. The massive steel door is shut against us, and to turn the lock three keys are necessary. These keys are in the hands of three trusty officials, and their kindly aid having been obtained the doors swing heavily back, revealing to our astonished gaze a stock of gold and silver representing a million pounds. Hundreds of millions—enough to pay the National Debt twice over —have filtered through this stronghold of gold. Ranged upon shelves in admirable order are ingots of gold and ingots of silver,

each one duly marked and numbered so that its identity can be established on the instant. These ingots—those of silver are worth £130 and weigh 1,100 ounces—have been carefully tested by the permanent staff of analysts in the Assay Department and are ready to be sent to the Melting-house.

There are two strongholds at the Mint to make a poor man's mouth water. The second is for coined silver, and it harbours £200,000 of coins packed away in neat bags. Five shilling pieces, half-crowns, florins, shillings, and sixpences are done up in £100 bags; threepenny pieces in £25 bags.

We will now proceed to the Melting-house to gaze upon the pleasant spectacle of £20,000 worth of gold melting like butter. There are twenty-two furnaces in all—eight in the gold Melting-house and fourteen in the silver. The eight men dressed in blue serge employed in the former have melted in their time enough gold to fill a small pond. With as little concern as a cook puts bones to stew over the kitchen fire they place each ingot with its proper proportion of copper alloy into a crucible and plunge it deftly into the red-hot furnace, where it remains until it is reduced to a liquid state. The melting done, the crucible is withdrawn from the furnace by means of hand tongs, and the contents—a white molten fluid—are poured into an iron mould, the result being that a number of narrow bars are produced each worth between four and five hundred pounds.

From the Melting-room we step into the busy Rolling-room, where the bars go through the various mills until eventually they are rolled down to the required thickness. Every man is in full work, and each one is touching gold in the form of beautiful yellow strips from one to two inches thick that would suffice to support him and his family in luxury for a good twelve months. More gold passes through the hands of these humble workers in a year than a millionaire sees in a lifetime.

The average visitor to the Mint cudgels his brain in vain to understand how a check can be kept on all this wealth, for there is scarcely any waste, and theft is unknown. The explanation is simple, however, for, contrary to general supposition, nobody is searched when

employés in that department have to find it before they go home. Several other precautionary rules have to be observed, not because there is any doubt as to the honesty of the workers, who bear the best of characters —the greed of gold is not for them, familiarity with the precious metal having removed all temptation—but in order to prevent the ingots from going astray.

Each department is kept locked throughout the day, and no man can visit a room other than his own without the sanction of the officer who is over him. Further, the metal is weighed as it is passed from room to room. The head of each department knows by his books the weight of metal that was given out to him in the morning, and consequently has no difficulty when work ceases for the day in ascertaining the exact amount of gold and silver, after allowing for waste, that should be in his hands. Even the dust

THE ROLLING-ROOM.

he goes home at night, and there is no system of espionage; but no employé engaged in the making of money is allowed to leave the building until the day's work is done— the men must take their dinner on the premises—and until every particle of metal has been weighed. If a valuable piece of metal is missing from any department, the

on the floor is taken into calculation. Before the bells sound for the nightly exodus each room is carefully swept, and the particles that have accumulated during the day having been collected they are put into water, with the result that any gold or silver that may be present soon separates itself from the dust by dropping to the bottom of the pan. It is interesting also to observe that the gold pieces are counted as well as weighed as they are carried from room to room.

But the Mint is a large place, and a personally conducted tour occupies an hour and a half, so we must get on. Leaving the Rolling-room we proceed to the Cutting-room, where perspiring men of all ages are occupied in putting into machines the bright clean strips of gold out of which are punched blank pieces the size and shape of the

CUTTING-ROOM.

coins. The "blanks" are afterwards placed into marking machines and reappear with a raised edge.

From the Cutting-room the "blanks" are despatched to the Annealing-room, for the rolling has rendered the metal so hard that before it can receive the impression it must be put into the oven to be softened.

The next process takes place in the Blanching-room. Here myriads of gold and silver blanks are treated with acid, the silver to obtain the desired whiteness, the gold to remove the black surface which has been

RINGING THE COINS.

caused by the annealing. Two men are at work here. Their joint wages do not, perhaps, exceed more than a few pounds a week, but during their careers each one of them has fingered his million. One of them has just finished blanching a couple of thousand silver "blanks," and to rid them of the acid he has poured them into a pan and is holding them under a running tap. With so little fuss does he clean his blanks that we inquire how many he loses in a week, and the startling reply is "None." Nothing is lost at the Mint.

It is now necessary that the blanks should be dried, and for this purpose they are shaken up in revolving drums containing warm sawdust. This drying process cleanses the "blanks."

By far the busiest place in the Mint is the Coining Press-room, which we enter after quitting the Drying-room. Here are engaged the livelong day—from 8 a.m. to 5 p.m. —eighteen presses turning out money at the rate of 110 coins per minute apiece. The Coining Press-room of the Royal Mint is Britain's Klondike, for within its four walls every gold and silver coin in general circulation in the United Kingdom is made.

The machines, to each of which there is but one operator, stand side by side. The blanks flow in from a receptacle one by one, and, behold: m the twinkling of an eye they fall into a little tray below, a finished coin of the realm.

Our final visit in our walk through the Mint is to the Weighing-room. In this extraordinary hive of industry from three to four hundred thousand pounds' worth of money is weighed in a day by machines which are not to be found in any other part of Great Britain, save at the Bank of England, for they not only retain the good coins, but they throw out the light and the heavy. Faulty coins are re-melted. Having been weighed, the gold money goes to the "ringers"—boys who test each coin by throwing it down on a steel block. Boys are also utilised for overlooking the silver coins.

The gold is now put up into £1,000 bags and stored in the Strong-room. The following day a van arrives from the Bank of England, and the money is quietly taken away. With silver and bronze the case is different. Coins made of these metals are counted by a wonderful machine, which in one way is a good deal more than human, for although it sometimes counts a ton of bronze

coins in the brief space of sixty minutes, it never makes a mistake. It is only on silver and bronze coins that the Mint earns a profit. On gold there is considerable loss; but on silver and bronze the profit is large silver being coined into any denomination at a fixed rate of five shillings and sixpence per ounce.

It is important to note that none of the gold in the Royal Mint belongs to the Government. It is the property for the time being of the directors of the Bank of England, who, whenever they require an addition to their stock of sovereigns and half-sovereigns, send a supply of bullion to the Mint, where it is turned into coins at the expense of the Government. The Bank pays nothing for the manufacture of its gold money.

Thus are the King's coins brought into the world. It may be remarked, in conclusion, that a high wall surrounds the Royal Mint, and that inside the wall there is a military path where sentinels—soldiers quartered at the Tower—are posted night and day.

IN THE COINING PRESS-ROOM.

LONDON STREET CHARACTERS.

By L. B. O'BRIEN.

"PIT' THE POOR BLIND!"

"A MAN likes 'is liberty!" That was 'is answer, sturdily given, when they asked him to go to the workhouse. He is an old man. His beard is silver. His sight is almost completely gone, and one leg is weak. But a Briton he is to the backbone, to freeze in winter and bake in summer —a free man always—under the grey walls of the National Portrait Gallery rather than become the guest of the Camberwell ratepayers.

The Metropolis is dotted with his brethren. It is noon. Turn into St. Paul's Churchyard. The grand old Cathedral stands for permanence, almost for eternity, whilst the hundreds hurrying to and fro through the close seem bent on throttling Time in the effort to keep pace with business. There is a grim figure on the pavement, his massive head and shoulders well above the jostling crowd. He wears a short white blouse, and the people open their ranks to him as though he were a prince. He is only a blind man, but better known in the City than the King's Prime Minister. Hush! and hear him speak: "Kind friends, buy a box of lights, poor blind!" "Kind friends, pit' the poor blind!" —this in a shrill, monotonous sing-song. He stands a minute or two, perhaps to rest, perhaps awaiting the help he pleads for. Then his iron-tipped stick beats imperiously on the pavement—tap! tap! tap! tap!—as he moves westward in his daily walk from the centre of business to the centre of fashion.

Most street characters stand or sit at a particular spot. But the blind Hercules in the white blouse spends all his time trudging backwards and forwards between Piccadilly and Cheapside. He often performs the journey between the City and the West-End twice a day. For an hour or two late in the afternoon he is lost to us. But as the night glides on, and pleasure-seekers pour out of theatre and restaurant, his haunting plaint is sometimes heard in Leicester Square —its pathos deepened by the feast of colour, the rich flood of glittering life and movement, which are buried, so to speak, from the hapless mendicant behind barricades of impalpable ebony.

Comedy has its popular representative in the highways in the person of smiling John Chinaman. Everybody knows him! He has no regular beat. To-day he is making acquaintances in Euston Road, to-morrow in Lewisham. Long ago he came from the East, and started life among us as an assistant in a tea warehouse. He was lost in the tea house. But as a man of the world— friend to all mankind, especially to himself —he justifies the pains Nature took with his moulding. He is our own Li Hung Chang. And the police are the Great Powers he has to keep in good humour. He is a

FROM CANTON.

tattered, picturesque gift from Canton, and on Canton he is always ready to dilate in the elegant jargon which he has adapted for his personal use from the smithereens of the King's English.

The street character is not, as a rule, uncertain in his movements. The Montenegrin in full national costume is, however, rather an exception to this rule. But, on the other hand, "Blind Jack," who stands outside Devonshire House, is seldom absent from his post. He is lucky in having the sanction of the police to seek for help in such a quarter; for sixpenny pieces and bright shillings are very small change indeed to many of those who, sauntering through Piccadilly, halt to greet this humble pensioner of the bounty of the tender-hearted. He differs from most of his brethren in being a man with an accomplishment, for he presides in a Marylebone church on Sundays at the organ bellows. In London it is quite unusual to see a dog guide a blind man. And amongst the best-known street characters there is only one partnership of the kind. To the Upper Street, Islington, on Saturday nights resorts the poor fellow who sits in a trolley selling matches. He has no legs, and contrives to work himself along with his hands. In a sort of tricycle chair, in the Seven Sisters Road, sits a cripple who loves his pipe. Near the Army and Navy Stores in Victoria Street a paralysed man manages to eke out a living, using a little vehicle mounted on what looks like a perambulator frame to hold his stock-in-trade. An industrious cripple woman sews untiringly in Stroud Green Road. But one of the most charming characters in our whole gallery is the old lady who wanders day after day to Clarence Gate, Regent's Park, to do her knitting. In her gipsy bonnet, white apron, and comfortable cloak she is a model of homely neatness. For years the Park has been her workshop, and now Clarence Gate looks lonely when she is absent. Long may she ply her needle there—a quaint, peaceful, old-fashioned figure whose proper setting would be the doorway of a straw-thatched cabin in a Munster vale.

The inevitable isolation of the deaf and dumb men who, with placards on their breasts, wander through the streets of London makes their situation singularly painful. To judge by appearances, they are almost always steeped in the most abject poverty. A whole troop of street characters, in company with a wife or partner or child, use the barrel organ to bring their misfortunes under the notice of the public. There is an emaciated man in the advanced stages of consumption. A card hung on his organ explains his trouble. There is the boot-finisher who has lost his sight, the cabinet-maker struck with paralysis, the "export packer," a chronic invalid, and the man who contracted hip disease through a fall downstairs in childhood. Each has recourse to organ-grinding for a living. Usually the placard contains, besides an appeal for charity, a few words explaining what the man has been and the cause of his helplessness. But the armless man who lost his limbs in a factory explosion is up-to-date in his methods, for he has pictures on his organ illustrating the accident.

See Regent Street and die—but it must be on an afternoon in the season, and not on Saturday, else you die in vain. It is almost as true to life as a scene in a first-class theatre! The women, the jewels, the pictures, the silks, the gowns, the hats, the furs—and one or two men, perhaps—are all worthy of immortality. Then the shadow creeps into the picture. It is a man with a board on his chest—that ghastly board always reminding one somehow of a graveyard stone! He is blind. Take his hand, and lead him across the street. He speaks a word of thanks in a pleasant voice, and his accent is unlike that of your other friends who garner their daily bread on the pavement. He is a German. His fair, handsome face hardens a little as he says it, as though he expected the confession to alienate sympathy. Pride was perhaps a stumbling block in his path in the fulness of health; but this symptom of it is almost lovable in the victim of crushing calamities.

He was a teacher of languages. A day came when the page was blurred, and a darker day still when he awoke to pitchy night—blind beyond hope of cure. Into the bread-winner's shoes at once stepped the wife. She opened a little shop in a humble street, and hard work and thrift kept the wolf from the hearth if not from the door. But the cup was not full! The brave woman, battling with feminine tenacity to save her home, was prostrated with an incurable disease. And just when Heaven seemed to have done its worst earth took the scourge into its hands. The house had to be vacated. Out went the blind German and his family

A BUSY CRIPPLE (STROUD GREEN ROAD).

BLIND (REGENT STREET).

BLIND (REGENT STREET).

PARALYSED (VICTORIA STREET).

"MATCHES AND LACES!"

BLIND (ST. MARTIN'S CHURCH STEPS).

CRIPPLED (REGENT STREET).

"BLIND JACK" (PICCADILLY).

lace vendor who is often seen in Farringdon
Street has had both legs amputated from
below the knee. Once he was a stalwart
man. He looks a sturdy fellow yet, one
who was made for action. But Fortune—
misfortune—has crossed his destiny.

Persons of education are few amongst the
more familiar characters of the streets. The
blind lady who sits on the steps of St.
Martin's Church, and reads with her fingers
the Bible and other literature, was the
daughter of a police inspector. She was
educated with a view to becoming a
governess. Another well-known literary
figure is that of an old blind man who
sits near Parr's Bank, Regent Street, reading
his Bible.

We are in the Haymarket now. A Juliet of

into the street, and there he now finds his
friends!

A few yards farther off—still in Regent
Street—you come upon one whom an
Academician might paint as the ideal type
of him who has seen better days. There
are plenty of legislators of less pleasing
appearance. He wears a silk hat and caped
overcoat. Every afternoon he takes up his
station near the same spot, except in very
severe weather, when he shelters himself
just round the corner of a convenient side
street. The crippled match-seller of Regent
Street is a sad sight; an accident in a
Staffordshire coal mine has condemned him
to the ranks of the stricken. The match and

CRIPPLED (SEVEN SISTERS ROAD).

thirty years ago passes, Juliet old and
shrivelled and deserted by Romeo, or perhaps Romeo died when the sun was shining
brightly and the world was very fair. Now
she is a street character in search of help
and pity, though she hides it from herself.
How pretty she once was! Then the sharp
little curved chin was rounded daintily with
dimpling flesh, and the glow of warm blood
was often in her cheeks. They are hollow
cheeks now. Thin grey hair falls in sorry
curls on her shoulders. Her faded blue
eyes are diverted shyly when they have

ON WHEELS.

A VETERAN (FARRINGDON STREET STATION).

caught the looked-for glance of pity; once a coquette, always. It is comical even while it is inexpressibly sad.

Another dainty little lady is she who sells studs and bootlaces at the east corner of the British Museum. She is a fragile creature, no taller than a man's elbow. Hail, rain, or snow, she is at her post, and conducts her sales with a dignity and directness that would do credit to Bond Street. At Farringdon Street station a veteran plies the same sort of trade, only that he includes pipe-cleaners in his stock, which is set out on a tray suspended from his neck. On Saturdays he is seldom far from the station. On ordinary weekdays he occasionally goes prospecting in other parts of the district. Farther east, in the neighbourhood of Finsbury Pavement, one comes upon a poor sightless fellow, the victim of a historic dynamite explosion. A brass plate hung upon his chest tells the story. Whitechapel, too, has its maimed dependant upon the match and bootlace industry. His infirmities compel him to ply his trade seated in a sort of bath chair.

Should Lord Tom Noddy in a fit of extravagance ride on a 'bus from Hyde Park Corner to the City he can buy a box of matches at Piccadilly Circus without alighting. The Circus has for years past been frequented

by a man who passes up matches and button-holes to omnibus passengers on the end of a long pole. This good Samaritan does not restrict his humanitarian zeal to Piccadilly. You find him manipulating his wand in Oxford Circus, at the Marble Arch, and at a dozen other places. He is a useful fellow. It is never a luxury to descend from the top of a 'bus. To do so for a box of matches would be heroic—indeed, Homeric.

There is a woman who sells matches at Charing Cross. What a romance is hers! She is old, but her figure is youthful still, and her big brown eyes can sparkle at times. Thirty years ago she was a pretty girl. Men looked after her as she tripped through the streets. Then she was a leading hand in a West-End costumier's. The frills and fripperies, the bows and rosettes, that make a débutante's gown bewitching were her speciality—now it is a box of matches.

In time she had a home and a husband.

"I never left 'im without 'is meals . . . never . . . And now I'm 'ere . . . 'is doing . . . I think 'e's dead . . . Wish I knew!" . . .

For several years she has sold matches at Charing Cross. Several long years! Yet she still remembers to herself with pride that she never forgot what was due to her

WITH THE AID OF A POLE.

lord's healthy appetite. And one fine day he went out with his milk-cart, for he was a milkman—and he has not yet come home.

Every day for many years a blind man has posted himself at the Russell Square end of Southampton Row. There he sits till late in the evening, a little cup hung round his neck for the coppers of the charitable. From infancy his eyes were weak. He became a hotel porter. Year by year his sight grew worse. The crisis came when in one day

WELL KNOWN AT CHARING CROSS.

to Heaven. They drift from mansion and hovel, from kitchen and factory, from boudoir and counter, from office and camp and stage, and the Spar of our Mercy is their only hope—too often, alas! an elusive spar, a sickening hope, an ever-fleeting mirage. Too often the shrivelled hand is outstretched in vain; the suppliant voice melts in the babble of the crowd, the hungry eyes plead to cuirasses of steel. From day to day recruits glide into the ranks, and now and again the frantic struggle ends,

he had to grope his way through the passages as though it were twilight. He tripped over boxes and stumbled upstairs; faces he should have recognised were strange to him. "What's the matter?" they said. What was the matter! The porter was blind. That was all.

Such are they—toll collectors on the road

and a tired wastrel goes down to rest beneath the waves of the world, leaving not an eddy behind, not a ripple, not a wrinkle on the face of the pitiless waters. It is the working of the Wheel of Life breaking human hearts — torturing souls; and why such things must be God alone knows. We can but love, and help, and pity

IN QUAINT ATTIRE (CLARENCE GATE, REGENT'S PARK).

MY LADY'S EVENING IN LONDON.

By MRS. ARIA.

"MONSIEUR HENRI not come yet?" and My Lady lifts her head from the latest edition of the *Globe* she is reading, while sitting in front of her looking-glass with her luxuriant locks in simple disorder.

And at that moment Justine announces, "The hairdresser is here," with all the portentous solemnity that the butler would say, "Madam is served," and My Lady closes the paper at once to greet the Frenchman, knowing that while he dresses her hair she will not lack food for the mind; for now, even as yesterday and the day before, does the barber temper the prose of his occupation with the poetry of scandal.

The hairdressing is soon over, the skilful fingers of the *coiffeur* have laid the locks of My Lady in shining waves, and twisted them into a coil at the nape of the neck, and clasped them with glittering diamonds; then, placing his feet together, he has bowed his adieux with all characteristic gravity.

The evening dress of softest chiffon and rarest lace is slipped over that sleek head, pearls are placed round the fair throat, the corsage shines with diamonds, the final puff of powder is applied to the glowing cheeks. Justine wraps

PREPARATION.

around her a lace cloak, and My Lady is ready to meet her husband in the hall and start for her evening entertainment. It has been a hurried dressing, for an early dinner is to be the preliminary to a gala night of much feasting and festivity.

The brougham is at the door, My Lord has been assisted to the adjustment of his coat to a nicety, after a careful survey of the effect in the mirror, and they are prepared to start for that corner table of their favourite restaurant, where behind a glass screen the attentive waiter soon gives evidence that he knows his customers and would attend to them well—would do even as it is advised we should all do, as he would be done by.

The little dinner is served with rapidity, and coffee and Kümmel are placed before them within thirty minutes of their arrival, and they are off to the Lyceum Theatre, for it is the first night after the return of Sir Henry Irving from one of his American trips, and all the world of wealth and fashion is to meet to hear and join in the tumultuous shouts of welcome which will greet the great actor when he steps once more upon the boards in London. The broad steps of the entrance are thronged with people, the aide-de-camp of the chief of British actors is receiving

A LYCEUM RECEPTION AND STAGE SUPPER.

all with courtesy and kindness. "Sir Henry will be delighted to see you on the stage after the performance" is whispered into the ear of My Lady, who feels inordinately proud of the privilege.

The lights are lowered and the play has begun, and the clapping in the stalls has been rapturously echoed in the gallery, when the best-beloved actor of his day comes forward to prove again his right to be regarded as the greatest artist. Between the acts the well-known in the world of Art and Letters exchange their greetings, and My Lady is confidentially told by a dramatist on her left that the new play at such-and-such a theatre was not a success because the acting was so bad, while during the second interval she learns from a leading light in the histrionic firmament that the real reason for its failure was because the author could not be made to see how stupid was his story and how dull was his dialogue. The appointment of a prominent painter to the Hanging Committee of the Royal Academy is the next news which reaches her. "The ideal man," "Too much of a crank for the position," "One of the fairest judges, he has no prejudices," is he voted alternately, and always with conviction.

When the play is over, and the storm of applause has subsided, and the few courteous words of acknowledgment have been spoken by Sir Henry, the curtains are drawn, and gossip takes place in the stalls, where there is much rustling in and out of cloaks when the invitation to go on the stage is forthcoming.

And what a change is there, my countrymen! The palace garden has disappeared, and on "such a night as this," outlining the back cloth in formal row, are there tables set with glittering silver and tempting food, presided over by eager black-coated waiters. A very quick transformation it has been, for already groups of people are standing about, hoping for a word with their host, who indeed seems to be here, there, and everywhere, greeting all with gracious gladness. To the side of My Lady he comes, to remember to ask after her prowess in golf, and to compliment her husband on his recent achievements in the war; then he is seized upon by a dignitary of the Church—and with what respectful

72

interest each attends to the other!—a distinguished lady novelist, whose advanced views are always advancing, finds in him a sympathetic listener; while the hero-struck girl, who is introduced by her proud parent, declares his smile "divine"; and when that friendly hand is laid upon his shoulder the enthusiastic schoolboy becomes at once and for ever a devoted disciple. The Minister of State drinks a glass of champagne to

READY.

Sir Henry's health; the gushing young lady is promised the autograph she seeks; and the young actor is encouraged by a word from the chief, who truly contrives to say the right word in the right tone to everybody.

My Lady follows the crowd which surrounds Miss Ellen Terry, and even after the fatigues of her work she finds the great actress in the highest spirits, and gay as a girl in her joyous welcome and responding sympathetic ally to My Lady's complaint:

"I'm so sorry we must hurry away; it is hard to leave this throng of interesting people, but we are bound to that reception at the Carlton Hotel, where Lady A. has arranged to receive her friends at supper, and an

"TITIVATING."

amateur finance committee is to sit upon the question of expenses at an amateur theatrical entertainment, given to-night in aid of a deserving charity."

Lightly stepping through the glass-covered portals of the hotel, My Lady hurries to the right into the little room, where the powder-puff may be indulged in without fear of notice, the faithful maid-maiden divests her of her cloak, and the hurried inspection into the looking-glass shows that so far the revels of the evening have not left any unbecoming traces upon her face.

Amid the garden of palms there are lounging and smoking many men of their acquaintance. There is Lord George, who is just back from Africa, and there is Charley L., full of enthusiasm over the splendid riding of his favourite jockey that afternoon, while Mrs. F. rushes forward to urge My Lady to confide to her where she bought her beautiful gown, and to ask her whether it is really true that the dresses at

a certain establishment in London are all stitched and made up in Paris. "You are only fitted here, my dear, I am told, and everything else is done in France."

They move to meet their hostess, Lady A., who is gowned in pale mauve velvet, and wearing all the diamonds which unkind gossip has credited to the possession of the family financier.

My Lady and her husband are soon directed to their places at the table, where it would seem they are the last arrivals. Animated conversation is being carried on about the wonderful theatrical entertainment which has been graced by all the favourites of Society, and there may be heard such comments as, "Miss N. ought really to make the stage her profession"; and "Lady S.'s manners are delightful; but don't you think her enthusiasm as a programme-seller might have been tempered with a little discretion?—her attitude was really too solicitous," and so on and so on.

However, the show has realised an amount of some thousands of pounds, and who shall say that charity does not number amongst the sins it covers an opportunity of gossip about our neighbour?

"We are really perfect slaves to-night," complains My Lady to Lady A. "I vowed I would dance at the Duchess of G.'s cotillon, and one o'clock is the hour arranged for, and it is a quarter to one now! I must be off; and it is so delightful here—you are surrounded by such amusing people."

"Yes, they are very kind; £5,000, I believe, we have raised to-night one way and the other, and the expenses were not quite £4,000."

My Lady says nothing, but thinks much, and, smiling her farewell, seeks again the little dressing-room, to drag her lace and chiffon mantle from beneath a myriad of cloaks and to hurry once more into the brougham, followed by the faithful one, whose duty as pioneer does not prevent him from saying, with almost pathetic emphasis, "I should have liked to finish my supper—that new salad was rippin'."

The hall door at — Curzon Street is thrown open, the silken stockings and powdered heads of the footmen proclaim the exalted position of their mistress, and My

Lady is at once mounting the tapestry-hung staircase, where, in a palm-shaded alcove, there sit those popular minstrels known as the Blue Hungarians, and called by Owen Hall "the band from Blue Hungary." She meets the Duchess half-way, and receives an enthusiastic "I was just becoming nervous lest you should disappoint us."

"As if I would," she replies, "when I had specially promised you, dear; and do not think I have a soul above presents either," she continues merrily. "I will be three moments getting ready, and you can warn the dancers, if I am really the last to come."

Soon the cotillon is in full swing, and no greater fun is evolved from any than from the old Mirror figure, and My Lady's hesitation, deliberation, and final selection are made with much coquetry. The postillions gallop round the room in fine style, Bluebeard's wives are chosen with great wariness, and My Lady finds herself possessed of a little gold looking-glass set with turquoise and more flowers than she can conveniently carry.

"It is charming here; I wish I could stay longer, but I am bound to go on to a reception—I ought to have been there an hour ago. If I only just put in my appearance I shall have done my duty towards my husband. You know it is for his sake I am going, for I do not want him to be sent out again; and it is rumoured that Sir S. is to retire from public life, and — well, vacancies must be filled, and there is a social side to every political question, and women rule the world, or at least we all think so — so you will excuse me, won't you?"

They are off again and within a very few moments at a well-known house in Picca-

dilly, where there is such a getting upstairs as would recall the doubtful pleasures of a Lord Mayor's Day spent on foot in the City. Shoulder to shoulder they fight for every step, the downcomers and the upgoers seem as if they would never extricate themselves; and a weary woman is to be found standing at the top, patiently saying, "How

AT THE RECEPTION.

do you do?" and "Good-bye" to the people who are pressing round her—occasionally, it must be admitted, greeting those who are just arriving and speeding the parting guest with convincing courtesy.

My Lady diplomatically fights and struggles until she succeeds in effecting the most casual meeting between her husband and *the* authority, and then turns to sympathise with her hostess on her fatigue. She has been standing there—poor lady!—for three mortal hours, with never a bite or sup: a social heroine of no mean parts. My Lady remains near her in silence, realising that nothing as a guest could so well become her as the leaving of such a tired hostess; yet she herself is still thrilling with the excitement of the cotillon, and feeling as if fatigue were an unknown possibility.

"I hate the idea of going home," she says to her husband when they are once more settled in the carriage; "it is so dull to go there, and I want something exciting to take place. Here is a beautiful dawn in a world alive, and I am to shut it all out, to sleep when the earth is awaking."

But the clattering hoofs of a galloping team may be heard amidst masculine shouts, and "A fire! a fire!" shrieks My Lady with delight; "just the very thing! Follow them, Johnson!" she cries to the coachman.

Past the Park they rush, waking the echoes of the silent Edgware Road, the inhabitants of a sleepful Maida Vale, and on, on they tear through a hushed world of villas set in green gardens, till they come to a small side street where there is assembled a small knot of anxious, silent

people, and the engines are blocking the way, the pavements are wet with tortuous lines of leather piping, and a slight smoke in the distance shows that the conflagration is exhausting itself, when the sight of a stalwart young fireman being lifted into a cab freezes My Lady's warm excitement into cold terror.

"Is he hurt?" she asks.

"Only stifled a bit by the smoke, ma'am, and he's broke his arm, I think; he got down the child that was burnt."

My Lady's mood has changed; she is no longer eager, glad, and gay—she shivers with the cold of the early dawn; the careless gaieties of the early evening are blotted out by this woful tragedy of human suffering; and she turns to her husband, "I am so tired, let us go home."

The horse's head is turned, and they reach their door just as the grey dawn is growing pink, and the birds in the Park are beginning their joyous song. My Lady's evening is done, and her day has risen, and My Lord, divesting himself of his overcoat, murmurs thankfully to himself,

"To-morrow is my evening at the club."

THE COTILLON.

BIRKBECK INSTITUTION: IN THE LABORATORY.

INSTITUTE LONDON.

By HUGH B. PHILPOTT.

THERE are few modern developments of London life that have so excellent a record and are so full of hope for the future as those we may conveniently group under the heading "Institute London," a term which, for the purpose of this article, must be held to include all those institutes of a partly educational and partly recreative character which have been established in the interests of young men and women of narrow means. Such institutions are now to be found in every part of London, for recent years have seen a great increase in their number; and to the many thousands who take advantage of them they prove a genuine boon.

All kinds of tastes and dispositions are catered for. Educational classes of almost endless variety, well-equipped workshops and laboratories, libraries, reading rooms, lectures, concerts, gymnasia, swimming baths, and athletic clubs galore are all at the service of a member of one of the great London institutes, at a cost that is often less than

that of the fire and lights he would require if he elected to spend his evenings in the dreary loneliness of London lodgings.

Of course, it is not every institute that offers all these varied attractions, though several of them do. Sometimes they concentrate their efforts on particular lines. Thus at the Birkbeck Institution, the oldest and one of the best known of any, there are no trade classes. But there is a very wide range of classes in scientific, commercial, and artistic subjects. Clerks, teachers, and candidates for the Civil Service form the bulk of the students at the Birkbeck, and much of the instruction given is of a very advanced character. In the laboratory especially, which is one of the best equipped in London, some very thorough work is done, and every facility is given for original research. No one goes to the Birkbeck for any other purpose than that of serious study. There is a quiet, thoughtful air about the place that would quickly frighten away those intent merely on pleasure. On Wednesday evenings the students unbend a little, and attend, with their friends, a lecture or entertainment of a popular though high-class character, but, with this exception, no provision is made at the Birkbeck for anything more frivolous than a game of chess or a cup of tea.

Of a very different character is the Polytechnic in Regent Street, the most popular and many-sided of all London institutes. It has 17,000 members; and it would not be easy to think of any legitimate human

men—entering or leaving the building, or stopping to chat with friends. At each side of the hall are long counters, behind which a number of clerks are busily engaged issuing tickets for classes and concerts, conducting the business of the Friendly Society, the Employment Bureau, the Savings Bank, and the Co-operative Holiday Trips, and generally imparting information on the various departments of the Polytechnic work. In the middle of the hall is a glass case containing cups and other athletic trophies won by

Photo, Brown, Gear & Co. Great Portland Street, W.
POLYTECHNIC, REGENT STREET : CARRIAGE-BUILDING CLASS.

interest for which it does not cater. It is an educational institute, affording technical as well as commercial and scientific instruction. The carriage-building class, which we illustrate, is one of the many trade classes which give young workmen a thorough theoretical and practical training in the calling in which they are actually engaged during the day. The Polytechnic, however, is much more than an educational institution. As soon as we pass through the entrance doors in Regent Street we get a fair impression of its wonderfully varied activities. We are in a spacious mosaic-paved vestibule, which proclaims, by means of the allegorical frescoes on its walls, the work and aims of the institution. If it be the evening of any working day the vestibule will be thronged with people—mostly young

"Poly boys," among whom are some of the most famous athletes of the day. In the entrance hall are always to be found one or more members of the Reception Committee prepared to welcome new members and show visitors over the institute.

For the Polytechnic is, above all things, a social club. To other institutes men go to learn this subject or that, and when the class is over return to their homes, caring little for the institute as such, and taking no interest in other branches of its work. At the Polytechnic everyone who enters seems to be surrounded by an atmosphere of good-fellowship. A man may be as diligent a student here as elsewhere, but, unless he be a singularly misanthropic person, he will not have been very long at the institute before he has grappled to his soul a few true and loyal friends, and become a devoted member of the great "Poly" clan, which has adherents in all parts of the world.

All the newer polytechnics have many features in common with the Regent Street institution, which has, indeed, served to some extent as the model for them, though each one has some features peculiar to itself.

Polytechnic at Chelsea, the development has been chiefly along educational lines, athletics and social life being entirely, or to a great extent, neglected.

Some, perhaps, will be surprised to find the People's Palace included in this category. To many the name suggests a great "Palace of Delight," like that described in Sir Walter

PEOPLE'S PALACE : SATURDAY EVENING IN THE WINTER GARDEN.

Probably the Woolwich Polytechnic is the institute which has most closely followed the original model ; and this is not surprising, seeing that it owes its existence to the efforts of Mr. Quintin Hogg, the founder of the Regent Street institute and the pioneer of the polytechnic movement. In some instances, as at the People's Palace in the Mile End Road, the Northern Polytechnic Institute at Holloway, the Battersea Polytechnic, the Municipal Technical Institute at West Ham, and the South-Western

Besant's "All Sorts and Conditions of Men," a book which undoubtedly helped, in the early stages of the undertaking, to promote its progress. It is true that the People's Palace is in a district where there are wider scope and greater need for a popular institution than almost anywhere else in London. But the idea of the governing body is that they can render the most valuable service to the people of the neighbourhood by providing educational facilities of the highest class. And so, after undergoing considerable

BOROUGH POLYTECHNIC INSTITUTE : BAKERY AND CONFECTIONERY CLASS.

vicissitudes, the People's Palace has settled down to a strictly educational work, which it carries on with singular success.

It is certainly remarkable that this East-End polytechnic should have achieved, through its students, higher scholastic distinctions than almost any similar institution. Several open scholarships at the Universities have been won by People's Palace students, and it is noteworthy that all these successful students, as well as many who have gained high honours at London University, are distinctly the products of the People's Palace educational system, having obtained all their education, since leaving an elementary school, in its day or evening classes.

It must not be supposed, however, that the extensive buildings are wholly and always given over to the comparatively few studious people who join the educational classes. At two or three points the institution touches the wider and more varied life of the district. In the great Queen's Hall entertainments and concerts of a popular character are given, and on such occasions the adjoining winter garden—a great iron and glass structure containing palms and other tropical plants—is used as a promenade,

and presents an animated picture of varied life. The gymnasium in winter and the swimming bath in summer are much patronised by those in search of healthful exercise; and in the reading room and library, which are free to all, many types of East-End life may be met with.

At the Northern Polytechnic and the South-Western Polytechnic we find the educational work even more exclusively the object of attention. Both institutions have modern and well-equipped buildings. At Holloway the building trade classes are the most notable feature of the work. These are very varied and complete. One can wander from class room to drawing office, and from drawing office to workshop, observing in actual operation nearly all the processes involved in the building of a cottage or a cathedral. The institute at Chelsea has distinguished itself by providing definite and systematic preparation for a career which few educational institutes seem to take into their calculations, a career which, nevertheless, is neither unimportant nor unpopular—that, namely, of wife and mother. In the Home Training Department women can undergo a complete course of study in such subjects as cookery, household management, dressmaking, sick nursing, physiology, hygiene, logic, account keeping, and general matters connected with children. This polytechnic is specially strong in women's subjects. Another interesting department provides training for women teachers of gymnastics; the martial exercises shown in the illustration on p. 195 forming the most picturesque, though not the most important, item in a very complete curriculum.

The social side of life is more cultivated at the Northampton Institute in Clerkenwell and the Borough Polytechnic Institute. Both these are primarily educational; but, in addition, many societies and clubs are organised to stimulate friendly intercourse amongst members, and enable them to ride almost any reasonable hobby they happen to favour. The Northampton Institute is planned and equipped on the most lavish scale. The classes are all of a technical and trade character; the work of the institute being complementary to that of the Birkbeck (scientific and literary) and City of London College (commercial); the three institutes together forming the City Polytechnic. It is a remarkable variety of trades that is taught at the Northampton Institute; and a walk through the workshops any evening is an interesting and encouraging

sight, when it is remembered that all these young men and women are not amateurs, but are actually engaged during the day in the trades they so assiduously study at night, and are thus seeking to perpetuate the best traditions of intelligent and skilful workmanship in British industries. In many of the classes—such as the brick cutting one, which we illustrate—the student gains an insight into the most advanced branches of his craft, and thus fits himself to undertake duties of which the workman who has had no such training is incapable. At the Borough Polytechnic the educational classes cover a wider range; but here, also, special attention is paid to trade teaching. An interesting feature, it may be added, is the fully equipped school of bakery and confectionery.

But for a thoroughly healthy social life mingled with the highest educational efficiency one cannot do better than go to the Goldsmiths' Institute at New Cross. Scarcely anywhere else have the two elements in institute life been quite so judiciously and successfully combined. Whether it is due to an exceptionally clubable spirit among the inhabitants of South-East London, or to the peculiar and

NORTHAMPTON INSTITUTE: BRICK-CUTTING CLASS.

WORKING MEN'S COLLEGE, GREAT ORMOND STREET : A DEBATE.

varied gifts of the secretary, the fact remains that the Goldsmiths' Institute is characterised by the same sociable, friendly spirit, the same *esprit de corps*, which we have remarked as existing at Regent Street. There is, however, this very important difference—that whereas the Regent Street Polytechnic is a young men's club, the Goldsmiths' Institute is a club for young women as well, and even for those who can no longer in a strictly literal sense be described as young. The Goldsmiths' Institute may not inaptly be called the Family Polytechnic. Fathers and mothers, whose sons or daughters are attending classes, are encouraged to join the institute themselves; and there have been cases of whole families becoming members. One thing which very greatly helps to keep the members together and attach them more closely to the institute is the fact that, alone among similar institutions in London, the Goldsmiths' Institute is in the happy position of having ample recreative grounds adjoining the building itself. There is a fine cricket field and bowling lawn encircled by a cinder track for running and cycling; there are also asphalt courts for tennis and quoits. With such attractions, in addition to the fine swimming bath and the reading and social rooms, it is not surprising that institute life is maintained in full vigour throughout the

year, instead of falling off, as is so often the case, when the classes close for the summer months.

A well known institution that is unique in character is the Working Men's College in Great Ormond Street. Founded by Frederick Denison Maurice, before the days of school boards or polytechnics, with the object of affording a liberal education and an elevating and humanising club life for working men, the college has numbered amongst its voluntary teachers such famous men as John Ruskin, Dante Gabriel Rossetti, Ford Madox-Brown, Sir Edward Burne-Jones, and Sir John R. Seely. The spread of education has necessarily changed to some extent the character of the work; but it is interesting to find that, while much of the teaching is of an advanced character, there are still men of mature years who, conscious of their deficiencies, but shy of exposing them in ordinary educational institutions, go willingly to the Working Men's College for elementary instruction. They find there a sympathy and a spirit of comradeship they might seek in vain elsewhere.

The characteristic life of the place is best observed in the Common Room, where men of varied types and many social classes mingle in friendly converse—University men, who have been lecturing or conducting classes, mechanics, law students, City clerks, and shop assistants. A typical feature is the Debating Society, which is surely the cheapest one of the kind in the world. If you are a student of the college you may become a life member of the Debating Society for the sum of one shilling; and that modest payment will entitle you, not only to attend the society's meetings, but also to smoke its tobacco during the progress of the debate.

In this brief survey of London institutes it is not possible to dwell at length on the work of the Young Men's Christian Association, which has its headquarters at Exeter Hall, and branches at Aldersgate Street and Cornhill, as well as in several of the suburbs. But among many interesting features this unique characteristic may be mentioned—that it has branches all over the civilised world, so that a young man who joins in London can, without further formality than a letter from the secretary, continue his membership in Calcutta or New York or Cape Town. The Young Women's Christian Association, which is run on very similar lines, caters in an admirably sympathetic and liberal spirit for the needs of young women of many different classes, and possesses at its headquarters in George Street, Hanover Square, some of the most comfortable and home-like club premises to be found in London. Nor is it possible even to mention the almost numberless institutes connected with churches and chapels—though some few of them, as, for instance, the Westbourne Park Institute, attain almost to the dimensions of a polytechnic—or the almost equally numerous clubs and institutes for working boys, of which the Telegraph Messengers' Institute in Throgmorton Avenue may be taken as a good type. Of these it must suffice to say that whilst they vary greatly in their methods, and to some extent in their aims, they are all sharing in varying degrees in a movement which makes strongly for a fuller, brighter, and nobler life for hundreds of thousands of workers in the great city.

SOUTH-WESTERN POLYTECHNIC: WOMEN'S FENCING CLASS.

REMOVING STREET REFUSE.

LONDON'S TOILET.

By P. F. WILLIAM RYAN.

DUSTMAN.

BEFORE we walk out into the highways and by-ways to look upon London in the hands of its cleansers, it is well to take as it were a bird's-eye view of the vastness of their task. The metropolitan area covers more than a hundred square miles and contains approximately thirty thousand streets, or about six hundred thousand houses, which if wheeled into line would extend across Europe and Asia, uniting the Thames with the Great Wall of China. No man knows every quarter of the capital. But its dingiest alleys as well as its most fashionable avenues are cared for at stated times by the municipal scavengers. As we pass through the streets it is possible to note only the most striking scenes in the routine of their work. But nearly every scene has a hundred counterparts; some have a thousand!

Most people are in their first sleep when the toilet of London is taken in hand. It has gone midnight; the deserted thoroughfares glisten under the gas or electric light, as though a heavy shower had fallen. The watering-carts have been doing duty for the clouds. In three-quarters of an hour after the bustle of the night has subsided the pavements are completely saturated. Some of the watering-carts waddle and waddle slowly. They are of the old-fashioned order. But when the motor watering-cart is used to soften the carpet of grease which overlays the streets after the day's traffic the work is disposed of more expeditiously.

Regent Street having its bath is a sight for gods and schoolboys. It is the dandy of West-End avenues. The men who valet it feel the seriousness of their office. In the words of a master of the ceremonies, "Hit hisn't clean till you could eat your vittles hoff hit!"

There is a dull red lamp in the middle of the street. Advancing, you hear a noise as of a million gallons of soda water "sizzling" madly. Beside the red lamp the water-main has been tapped by a great length of hose. At the loose end of the hose, twenty, thirty, forty yards away, is a nozzle—and a man. The man is having a glorious time, for the nozzle is a playful weapon. As he aims high and low he sends seas of water flying over the pavement. To be in his place many a mother's darling would give half his head! When the nozzle is lowered within a few inches of the ground, quaint, foamy waves rise round the operator's feet—wet feet, very likely. But the ricochet performance is, from the gallery standpoint, the nozzle-man's finest effort. The instrument is held almost horizontally; the water, leaping out like a cable of crystal, grazes the ground far ahead, and, opening in a great fan of spray, baptises the lady and gentleman in the advancing hansom.

Piccadilly has mysterious rites of its own. The frivolous nozzle and the plebeian watering-cart are never seen there. Its delicate complexion stands cold water badly! The aristocratic boulevard must be tickled gingerly by a broom—a horse-broom to begin with. The huge cylinder of bristles is just like what a patriarchal hedgehog must have been in the days when the world bred generous types. The framework in which it revolves is, to the eye of the layman, a medley of iron bars, ugly, bare, and complex, with a sort of cycle-shaped seat for the coachman. And who can do him justice? From head to foot he is cased in waterproof, except, perhaps, his face, which is lost somewhere under his sou'-wester. There is nothing flighty about his horse! For the

CLEANING REGENT STREET AT NIGHT.

thing at his heels is "hover the draft o' 'alf a ton"—a solid subject for equine reflection.

The horse-broom does not penetrate into Piccadilly Circus; for it, too, is in a measure exceptional. It is vulgar enough to endure the attentions of the watering-cart; but the nozzle is taboo. After the watering-cart has had its innings its driver may, if the Fates are propitious, retire to the shelter of a friendly porch and snatch forty winks while the squeegee-men and sweepers deploy for attack. When the horse-broom has done parading Piccadilly, two parallel creases of mud or dry rubbish, according as the day has been wet or fine, run the whole length of the thoroughfare. The road-sweepers break these up into small heaps for the convenience of the men who feed with their shovels the indispensable dust cart.

The squeegee-man deserves to rank as a popular benefactor.

MOTOR WATERING-CART.

For his regular night-work there is no audience; but on a rainy day we all recognise in him a valuable imperial asset. A dozen squeegee-men clearing Ludgate Circus or Oxford Circus on a drenching November day is a sort of hygienic Waterloo—for the mud literally runs before their spirited attack. Imaginative gentlemen sometimes swear that patent leather boots exercise a magnetic influence upon squeegees. Certain it is that the wheels of passing 'buses and cabs fresco wonderful patterns on white collars and aquiline noses, with the help of the gigantic mud-pies they create. But the dust cart soon comes along. Into it are shovelled the mud-pies; and the artistic vagaries of wheeled traffic are checked, to the chagrin of the Comic Spirit.

In the City proper there is practically only a two-hours' interval between the cessation of day-work and the commencement of night-work. The night men are at their posts at eight o'clock; about midnight there is an interval for supper; at six in the morning their spell of labour is finished. The toilet of the Lord Mayor's territory requires the services of between seven and eight hundred hands, including two hundred orderly boys, and no fewer than a hundred horses. The toilet of all London gives employment in round numbers to eight thousand hands. Probably no

ORDERLY BOY.

fewer than twenty thousand persons are dependent directly or indirectly upon this department of municipal work for their daily bread.

For cleansing purposes the City is divided into four districts. There are two foremen for each: one to keep an eye on the sweepers, the other to keep two eyes on the orderly boys. By eight o'clock in the morning the streets of the City are in apple-pie order. At that hour the zinc bins or pails of cinders, which ornamented many door-steps an hour previously, have been emptied into the fifty or sixty dust carts which are detailed for day duty. But before the Corporation employés have gone their rounds the refuse is often overhauled by "chiffoniers."

HORSE-BROOM.

Every free-born Briton is not privileged to put a zinc pail outside his door. But, if he is not amongst the elect, then the dustman pays him a visit during the day. This is the rule in all parts of London. The dustman sometimes condescends to plait a bow of ribbon in his horse's mane. But, more generally, he is a sedate fellow, above such flights of fancy, whose only intellectual enjoyment in business hours is derived from a "tip." The Borough Councils do not approve. But no municipal imprimatur could enhance the spiritual beauty of minted bronze.

The orderly boy is seen in all the principal streets, east as well as west. But he is on his mettle, as it were, in the City. He darts in and out through the traffic as though he were on rail-fellow terms with the hundreds of 'bus and van and cab horses trotting past

STREET SWEEPER.

PICKING UP PAPER IN THE PARKS.

his station. Everyone assumes that he bears a charmed life. And the little fellow, armed with hand-brush and scoop, would feel a slur cast upon his professional reputation if a driver pulled up his team, even when the horses' noses were within an inch of his ear.

He has wonderful luck, as a rule; but sometimes an illustration of the proverb of the pitcher and the well is flashed upon the screen of London street life. At Hyde Park Corner or Temple Bar or Ludgate Hill, wherever, in fact, the fever of London bustle runs highest, a small crowd attracts you. Over the shoulders of the people you catch a glimpse of a boy with soiled clothes stretched on the broad of his back. The dirty little paws still grasp the scoop, on which he has often rattled the devil's tattoo, grinning up at his friends the passing coachmen. The face is pallid now, beneath its layer of dust; the prone figure is the more pathetic, because usually he is such a bright, cheery, little fellow. In a day or two he will probably return from hospital to his post, not a penny the worse for his collision with a hansom, and rather proud of having been on

the casualty list. If the doctors fail to mend him, then he overleaps the years, and attains at a bound the dignity of a pensioner to the tune of ten shillings a week for life.

The City and the West-End are typical of what goes on all over London — with this difference, that, while in the City the routine of the toilet may be said to begin at eight at night, and in the West-End at midnight, in the suburbs the lightness of the traffic precludes the necessity of night work. And, while Westminster keeps 900 men busy, Fulham can manage with 200, and Stoke Newington with fewer.

The crossing-sweeper—Heaven help him! —is the free-lance of the scavenging profession. The accredited grooms of the capital are sturdy fellows. The crossing-sweeper is often a human wreck waiting for Death where meet the effervescing streams of life! Sometimes the match-seller of Saturday is the crossing-sweeper of Sunday: the weather decides his calling. The Moll Whites of old rode the air on a broomstick. With the help of the same sober steed the crossing-sweeper rides calmly through the statutes against begging. Armed with what was once a broom, but with the bristles now worn to the timber, he hardly tries to deceive anybody into the belief that he is a labourer. When night falls he is still at his corner, resting on his broom. He rubs his numbed hands together, and blows upon his fingers —not that he hopes to warm them. It is

CROSSING-SWEEPER : A MUTE APPEAL.

SORTING A DUST-HEAP AT A COUNTY COUNCIL DEPÔT.

only his way of announcing his existence, of inviting your gaze to his sunken, hungry eyes—eyes that follow you home, and peer weirdly into yours, as you smoke before the roaring fire on your own cheerful hearth.

The men who keep the parks in order are, in a sense, the aristocrats of the business. He of the spiked stick, tilting at pieces of paper in Hyde Park, is a Government servant, for his employer is the Office of Works. In addition, however, to the hands permanently employed about Hyde Park, St. James's, the Green Park, and Kensington Gardens, a

OVERHAULING A ZINC BIN.

private contractor is entrusted with the task of keeping the roads in proper order. The contractor's foreman drives through the parks each morning, notes what requires to be done, and puts on the requisite number of men

After a big public demonstration Hyde Park gives its valets many busy hours. In summer time a fair proportion of the people who go to the parks for a breath of air are careful to speckle the swards with pieces of newspaper, penny novelettes, remnants of sandwiches, and orange peel. These things are consigned to holes specially dug in the earth, and burnt. Empty bottles and sardine tins, and all the less inflammable sorts of rubbish, are sent to the County Council depôts. The bottles are valuable prizes to the women and men who turn over the dust heaps at these places. Neither, as we have said, are the zinc bins in the streets neglected in search of the hundred and one odds and ends which can be turned into an honest penny. Pieces of metal, old hats and boots, and rags—everything is grist for the humble mill.

No complete notion of all that London's toilet involves can be obtained without visiting a dust destructor. They are to be found here and there in all quarters of London; but Shoreditch probably stands first in this respect. Imagine a massive iron cube, a veritable iron house of fire. The roar of the furnaces within is fierce as a gale at sea. The doors are thrown open, revealing what words cannot describe—fire! bright as great banks of burnished gold, only with soul quickening the flaring mass of yellowish-red — hungry, tigrish soul! In the glowing slabs there is a strange shimmer, as though each of the hundred million atoms at white heat quivered in glorious, devilish, meaningless conflict. Had Dante but known the dust destructor, to what exquisite agonies could he not have condemned some of the wretches of his "Inferno"! It is grand, ugly, choking, diabolical; it is a place to fly from. But its very ugliness, while repelling, holds you fast.

Half a dozen men with long iron rods act as stokers. Their faces glisten with perspiration; and they are black as negroes. The atmosphere is dust, nothing but dust; it shuts out the roof, you blink it into your eyes, it enters your nostrils, it settles on your lips. An immense iron lift, large as a railway waggon, is above your head. It is rising steadily higher and higher. It holds tons of refuse. When it reaches the top of the iron scaffolding in which it slides, its cargo is emptied into cars that run on tracks laid on platforms above the destructor. The mouths of the receiving chamber are beside the platform, and into these are heaved the contents of the cars. The furnaces are beneath, devouring everything with the ravening appetite of a monster that would feast upon its own vitals. Massive iron girders cross from wall to wall, and others meet these transversely. Everything is big, coarse, forbidding; and yet the gloomy, brown pavilion of fire holds the eye; its ugliness redeemed by the majesty and power of the mysterious force within—the god of Zoroaster, a very slave in the service of despised Bumble!

IN A DUST DESTRUCTOR (SHOREDITCH).

TAPE AND TELEGRAPH ROOM
("DAILY EXPRESS").

NEWSPAPER LONDON.

By HENRY LEACH.

OUTSIDE THE "GLOBE" OFFICE.

LOOKING upon the Fleet Street of a comparatively early newspaper era, Thackeray, in the person of one of his characters, was moved to the profoundest reflections when he contemplated the great engine of the Press which never slept. And if the great engine was so wakeful in the days of " Pendennis," how much more does she seem to palpitate and revel in the very joy of existence in these far more strenuous times.

It is an accepted truism that one of the most wonderful things of our up-to-date civilisation is the Press, and most particularly the London Press. Its history is a romance, and each and every day's work is made up of a series of seeming miracles. London and the country see the result, and in reflective

moments marvel that it is all for a half-penny or a penny. This is just where Fleet Street is an exception to most other institutions which have this magic glitter. Rub it away, and so very often the substance underneath is as mean as clay; but, in the case of Fleet Street, the wonder and admiration only increase. The outside world, however, is seldom privileged thus to probe into the soul of Newspaper-land. It occasionally scans a brief report of the meeting of some such exclusive Press institution as the Institute of Journalists or the Newspaper Press Fund; but beyond this Fleet Street behind the scenes is forbidden to the person who has no business with "copy" or with proofs. He speculates upon the happenings there, draws inevitable and erroneous conclusions as to the functions of editors and the ubiquity of reporters, and passes on. For a little while a corner of the curtain shall be raised, and some real perception gained of the inner life of this place of wonder and of mystery.

In Newspaper-land there is no time for sleep. There is just one short period in the whole double round of the clock when she is a little inclined to drowse, and that is between five and seven o'clock in the morning. The heavy labours of the night are over, and, still with some show of vigilance, she pauses as if to gather strength for a vigorous grappling with the events of the dawning day. Obviously this is the time to steal in stealthily and watch her recommencement.

The Street itself has less of life in it now than at any time. The paper carts have done their turn, the staffs of the various departments, down even to the managers of machines, have sought their beds, the boiler fires are burning low, and there is only here and there, besides a few menials, an emergency editor reclining, with what comfort he can muster, till the day staff returns and relieves him of his guard. On him, for the time being, devolves the responsibility of watching London and the world, and of bringing out a special edition if a cablegram should warrant it.

And now, just when the sunlight of a summer morning is encircling the dome of St. Paul's with a golden fringe, the day workers of Fleet Street living in the suburbs turn uneasily on their beds, and the earliest of them rub their eyes and rise. Necessity makes a simultaneous demand upon the sub-editors and compositors, and by seven o'clock tram and train have taken many of them to Fleet Street, and the programme for the evening papers of the day has already been entered upon.

CYCLIST "RUNNERS" ("THE STAR").

Alone in his room the earliest sub-editor seizes a pile of the morning's papers, and, scissors in hand, scans them in search of the most striking events of the evening and night which have passed ; for the feature of his earliest edition, due in the streets in a few hours from now, must be a more or less comprehensive summary of all the news and thought that is in this pile. Paragraphs are cut out, trimmed up, striking headlines put upon them, and are whisked away per boy into the composing-room, where there is either an army of inky-aproned compositors at their cases, or a row or two of Linotypes—most wonderful machines which almost seem to think.

The tape machines begin to click out telegraphic news from the country and abroad. The first yard or two of this curious ribbon will tell, perhaps, of the death of a great celebrity in the small hours of the morning, and—click, click, click—the text of a big fire which is raging in the East-End. Before the last edition is printed, this tape will have spun off the best part of a mile of news, will have conveyed the first intelligence to the sub-editor of battles and murders, legal trials and kingly functions, the winners of horse races, the movements of markets,

ARRIVAL OF CART WITH "SPECIALS" FOR STREET SELLERS.

the totterings of Governments—everything! One minute there are ticked off half a dozen choice sentences of Sir Somebody's great speech in the House of Commons commenced but half an hour before, and this is suddenly interrupted for the quotation of starting-prices at Ascot. An accident in the street outside the office comes through, and is followed by the news of disturbing events at Pekin and great enterprises at New York. The serious drama of the world, and its tragedy and comedy, are mirrored on tape; and the tape-boy cuts it up, and pastes it on sheets of paper, stoically unmoved. To him in the lower degree, and to the sub-editor, who receives it, in the higher, it is

·II. 7· AIN. EX: TTEL 'COS' DEVONPORT TGM SAYS A BRILLIANT FUNCTN TOOK
PCE: AT II. RYL. NAIVAL BARRACKS DEVONPORT TODAY WHEN II KING PRESENTED .
MEDALS TO I. FLLWG OFFICERS. FR. SRVCE. IN CHINA AND S AFRICA
ADM. SIR E SEYMOUR CAPT. J. R JELLICOE CAPT LAWRENCE

REDUCED FACSIMILE OF A TAPE MESSAGE.

but "copy"—good "copy," passable "copy," worthless "copy," but merely "copy," after all, with which to feed voracious compositors.

And in the meantime little brown packets of "flimsy"—another species of "copy"—have begun to pour in from the news agencies, home and foreign, dotting the i's and crossing the t's of the tape, and telling of still more happenings of the day. A glance decides their fate, as far as the day's paper is concerned. In the majority of cases they are cast into the oblivion of the waste-paper basket; but this story of the strange disappearance of a City man is worth a double headline; and it is swallowed by the "comps.," whose hunger but increases. For their satisfaction more sub-editors have arrived to back up the early man, and the reporters are coming in. All this vast news received is not enough. The news editor is at work hatching a plan for a "scoop" for the day, for beating all his rivals with some fine, sensational story, or an exclusive interview. When the idea is formed it is passed on to a reporter, who, on the moment, hurries away, perhaps only to the West-End of London, perhaps to Waterloo, *en route* for Southampton, to meet a passenger on board an incoming vessel. Others are spread out on the day's engagements—some in the

Law Courts, one at a gathering at the Mansion House, a third has departed for the scene of a colliery disaster, and a fourth, possessed of a special detective faculty, is endeavouring to beat Scotland Yard in the unravelling of some great mystery.

By half-past ten the high pressure of the early morning's work inside the office begins to slacken. Most of the news, and the leading article, are in type; and the early sub-editor, having seen that the contents bill is of proper spelling and effect, has time now to go out for breakfast. Before very long one hears, in regions far below, the sharp rattling of metal plates. The "comps." and the stereotypers have done their duty, the machine-man pulls his lever, a roar rises up, and the reel of paper is being converted into early editions at the rate of thousands an hour.

Now come the publisher's most anxious moments. The paper is ready for the people, and by divers methods he must give it to them. At his counter there is a huge crowd of urchins rending the air with savage shrieks and yells. Like the editors, their one desire is to be the first in the field. Presently the papers come up from the machines, with the ink still greasy on them; the babel of cries increases till the din is deafening; and then, from the back of the counter, quires and half-quires are hurled into the air, to drop into pairs of eager arms, and be carried out with a mad rush exultingly into the streets. Away from four or five centres in Whitefriars Street, Tudor Street, Stonecutter Street, and so forth, they are carried at a gallop to the four points of the compass, the topic of the morning being yelled from these lusty young throats till Fleet Street and the Strand and Ludgate Hill resound with it.

This is the minor distribution: then come the cyclist "runners," as they are called. A corps of sturdy riders are ready on the kerb-stone; the bags on their backs are filled with the white or pinky sheets; and they wheel away from the side streets into the main thoroughfares, threading their way through the traffic, darting across streets at right angles, dashing in front of horses' heads, risking their lives in the most daring

PRINTING THE "DAILY TELEGRAPH."

EARLY MORNING AT MESSRS. W. H. SMITH AND SON'S: DESPATCHING NEWSPAPERS.

MAKING CURVED PLATES OF PAGES
("DAILY CHRONICLE").

manner at every turn of the cycle pedals. This in itself is surely an object lesson in the strenuousness of London life. The carts which carry huge bundles of papers to the stations and the suburbs and feed the boys in the main thoroughfares with them complete the great distributing work.

These are the halfpenny papers. A little later the penny evening journals follow them in somewhat more dignified style ; and, from now till the close of the afternoon, edition follows upon edition, the "Special" is followed by the "Extra" and the "Second Extra" and the "Late," and the vendors' street-corner and other pitches are covered with a constantly changing series of contents bills, in white, pink, buff, green, and other tints. Not a few of these vendors are famous characters in their way, and

have "specialised," as it were, in some cases—one is pictured on page 202—for years and years.

The tapes, the sub-editors, and the reporters have been as hard at work as ever ; and a very different paper is the complete and polished "Late" edition from the immature effort of the morning. So at six o'clock, or thereabouts, the evening newspaper day is over, and the offices are deserted again.

How clean and tidy were these sub-editorial apartments in the fresh hours of morning—and see them now! One may approach the desks and tables only over hillocks of rival papers, piles of rejected "flimsies," and entanglement in hundreds of yards of confused tape is certain. The air is heavy

REELS OF PAPER ON THE WAY TO A NEWSPAPER OFFICE.

with a peculiar odour resulting from paper, ink, and tobacco smoke. The scene is chaotic, and it is a little melancholy as well, for all the great—in a sense, magnificent—efforts of the day are of no more consequence now. Already the evening paper is being discarded in the railway train; to-morrow it must all be done over again, and the next day, and the next. Several miles of paper, wheeled to the offices in great reels daily through the streets, have been used up to-day; hundredweights of printers' ink have been spread over millions of copies of nearly a dozen journals.

But there is no rest for Fleet Street yet; its more serious work is only just beginning. Quietly, less obtrusively, the day staffs of the morning papers have long been busy. Special correspondents and reporters at home and in every part of the civilised

centres. These messages are costing the paper thousands of pounds. A simple, two-line "Reuter" may announce the quite unexpected death of a European monarch or a great statesman; but his biography in full is already written and pigeon-holed, and there is little to do but pass it on to the composing department. Intelligence which is coming in may create consternation throughout the country in the morning, but the sub-editors are quite unmoved. To them it is only "copy" after all; and all is well if

SUB-EDITORS' ROOM ("DAILY MAIL").

world have been gathering their harvest of news, and now it is speeding over the wires to its great headquarters, where the night sub-editors, turning in at six o'clock, sit with blue pencils for its reception.

Necessarily, the task being greater and less hurried, a more thorough organisation is apparent than was the case during the daytime. Special departments are now working for the completion of separate sections of the paper. The sporting sub-editors are dealing with all the racing and athletic news, the home news department is covering all the events happening in the United Kingdom, and the foreign sub-editors are receiving agency and special cablegrams from New York, Paris, Berlin, Rome, Vienna, and a score of other world's

it is through before one o'clock. If "The House" is sitting, columns are pouring in from the special corps of reporters in the Gallery, the tape machines are still clicking as briskly as ever, the news agencies are vieing with each other in the quantity of "flimsy" which they are contributing, and the liners of Fleet Street are adding to the gigantic store of "copy." So the night wears on. By two o'clock in the morning, when most of London is fast asleep, the great night's work is nearing its end. The tapes click feebly, the desks are clear of "copy," the order has been given to "close up," and presently the chiefs move off to the composing-room to superintend the "make-up," as it is called, arranging in the printers' forme the precise place which each item shall

occupy. Then, when this is done, the formes
are locked, moulds in *papier-maché* are
taken of each page of the paper, and from
these metal curved plates are made in
the foundry by the perspiring foundry
hands with their ladles of white molten
metal; and so the chiefs, having thus seen
the paper "put to bed," as they say, are free
to gossip with each other for half an hour or
so on the events of the night and things in
general.

Presently there comes again that hoarse
roar from below. The machines have been

PUBLISHING THE " SPECIAL " EDITION OF THE " EVENING STANDARD."

started. There is a momentary lull while
the first papers are examined, and then
every one of these great mechanical monsters
is off again at its topmost speed.

Looking through the window out into the
street it is observed that the scene, which
was quiet and tranquil but an hour ago, is
now full of bustle and excitement. There
is a long line of carts, with fresh, mettlesome
horses between the shafts. Scores of busy
hands are loading them up with huge bundles
of the freshly printed papers which palpitating
machines are belching forth by thousands
to the minute. At this moment not in the

whole world is there so busy a place as this
wonderful Fleet Street.

There is a cracking of whips, and the first
carts are away. Some are off to the great
distributing house of Messrs. W. H. Smith
and Son, Strand, and other well-known
wholesale agents; and some are hastening
to railway stations to catch the newspaper
trains. The first thought is for the
country; and not till the country's needs are
satisfied is attention given to the later
demands of London, for which a special
town edition will very likely be printed off.

Then away go these home papers to the
distributing agencies; by and bye they filter
through to the newsagents, and before eight
o'clock in the morning the sellers are going
their early rounds.

By five o'clock the famous street has
quieted down again. The compositors have
gone home, and the gentlemen of the staff
—a few of them—have sought an hour's re-
laxation at the Press or some other club.
For all these busy folk the small hours of the
morning are but the equivalents of the ordinary mortal's ten p.m.
Then each to his suburban home by all-
night tram or early train.

One more of Fleet Street's daily cycles
is made complete, and, just when the City
man is waking and speculating upon the
contents of his morning's paper, the sub-
editor who made it for him is slipping away
into a dreamland where all things happen
before eleven at night and editorial crises are
unknown.

He has earned his sleep; no man better.
Do not disturb him. Let the curtain fall
again upon Newspaper London.

A WORK ROOM.

LONDON'S DRAPERS.

By MRS. BELLOC-LOWNDES.

LONDON has long been, in the business sense of the word, the market of the world ; but only comparatively lately have been established, especially in the West-End, the well-known emporiums which now cater successfully not only for Londoners, but for those American and Continental visitors who formerly took the whole of their dress custom to Paris.

A volume might well be written concerning life at the draper's ; the more so, that not content with what was originally their mainstay—namely, drapery, millinery, dress-making, and underclothing departments—many now join to these separate sections, where every household want is satisfied, from the morning tea and milk to the costly fruit and liqueurs required for a Lucullian banquet.

The time may come when no drapery business will be able to live without these adjuncts ; but there are still many prosperous establishments which, like their French rivals, deal almost entirely with the art of dress. Let us content ourselves with, as it were,

taking off the roof of one of the half-dozen busy London hives which cater almost exclusively for the lady customer. It may be doubted whether this can be done more effectively than in tracing the various incidents connected with the brief existence of one of the many pretty items, say a hat or toque, dear to the feminine heart, from the day when it takes its place in the stockroom of a big West-End establishment to the moment when it is finally handed in at its purchaser's door by one of the army of *employés* belonging to the distribution service of the emporium in question.

Paris is·still supposed to hold the sceptre where feminine dress is concerned : accordingly, the managers of each great London drapery business have to make a point of being in constant communication with the gay city, and their buyers—many of whom are paid salaries averaging from six to twenty guineas a week—are always on the look-out for new ideas, and huge prices are paid without a murmur for really original model

75

A PACKING ROOM.

gowns, model hats, and even model under-clothing.

"What," the reader will ask, "has this to do with the progress of any special article from the workroom to the customer's hat-box?" Everything; for the hat or toque in question owes its very existence to the care exercised by the buyer, whose business it is to keep himself in touch with the great Paris millinery houses; and the piece of headgear under discussion is almost certain to be a clever modification of a Paris model, so arranged by the important lady whose business it is to superintend the millinery department. It is she who decides of what materials the hat or toque is to be made, and what price is to be asked for it.

At the London draper's each day, properly speaking, begins at 8.30, but as early as 7 o'clock the young men assistants, known to the trade as "squadders," have started work, cleaning, dusting, and finally un-packing the goods which are to be shown and offered for sale that day. The young ladies, who, in some great establishments I could name, number as many as 250, have nothing to do with what may be called "squadder" work, although they dress the windows of their departments; and, of course, the more delicate goods—and this especially applies to millinery—are taken out of boxes

and from the tissue paper in which they were carefully wrapped up the night before, to display them to the best advantage. It may be assumed that particular care is bestowed on those windows where the newest millinery is dis-played, as so much depends, when headgear is concerned, on a first impression. In most good houses every article for sale is marked in plain figures, and there is a "marking-off room," where everything is priced; but this only applies to goods that are not made by the firm. Before a hat or toque, for instance, has left the workrooms it is marked by the head of the department, for she alone can know what it has cost and what the profit should be. It may interest some of those ladies who spend much of their time "at the draper's" to learn that the best and newest goods, especially those copied from the more recent Paris models, are always at once put in the window. It is there that they are first seen by the public.

The best-looking young lady assistants are generally to be found in the millinery department; for human nature being what it is, many a middle-aged plain customer will the more willingly invest in a hat when she has seen it gracefully poised above the pretty face of the young lady who has been told off to attend to her wants. Once the piece of headgear has been chosen, the delicate matter of payment comes. If the customer has an account, and is known to the as-sistant, the amount of her purchase is simply debited to her; if, on the other hand, she is a casual purchaser, she is, of course, asked to pay ready cash, but it is also open to her to pay on delivery.

The question of payment satisfactorily settled, the hat or toque is packed by the vendor, and sent down to the despatch-room, where—and this is rather a curious fact—the parcel is opened, to see if everything is all right, by one of the many porters and packers whose duty it is to finally do up the hat-box and place it in the delivery cart.

Few ladies seem to care to begin their shopping before 11 o'clock, but by midday business is in full swing, and the outside porters are busily minding the pet dogs which, by a wise rule, are not allowed to accompany their mistresses through the great glass doors which admit them to the modern woman's El dorado.

The busiest times of the day are from 12 to 1 o'clock and from 3 to 5 o'clock; but time has to be found for dinner, and the shop assistants in most great emporiums take their meals in five parties—half an hour being allowed for dinner and twenty minutes for tea. The mid-day meal consists of an ample supply of well-cooked food—not in winter and generally cold in summer, everything being done to vary the diet and to make it palatable.

Time was when much of the drapery business consisted of unmade-up goods. Ladies preferred to buy their materials, and have them made up either at home or by their own dressmakers. Now, however, the largest and most profitable side of the drapery business is the sale of made-up goods. Customers will sometimes arrive in the middle of the morning and ask to be shown a gown that they can wear the same evening! Accordingly, an important side of the business is that of altering bodices and skirts to fit the buyer's figure; and the workroom, though never seen by the public, is a very busy department of a modern drapery business.

The bi-annual sales, which play so prominent a part in the lives of those connected with great drapery businesses, and also, it may be added, in that of some of their customers, who are always looking forward to "sale time," take place soon after Christmas and about Midsummer. During the days of the sale everything in a really good shop is, as a rule, "marked down," especially everything in the shape of a made-up garment, for these must be cleared off at an "alarming sacrifice" if need be; and amazing bargains may be secured in the millinery departments, for the simple reason that a winter or summer piece of headgear, if it be put away for

AT DINNER ON A BIG SALE DAY.

LEFT OUTSIDE.

twelve months, always acquires a worn look.

The preparation for a season's sale goes on for many days previous to the date advertised, for, as we have said, in respectable establishments all the articles offered during the days of a sale are "marked down"—that is, their price is lowered—and this means an extraordinary amount of careful work and thought for all those concerned. On the days of a sale, especially when some attractive "line" is offered at what seems to the average shrewd customer an exceptionally low price, it is quite usual for a large crowd of ladies, each and all eager for the fray, to gather outside the large plate-glass doors some half an hour before they are actually opened; and the scene, when the magic hour of nine is struck, recalls nothing so much—if one may credit the remark made by a certain stalwart soldier who had been through more than one campaign—as that of a town being taken by assault! Once the establishment is full the doors are again shut, and impatient customers are often kept waiting half an hour before they also are allowed to join the eager throng.

The more popular "lines," especially cheap footgear—shoes, for instance, at a shilling a pair—and very cheap gloves, are cleared out in the first hour. But there still remains plenty to satisfy the bargain hunter, the more so that, as the day goes on, fresh supplies are brought out; and the woman who is aware of such simple facts as that light silks cannot be stored for any length of time without becoming spotted, or that a very showy Paris model will generally be "marked down" to a third of its value, can often pick up, at any period of a genuine sale, articles for which she would have to pay at least fifty per cent. more under ordinary circumstances.

During the sales weeks of the year the assistants have scarcely time to breathe, and the pleasant room which the managers of most leading emporiums provide as a resting-place for their "young ladies" is practically deserted, the latter finding it as much as they can do to get their meals within an hour of the proper time.

Strangely enough, the *employés* of a drapery emporium rather like sale times, and it may be hinted that those shop assistants with any sense of humour thoroughly enjoy the experience, for all that is eccentric and peculiar in London femininity is there seen to most advantage. Again, the lady customer attending a sale is generally far less hard to

A CASH DESK.

please than she is on ordinary days; the delightful thought that she is acquiring a series of bargains—even if the articles purchased by her will never be of the slightest use to either herself or her family—filling her with unwonted self-satisfaction. Many more sensible people, however, wait patiently for sale time and deliberately buy with a view to what is to fill their wardrobe the following year; yet it is, from the manager's point of secure their bargains at once. One type of customer whom the experienced saleswoman can detect almost at a glance is she who orders a great number of things to be paid for "on delivery," and who then instructs her parlourmaid or butler to refuse the parcels when they arrive the same evening or the next morning.

The shop-walker, that elegantly dressed individual who seems to the casual observer

A POSTAL ORDER ROOM.

view, surprising to note how often a customer who has a chance of securing a real bargain in silk or fur will pass it by, and perhaps spend just as many pounds in purchasing cheap articles of wearing apparel—gloves, veils, and last, not least, blouses—which have only been "marked down" a few pence, or, in the case of a blouse, a couple of shillings.

Although a considerable strain is put on the parcels department, generally situated, by the way, under the showrooms, it is remarkable how many ladies, when attending a sale, are content to take away their purchases, even if the latter be great in bulk. They seem to think that they must to have so little to do, and yet who is considered so important a member of his staff by the managers of each emporium, finds his duties greatly lessened on the days of a sale. It is at ordinary times, when business is more or less slack, that the shop-walker who knows his business shows to advantage. It is he who then indicates to the hesitating customer where she may hope to find exactly what she is seeking, or, better still, where she may be persuaded to purchase some article of which she is not in any sense in want.

It has often been asserted that women cannot be taught the business side of life.

A SALE DAY AT PETER ROBINSON'S.

The best answer to this charge is that in the great drapery establishments the cash desk is almost always occupied by a girl clerk, who does her work well and civilly.

An important and profitable branch of the work performed each day concerns what may be called the shopping by post department. This is carried on in the Postal Order Room. Many country cousins have an account at a London shop, and all such important customers must be answered by return, and their wants, if it be in any way humanly possible, supplied.

On one side of life at the draper's it is not quite easy to touch, yet it plays a part of no small importance. Now and again, under "Police News," appears a paragraph stating that "Mrs. or Miss So-and-so, of such-and-such an address, was charged with stealing various articles, valued at so much, from Messrs. ——, Ltd." Of course, the world at large never hears of the innumerable cases when ladies, detected in appropriating more or less valuable articles from the counters and stands, are not taken in charge, either because they happen to be connected with old and valued customers, or, more often still, because it is extremely difficult to actually catch such persons in the act.

One method, often pursued by an intelligent and well-dressed shop-lifter, is to actually purchase and pay for, say, a pair of gloves, or a piece of real lace, and, while the shopwoman is obtaining change, or even when she is only making out the bill, the thief manages to pull over the counter several other pairs of gloves or pieces of lace, and then, stooping down, stuffs them into her hand-bag, which has been previously placed on the ground in readiness for the operation.

The true kleptomaniac, as differentiated from the ordinary thief, not content with taking a number of valuable articles from one counter, will go through the whole shop annexing pieces of dress material, rolls of silk, half-a-dozen pairs of stockings, veils, and even such articles as pairs of boots and shoes, not one of which will fit her! This type is far more easily detected and punished than her wiser and more artful sister who contents herself with only stealing articles from one counter, and who chooses pieces of valuable real lace, or lengths of beautiful embroidery, in preference to heavier or more cumbersome articles.

In connection with each emporium is a regular detective service, and during a big sale twelve to twenty detectives are present in the shop. At these times every drapery business loses, in spite of the vigilance on the part of the detectives, a great deal of real value, mostly in fur and lace.

It is difficult to over-estimate the responsibility borne during sale days by these detectives. Much is left to their discretion and tact, for it is not too much to say that the making on their part of a "mistake" —that is to say, the arresting of an innocent person—would do the establishment with which they are connected incalculable harm. So true is this, that often when a detective sees a lady walking off with, say, a valuable piece of lace, unless he has reason to suppose that the lady in question is really a professional thief, he simply follows her to the door, and, taking the article, which still bears the ticket on it, from her hand or from under her cloak, remarks suavely, "Excuse me, madam; I will have this sent home for you." As a rule, the thief quickly disappears in the crowd, but if she is a hardened kleptomaniac she may reappear the very next day.

Once the day's work is over—that is, once the doors are closed—the young lady *employés* have the whole evening to play in or to work for themselves; they also have Saturday afternoons from two o'clock. They are not, however, allowed to go out from Saturday to Monday unless they can show a letter from their parents authorising them to do so, and stating where they are going. Those young ladies who remain in have pleasant sitting-rooms in which to spend their time, and plenty of books and games; while the young men have various forms of indoor amusements, including billiards, and on fine Saturday afternoons can enjoy the national games of cricket and football, large pieces of land near London having been secured for that purpose by several of the leading drapery firms.

A WELL-KNOWN ESTABLISHMENT IN ST. JAMES'S STREET.

HOUSE-HUNTING LONDON.

By GEORGE R. SIMS.

EVERY day in the year a certain number of people are consulting agents, or referring to the advertising columns of the newspapers, or driving or walking round the residential portions of London in search of a roof for their heads. The bulk of them are people who are already householders, but who wish to change their addresses. Sometimes the change is due to prosperity, sometimes to adversity, frequently to the increased accommodation required by the growing up of little boys and girls. In some cases, in fact in many cases, it is the mere desire for change. But we have not, fortunately, to concern ourselves with motives—our task is the lighter one of accompanying the Londoner in that series of adventurous expeditions commonly known as "house-hunting."

For the wealthier class there are West-End firms who undertake the whole business. These firms have always in their hands the letting of a certain number of first-class residences in the localities favoured by rank and fashion. The fashionable house-hunter cannot go very far afield in search of his new address. Society has certain quarters in which it keeps itself "to itself" as much as possible in these days of the millionaire, native and imported; therefore the fashionable house-hunter is confined to one of the aristocratic squares or streets of the West or South-West. These houses are not generally advertised, nor do they display as a rule the notice boards which allow the passer-by to know that they are to be let. They are placed in the hands of a firm whose speciality it is to deal in "town mansions." The people who desire such a property send to such a firm and request it to find them a residence. The firm indicates the residences on their books, and the rest is merely a matter for the solicitors of the two parties to the transaction. When the purchase or the leasing is completed the world is informed in the "Society" columns of the daily papers that Lord This or Lady That has taken Number So-and-so, Berkeley, or Cavendish, or Portman, or Eaton, or Grosvenor Square, or Park Lane, as the case may be.

Occasionally photographs are taken of residential properties of the first class and may be seen in the front windows of, let us say, Messrs. E. and H. Lumley, in St. James's Street. The higher-class house furnishers are also house agents, and have generally on hand a number of photographs, thus enabling their clients to see what a house looks like without the trouble of going to it. If the photograph makes a good impression, personal inspection follows; but in some cases houses, principally furnished houses let for the season or a limited period, are taken for clients abroad who see their new home for the first time when they drive to it from the railway station.

But for the great body of house-hunters, the ordinary family folk who have many things to consider before their address is altered in the Post Office Directory, the process of house-hunting is at once more absorbing, more anxious, and more fatiguing.

The time has come when Mr. and Mrs. Horace Brown feel that their present house is not large enough for them. They started housekeeping two in family, with a couple of servants; now they are five in family, and they have three servants. Mr. Brown is in the City, and a busy man. He hates the idea of

SHOWN INTO THE DRAWING-ROOM.

moving, but his wife has dinned into his ears morning, noon, and night that it is quite impossible they can stay where they are any longer, and has at last induced him to consent to the taking of a more desirable residence.

But he absolutely refuses to take any part in the preliminary search; he has his business to attend to. Once or twice on a Sunday he has been cajoled into taking a drive round the suburban district which Mrs. Brown "fancies" in order to look at the houses which are exhibiting boards; but none of them have seemed quite the thing, and he has declined to make any further sacrifice of his Sunday's

rest to the contemplation of house agents' boards stuck up in front gardens; though these boards, as will be seen in our photographic illustration, "A Choice of Agents," sometimes make a brave show and furnish quite a large amount of reading.

So Mrs. Brown has to go hunting alone. Her instructions are to find the place that will suit, and then Mr. Brown will try to get away from the City for an hour or two to look at it. It is an anxious time for poor Mrs. Brown. She reads the advertisements in the papers, she calls at house agents', she gets their lists, day after day she hurries off hither and thither to look at this desirable residence and that eligible villa; but there is always a "something." At one house which she would have liked very much there are an absurd number of fixtures to be taken; another, which is all that could be desired in the way of accommodation, is next door to a church with a powerful peal of bells. In

AN INSPECTION BY THE DOG.

another she discovers that the drainage is not above suspicion; in yet another that a railway runs at the bottom of the garden, and that every ten minutes the "desirable residence" rocks with all the premonitory symptoms of an earthquake.

She goes back to the house agent and enters into fresh explanations, and he supplies her with a list of six houses, each of which he thinks will exactly suit her requirements. This time she insists on her husband accompanying her. She is most anxious to settle; she wants his moral support in assisting her to a decision. Mr. Brown is grumpy, but eventually consents to sacrifice an afternoon, and they set out together.

The first house is empty, and in charge of a caretaker. The caretaker is a woman with two children and a husband. The husband is out of work, and at home; he is smoking a pipe, and has it in his mouth when

he opens the door. Mrs. Brown boldly attacks the situation. She has come to see the house, and hands the man the agent's order to view. The man scowls, goes to the top of the stairs, and calls out, "'Lizer — somebody to see the 'ouse."

'Lizer appears, wiping her hands on her apron, takes the card gingerly, and flings open the dining-room door without a word. Mr. and Mrs. Brown look at the dining-room, exchange a few remarks in a low voice — nobody ever talks loudly while viewing an empty house, for there is always a sense of restraint in the process—and come out into the hall. 'Lizer flings open the door on the other side, and says, "Drorin' room." While Mr. and Mrs. Brown are looking at the drawing-room and mentally measuring it a baby begins to cry in the basement, and 'Lizer goes to the top of the stairs and shouts down some domestic instructions to her husband. When Mr. and Mrs. Brown come out of the drawing-room 'Lizer conducts them upstairs. She walks much after the manner of a clergyman preceding a coffin to the graveside. She flings open the bedroom doors one after the other. Presently she gathers from the remarks of the visitors that the house is likely to suit them, and instantly her manner changes. She becomes more friendly, she volunteers little communications as to the length of time the house has been empty, she thinks that the reason no one has taken it is that it is damp. She even confesses that she and her husband have suffered from rheumatism a good deal since they have lived in it. She doesn't quite *volunteer* this information, she allows it to be *dragged* from her as it were. Mr. Brown is impressed with her candour; Mrs. Brown is grateful. When the inspection is completed 'Lizer is presented with a couple of shillings. "Thank goodness that woman was honest," says Mr. Brown when he gets outside; "I shall save doctors' bills for the next seven years; for I *liked* the house."

Inside, 'Lizer joins her husband in the kitchen. "They looked like taking it," she says; "but I told 'em it was terrible damp, and that settled 'em." The man heaves a sigh of relief. To have had to turn out just now would have been decidedly inconvenient.

The next house visited by the Browns is occupied. The family are still in it. The housemaid, who opens the door, looks at the card and says, "Oh, to see the house!" and vanishes, leaving the visitors standing in the outer hall.

When she returns she says, "This way, please," and opens a door. Mr. and Mrs. Brown are about to enter when they discover that members of the family are there. The members of the family try to look agreeable, but glare. Mr. and Mrs. Brown remain on the threshold and just peer in. "Thank you, that will do," says Mrs. Brown. The same process is repeated in the next room, where a young lady is practising at the piano. "I—er—think *you'd* better go and see the bedrooms," says Mr. Brown somewhat nervously to his better half; "I'll stay here." And he remains patiently in the hall, like a man who has brought a parcel from the draper's and is waiting for the money. The dog of the family suddenly appears and eyes him suspiciously. Mr. Brown feels rather nervous, especially as the dog approaches to make a closer scrutiny of his legs. For the

first time in his life Mr. Brown is sorry he has never kept a dog; he has always understood that if you keep a dog strange dogs discover it quickly, and become friendly. Just as he is wondering whether it would not be wise to call for a member of the family, in order that it may be explained to the animal that he is not there with dishonest intentions, a young gentleman makes his appearance, and, hurriedly seizing the dog by the collar, drags him away and pushes him through the swing door at the top of the kitchen stairs. "Keep Bill downstairs," he calls out; "some people are looking over the house." Then he turns to Mr. Brown half apologetically. "'Bliged to be careful with him," he says; "he bit the washing man yesterday."

Presently Mrs. Brown comes downstairs, looking hot and flurried. "Do you want to go into the kitchen?" says the housemaid. "No—I—er—think not," Mrs. Brown stammers. Mr. Brown is greatly relieved. In a few seconds he and his wife are outside. "Oh, my dear," she says, "I didn't see the house, I only went into two bedrooms. The eldest daughter was lying down in one with a bad headache, and there was an old lady in the other—the grandmother I think—who has epileptic fits. She was in one then, and, of course, I said I wouldn't disturb her." "And I've nearly been bitten by a savage dog," exclaims Mr. Brown. "No more house-hunting for me!"

LET AS FAST AS BUILT.

A CHOICE OF AGENTS.

But the afternoon is still young, and a house *must* be found, so at last he is pacified, and calls with his wife at the next address. Here everything is satisfactory. The house is admirably adapted for their requirements; it is sunny, it is dry, there is an excellent garden, a good view from the windows, and the caretaker says there are two "parties" after it. Mr. Brown says, "Ah! this will do; we'll go to the agent's at once, and see about the fixtures, and settle." The agent is at the West-End. They take a hansom and drive to his place of business at once. On the way they discuss the rooms. Mr. Brown selects one for a smoking-room, Mrs. Brown decides on one with a sunny outlook for her boudoir. In two of the rooms the old carpets will fit, which is a great blessing. They arrive at the agent's, and inform the clerk that they will take Laburnum Villa. The clerk goes into the private office, and returns quickly. "Mr. —— is very sorry, sir, but he has just had a telegram to say a gentleman who looked over the house yesterday, and had the refusal till to-day, has wired to say he will take it."

What Mr. Brown says does not matter. Mrs. Brown feels inclined to cry. It is *so* annoying; and it is getting late. Instead of seeing any more houses, the Browns go home, and the evening repast is a gloomy one. Mr. Brown is "sick of the whole business." He talks wildly about staying where they are—

they will have the children's beds moved into Mrs. Brown's room, and he will sleep in the coal cellar.

But with the morning comes reason, and more house-hunting. Eventually the Browns succeed in securing a house after their own hearts, and, after paying for about forty pounds' worth of fixtures which are of no earthly use to them, they move in. And once in Mr. Brown declares that he won't move out or go house-hunting again as long as he lives.

Flats, with all their advantages, do not always retain their charm for Londoners. There is a great difficulty in getting good servants, for Mary Jane looks upon life on the third or fourth floor of a huge block of buildings as too far removed from the world below. In many flats the kitchen and the servants' rooms look out on back streets or back gardens, and so the servant difficulty forces many a flat family into house-hunting. Then comes the difficulty that the furniture of a flat does not always suit houses which are differently arranged, and generally much more spacious in their room measurement. The flat house-hunter therefore hunts generally for a house which can be fitted and furnished with the flat "belongings," and makes many anxious inquiries as to rates and taxes, which were covered by the flat rent. The flat people invariably want more garden than anyone else, because they have been without a garden for so long; and, having had the use of a lift, they look at stairs with a critical eye. To find a house that will satisfy the family moving from a flat is one of the house agents' most difficult tasks.

The small house-hunter is perhaps the most genuine hunter of all. She—it is generally the wife, for the husband is in employment and not his own master—covers ten miles in her search to the better class house-hunter's one. She has no agent to assist her, and not only is the rent a great consideration, but she must make sure that the 'bus or train service is convenient for her husband's daily journeys to and from his place of employment. As quarter day approaches the young wife becomes feverish in her anxiety. Notice has been given to her landlord, and another tenant has been secured. Visions of her household goods piled on a van with no address to be given to the driver, and herself and little ones homeless in the street on a pouring wet day, haunt her imagination. At last she is in the condition when she will take anything. She sees a place that will suit—though it is not *quite* what she would have liked—and she hopes and prays that it will remain vacant till Saturday, for on Saturday afternoon her husband can go and see it. If *he* says it will do, her principal terror is removed—men's ideas of houses differ so much from women's. At last the house is

taken, and the references given. The references are a worry to many men who have no banker. It is a delicate thing to write to a friend in a good position and say "Will you be my reference?" As a rule, in small properties the last landlord's reference is sufficient. But many landlords ask for two. The second reference keeps many an honest man awake of nights just before quarter day.

The way in which the population of London drifts and changes, and flits from house to house and from neighbourhood to neighbourhood, is always wonderful, but the most remarkable feature of the "general post" which takes place on the great moving days—Lady Day and Michaelmas Day—is that all the new villa residences springing up in every direction around the Metropolis are snapped up almost before the slates are on them. Hardly are the windows in before a large "Let" is writed on them. The old neighbourhoods are still densely inhabited, the boards after quarter day are few and far between; but in some mysterious way a new population is continually entering the capital, and the stream of house-hunters spreads itself over neighbourhoods that a year previously were green fields and meadows and country lanes. A year later they will have their streets of thriving shops, their pawnbroker and hotel, their local Bon Marché, their telephone call office, and their local newspaper.

MOVING IN.

MUSIC-HALL LONDON.

By H. CHANCE NEWTON.

ONE of the most remarkable developments in Living London of late years is that of the modern music-halls—or Theatres of Varieties, as they are mostly called, except when they are described as Empires or Palaces. The variety form of entertainment now so prevalent is a real boon to those amusement-seekers who cannot, even if they would, indulge in playgoing at the so-called "regular" theatres. Working hours have for many to be continued until it is too late to reach home in time to come out again to the play—especially for those who are only able to afford unbookable seats.

For these hampered toilers the music-hall or variety form of entertainment is the only thing of the show kind available. They can take or leave the entertainment at any hour they please—the programme given being, of course, everything by "turns" and nothing long. Besides all this—and it is an important factor—there is the chance of enjoying a smoke, a luxury prohibited in all theatres run under the Lord Chamberlain's licence.

The most striking examples of the modern variety theatres in London are the Empire, the Alhambra, and the London Hippodrome. Next to these would undoubtedly rank those other popular West-End resorts, the Palace Theatre, the Oxford, the Tivoli, and the London Pavilion.

The Empire is one of the most beautiful buildings, as regards its interior, to be found in the Metropolis. Its entertainment is of a high class, and its gorgeous ballets and other extensive and expensive spectacular productions are patronised not only, in addition to its large general audience, by our "gilded youth," but by all sorts of society folk, who need an hour or two's bright and ever changing entertainment after dinner.

The Alhambra—a huge Moorish building—is, in its status and its style of entertainment, similar to the Empire, with the difference that it claims—and rightly—precedence

of all neighbouring places of the sort. Indeed, its own proud description is, "The Premier Variety Theatre of London." This house was certainly the first to introduce the big ballet and spectacular form of entertainment. For many years a large proportion of visitors to the Metropolis made the Alhambra their first variety "house of call." Nowadays, however, these visitors must perforce take in the Empire and the other important variety palaces.

A few steps from these huge halls is the London Hippodrome, one of the most remarkable buildings in the great city. Although so close to the Empire and the Alhambra, the entertainments and the audiences are of a totally different character. The Hippodrome programme is principally made up of equestrian, gymnastic, and menagerie "turns," plus a burletta or pantomime. This last must include at least one aquatic scene of some sort, in which the comedians (most of them expert swimmers) disport on or in the large lake which, by a wonderful mechanical process, when required, fills up the circus ring. The Hippodrome's audiences are not of the lounging "after dinner" or "round the town " kind, but are in a great measure formed of family groups, headed by pater or mater, or both. Indeed, most of its patrons are of the sedate domestic sort. There is no doubt that the fact of the Hippodrome being, like so many of the new large variety theatres, forbidden a liquor licence, is in itself (however unfair it may seem) an attraction for most of those who take their youngsters to such entertainments. The Hippodrome—the auditorium of which is a sight—resembles the Alhambra and the Empire in one respect, namely that not a few of its artistes are foreigners, and that many of its performances are in dumb show. Our photographic illustration on page 224 depicts a scene beneath the arena of the Hippodrome. Here are heavy wooden

READY TO PASS IN ("WONDERLAND").

WAITING TO GO ON (ROYAL MUSIC-HALL).

"properties" about to be conveyed above, while "supers" and stage hands are crowded together in readiness for their particular duties.

The Oxford, the Tivoli, and the London Pavilion are likewise sumptuous if somewhat smaller establishments. At these resorts, however, comic and "serio" singing, sandwiched with short acrobatic, dancing, and trick cycling "acts," and fifteen or twenty minutes' sketches, are the rule. The best

André Messager's *Le Basoche*, Fortune frowned upon the enterprise. Ere long Sir Augustus Harris transformed it into a variety theatre, with its present name. Under Sir Augustus's successor, Mr. Charles Morton, who deserves special mention here as being "the father of the modern music-hall," the Palace Theatre was lifted into the high position it has since sustained. Its entertainment is one of the best of its class, not only as regards its singers and dancers, pantomimists, mimics,

BENEATH THE ARENA (HIPPODROME).

available artistes are engaged at these three houses. Oftentimes the same "stars" appear on the same evening at the three halls, which are virtually run by one syndicate. When a comic or a "serio" "star" books an engagement with this syndicate, he or she is required to stipulate by contract not to appear at any other hall within a radius of so many miles. This "barring out" clause, as it is called, has also of late prevailed in connection with certain of the larger music halls in suburban London.

The Palace Theatre, in Shaftesbury Avenue, is a beautiful building, which was opened by Mr. D'Oyley Carte as the English Opera House. In spite of such excellent operatic works as Sir Arthur Sullivan's *Ivanhoe* and

sketch artists, and others of all nations and denominations, but also its beautiful and realistic *tableaux - vivants* and biograph pictures.

It is no wonder that the old-time stuffy music-hall has been killed by such places as the splendid variety houses just named, to say nothing of those other large and admirably conducted halls such as the Royal in Holborn, the Metropolitan in the Edgware Road, the Canterbury in the densely crowded Lambeth district, and the Paragon in the still more densely crowded Mile End region. Besides these resorts there have sprung up several vast "Empires" such as those respectively at New Cross, Holloway, Stratford and Hackney, all under the direction of the wealthy syndicate that runs the London Hippodrome and a number of "Empires" in the provinces.

If one should desire to get some notion of how the "toiling, moiling myrmidons" (as Béranger calls them) patronise these new "Empires," he has only to watch outside any of them just before the doors are opened for the first or second "house." For be it noted that two entire performances are given at each nightly, and at small prices of admission. Moreover, the programmes always contain several highly-paid variety artistes—whether of the comic singing, acrobatic, canine, or sketch kind. Indeed, it is not at all unusual to find here a favourite performer in receipt of at least one hundred pounds per week; not to mention this or that leading serio-comic lady or "Comedy Queen" at a salary not much lower. Yet, in spite of such princely salaries, the prices of admission are small, ranging, say, from two shillings or eighteenpence in the best parts to threepence in the gallery.

That these "Empires," "Palaces," and similar halls are run not only with excellent programmes but also on strictly proper lines is proved by the fact that, moderate though the admission prices may be, the patrons come from some of the best parts of Hampstead, Stoke Newington, Catford, Blackheath, Woodford, and so forth. Here recreation-seekers may—and do—have

placed before them all sorts of "turns" besides those above-mentioned, and comprising many examples such as conjurers, acrobats performing elephants, seals bears, instrumentalists—comic and otherwise. Often will be found certain old stagers or juvenile performers of dramatic sketches made up of boiled-down plays—even of *Hamlet*, in a twenty-minutes version of that play.

To those amusement-seekers who may prefer to take their variety entertainment in a rough-and-ready form there are still such haunts as that Whitechapel resort fancifully named "Wonderland." In this big hall are provided entertainments of the most extraordinary description. They include little plays, songs, and sketches, given first in Yiddish dialect and afterwards translated into more or less choice English by, as a rule, a Hebraic interpreter. This interpreter often improves the occasion by calling the attention of kind—and mostly alien—friends in front to certain side shows consisting of all sorts of armless, legless, skeleton, or spotted "freaks" scattered around the recesses of this great galleryless hall. When once the "freaks" have been examined, or the "greeners" and other foreign and East-End "sweated" Jew toilers have utilised the interval to indulge in a little light refreshment according to their respective tastes, the Yiddish sketches and songs—comic and otherwise—are resumed until "closing time."

It is, however, on its Boxing Nights (which in this connection means

TYPES OF MUSIC-HALL PERFORMERS.

Mondays and Saturdays) that "Wonderland" is to be seen in its most thrilling form. Then it is indeed difficult either to get in or to get out. In the first place it is hard to get in because of the great crowds of hard-faring—often hard-faced—East-End worshippers of the fistic art; several types of which are to be seen in our photographic illustration on page 223. In the second place, if you do contrive to get in you

Photo Harcea

PERFORMING DOGS.

speedily find yourself so hemmed in by a sardine-like packed mob that all egress seems hopeless.

Several other extremely typical East-End variety resorts, each of a totally different kind, are close at hand. One is the huge Paragon Theatre of Varieties, further east in the Mile End Road. Another is the much smaller Cambridge Music-Hall, which is in Commercial Street, a little way westward from Toynbee Hall. There are also the Queen's Music-Hall at Poplar, the Royal Albert at Canning Town, and the Eastern Empire at Bow.

In spite of its cheap prices and its seething audiences, the Paragon entertainment is exactly on a par with those given in the West-End and South of London Variety Theatres. Indeed, the entertainment at the Paragon is mostly identical with that supplied at the Canterbury, Westminster Bridge Road, and is under the same syndicate. As for the Canterbury, the better class South London

tradesfolk and toilers go there, excepting, of course, when they visit the newer and equally well managed South of London variety shows.

The Cambridge Music-Hall, between Spitalfields and Shoreditch, deserves a few special lines. In point of fact, ever since the time when, years ago, it was converted from a synagogue into a music-hall, the Hebrew residents of the locality have made it a point of honour to attend the Cambridge. With them they often bring not only their wives, but also their black-curled, black-eyed infants, who may often be seen toddling calmly about the stalls — especially during the earlier of the two "houses" per night.

Round the corner in Shoreditch is the London Music-Hall, wherein the stranger who pays his first visit will undoubtedly fancy for the nonce that he has lost his way and has by accident strayed into one of the best West-End halls.

Further north there are several more or less large and more or less "classy" variety houses: for example, the new two "houses" per night resort, the Euston, opposite St. Pancras Station; the Bedford, in Camden Town; the still newer Islington Empire, next door to the Agricultural Hall; the old-established music-hall, Collins's, on Islington Green; and the still older Sadler's Wells, adjoining the New River Head in Rosebery Avenue.

The west-central district and southern suburbs are also well provided for in a music-hall sense. Among others, one notes the old Middlesex, or "Mogul," in Drury Lane; a Theatre of Varieties at Walham Green; Empires at Balham and Deptford; an Empress at Brixton; a Royal Standard at Pimlico, and a Star at Bermondsey; and Palaces at Camberwell, the London Road (Southwark), and Croydon. Besides these may be mentioned Gatti's in the Westminster Bridge Road, another Gatti's at Charing Cross, and a Grand at Clapham Junction.

Like the halls themselves, the agents who supply the managers with artistes at so much per cent. commission on the salaries have, too, not only much improved in character, but have in many cases migrated from their former dingy haunts in the York Road, Lambeth, to more commodious—not to say palatial—offices in or around the Strand, the Haymarket, and elsewhere. Some few of them, however, still have their offices near a well-known tavern at a corner of York Road; and at certain hours a large number of minor music-hall entertainers and

Nowadays the music-hall ranks include large numbers of the worthiest of citizens. And, what is still better, they have combined together of late years to organise several protective associations, such as the Variety Club and the Music-Hall Railway Rates Association, as well as to found some excellent charities for benefiting their brethren out of health—or out of work—and to provide for the widows and orphans of comrades who have fallen by the way.

The chief of these charities is the Music-

AT THE CORNER OF YORK ROAD.

their agents may—as shown in the above illustration—still be seen congregating near this old-established hostelry.

Music-hall "artistes" (as they love to call themselves) have also vastly improved. Not many years ago these were mostly shiftless and thriftless from the "stars" downward.

Hall Benevolent Fund, a very fine organisation, the committee of which consists of many of the most important and most honourable men to be found in any department of life. From time to time the smaller associations assist their parent fund, or the Music-Hall Home for the Sick and Aged, by arranging matinées or sports. In the case of the Music-Hall Railway Rates Association all the surplus of the money subscribed thereto for the purposes of getting the fares reduced for travelling "artistes" is handed over to one or other of the aforesaid charities.

And though the members of the smaller music-hall societies delight to call themselves by such names as "Water Rats," "Terriers," and "J's," and to dress themselves as ostriches, savages, cowboys, Red Indians, and so on at their annual sports, or to disport as comic cricketers in all sorts of extraordinary costumes—what does it matter, seeing that they do it all for charity's sake? Thus, by drawing vast crowds of the general public, they add substantially to the funds of their excellent charities. In these benevolent affairs Mr. Dan Leno is mostly at the head (as he is with regard to his profession). On such occasions he is indeed a Jack of all trades and master of most.

As will be seen from the photographic illustration on page 223, the "behind the scenes" life of Music-Hall London is not without its humours. In "Waiting to Go On" we have, indeed, a motley throng of variety "turns." These include a famous "serio" in Early Victorian "dandy" costume; a popular "comic" in the usual

battered hat and ill-fitting clothes which such comedians always adopt; a celebrated conjurer, a couple of clever "descriptive" singers, a noted strong man, and several others. This "Waiting to Go On" represents, of course, quite a different state of things from the arrangements in a regular theatre, where every entrance and exit is fixed, and where the players have to report themselves, as a rule, some time before the curtain rises. Music-hall entertainers must, if they wish to earn a remunerative amount per week, do three or four "turns" a night; and in order to travel from hall to hall, a brougham—or, in the case of a troupe, a private omnibus — has to be provided. When they arrive they are naturally in a hurry to get their work over, and are apt to get in each other's way, either in the dressing-room or at the wings. As most music-hall entertainers start from home already "made up," and even sometimes "change" in their vehicles *en route*, it does not take them long to be ready for their respective "turns"; and their punctuality is remarkable.

To sum up, it may in common fairness be said that without its Palaces of Variety and its Music-Halls Living London would only be half alive.

BEFORE THE DOORS OPEN
(LONDON PAVILION).

ATTACKED BY TWO.

HOOLIGAN LONDON.

By CLARENCE ROOK.

IF you will take a walk—it will be a pretty long one—round the inner circle of London, and keep your eyes open, you will see many interesting things. And, if your eyes are open for human character rather than for buildings. or historical associations, there is one type that will probably remain as a lasting impression. Start from the Elephant and Castle, and work westward through Lambeth, cross the river to Chelsea, fetch Notting Hill in the circuit round by the Euston Road and Pentonville, and then take Bethnal Green on your way down to the Commercial Road, and back again across the Tower Bridge for a glance at the Old Kent Road and Walworth and the Borough.

Whatever else you fail to notice on that walk, you will scarcely fail to notice this: the persistence of a particular type of boy. He is somewhere between fourteen and nineteen years of age, but he is under-sized and underfed. You will find him selling newspapers, or sitting on the tail of a van, or loafing among the cabs at a stand;

you will find him playing pitch-and-toss, with a sentry on the look out for prying policemen, on any convenient bit of waste ground; or you may spy him at a game of cards—more especially on Sunday—on a deserted barge in the Pool. But you will not find him among the crowds that come at twelve and six o'clock out of the factories, or filter at odd hours from the big printing establishments. The boy of this special type which you cannot fail to notice has no fixed purpose or permanent employment, and he shows it in his face. He has found no place in the orderly evolution of society. He is a member of his Majesty's Opposition—the permanent Opposition to law and order which every big city develops.

Before you cross the river again on your return journey, look a little closer. It is Saturday night, when half London is at leisure, and the other half ministering to its demand for "bread and games." The man who keeps the big coffee-stall near the end of the bridge is making ready for his customers; and the policeman who stands hard by stamps his feet to keep them warm. He is not permitted to take a walk, for it is his business to see that the disorder about the coffee-stall does not pass reasonable limits. But things are quiet enough at present, and the man in a reefer jacket,

shoulders slightly hunched and elbows close to the side, which marks the London street boy. The policeman at the coffee-stall looks knowingly at them as they pass. He knows well enough that the belt which this boy is carefully tightening serves other purposes

PITCH AND TOSS.

bowler hat, and thick boots, who ostentatiously ignores the policeman, is quite conspicuously a plain clothes constable. Now and then, among the strollers and the women returning from market, there passes along a boy— sometimes two or three together—walking swiftly and with evident purpose. They are not nicely dressed; though the night is cold there is not an overcoat among them; but their jackets are buttoned tight, neckcloths supply the place of collars, and they walk with the curious light tread,

than that of dress; he knows that the unusual stiffness of that boy's arm is probably due to the presence of an iron bar up the sleeve. But there is no law which compels the wearing of braces instead of belts, and the policeman, from experience of his own, deduces the task which lies before some of his colleagues across the river.

On the other side of the bridge these furtive figures scatter through the streets to left and right; for they are moving to an attack on Pentonville, all directed by one

A BROKEN WHIP.

WAISTBELT.

master mind. These are the boys from the Borough who have developed a feud with the boys of Pentonville, and their leader, a lad of seventeen, with a cropper in his breast pocket and some notion of tactics in his head, has foreseen the position of the enemy and designs to place him between two fires. A quarter of an hour later the movement has been developed. The Pentonville boys have been caught in one of those little streets off the Goswell Road. Belts are off, and the buckles swinging; sleeves lose their stiffening of iron; here and there a fortunate boy has a cheap pistol, which startles quiet citizens and occasionally kills them. The fighting is independent of the Geneva Convention; there are no rules, only a general desire, born of the instinct of self-preservation, to get at once to close quarters, for fist and muscle are less deadly than buckle and bar and pistol. Then come the police— if there are enough within earshot. But that is generally after the fight is decided, and only the wounded appear next morning at the police-court and give texts for letters to the papers. The rest scatter and run, to gather again at the river. And if you are at the aforesaid coffee-stall at one in the morning you may see and hear the whooping victors wheeling back the disabled leader on a barrow—doubtless borrowed.

That is a typical instance of the feuds which rage between the street boys of the various London districts. In this case the cause of war was the oldest in the world, a Borough Helen abstracted by a Pentonville Paris. But these mysterious feuds exist, and are fought out, between many London districts, and there are times when a Lisson

Grove boy would go east of Tottenham Court Road at his peril. All round London these gangs are ready for provocation. The organisation is loose, and depends mainly on some masterful spirit of lawlessness in direct succession to the original Patrick Hooligan, of Lambeth. But whether at Bethnal Green or Wandsworth, Pentonville or Fulham, so soon as the King of Misrule arises the ground of quarrel is assured.

Sometimes the leader of a gang develops qualities of organisation and command which inspire respect among the police, who know quite well that the Hooligan is always on the verge of crime, and often topples over. Such was the head of a gang which terrorised Lambeth. He was only about seventeen years of age, but he had had a thoroughly good criminal education, and, while he had effected a burglary or two, picked up his living mainly by petty thieving. But he had acquired a remarkable influence over the boys of Lambeth. He made it a point of honour for every boy who aspired to membership of his gang to show a shattered window, a smashed door, or a broken head—the broken head opened the way, as it were, to a commission in the gang. He had no settled residence; that were unadvisable; but the boys knew where to find him and ask for their orders for the day. And he collected about him as enterprising and capable a horde of young ruffians as you could wish to avoid on a winter's evening.

For this lawlessness inevitably leads to crime. Street fighting is fun; but why should not the lessons it teaches be turned to profit? From cracking heads for love to bashing "toffs" for gain is a short step, and the boy who has served his apprenticeship in a gang—such as that

I. CRUCIFIX. II. A KIND OF DAGGER. III. LOADED STICK.

WAISTBELT.

WAISTBELT.

LOADED STICK.

HOOLIGAN WEAPONS.

of Lambeth—is quite willing and able to commit an unprovoked assault on another's enemy for half-a-crown down and another half-a-crown when the job is done. And we often read the result in the "police intelligence" without a thought of the power of the capitalist who has five shillings and an enemy. Nor is the step from street fighting to highway robbery much longer. Imagine a couple of boys, brought up to the street fighting in which there are no rules, with no fear of God, man, or constable before their eyes, and with no money in their pockets— imagine them face to face with a lonely wayfarer in evening dress, carrying presumably a watch and a sovereign purse. It is the simplest thing in the world. One boy whips the overcoat back and imprisons the victim's arms ; the other goes through the pockets. The work of a moment, and so easy ! No wonder the Hooligan turns his sport to account ! The sandbag, too, is handy. It is an American importation, and has made some reputation in New York. Unlike the bludgeon, it leaves no visible mark ; unlike the cheap pistol, it makes no noise. It is easily hidden up the sleeve till required ; and a well-directed crack over the head with a sandbag—especially if the sand has been damped—will stun the strongest man for several minutes. Not only gain, but also revenge, is a motive for the Hooligan assault, and the existence of a gang which had not been suspected was proved by the following letter which— marked "urgent"—turned up beneath the nose of an editor of a morning paper :—

" Sir,—For your ——— cheek in put one of our gang away we have Past a Rule that we will have your Life you will not know when we will be in your Liver tomorrow Saturday."

This note, grubby from the hand that delivered it, was signed by the name of the boy who was "Secretary" to the Camberwell gang. The editor is still alive. But shortly afterwards, in the small hours of the morning, one of the compositors was set upon and nearly killed by a gang of boys who caught him at the southern end of Blackfriars Bridge.

The Hooligan is a worshipper of muscle, quite apart from criminal application, and

to him the latest hero of the ring is a god. His saints are the wearers of the gloves in those obscure boxing contests which take place, mostly on Saturday night, in all kinds of dim holes and corners of London, where if you wear a collar you are assumed to be a detective. There is one of these places tucked away under a railway arch in a certain dark street off Lambeth Walk. You enter through a sort of hole in a big gateway, and after stumbling forward tumble into a square room, lighted by a flaring gas-jet swung from the roof Space is limited, and you sit close packed around the square—which is called a ring. Row upon row of eager faces ; eyes fixed on the proprietor, in whose breast is locked the secret of the next fight. The lowest row is composed of the youngest—those who came first. Above are men who have fought their fights and apparently lost them. Highest of all appear the cap of an inspector of police and the helmet of a constable, for we are within the rules. The boys step into the ring ; their names are announced—not their real names, for the ring's traditions are as insistent as those of the stage, and with better reason. But the inspector, cocking an eye at the boy who turns out in fighting tights with a torso as clean and bright as a new pin, recognises the boy he knows as a grimy, grubby loafer in the street. Absolute cleanliness and neatness of attire are a point of honour in the obscurest boxing saloon, and that is something in its favour.

It is a disillusion to see these boys, so lithe and clean in their fighting trim, huddle on their trousers and coat—they do it in a corner raked by the eyes of the audience —tie the wisp of cloth round their necks, and revert to the slavery of their usual habit. But the most remarkable feature of this saloon—and of others of its kind—is the expectant row of juniors, who got the front places by waiting. At the least hint of a hitch, if an expected combatant delays a moment in facing his antagonist, half-a-dozen coats are off, half-a-dozen shirts are pulled over head, and half-a-dozen clean, trained, eager boys are calling out " I'll tike 'im on." For these boys who sit patiently night by night are waiting to get a foot

HOOLIGAN *V.* HOOLIGAN.

on the first rung of Fame's ladder, and are not going to miss a chance. Some day, if luck is theirs, they will box at "Wonderland" in the Whitechapel Road, where the audience is numbered by hundreds and wears collars; and if the luck holds at the National Sporting Club, where the audience wears evening dress.

To catch the street boy in his softer mood you need not wait for a Bank Holiday or travel so far as Hampstead, much less to

78

Epping Forest. On Saturday evenings they stand in long lines at the gallery doors of the less fashionable theatres and music-halls, having somehow acquired the price of two seats apiece. For every boy who has started life on his own account considers it a point of honour to possess a girl. The girls who stand at the gallery door waiting for the treat which they demand of their cavaliers are neither particularly clean and tidy nor very picturesque. They wear the clothes in

SANDBAGGING IN THE FOG.

which they work all the week at cardboard-box making, jam packing, match making, and so on—with the addition of the feathered hat which is the glory of a woman in this rank of life. But, on the whole, they are reasonably good. And it is a curious fact that the Hooligan boy seldom finds an ally in his girl when he wants to be flagrantly dishonest. She does not ask too many questions—she does not, for instance, inquire where he got the money to pay for a riot supper after the entertainment; but she would prefer to think that her boy is " in work " and " earning good money," and she is perfectly capable of maintaining that proposition—with tooth and claw, if need be—against any other lady who presumes to doubt it.

The street boy of the type I have tried to describe is full of a certain spasmodic nervous energy, but he has neither ballast nor settled purpose in life beyond the present day. Long ago the Ragged School Union set to work to catch this continual growth of possible criminals and train it aright; and to-day the energetic Secretary from the centre influences many institutions and workers. Our illustrations suggest some of the difficulties encountered in Hoxton by a devoted teacher who to this day is engaged in making silk purses out of unpromising

material, with no little success. The waist-belt near the top of page 231, for example, was laid about the teacher's head by a voluntary scholar who had changed his mind about the charm of education. The loaded stick at the foot of the same page is a relic of a great street fight outside the school ; the missing piece was broken off over a victim's head. But perhaps the quaintest of this little collection is the crucifix. It is the offering of an apostate of eleven. He had joined a High Church club. But the world called him ; he enlisted under the leader of the Hoxton gang at the time, and, having chosen the life of disorder, presented his teacher with the symbol which had ceased to symbolise.

A further impetus to the movement started by the Ragged School Union was given by the institution of Toynbee Hall, in memory of Arnold Toynbee, of Balliol. The public schools and the universities caught up the idea of " boys' clubs " which should be impregnated with something of the public-school spirit. At present East, South-East, and North-East London are the main seats of these settlements, while London is breed-ing boys from Wimbledon to Leytonstone whom careless parents throw upon the streets so soon as they can run alone. Oxford House is a notable centre. It owes its success to Dr. Ingram, who before becoming Bishop of London was Bishop of Stepney. Go down to Bethnal Green—on a Saturday evening for choice—and at Oxford House you will find an interesting dining-hall and common-room. They are all of them young graduates. Some are barristers or journalists at work all day at their own affairs; others are intending clergymen who wish to take a close look at the souls they shall save. A hurried meal, a snatched smoke, and they scatter to the clubs where they have to take control.

We will go to one, typical of many, within a short walk of Oxford House. It is in a quiet street, but near the door boys with knitted brows are hanging about. The entrance fee is sixpence; and just inside a genial official is receiving this sum—usually in pennies—from a new member. We go upstairs, and find a room full of boys playing billiards and bagatelle. There is an evident effort for cleanliness and neatness in attire. One lad with a note-book marks down the games and takes the money; for the club is run, under supervision, by the members, and public spirit is strong against peculation or disorder. We go further, led

by the sound of tramping feet, and find the newest recruits to the cadet corps at their drill. One of them, in an interval, tells you he has just joined the football club, having secured an income of a halfpenny a week. He is fifteen, he says. He would pass for twelve on a railway, and for eleven in an Eton preparatory school; the London street boy is terribly undersized. In the basement we reach the theatre, where the minstrels of the club perform; here, too, we find a boy solemnly punching the ball —for as boys will fight anyhow, they may as well join the club and learn to box at an initial and final outlay of one shilling, under the sanction of the Church and the Queensberry rules. But the boy who joins the Webbe Institute may get a great deal at cost price. He may even get a week in a seaside camp every August. This is only one of the clubs which are scattered about the confines of the inner circle. And music, too! The drums and fifes cease for a minute, and you see the contingent of cadets join the main body and march off to the evening service at St. Matthew's Church, clean, erect, and enlisted from the forces of disorder on the side of law and right.

A STREET GROUP.

MANAGER RECEIVING GUESTS (HOTEL VICTORIA).

HOTEL LONDON.

By J. C. WOOLLAN.

PAGE.

HOTEL London is great and growing. Perhaps no feature of London life was more conspicuous for a smart advance in the closing years of the last century and the opening of the new than hotel accommodation of every variety, and what might be called the hotel habit — the living in hotels of even Londoners themselves. There was a time, not so very long ago, when London had to bear the reproach of giving less satisfaction in the hotel way to the visitor than almost any other great city. Even yet the foreigner has his complaints to make, especially when he comes to settle the bill, but in a general way the Metropolis has responded excellently to an increasing demand. To-day she can fling at the cities of the European and American continents a boast that she will name twenty of her hotels, and challenge each of her rivals to produce twenty that are better, or even as good.

You may never have reflected, and perchance may not have had the materials for reflection, upon how vast and of what infinite variety is the Hotel London of to-day. Let us consider the first of the two points just named, and estimate in some small way the dimensions of Hotel-land within the confines of the capital.

The most careful of calculations brings one to the safe conclusion that there are daily no fewer than 120,000 visitors in the Metropolis. Not all of these stay over a single night, and of those who do a fair proportion welcome the hospitality of friends in private houses. Yet, when all deductions have been made and we have nursed the figures down to those of the net hotel and boarding-house population, it is discovered that there are, on an average, between 50,000 and 60,000 people who daily come within this category. Of this great number it is reckoned that the recognised hotels, licensed and of varying pretensions, are capable of accommodating just about half, and the boarding-houses and private hotels are well able to account for the rest, existing as they do in their thousands. It has been found in actual practice that over 8,000 guests have slept in twenty of the chief hotels on busy nights of the season. One single hotel has about 1,000 bedrooms, and there are five others with 500 or more. A dozen of the chief hotels make up an aggregate of only a few short of 6,000 bedrooms, a proportion of which contain a couple of beds, so that in the whole these sleeping apartments will very likely accommodate 12,000 people—the population of a small town. And the directory gives you the names of over 300 big licensed hotels in London.

The story of the growth of Hotel London to these vast proportions is tinged with not a little of romance. Once upon a time there was an enterprising servant in a West-End mansion, which he forsook in order that he might start a boarding-house. The latter in due course developed into an hotel, and the hotel so thrived and grew that to-day it is one of the biggest in the Metropolis, whilst the quondam servant, for his part, is a rich country gentleman with large lands. He is not alone in his great success. And on the other hand, showing again the vast outcome of the enterprise of the pioneers in the making of modern Hotel London, it may be cited that a score of the chief hotels among them represent a capital of about eight millions of money, and even the little group of Gordon Hotels are capable of accounting for three and a-half millions.

But it is not our purpose to weary with statistics, though such few as are in the foregoing lines will be pardoned for the tale of immensity which they alone can tell. We will discover now the variety of our Hotel London, and the even greater variety of its patrons. Each hotel is not for every patron. The Americans have claimed the biggest; and have, indeed, made the success of some of them. The Germans preponderate at others, and there is another where we may find a regular *potpourri* of highly respectable foreigners of different nationalities. Such is De Keyser's Royal, at the eastern extremity of the Victoria Embankment. Do not even the names of the hotels of the west tell their own little tales of foreign individuality and of cosmopolitanism? There are the Hotel Continental and the Hotel de l'Europe with expansive titles; but there are so many others, many of which you may not know, but all by their names alone making a mute and often successful appeal to particular classes.

However, with this brief general survey, let

ARRIVAL OF AN ORIENTAL POTENTATE (CLARIDGE'S)

us particularise. With the duty we owe to rank let us return to the kings and nobles, and see where they most do congregate.

You may find their majesties at two or three places in the fashionable west. Some time or other they are certain to be at the pre-eminently aristocratic Claridge's, in Brook Street, away from all the din and bustle, and in an atmosphere which is positively scented with exclusiveness and distinction. There are not many hotels in the world which have the extremely restrictive peculiarity of Claridge's. This is no place for the mere man of money, who is nothing more than that—with not even a social aim. Whatever king he be, he may live here and move about in no disguise and with perfect freedom from any vulgar gaze. For here, tenanting the grand and costly suites of rooms, are men and women who are numbered amongst the foremost of their respective lands, men and women who would make up for this king a court of which he might well be proud. There is an English duke, a Spanish princess, a Russian grand duke, a variety of counts, several leaders of London society, and, generally, a collection of people in whose veins runs the best blue blood of every nation. Wealth, rank, and power are represented. On a winter's evening, as we pass along the street, a carriage with a fresh arrival rattles up to the entrance, and with a passing fancy that we will stake the reputation of Claridge's, as it were, on this one haphazard throw, we pause a moment to discover the new comer. Claridge's wins. The American Ambassador has just arrived from Washington, and has driven straight to Claridge's, where he will stay for a few weeks. Another time an Oriental potentate comes driving up, and with some form and ceremony and his own native servant in attendance he passes within.

Yet even Claridge's has not a monopoly of the greatest. You may find royalty and nobles at the Albemarle, in Piccadilly, or at Brown's, in Dover Street, or at the Langham, in Langham Place, upon which King Edward, when Prince of Wales, set the aristocratic stamp by opening. The grand and highly fashionable Carlton is, again, one of the most likely places in London for the foreign potentate or the social star of some to be temporarily housed in, especially if there is a

desire to be, in the colloquial term, "in the thick of it." In the Palm Court here one may lounge to perfection amongst the best-known people of at least two continents. Different celebrities, too, have their own conservative tastes and their own hotels; and there are old-fashioned country families, most highly respectable, who would prefer to pay Claridge's and Carlton prices at hostelries of far less renown but of guaranteed "tone."

To leave the rank and fashion pure, and seek the greater rendezvous of wealth and luxury we must proceed a trifle eastward and southward, dip down to Trafalgar Square and Northumberland Avenue, and walk a few score paces along the Strand. In the maintenance of such hotel luxury as we are speaking of, the American contribution preponderates. Our cousins of the States are a very notable factor indeed of Hotel London. At the opening of the bright summer season they arrive with their trunks and their money in thousands, till the Transatlantic accent hums in the region to which we have just passed. Always for the biggest, their first thought is for the Cecil; and so pass into the courtyard any fine morning in the season, and walk up to the tables and chairs at the foot of the steps, where the loungers recline preparatory to their day's assault upon the lions of London, and you will not need to search for the man with the American voice, or for the girl with American smartness. They are everywhere—here outside, inside, there still dallying at the breakfast table, penning picture postcards in the writing-room, and—just a few thirsty souls are these —sipping iced concoctions downstairs at the American bar. There is special accommodation for the American, even to the chef. This middle-aged man, with the kindly face and the grey moustache, stepping into a hansom is a great American railroad king who means to revolutionise railway London; the slight dark figure in the porch is that of a man who is an engineer of monopolies and trusts. These are men who are feared. The richly-apparelled lady who is sweeping along a corridor is an American society woman who recently gave a dinner in New York which cost twenty pounds a head.

You will discover also a great American

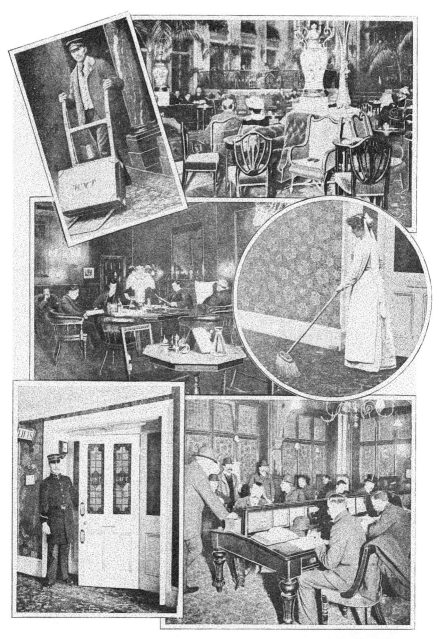

I. PORTER. II. THE PALM COURT (CARLTON HOTEL). III. SMOKING ROOM (GRAND HOTEL).
IV. CHAMBERMAID. V. LIFT MAN. VI. COMMERCIALS " WRITING UP THE MAIL " (MANCHESTER HOTEL.

contingent, as well as a fine smattering of other nationalities, at the Métropole, the Victoria, and the Grand—all Gordons, all in Northumberland Avenue, and all palatial and luxurious. The great First Avenue in Holborn and the Grosvenor at Victoria are also Gordons. Well-to-do Frenchmen, well-to-do Germans, and many besides are here in numbers; but then, as has been said, De Keyser's Royal, on the Embankment, is the particular resort of the Continental visitor. Germans are here in force, and if you move still more eastward and come to Finsbury Square you will find a further batch of hotels with great German reputations. There are Klein's and Seyd's in the Square, and there is Bücker's in Christopher Street just off it. In Finsbury Square, where beef is "bif," the sons of the Fatherland may live precisely after the manner of the German fighting cock.

Other nationalities, other hotels; and many more, especially in the east, could be added to this already long list. In these followings of the foreigner we are neglecting the strangers of our own country who are temporarily within the hospitable gates of the Metropolis.

Whence comes the provincial? We discover that he comes very largely viâ the termini at Euston, St. Pancras, and King's Cross, and here we find the great railway companies have raised palaces for his temporary residence. The railway hotel is essentially the hotel for the busy man who must live in style and comfort, but who is always catching express trains, or who in catching but a few must make a quick certainty of them. Of course, such hotels as the Midland Grand—truly grand—the Euston, and the Great Central are for other people besides—for families and for pleasure folk as well. All sorts and conditions of British people, but especially business people, are here. One of the greatest financiers of modern times has worked his deals from a suite of rooms in the Midland Grand, and such is high commercial loyalty that in another suite may be found a celebrated director of the Midland Railway itself. At Charing Cross Station is another railway hotel, and at Cannon Street, in the heart of the City, one more—which is perhaps the most business-like of all, for a long programme of big company meetings is negotiated here every day. Shareholders have

DRAWING ROOM (HOTEL CECIL).

rejoiced and sorrowed, congratulated and stormed, in the Cannon Street Hotel as in no other. Then there is the more purely commercial hostelry, of which the Manchester, in Aldersgate Street, the Salisbury, off Fleet Street, and Andorton's, in the middle of newspaperdom, are great examples. You may witness a busy scene at the Manchester in the evening, when the commercial travellers, their City

DINING ROOM (OAK SALON, HOTEL MÉTROPOLE).

wanderings over, send their reports and instructions to headquarters, or, as they call it, "write up the mail."

Forsaking commerce, we will seek out the hotels of the studious, and we shall find them in Bloomsbury, hard by the British Museum, busy hive of brainworkers. The Thackeray, Kingsley, and Esmond trade, one might almost say, upon the Museum; even the telegraphic address of one of them is "Bookcraft." These three are temperance hotels; and in, passing, let it not be forgotten that London accommodates excellently the thrifty people who prefer the teetotal establishment and its moderate charges. Wild's, in Ludgate Hill, and the Buckingham, in the Strand, are two more among many.

If we tried we could not before leaving Bloomsbury miss the magnificent Russell, fashioned on the Gordon system, and bearing the Frederick name. For patrons of a different character, in the long street arteries which feed Bloomsbury are countless private hotels, which faithfully serve a mission of cheapness. Mostly they are numbered, but some of them take names to themselves; and, being bound by no traditions, desiring only to be up to date,

79

fearful and wonderful specimens of hotel nomenclature are prepared in a single night. What was a modest title at eventide glares forth pretentiously as "Hotel Pretoria" next morning, wars and patriotism just then making the blood to leap. And by the same token when there was a scamper for Alaskan gold fields an "Hotel Klondyke" came topically forward. In these days, from highest to lowest, it is Hotel this and Hotel that—à la mode "hotel" comes first.

Away in the farther West-End are many other hotels of great reputation. Beginning at Westminster, there are the cosy St. Ermin's and the Westminster Palace. At South Kensington there is Bailey's; overlooking Rotten Row in Hyde Park is the Alexandra, of most pretentious appearance; hard by is the Hyde Park Hotel, carried on in conjunction with the Carlton Hotel; whilst the Buckingham Palace, the Royal Palace, the De Vere, and many others are all institutions of the Metropolis, and there are others, such as Morley's in Trafalgar Square, the Holborn Viaduct Hotel, and the Queen's in Leicester Square, which a London visitor can hardly help but see.

Of the oddities, peculiarities, individualities

of Hotel London—an! they are so many, too many for one short survey. The trades and the professions have their own hotels. To take two widely different examples, one might point out that, whilst all who attended the great wool sales from the country and abroad would stay at the Great Eastern, country lawyers and clients whose business is at the Law Courts would favour Anderton's or the Inns of Court, which vie with each other in proximity to the great headquarters of Justice. And the space in between these two could be well filled. Come with me to Covent Garden, and I will show you a big hotel with 200 rooms which will not admit ladies—it is "for gentlemen only." There is another hotel far away which has obtained a peculiar patronage from persons arriving in London by P. and O. steamers, who know nothing whatever of Hotel London, and have gratefully accepted a hint that was given them. There is a clerical hotel; ships' captains have their own in dock-land; there is a Jewish hotel; and in the neighbourhood of Regent's Park there is even one which is advertised as "the only Spiritualist hotel

in London." After that, it would be futile to attempt a further illustration of the possibilities of hotel individualism in the great Metropolis.

We will go back to the Strand, and see that each street as it runs from the great thoroughfare southwards to the Thames is honeycombed with hotels of different sorts and sizes. And in perambulating westwards again we may this time note the Savoy, with its abundance of fair fame, which we could on our last journey hardly couple with the Cecil, though they adjoin. The Savoy is as æsthetic as it is big.

Such is Hotel London in all its magnitude and with all its wonders. And in the enumeration of so many wonders we dispel at least one. There is such a variety and such a choice in hotel life that more and more are Londoners of means forsaking their homes and living only in hotels, with all their careless freedom.

For years Hotel London has been passing through an interesting process of evolution, and the end of the process will not be in the twentieth century.

LOUNGE (HOTEL RUSSELL).

Photo: H. Mayes, Putney, S.W.

THE OXFORD AND CAMBRIDGE BOAT RACE.

THAMES PLEASURES AND SPORTS.

By JOHN BLOUNDELLE-BURTON.

THE pleasures and sports of the Thames are principally above bridge; the business part lies below. Yet let none forget that there is plenty of pleasure and sport and fun to be obtained below bridge also, and found at Greenwich, Gravesend, Southend, Margate, Ramsgate, and elsewhere. But, even to start for these places beloved of a certain portion of Living London's population—and visited often enough by a totally distinct stratum of that population, whose cry, as a rule, is "anything for a change"—one sets out by water from above-bridge : *i.e.* from the Old Swan Pier. Whenever one does so in the summer time, and providing the weather is fine, the cruise is certain to be an amusing as well as an enjoyable one. There is always a band on board (harp, cornet, and flute), refreshments may be obtained, all are determined on enjoying themselves, and lovers are abundant and shed a rosy glow around. In the case of the "husbands' boat"—for Margate on Saturdays

Photo: Russell & Sons, Baker Street, W.

DOGGETT'S COAT AND
BADGE.

—it is the married men, hastening to join their wives until Monday, who represent the votaries of Hymen, late Cupid ; yet they too are happy.

But we will turn to the absolute subject of this sketch, the pleasures and sports of the Thames.

By priority of age comes the race for Doggett's Coat and Badge, a sum of money having been left by Thomas Doggett, a Drury Lane actor of the early Georgian period, to commemorate the accession day of the first Hanoverian monarch, *i.e.* August 1st, 1715. This furnishes a waterman's coat and a silver badge—the latter as large as a pie-dish and bearing the white horse of Hanover on it—and is open to any six young Thames watermen who desire to compete, the course being originally from the "Swan" at London Bridge to the "Swan" at Chelsea. As the event has existed for nearly two hundred years, the old actor's loyalty and enthusiasm have been pretty well stamped

EXCURSION STEAMBOATS LEAVING FRESH WHARF, LONDON BRIDGE.

BATHING IN THE RIVER.

into the minds and memories of several generations of Londoners. The ground, or rather water, covered by this course, and the shores from London Bridge to Chelsea, not only comprise almost all the chief historical portion of the river as regards sport and pleasure, but also the grandeur and might and power of the greatest city in the world. And—which should give us further food for reflection—Father Thames is still adding to our history while even now serving the purposes of recreation and amusement.

Lean for a moment over Chelsea Suspension Bridge on a summer day and look around and below you. Passing under the bridge is a steamer on its way to Kew and Richmond and Hampton Court. Here, too, you may see, especially if it is Saturday afternoon, single, double, treble sculling boats with young maidens, and, of course, their swains, prepared for an outing, or jaunt—for a Saturday "up the river." You may observe, also, men of sterner metal and intentions passing beneath you—brawny and muscular oarsmen sculling in wager boats, and practising for some race the stakes of which may be well worth winning—stakes that may enable whosoever gains them to set up in business as a boat-builder and a man who will have "Boats to let," or as the landlord of some riverside public-house, which, as every riparian resident knows, is the "be all and end all," in the majority of cases, of the professional sculler's existence.

On one side of this bridge is Chelsea Hospital, where once stood, close by, the celebrated Ranelagh Gardens: on the other is Battersea Park, formed out of what was originally a marshy, undrained piece of submerged land. Now it is a very pretty place, much given up to cyclists, especially beginners who do not care to roam too far afield at first or to encounter their latest rival, the motor car.

In this park, especially in summer—since it is then green and leafy and at its best—youths and maidens make and keep their rendezvous, as they have always done and always will. The nursemaid loves to saunter on its paths with the inevitable perambulator, whilst the warriors from Chelsea Barracks across the river cast admiring glances at her. Once, in

the early sixties, the West-End terminus of the Brighton line was near here, before the railway came farther into town and before Victoria terminus and the railway bridge were built. Beyond this, as we proceed up the river, there is nothing much to call for special remark in the present day until we come to Putney.

Putney is the metropolis of boating men; and on its embankment are the boathouses of the Thames, Vesta, Leander, and London Rowing Clubs — world-renowned establishments, if not for their own celebrity, which is considerable, then because, also, it is from one or other of these that the boats of the Oxford Rowing Club and the Cambridge Rowing Club put off for their practice daily during the fortnight before the 'Varsity Race, and also on the momentous morning of the race. This they have practically done since the year 1849, when, in consequence of there having been no race in 1847 or 1848, two races were rowed in the former year, while previous to 1849, with one solitary exception, the race was rowed from Westminster to Putney.

We witness a busy scene when the start for the great race takes place soon after the steamers for the Press and the Universities arrive from London; when the river is cleared for what the reporters call the great "aquatic contest," much as the Epsom course is cleared for the Derby, and when hansoms, drags, char-a-bancs and omnibuses line the esplanade, as they line every spot where vehicles can go. The ladies all wear favours and rosettes of their favourite University, or, as the cynics say, of whichever blue suits their complexions and toilettes the better; and it has been whispered that some who have sported the losing colours before the race change it for the winning colour afterwards. This is, however, probably scandal.

Once off and the start made, horsemen and light vehicles, such as hansoms, tear off from the starting-point, make a dash across Barnes Common to the "White Hart" at Barnes or the "Ship" at Mortlake—the huge bend north of the river favouring the short cut—and so get in in time for the death, or, rather, the finish: the result being made known by the hoisting of the winning colour above the

READY FOR A ROW.

Only a passing line of reference need be made to Hurlingham — especially as it is a little below Fulham and Putney — since every one knows that this is the most fashionable place in the world for pigeon-shooting, or, as students of human nature say, for the "massacre of the Innocents." Every one does not know, however, that some of the nondescript beings who are to be found alongside the river from mouth to source, and who are generally spoken of as "waterside characters,"

losing one on Barnes Railway Bridge, after which a scene of wild excitement takes place. Old Blues—and young ones, too—clergymen from distant parishes and lawyers from town shake hands and nod pleasantly to each other if their 'Varsity has won, while those belonging to the losing side swallow their disappointment as best they can. The negro minstrels commence their soothing strains and the men who swallow not tow or allow stones to be broken on their bare chests give their performances; the adjacent public-houses become crowded; a few fights take place; pigeons are let loose for distant villages; air-balloons bearing the names of theatres and their performances, or of enterprising newspapers or Turf-tipsters, are sent up. The vehicles either speed back to town or take their occupants to Richmond; the steam-launches turn their heads Londonwards, and the sight-seers on foot stream off to the railway stations; while the "sportsman" who invites you to back the "'art, the marker, or the diaming," or find the queen as he performs the three-card trick, packs up his traps and departs. The boat race is over and done with for another year.

pick up in this neighbourhood a few shillings occasionally by appropriating the escaped birds, which avoid one fate only to find another. Few birds, however, escape the marksmen of Hurlingham.

The river—especially its pleasures and, in a smaller way, its sports—would not, however, have full justice done to it if attention were not called to one of its most popular haunts —i.e. Kew. For here, indeed, the home of pleasure for many holiday-makers is established, and there are those who think that the succulent winkle and shrimp may be found at their best in this resort. Bread and

A "PENNY SWEAT."

butter, too, are, as all the world knows—or should know—partaken of in large quantities, accompanied by the health-giving watercress while washed down by a strong highly-flavoured tea, good for promoting digestion after a stroll in the celebrated gardens. Who has not seen the mystic legend inscribed over many a riverside door here—the legend announcing "Tea and hot water, 9d."? and who has not gently wondered why the hot water should be so emphatically mentioned, since, to make tea without hot water, is at present regarded as an almost unattainable feat?

Kew has its visitors, however, for other things besides the Botanic Gardens and the above appetising

river can provide. And here is the spot where sweet-scented and beautifully variegated bouquets have been sold near the steamboat pier and the south side of the bridge—the old bridge—from long past days, and are still sold.

One wonders sometimes what Londoners would be like if it were not for the river. Its waters have not, it is true, been pellucid for many a day; salmon is no longer caught at

I. AT PRACTICE.   II. "BOATS TO LET."

Putney as it was in the middle of the eighteenth century, and the nightingale no longer sings outside Barn Elms or Craven Cottage, where Bulwer-Lytton lived some time. But boys have bathed from time immemorial in the stream, and

refreshments. Anglers come here to fish for barbel, of which there is still a famous "swim" even lower down, namely, at Barnes; and there is an eyot where skeleton leaves can be obtained in large quantities—the kind of leaves our grandmothers pinned and pressed between the pages of books with, often enough, an auspicious date marked against them and the initials of what was, doubtless, a masculine name. Here, too, are rowing clubs capable of producing crews and scullers of no mean prowess, quite fitted to contend for victory in any regatta or water contest which the

will continue to do so; they have also for a long while hired boats in which to take what is called "penny sweats"—i.e. enough of them band together to hire a boat (not generally the best the boatman has to let), and so get their modicum of exercise. Who, too, has not rowed on the classic stream, either in outrigger, racing-boat, or randan?—who that is a Londoner has not plunged "the labouring oar" into its waters and rowed his lady-love up river, or, if the tide is very strong, gone ashore and towed the boat containing the fair one, the luncheon-basket and the tea-kettle, as well as other things? Who, too, has not fed the swans that abound on the river, and alternately teased or played with them, while some, perhaps, have even witnessed the ceremony of swan-upping, which is occasionally called "swan-hopping"? This ceremony consists in marking the birds on the upper mandible of the bill with nicks; the Royal swans, of which there are many, having two diamonds, those of the Dyers Company one nick, and those of the Vintners Company two nicks. From this old practice comes the corrupted inn-sign, "The Swan with Two Necks."

Of late years old customs have been revived on the Royal River which had quite sunk out of fashion, and they now share with the boat-clubs of men and women the office of furnishing both pleasure and sport upon it. Regattas have much increased and multiplied; so, too, have water carnivals. Richmond, amongst other places, organises several of the latter, and the beauti-ful and brilliant scenes on the illuminated water and the river banks on a summer night are not unworthy competitors with those of Venice. Indeed, the Thames above bridge, while having its fair share in utility, is the greatest contributor to the Londoner's open-air enjoyment, and is without a rival. For the pleasure-seeker can bathe and row, if he chooses; he can, on the other hand, if he is not athletically disposed, be conveyed upon it in steamers or launches or sailing-boats, and he can dwell on its shores at any point which he chooses to select; while, when he has left London a few miles behind him, he can, if an angler, fish to his heart's content. Moreover, no part of England is better fur-nished with good hotels and inns where everything that the heart of man can desire is to be found, so that, as one poet has remarked, the holiday-maker can "take his ease at his inn," and, in the words of another, "find his warmest welcome there."

RIVER STEAMER.

ROMAN CATHOLIC LONDON.

By WILFRID MEYNELL.

LONDON entertains, perhaps unawares, some half-million of persons professing the Roman Catholic faith. Not all of this multitude actually practises its religion cover a larger total area of earth, and Westminster Cathedral boasts the broadest nave of all. A bold man is he who builds a cathedral; he has about him the tongues of Babel, and

LEAVING THE ORATORY, SOUTH KENSINGTON.

by going to mass on Sundays and to its "duties" (confession and communion) at Easter. "The world is too much with us" is a Wordsworthian sigh upon the lips of nominal adherents of every creed.

"Nominal Catholics," therefore, exist; otherwise the antithetical term "practical Catholics" would not need to be very commonly heard among them. Of the number of these practical Catholics, failing an official census, nothing can be certainly known. But London has no fewer than eighty churches for their accommodation—and in nearly all of these a succession of masses on Sunday morning, so that every seat may have been occupied twice or thrice. The Westminster Cathedral, dreamt of by Cardinal Manning and realised by Cardinal Vaughan, possesses that ideal conjunction—an actual as well as an official pre-eminence. Only the Abbey and St. Paul's of all churches in London

in this Westminster case nearly Babel's tower. Cardinal Vaughan heard, and, more difficult still, did not hear. He wasted no idle discussions none of the energy which was otherwise required. Fortune and generosity supplied the £200,000 that had to pass into the bare outwork of bricks.

Next to the Westminster Cathedral in size comes the Oratory Church at South Kensington. It is served by over a dozen fathers. These do not belong to an "order" in the sense in which Franciscans or Benedictines do; but they live in community. Their rule is that of St. Philip Neri, adapted to English life by Cardinal Newman. He (from Birmingham, too!) was the nominal founder of the London Oratory; but its actual founder was Father Faber—he whose hymns, sung within their native walls at Sunday and week-day evening services, are echoed in churches and chapels of every other creed

—in truth, a great "conspiracy of song." Its site lies where several ways meet and part — types of the many crises of the spiritual life its walls have witnessed—the farewells involved by "conversions," the meetings, the marriages, the last rites over the dead. In this church, or in its predecessor on the same site, Lothair (the third Marquess of Bute) was married (but not to Corisande), Lord Beaconsfield languidly looking on. Here, too, the Marquess of Ripon laid down his wand as Grand Master of the Freemasons, Mr. Gladstone metaphorically observing anything but languidly; forging, indeed, out of that not mood, a famous new arrow-head for his quiver as an anti-Vatican pamphleteer. Here was the Requiem sung over beloved Cardinal Manning's bier; here was held the Victorian Diamond Jubilee service of 1897; here Edward VII., when Prince of Wales, has assisted at a nuptial mass; and here, too, is a bench which has been the judges'—all gathered together to pay the last tribute of homage to Lord Russell of Killowen.

ARRIVAL OF THE CARDINAL AT SARDINIA STREET CHAPEL.

History gets made quickly, you perceive; for it is only about fifty years since the first Oratorians in England (most of whom were Oxford and clerical converts) settled on this site, and were stoned in the streets for their pains. Their own pile of stones is that which remains, and the noble dome which crowns the edifice is an admitted adornment—amid a hundred modern defacements — of London. Apart from its memories (and a full share of sad ones) the church is a "show" one, by reason of its size, its abundance of marble, its many altars, its saints and cherubs, with all the flourishes and flying draperies of the Italian Renascence.

I dwell on this very representative church because what is said of it can be more or less applied to the other seventy and nine churches which need, for the most part, no special description. But "Farm Street"—the church of the Jesuit Fathers, planted amid the glories of Grosvenor Square—demands its own word. Between Oratorians and Jesuits may be supposed to exist a certain "holy rivalry," which the westerly and south-westerly trend of the social stream, perhaps, intensifies. But the sons of St. Ignatius, who are sometimes called the "Apostles of the Genteels," are really of no fixed time or place. They are a floating population, sent hither and thither by their superiors —it may be to martyrdom in Japan, or in the London slums, or in the fumes of Widnes. They come and go. At one of these altars, where members of the devout female sex, and of the sex that is not devout, may be seen kneeling at all hours to-day, Manning said his first mass. Only a few weeks earlier he was "charging" Chichester as its archdeacon; and in later years, by another great change of domestic sentiment, he ceased to love Jesuits.

The mention of Manning recalls his saying that pulpit oratory is one of the three wounds of the Roman Catholic Church in England. Sermons, in fact, take a secondary place to-day, as ever, in Catholic services; preaching is not practised as an art. "Farm Street," however, has its eloquent preacher in Father Bernard Vaughan, as the Oratory has in Father Sebastian Bowden (formerly an officer in the Guards) its direct one. Of this Mayfair church Mrs. Craigie ("John Oliver Hobbes")—herself a worshipper there—says, in "The Gods, Some Mortals, and Lord Wickenham," that her hero "used to sit near the altar of Our Lady of Lourdes, where he could see, at the end of the aisle, another altar and the pendant lamps before it. The odour of the flowers, incense, melting wax, and that something else, like the scent of goodly fruit stored away for

THE RED MASS AT SARDINIA STREET CHAPEL, LINCOLN'S INN.

the hungry winter, gave him a welcome. The little silver hearts which hung in a case by the altar had each some story to tell of a faithful vow." This is the literature of fiction. The literature of fact has its devotees inside the large red-brick house adjoining the church; and among the busiest researchers at the British Museum are sons of St. Ignatius.

To the east and to the west, two miles each way from the Marble Arch (the site of old Tyburn, where many a Jesuit was hanged, drawn, and quartered in those palmy days that have no date), lie the churches of St. Etheldreda and of St. Charles Borromeo. The "Tube" covers in a few minutes the four miles between them. In Ely Place, an enclosure on the very confines of the City, and within sight almost of La Belle Sauvage Yard, stands St. Etheldreda's Church, with its thirteenth-century crypt—an ancient fane, and one of the few of the actual churches of "The Old Religion" restored to the ancient rites. It somehow got into the market, and was bought by Father Lockhart, a relative of Walter Scott's son-in-law, and himself the first of Newman's young community at Littlemore to secede from the Anglican Church. Long will the memory remain of his handsome face and figure, as he stood in the surrounding streets preaching on the tee-totalism he practised. He belonged to the Fathers of Charity; and there was full accord between his aim and name. The church of St. Charles Borromeo (he was an archbishop of Milan, who loved the poor

and fought the plague and established Sunday schools) was planted by Manning among rather mean streets in Bayswater. You note the meanness, because it contrasts with the reputed "ambition" of its founder. Hither to him came the world to which he would not go; and "receptions into the Church" —the only receptions he ever loved—have not ceased to be an order of the day.

To churches with specialised congregations —for Italians, in Hatton Garden, and others —reference is elsewhere made in this work. The Sardinia Street Chapel, Lincoln's Inn, once tolerated and protected only as a chapel of an ambassador, became in the fulness of time the scene of the Red Mass (so called in Paris from the colour of the legal robes), where Roman Catholic members of the Bar gathered at the beginning of a term to invoke a blessing on its labours —a notable gathering in which might be seen, at one time or another, Lord Brampton, Lord Russell of Killowen, Sir John Day, Sir James Matthew, Sir Joseph Walton, and Lord Llandaff. Cross the water to Southwark, and you find its own cathedral, famous for its congregational singing, and the centre of a circle of spiritual and temporal activities for the amelioration of the lot of the poor who, as Charles Booth shows, are poorest of the poor in that region.

The Religious Orders are dotted about London, which loses in picturesqueness by the non-appearance in the streets in their own religious dress of Friars of Orders Grey and of monks who make their habits, though habits do not make the monk. By Act of Parliament they are forced into the coats, trousers, and headgear that mean despair for the artist. The Carmelites abstain from flesh, and rise by night to sing the Divine Office, in Church Street, Kensington; the Dominicans are at Haverstock Hill, the Capuchins at Peckham, Franciscans at Stratford, Passionists at Highgate, Benedictines at Ealing, Augustinians (whose habit Luther wore) at Hoxton Square; and there are Canons Regular, Redemptorists, Servites, and many more. Congregations of women abound; and their habits are seen

UNLOADING A CART AT NAZARETH HOUSE.

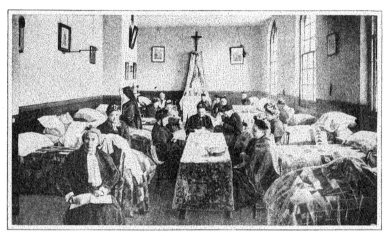

OLD WOMEN'S WARD, NAZARETH HOUSE.

in the streets, for in this matter of the religious dress, as in most others, it is women who lead. Carmelite nuns, with St. Teresa's habit, and Poor Clares, do not come from their enclosure. But Sisters of Nazareth will call anywhere in their carriage—they name it a cart—on anyone in "the world," and they do not always wait for invitations. They beg in fact from door to door for food for the six or seven hundred poor whom they entertain at Nazareth House, Hammersmith. In this great family are young children and old men and old women, into one of whose wards our illustrator has taken no idly intrusive peep. The Little Sisters of the Poor are of their kindred; and there are Sisters of Mercy, who, among their works of the same kind, include the Hospital of St. John and St. Elizabeth for suffering children at St. John's Wood; nuns of the Good Shepherd, with their great laundry worked by penitent women; the nuns who manage the French Hospital; the Sisters of Zion, those of the Sacred Heart, and those at the Convent of the Assumption, to all of whom flock girls of Catholic parents for education—these and many more; the Sisters who go out to nurse (and do not refuse a small-pox

case), and the Sisters who carry on the great night Refuge in Crispin Street; those who assist the Rescue Crusade among boys, and, last but not least in a list not easily exhausted, the Sisters of Charity, in whose great house, in Carlisle Place, Lady Etheldreda Howard amid other all noble women has chosen the life of sacrifice.

Come, finally, to Archbishop's House, Westminster, where Cardinal Vaughan, a stately red-robed host, receives his flock on afternoons in early spring. "The Faithful" kneel to kiss the ring of the Archbishop, who is also a Prince of the Church. He has a word for all—well judged, shrewd, fatherly. Forms and formalism are not necessarily related; and, when visitors have ceased to offer homage and pass to the tea-table, no one will be more homely than a Cardinal who, if you are a lady (and look hungry), will suddenly hand you the bread and butter. You are charmed, if a little taken aback. Then you see an ex-Army chaplain, wearing military orders; and you have been able, perhaps, to tell Monsignor Johnson how indebted to his "Catholic Directory" is any writer (and therefore any reader) of a paper such as this—crumbs gathered from his abundant table.

THE NATIONAL PENNY BANK (HACKNEY ROAD).

LONDON THRIFT.

By SIDNEY DARK.

IT is doubtful whether, both from the nature of his being and the character of his environment, the Londoner of any class can be said to be unduly addicted to thrift. In the sense in which the French peasant and the Paris bourgeois, the Scotsman and the Cornishman, always save a little, however small may be their income, the Londoner is a monument of extravagance. It must, of course, be remembered that expenses of living in the Metropolis are immeasurably greater in proportion to income than they are almost anywhere else, and the storm and stress of life in a great city practically compel a man to spend a certain part of his income in amusement and distraction which in healthier circumstances he would not require. At the same time, alongside the manifold agencies for spending money that exist in our city, there are innumerable agencies for the encouragement of thrift, from great institutions like the Post Office Savings Bank, with its millions of depositors, to the humble Slate Club held in the top room of a public-house, with its constant difficulties of obtaining subscriptions from its members and

sometimes of getting them back from its treasurer!

The baby's money box may be said to be the beginning of thrift; but in these progressive days the money box, from which ingenuity and a dinner knife can extract the pennies, is naturally regarded with suspicion. So the modern baby obtains, presumably through his legal guardians, a form from the nearest Post Office, turns his pennies into stamps, and sticks them on to the form, and then, when he has collected twelve, lodges them at the nearest Post Office, where the money, instead of lying idle and unproductive like the talent of the unfaithful servant hidden in a tin money box instead of a napkin, earns, as soon as a pound has been accumulated, two and a-half per cent. for the thrifty infant. Or, if the legal guardian to whom I have referred is a person of individualistic tendencies who regards the enlargement of governmental action with suspicion, the child may take his pennies to the nearest branch of the National Penny Bank, which receives deposits from a penny upwards, and there the directors will guard his money for him, and also give him a certain rate of interest. There is even for the budding capitalist a third alternative. The Salvation Army Reliance Bank will provide him with a money box not of unsubstantial tin or brittle wood which will enable the greed for chocolate of to-day to break through and steal the careful forethought of yesterday, but a strong receptacle, recalling in a miniature manner the masterpieces of the great safe-makers. This box is supplied with a strong padlock, the key of which is in the hands of the Salvation Army agent, who at certain periods visits the house, unlocks the box, counts the pennies, for which he gives a receipt, and, going one better than the Post Office allows the youthful depositor three per cent.

In any account of the way London saves, the Post Office, both from the magnitude of its transactions and its governmental position, naturally claims first consideration. More than £140,000,000 are deposited in the Post Office Savings Bank, and of this huge sum, though there are no official figures, London may be assumed to own a quarter. Of the total number of depositors sixty per cent. are women and children, ninety per cent. own less than fifty pounds, and probably seventy-five per cent. belong to the industrial classes. It is natural and inevitable that amongst the folk, who in their most prosperous times are only removed one hair's breadth from semi-starvation, the women should be the most thrifty. This fact is illustrated in the figures issued by institutions similar to the Post Office Savings Bank. There are a thousand branch savings banks in London. At the central office 3,000 persons, of whom nearly half are women, are engaged in managing the savings of the poor man. The Post Office encourages youthful thrift by allowing school teachers to collect the pennies of their pupils either by the use of stamp forms or by instituting penny banks, the funds of which are placed in bulk in the Post Office Savings Bank.

Very similar in aim and somewhat similar in method is the National Penny Bank, founded by Mr. Bartley, M.P., with the late Duke of Westminster, the late Earl of Derby, and other friends, in 1875. The Penny Bank, which began as a philanthropic institution, has by careful management been put on a thoroughly sound commercial basis, and its depositors have the satisfaction of knowing that they are obtaining the benefits of a genuine business and not of a mere charity. The National Penny Bank has

SCHOOL TEACHERS RECEIVING PUPILS' PENNIES.

SALVATION ARMY RELIANCE BANK, QUEEN VICTORIA STREET.

thirteen branches, of which that in the Hackney Road is one of the busiest. As an illustration of its operations, during one week before Christmas £150,000 was withdrawn by its depositors, while during the week previous the weight of money paid over the counters was 1 ton 18 cwts. 111 lbs., of which ninety per cent. was silver. The ledgers are probably the most remarkable documents owned by any banking house. Here is a typical account. It began on the first day of a month with the deposit of a penny, which was increased four days afterwards to eighteenpence. Two days later it was brought down to twopence by the withdrawal of sixpence. It then rose again in three jumps to one and twopence, fell again to threepence, then to a penny, and after an interval of three months the account was closed. This is an instance of the intricate nature of the bank's account. Some years back there was, for various reasons, a run on the bank. Customers poured in demanding their money. Everyone was paid, including two costermongers, who drew out between them in gold and silver something like fifty pounds. About an hour afterwards they returned and asked the cashier if he would kindly take their money back again. "What has made you alter your minds?"

said the cashier. "Well, guv'nor," said one of the costers, "me and my mate, w'en we got outside, didn't know wot to do with the stuff, so Bill sez to me, 'Let's tyke it to Coutts's.' We went dan the Strand, guv'nor, and blowed if Coutts's man didn't refuse to tyke it! So we've come back to you."

The Salvation Army Reliance Bank, which has its headquarters in Queen Victoria Street, is, as far as its deposit side is concerned, worked in much the same manner as the Post Office. The bank itself, with its counters and brass railings, flanked with clerks in red jerseys with "S.A." on their collars, has a novel and unexpected appearance; and on my visit I could not help being impressed by the unusual cheerfulness and civility of everybody, from the happy-looking old gentleman acting as hall door porter, who directed me when I entered, to the able and courteous manager—also in a red jersey—whose manner and appearance were about as unlike one's ideas of a financial magnate as well could be. The curious mixture of spiritual fervour with business acumen which is characteristic of a great deal of General Booth's organisation was exemplified by the fact that this officer was reading when I was shown into his room a copy of the latest Stock Exchange prices, to settle, no doubt, in which direction to invest his bank's money.

Turning to another branch of the subject, it would be impossible to attempt even to enumerate the different benefit and friendly societies of one sort or another that exist in the city of London. Inquiries go to prove that in almost every large business—railway companies, foundries, manufactories, and so on—there is, in addition to the larger outside societies, some sort of benefit fund attached to the firm itself, in which the men's subscriptions are often augmented by subscriptions from the masters. These funds are looked upon with a very great deal of distrust by the trade unions and friendly societies' leaders, and there seems some reason to believe that in certain cases they are administered too much by the master and too little by the men, though I am inclined to think that this is rather the exception than the rule. A large number of publicans and licensed grocers in working class localities also start goose clubs and Christmas clubs amongst their customers, in which, again, the few pence or shillings put by every week for the Christmas festivities are often increased by the publican.

Perhaps more important and more interesting are the great friendly societies and their host of small imitators. Briefly, the object of a friendly society may be stated to be the payment of a certain weekly sum to the members in time of sickness and sometimes, also, when out of work, and of a certain sum to the widow or orphans on the decease of a member. No one unacquainted with the London poor can have any idea of the extraordinary desire, especially amongst the women, for what is called a decent funeral; and I find by inquiries amongst clergymen in the poorest districts of London that the burial club is a far more popular institution than the organisation which provides funds to tide its members over bad times, whether from sickness or from want of employment. There is a well known story of a poor woman who dearly loved her son, but who, rather than spend certain money in buying port wine and risk his having a pauper's funeral, left him to die without the wine, and had a burying which astonished the neighbourhood. I myself once overheard a conversation in an omnibus between two elderly matrons, one of whom said to the

BIRKBECK BANK, SOUTHAMPTON BUILDINGS.

HEARTS OF OAK CERTIFICATE.

the Sons of Temperance, and the two Orders of Sons of the Phœnix—the last four being teetotal organisations. Their ramifications are very difficult to follow, and much of their proceedings is kept secret from the outsider. But generally they may be fairly accurately said to be a combination of freemasonry and an ordinary friendly society. The Foresters, for example, which is the most interesting of them all, is said—I do not vouch for the accuracy of the statement—to have been founded by Robin Hood. Anyhow, a court was in existence in Leeds in 1790, and Forestry was introduced into London in 1837. It consists of nearly a million members, male, female, and juvenile, and its funds are approaching seven millions sterling. The admirable objects of the Foresters, which again may be taken to be fairly typical of these societies, are:—

To establish and maintain benefit funds, from which, on satisfactory evidence of the death of a member of the society who has complied with all its lawful requirements, a sum shall be paid to the widow, orphans, dependents, or other beneficiary whom the

other, "Oh, it was a beautiful funeral! After we come back we had wine and biscuits and sangwitches; and it must 'ave done 'er 'eart good, pore thing, to 'ave been able to bury 'er 'usband so nice." Of course, it is easy to philosophise over the wastefulness of money spent on elaborate funerals, but it is all very human and very touching.

Christmas goose clubs are held in connection with many institutes and clubs. The Aldenham Institute, St. Pancras, has a club consisting of nearly 2,500 members, who pay weekly contributions towards a Christmas dinner, the distribution of the good things taking place on Christmas Eve. Thanks perhaps to Dickens, putting by for Christmas Day is one of the most popular forms of London Thrift.

Among the friendly societies having branches in London are the Foresters, the Buffaloes, the Druids, the United Patriots, the Oddfellows, the Rechabites,

FORESTER'S CERTIFICATE.

member has designated, or to the personal representative of the member, as laid down in the said laws.

To secure for its members such other advantages as are from time to time designated.

To unite fraternally all persons entitled to membership under the laws of the society; and the word "laws" shall include general laws and byelaws.

To give all moral and material aid in its power to its members and those dependent upon them.

To educate its members socially, morally, and intellectually.

To establish a fund for the relief of sick and distressed members.

A characteristic of the Foresters and most

called "death money." Young men in good health in receipt of a wage of not less than 24s. per week are eligible for membership between the ages of eighteen and thirty. The entrance fee is 2s. 6d., and the subscription about £2 a year. For this the benefits include 18s. a week in case of sickness, £20 for a member's funeral, and £10 for the funeral of a member's wife—ladies apparently costing less to bury than gentlemen—30s. for a wife's lying-in, and £15 for loss in case of fire. The tremendous business done by the Hearts of Oak, as well as the fertility of its members, may be gauged

A CHRISTMAS EVE DISTRIBUTION OF TURKEYS, GEESE, ETC. (ALDENHAM INSTITUTE).

of the other societies I have mentioned is found in their picturesque regalia.

The older trade unions also very largely act as benefit societies, and offer much the same advantages to their members. But it will be remembered that when the new Unionist movement started after the Dock Strike, it was made a great feature that the trade union should be exclusively a fighting body, and that its power to fight for higher wages and better conditions of labour should not be weakened by including within its functions those of a friendly society.

The Hearts of Oak, which has its headquarters near Fitzroy Square, is a benefit society worked from a central office. It, too, offers to its members sick pay and what is

by the fact that from 1842, when the society was founded, to the end of November, 1901, no less a sum than £1,045,656 was paid for lying-in claims, while the total money disbursed amounted to over six and a-quarter million pounds.

Before leaving this branch of the subject it is interesting to notice that the Jewish and the foreign quarters of London have their own friendly societies, with their own peculiar names, of which the following may be taken as specimens:—The Podumbitzer Friendly Society, United Brothers of Kalish, Socheti bover Sick Benefit, Grand Order of the Sons of Jacob, and so on.

The building society is the favourite means of thrift among the artisan and clerk classes.

DRUID'S CERTIFICATE.

There are innumerable building societies all over London, some of which are, rather oddly, connected with Dissenting chapels, and often have the minister of the chapel as one of the trustees. The method of the building society is to collect money in small sums from a large number of persons and lend it to others upon real security. The method has many variations. Usually after a member has deposited a certain amount with the society sufficient to pay a proportion of the price of a house, the directors, after an investigation by their surveyor, advance the balance of the purchase price, holding the deeds as security, and this advance, together with interest, has to be repaid in instalments over a specified number of years, the result, of course, being that the borrower pays probably rather less a sum than would be demanded of him for rent, and in the course of a few years owns a house of his own. In one instance which has come to my knowledge a doorkeeper of a factory in the Euston Road has in the course of forty years acquired about twenty houses in this manner, and has become possessed of a comfortable income which he will, of course, be able to bequeath to his heirs.

There are between 2,000 and 3,000 building societies in England and Wales, and the amount of business they do may be gauged by the fact that in the Birkbeck—one of the best known London societies—during 1901 5,754 persons became depositors with the society, and the total cash received during its first fifty years of existence amounted to over £290,000,000 sterling. Our photographic reproduction on page 257 depicts the interior of the well-known Birkbeck Bank, where the business both of the building society and of the bank itself is transacted.

Among interesting minor thrift societies mention may be made of a very admirable idea which has been started in West London by one or two ladies, whereby servant girls contribute a small sum monthly to the funds of what is called a Clothes Club, and are provided with rather more than the value of their subscriptions in garments.

I have endeavoured to give a kaleidoscopic view of the many varied organisations, some entirely engineered by the members themselves, others guided and fostered by clergymen, philanthropists, Government officials, and employers of labour, which have for their aim the encouragement of putting by for a rainy day — the enunciation of the doctrine that to look after the pennies is a sure and certain way of finding that the pounds will look after themselves, and that by the help of that marvellous institution called interest, if you cast your bread upon the waters, it will come back to you largely increased in bulk.

Postage Stamps for a Deposit of One Shilling in the Post Office Savings Bank.

12 Penny Stamps to be affixed below.

POST OFFICE SAVINGS BANK STAMP FORM.

DURING A SUMMER HEAT WAVE.

LONDON UNDER THE WEATHER.

By GEORGE R. SIMS.

ON THE KERBSTONE :
SUN HATS.

THE staple commodity of London conversation is the weather. In the street the usual greeting among passing acquaintances is "Fine day," or "Wretched weather," as the case may be. At the social gathering the weather is the subject which usually breaks the ice, and at the clubs the members meeting in the hall, or gazing out of the big front windows, invariably refer to the atmospheric conditions. Of late years it has been the fashion to describe most of the seasons as "trying," and to-day the newspapers have taken to headlining their meteorological paragraphs. The word "phenomenal" has come into vogue for the autumn that is hot and the spring that is cold. The Londoner seems to be always hardly used by the atmosphere, and the elements are continually against him. If it is hot, it is a "heat wave" and unbearable; if it is cold, it is a "blizzard" and murderous.

Having made up their minds that the weather is extraordinary, Londoners comport themselves under its variations in a more or less extraordinary manner. They are never prepared for heat or cold. A few days of blazing sunshine fill the streets with eccentric costumes for man and beast alike. A few days of snow drive the borough councils to the end of their wits, and paralyse the traffic of the busiest city in the world.

But though only the extremes of heat and cold emphasise the Londoner's helplessness to the point of ridicule, the weather in all its phases frames a picture of serio-comic suffering which is well worth the attention of the student of men and manners.

London in the heat wave is always interesting. The streets suddenly become white with the straw hats of men and women. The waistcoat of civilisation is abandoned, and daring young men wear sashes of colour around their waists which are dignified by the name of "cummerbuds." The ladies in their lightest array anxiously shield their complexions beneath umbrellas or parasols of sufficiently large dimensions to be of use as well as ornament. Aristocratic London in the heat wave—so much of it as remains in town—seeks the shade of the Park at an early hour. Occasionally it breakfasts in Kensington Gardens; it dines at night with its windows wide open amid shaded lights;

HIGH HOLBORN IN A STORM.

tattered humanity reclines in the streets, after the manner of the Neapolitan *lazzaroni*. The steps of St. Paul's in the height of a heat wave are frequently used for the *al fresco* siesta of worker and loafer alike.

London in a thunderstorm is a scene of panic. At the first clap women utter a little cry of terror in chorus, and make hurried darts into drapers' shops or convenient doorways. Presently the heavens burst, and a terrific storm of rain sweeps over the town. Instantly, as if by magic, the streets are cleared: where the pedestrians have vanished to is a mystery. But the 'buses and the cabs cannot escape. The 'buses are full inside; the outside passengers bend their heads to the pitiless storm, cowering under umbrellas if they have them.

The cabmen turn up their coat collars, and the wet reins slip through their hands; but the cab horse plays no pranks in the heavy downpour. The rain rattles against the lowered glass; a small Niagara pours off the brim of cabby's hat, and further impedes his view; the wheels splash through small rivers

and the balconies of the west have an Oriental character until the midnight hour.

Ordinary London—working London and loafing London—maintains no dignity in the heat wave. Its coats come off in unaccustomed places; the business man carries his pyjama in his hand, and mops his brow; the 'busmen and the cabmen adorn their horses' heads with straw bonnets, and tuck handkerchiefs under their own hats, after the fashion of the Indian puggaree. "Ice" becomes the legend in the public-house windows; the sale of white linen hats becomes a trade of the kerbstone; and

of muddy water; and presently the shop windows and the adjacent rails are mudbespattered, as if they had been pelted by an indignant crowd. When the storm abates, macintoshed stragglers appear in the streets, but the outlook seems dark and miserable. The ladies compelled to be abroad tread gingerly on the tips of their toes. A cat has no greater horror of wet under foot than a female Londoner.

London in a fog! The "scene" is unique; no other capital in the world can show the equal of "the London Particular." When the yellow, choking mist commences to roll up in the daytime, London is filled with Rembrandtesque effects even at night noon. The lights in the shops are flaring, the lights in the private houses are full on. You see more of the "domestic interior" on a foggy day than at any other time, for the blinds are not drawn. There is no more picturesque peep-show than the London "domestic interior" lighted up in the daytime with the firelight flickering on the walls.

AT THE MERCY OF THE WIND.

Towards night, when the fog has not lifted, the situation becomes tragic. Fog signals explode with startling detonation on the railways; Dante's Inferno seems to have been transported to the town upon the

BY TORCHLIGHT.

Thames. Boys and men wander here and there with torches, and lend a diabolical element to the Cimmerian gloom; the warning shouts of 'busmen and cabmen, as they move slowly forward, now getting on to the pavement, now colliding with a lamp-post, come from the unseen. Wayfarers, business men returning from their occupation, belated travellers bound for distant parts of the Metropolis, grope their way blindly along, clutching at the railings of the houses to make sure that they do not wander into the roadway; when they come suddenly upon something that looks like a policeman, they ask in plaintive voices for topographical guidance. But somehow or other everybody gets home—the cabmen find their stables, the 'busmen their yards. On the morrow, when the gift of sight is once more of practical use, we relate our adventures as humorous experiences to our friends who had the good fortune to remain indoors during "a London fog."

London in a gale. London, when the wild north-easter blows over a wind-dried city, is trying alike to the temper and the dignity. As the sign-boards swing the nervous pedestrian glances uneasily aloft. At times he ceases to glance anywhere, and, turning his back on the blast, closes his eyes;

LUDGATE CIRCUS IN A FOG.

for the dust which has eddied and swirled in the roadway comes on a sudden gust, in a thick cloud, straight at him. In this position the male pedestrian is uncomfortable enough, but the female pedestrian is an object to melt the heart of a woman-hater. To keep her hat on and stand her ground, as the wind blowing fifty miles an hour spends its fury on her ample skirts, is a feat that requires long practice. If she is wise she clutches at a lamp-post or a railing; if she trusts to her own unaided efforts she is generally blown along in a series of undignified little jumps.

When the wind blows furiously in London the pavements and roadways are strewn with rubbish and torn paper, fragments of news-paper contents bills, and shop sweepings. It is as though a caravan of dust-carts had strewn their contents about the Metropolis. The newspaper bills have a partiality for the middle of the roadway, where they frighten horses or, occasionally rising like kites in the air, wrap themselves round the face of a carman or an outside 'bus passenger. The theatre boards and newspaper boards outside the shops are blown down here and there with a sharp little bang, and the spectacle of a gentleman wildly careering among the traffic after his hat is common. A gale is usually more prolific in accidents than a fog, and there is always a long list of casualties.

London in a drizzle—the damp, warm drizzle that goes on and on and colours all things a gloomy drab—is a misery unto men and a woe unto women. There is a penetrating dampness about the London drizzle that seems gradually to mildew the mind. The weather is repeated in the countenance of everybody one meets. The pavements have become gradually like the sea sand at low tide. They are a series of small puddles relieved by pools where the stones have been removed for repair. The nice conduct of an umbrella is not within the genius of the Londoner, and so where the crowd waits for the 'buses that are always full inside, or in the busy streets where there are always two opposing streams of pedestrians, there is constant collision and apology, and occasionally one man's umbrella drips down the neck of his neighbour. The bestowal of wet umbrellas in omnibuses and tram-cars is a fertile source of trouble. With

twelve saturated umbrellas all draining at once on to the floor of a crowded vehicle, and frequently down the garments of the passengers, the inside of a public conveyance closely resembles a bathing machine.

There is a peculiar blight that descends on London occasionally and lies heavily upon it for days. The skies are of a smoky grey, a yellowish haze narrows the horizon; in the parks and open spaces a light blue mist hangs upon the grass and envelops the trunks of the trees. The birds are silent, the church clocks strike with a muffled sound. The depression extends alike to beast and man. The cab and 'bus horses go lazily, the crowds of human beings move about as though they had a silent sorrow. It is then the words "Beastly weather" are heard everywhere, and men yawn publicly. There is even a pessimistic note in the public Press, and if Parliament is sitting a dyspeptic tone pervades the debates.

But it is when London has had a snowstorm that the Londoner is seen under the most depressing conditions of all. The beautiful snow of the Christmas number has no joys for him. Short spells of frost may come now and then, but they are marred by the dread anticipations of the thaw that must follow. London under a rapid thaw is the paradise of plumbers, but it is the other place for everybody else.

Yet London half-flooded by thaw is but a minor evil compared with the flooding of certain low-lying districts that follows a long period of heavy rain. South London is sometimes the scene of an extensive inundation. Lambeth Marshes are under water; houses in this neighbourhood are flooded in cellar and basement, founda-tions are rendered unsafe, and the inhab-itants are for many days amphibious. The Thames once extended as far as the Elephant and Castle and Newington Butts, and at times of heavy downpours the dwellers in this district are unpleasantly reminded of the fact.

But to return to the snow. When the Londoner wakes up in the morning and sees that it has fallen heavily in the night —when the Londoner looks out upon a "white city"—he for a moment appreciates the poetry of the picture. But directly

London begins its day's work the scene is changed. The traffic, foot and horse, rapidly crushes the snow into a slushy paste resembling chocolate in the early process of manufacture. The pavements become slippery, the wood and the asphalt are skating rinks. If the snow still continues and the roads freeze hard, or only partially thaw, London does nothing. The unemployed are immediately remembered, and indignant citizens rush into print, demanding an army of men for the relief of the situation.

Presently the authorities summon up courage to attack the difficulty. The householder has felt compelled to clear so much of the pavement as lies in front of his habitation, or has employed the men with spades who perambulate the suburbs shouting, "Sweep your doorway." But the municipal officials have "waited." When they set to work they generally clear the roadway by shovelling the snow into great heaps on either side. London then becomes a miniature Switzerland with a small Alpine range running along its roadways.

If the frost holds and the London lakes freeze over, then the Serpentine and the ornamental waters in Regent's Park revive for a day or two the vanished glories of the Ice Fair. The banks are lined with men who bring old cane-bottomed or Windsor chairs with them, and do a roaring trade in affixing skates to the boots of the select. Sliding is the sport of the small boy, who is largely represented on these occasions. Picturesque figures are the Royal Humane Society men in their cork jackets, and not infrequently their services are required to rescue an adventurous skater who has disdained the warning notice-board of danger.

London while the frost holds and the snow is hard is exhilarating for the young and the idle; snow-balling is indulged in in spite of police prohibition, and in some parts of the suburbs you may come upon the juvenile sculptor's effort at a snowman. But snow disorganises the traffic, and the business man suffers and growls, while the poor feel their situation acutely. Many trades cease. Frozen-out gardeners and bricklayers make their appearance in slowly walking little groups, and seek to open the purse strings of the charitable by chanting doleful ditties.

But London under the snow that is half snow and half slush—London under a week of alternating snow and frost—is a piteous spectacle. A general paralysis attacks the whole working organisation. The train service gradually dissociates itself from the time tables, the omnibus service is cut down to infinitesimal proportions, and the newspapers are filled with sarcastic comments concerning "The Beautiful Snow." Then indeed is London "Under the Weather."

SKATING ON THE SERPENTINE.

SCOTTISH, IRISH, AND WELSH LONDON.

By C. O'CONOR ECCLES.

EVERY year from Scotland, from Ireland, and from Wales young men flock in hundreds to London. They are of all classes, all degrees of education, united in one common aim, that, namely, of making a living. The new-comers find employment squares to struggling practitioners in Whitechapel and Southwark. Irish barristers are numerous, and, thanks to the eloquence which is their birthright, win fame and fortune in their profession. Journalism likewise attracts

PLAYING IN THE HAGGIS ON ST. ANDREW'S NIGHT.

a living. The new-comers find employment in many different ways. Scotland and Ireland largely recruit the ranks of the police force. The Civil Service, too, in all its branches employs many Irishmen, whose brilliant talents often enable them to rise from small posts to places of high emolument and power. Mercantile clerkships attract the Scot, who has a happy knack of coming South with the traditional half-crown in his pocket, and by thrift, ability, and industry amassing a fortune. Scottish and Irish doctors, too, abound, from men who have made a name and dwell in fashionable large numbers of Scotsmen and Irishmen so that it is a saying in Fleet Street that English editors are kept simply to correct the "shalls" and "wills" of their colleagues.

Welshmen in their pursuits are usually either musical or mercantile, and frequently both. Many of London's leading singers, both men and women, are Welsh, though both Ireland and Scotland contribute their quota of musical talent. Indeed, perhaps, the gayest and most picturesque figure to be seen in London streets is the itinerant Scottish piper with his bagpipes, a man who, if he does not rank in the eyes of the

PRACTISING THE SWORD DANCE
(ROYAL CALEDONIAN ASYLUM).

world with the musical celebrities of his nation, would seem to have a "guid conceit" of himself, and to enjoy mightily the interest he rouses in quiet residential quarters.

From music to milk is an easy transition, if we may judge by the innumerable old Welsh ballads which begin by stating that "Winnie" or "Nesta" was a milkmaid. It is consequently interesting to learn that the milk trade of London is to a great extent in the hands of the Welsh. Several drapery establishments, too, are owned by enterprising Welshmen.

Very many Irishmen of the poorest class likewise drift to London in search of employment. Debarred by lack of means from lodgings where the rate of payment is high, and yet compelled to be near the great industrial centres where chance jobs may be most easily picked up, they and their families are automatically forced into slum dwellings in such neighbourhoods as Poplar, Islington, and Southwark, where they form colonies of people wonderfully good and helpful to each other, but over-crowded, deprived of all that brightens and beautifies existence, and compelled to bring up their children under circumstances that give the little ones but a slender chance of developing their highest possibilities.

The Scot who comes to London is sure sooner or later to find himself in touch

with the Scottish Corporation in Crane Court, Fleet Street. This body occupies No. 7, a spacious building at the extreme end, with high-pitched roof, small turrets to the front, and other features of Scottish architecture. Scottish life in London centres round the spot. It is the headquarters of many county associations, of the Highland Society, the Caledonian Society, the Gaelic Society, and various other organisations. Because of the innumerable activities and interests concentrated there, 7, Crane Court, has been called "The Scottish Consulate." The house is modern, having been rebuilt in 1880 on the site of the old hall purchased at the end of the eighteenth century by the Corporation from the Royal Society. Sir Isaac Newton's presidential chair was saved from the fire which destroyed this original building as well as many valuable paintings and records; it now stands in the board room.

Ever since 1665 the Corporation has held an annual dinner on St. Andrew's Night, where the guests in full Highland costume are marshalled to their places by skirling pipers, who later in the evening lead a majestic procession of cooks, each bearing on a trencher a haggis, "great chieftain of the pudding race," the national dish which to the palate of the true-born Scot surpasses all that the South can offer. At this festival some prominent Scottish nobleman presides, and on the walls appear Scottish emblems, "the ruddy lion rampt in gold," the banners and shields of Highland clans, with claymores, dirks, and pistols. Funds are collected for the relief of distress, and thanks to Scottish benevolence many a humble home has been kept together, and many a decent body, brought low by misfortune, has been pensioned and enabled to spend his last days in peace. It is an interesting sight

clad in the Stuart tartan, and ready at their teacher's word to sing plaintive Jacobite ballads in sweet childish trebles. Their soft notes have more than once melted the hearts and loosened the purse-strings of Scottish visitors. Practical good sense is shown in the training given.

Scottish gentlemen of position, officers of Scottish regiments and others, foregather at the Caledonian Club, 30, Charles Street, St. James's. The house is roomy and old-fashioned, with wide corridors and lofty, spacious apartments. The Club, though only established in 1898, numbers over a thousand members, and, like the famous

LEARNING IRISH REELS (ATHENÆUM HALL, TOTTENHAM COURT ROAD).

to see the old people come for their pensions once a month.

Should an indigent Scotsman die in London, or a Scottish soldier, sailor or marine be disabled when on active service, his children will be received at the Royal Caledonian Asylum, which has given its name to the Caledonian Road. It is worth while to go down any morning and, escorted by the kindly Secretary, see the kilted boy pipers march up and down skirling bravely, or watch the little lads dance the Reel, the Highland Fling, and the Sword Dance. There are about seventy of them, all well-fed, well-cared-for, well-taught, and bright-faced. Across a passage from the boys' schoolroom are to be found some sixty bonnie lasses,

giantess, is "still growing." Ladies are admitted as guests daily to lunch and tea, and once or twice a week to dinner. The fine reading-room with its panels of dark green silk brocade is given over to them, and a special dining-room is reserved for them and their hosts.

The Scottish Golf Club at Wimbledon, founded in 1865 by a group of London Scotsmen, has a large body of members, devotees of the national game.

Seldom is a London winter sufficiently rigorous to admit of curling, but when the ice bears, the members of the Shinto Curling Club are there, ready to take advantage of it for this exciting game.

The Irishman finds in London his own

literary, athletic, political, and social institutions. He may join the Irish Literary Society, and stroll down to its headquarters, where he can read all the Irish papers, have luncheon, tea, or dinner, and meet his friends, since this organisation combines the advantages of a club with lectures, concerts, and other attractions, and is becoming more and more the chief centre of social intercourse for the Irish in London. It is non-sectarian and non-political, and, as its primary object is the advancement of Irish literature, appeals to all parties. To it belong many literary men and women of Irish nationality. Several of these are members of a kindred association, the Irish Texts Society. This was established to publish, with English translations, glossaries, and notes, the large and interesting body of Irish MSS. which still exists.

The most Irish of the Irish belong to a flourishing young organisation which is friendly in its relations with the Irish Literary Society, though quite independent of it. I allude to the Gaelic League, which attracts a number of the most energetic and practical of the younger generation, and has its headquarters at Duke Street, Adelphi. Its direct object is to extend the living Irish language, and preserve the store of fine Irish songs and traditions that, without such

IRISH GUARDSMEN.

timely help, might die out; indirectly — being based on principles of national self-reliance — it stands for the revival of Irish industries, for all that is at once national and progressive. The visitor to the Athenæum Hall, Tottenham Court Road, will find on any Monday evening some two hundred young men and women assembled

SHAMROCK SELLER.

to study Gaelic. There is always a large mixture of Irish speakers who make it a point of honour at these meetings to speak in Gaelic only. Amongst them are some who, though born and bred in London and speaking English without a trace of accent, are well acquainted with the sweet native tongue of their forefathers. The League has fifteen Irish schools in the Metropolis. Recreation, on traditional lines, is not lost sight of. The Irish dancing classes are always popular, and in addition there are in summer pleasant *Seilgi* and *Scoruidheachta*, or excursions and social gatherings, with now and then a *Pleraca* or dance, while an annual musical festival is held at the Queen's Hall. This has a large number of Gaelic songs on the programme, and the music is exclusively traditional. This festival is now considered the central event in the Irish musical year. It is distinct from the Irish concert always held at St. James's Hall on St. Patrick's Night, which is on the lines of the popular Scottish concert on St. Andrew's Night, and attracts the same kind of audience. On St. Patrick's Day there is a wonderful sale of so-called "shamrock" in the London streets—most of it, alas, pure clover that grew probably in Surrey meadows. It is often decorated with sparkling bits of gold foil, and to the uninitiated looks cheap at a penny a bunch. The expert, however, notes the white dot on each leaf and the hairy stems, and prefers to get his button-hole direct from Ireland, where, indeed, there is a considerable export trade in the genuine article about this time. The religious service in honour of St. Patrick at the Roman Catholic Church, Dockhead, is unique, the hymns, sermons, and responses being respectively in Irish and Latin. It attracts a crowded congregation.

The Gaelic Athletic Association possesses some eight or nine clubs, mostly in North London, devoted to hurling, football, and athletics generally, their chief grounds being at Muswell Hill and Lea Bridge. They hold no matches or competitions with English clubs. The "G.A.A." has its headquarters in Ireland, and Great Britain ranks as one of its provinces, London being con-

pected later to play All Ireland for the championship.

In Holborn there is an Irish club the members of which are civil servants, medical men and others; the medical men having also an association of their own at 11, Chandos Street, one of the objects of which is to secure the recognition of Irish degrees by London hospitals, which in distributing appointments often refuse to accept Irish qualifications, however capable may be the men holding them.

A LONDON IRISH HURLING MATCH.

sidered a county. There are in the Metropolis a large body of members, of whom over 200 belong to the Hibernian Athletic Club, the oldest of the group, which was founded in 1895. Hurling, as practised by Irish teams, differs in certain respects from hockey, and is a more dashing game; while the Gaelic Athletic Rules for football prohibit handling, pushing, or tripping, which are permitted by Rugby rules. When the grass is very wet, however, some of the players discard boots and stockings. The various G.A.A. clubs in London challenge each other, and then the winning team challenges some other county, as, for example, the Manchester and Liverpool G.A.A. The winner in this latter match is always ex-

While the various Irish counties have no such societies as the Scottish for bringing natives together, a province, Ulster, has its own association. It owes its origin to the casual encounter of two or three enthusiastic Northerners who lamented that, proud as was the position of their compatriots in London, they had no general meeting place. Its inaugural banquet was held in January, 1897, when many recruits joined the Society, and, thanks to excellent management, the membership has since greatly increased. Balls, concerts, cinderella dances, banquets, and a river trip are among the entertainments offered. The headquarters of the association are at the Hotel Cecil.

In the days of Parnell, the Westminster

LONDON KYMRIC LADIES' CHOIR.

education to a certain number of the London born children of Irish parents, preference being given to those whose fathers were soldiers or sailors. This Association also offers small prizes in Ireland for the best kept cottages.

Since the establishment of the Irish Guards by Queen Victoria, in compliment to Irish valour in South Africa, the uniform and the

Palace Hotel was a favourite rendezvous of the Irish Nationalist Members of Parliament. Nowadays, however, they have no recognised centre, but hold their meetings sometimes at one place, sometimes at another. Some of them have town houses, others live in apartments, others again club together and have rooms or chambers in common, whether in localities like Kensington or Chelsea, or on the Surrey side, which, if less fashionable, is within easier reach of the House of Commons. There are, it may be added, many purely political associations for Irishmen in London.

The above may be taken as covering Irish Ireland in London, but there is also fashionable Ireland, which, if the bull may be pardoned, is not Irish at all, since it includes wealthy non-resident Irish landlords who, for the most part, like the Duke of Devonshire and the Marquess of Londonderry, are Englishmen born and bred, but hold estates across the Channel. Many wealthy women, however, in this circle do good work in buying Irish manufactures, and no trousseau of an aristocratic bride is complete unless the dainty stitchery, the fairy-like embroidery, and the costly lace are provided by workers in some Irish convent. The Irish Peasantry Association at Stamford Street, Blackfriars, offers a free

flat cap with its green band have become familiar in the London streets. The three figures in our photographic illustration on page 270 are shown standing in front of a coat of arms affixed to a wall in the Tower of London. There is also a well-known Irish Volunteer regiment, the London Irish Rifles, already mentioned in the article on "Volunteer London."

The Welsh inhabitants of London, though they number some fifty thousand, have no

PUBLISHED IN LONDON.

such central meeting places as the Scots and Irish. True, they possess an admirable literary society, the Cymmrodorion, which gives aid to necessitous members of the community, but Welsh life in London centres chiefly in the chapels, and its activities for the most part are religious, or, at any rate, connected with religion. To gain some idea of its true inwardness, one cannot do better than attend the New Jewin Chapel or the Welsh Tabernacle in the Pentonville Road some Sunday evening when a popular preacher has come up to address the congregation. The stranger will find the building thronged with well-dressed people, for the most part prosperous business men and women, the number of the former sex being remarkable. The majority are Calvinistic Methodists, for to this body the bulk of the London Welsh population belong, though there are also many Welsh Congregationalists, Baptists, and Wesleyans in the capital, while the Established Church finds a certain number of adherents. The sermon, the hymns, the announcements are all in Welsh, so that the visitor feels himself an outsider and a foreigner, despite the familiar aspect of everyone and everything. As might be expected where a race is so musical, the congregational singing is exceptionally good. The talented organist at the Welsh Tabernacle, Miss Frances Rees, is conductress of the London Kymric Ladies' Choir, of which Lady Puleston is president. The members

are selected from all the Welsh chapels, the best voices only being picked out, with the result that this choir was awarded the first and second prizes at the Royal National Eisteddfod of Wales, and has appeared before royalty. All the singers are dressed in their national costume, with the Welshwoman's characteristic hat.

On St. David's Eve Welsh people have a special service at the City Temple, and on St. David's Day, though few of them sport the leek as the Irish proudly sport the shamrock, they eat it at their annual dinner in the agreeable form of Cawl Cennin, a favourite soup. The Welsh in London possess a political society, the Cymru Fydd, which is Radical in its tendencies, and to which most of the Welsh Members of Parliament belong. Moreover they have a newspaper of their own. printed in their own language, and bearing the title of *Celt Llundain* (the "London Kelt"). Thrifty, cleanly, industrious, neighbourly and united, the London Welsh form an important and valuable addition to the population.

Indeed, the Scottish, Irish, and Welsh elements do and have done much towards making London a world city, and in leavening the Anglo-Saxons with Celtic impetuosity and mental alertness have, with other causes, given to metropolitans a width of outlook and a receptivity not to be found in provincial towns where these elements do not bulk as largely or act as potently.

HIGHLAND PIPER AND DANCER IN LONDON.

LAYING ELECTRIC CABLES (WIGMORE STREET).

LIGHTING LONDON.

By DESMOND YOUNG.

IF one could only hover in a balloon over Central London as night falls! To see, as the man with the long stick makes his round and switches are turned on and levers pulled behind the scenes, the transformation scene gradually unfold and the myriad lights spurt out of the grey gloom beneath: the sinuous Thames become outlined by moonlike arc lamps; the bridges start up as if set pieces of fireworks; Leicester Square assert itself as the hub of Pleasure London in a blaze of bluish-white refulgence, more than ever eclipsing its sedate neighbour, Trafalgar Square; long lines of stars shoot out from the busy, pulsing heart below, radiating in all directions, beginning with steady white orbs and fading away in glimmering specks of yellowish luminosity —what a picture it would be! Innumerable are the lights of London and well-nigh in-

LAMP LIGHTER.

conceivably vast is the system by which they are produced and maintained. Scores of private companies, as well as a number of public bodies, including the County Council, are engaged in the work; the capital sunk in it is fabulous in amount; and the pipes and cables connected with it form an amazingly complex subterranean network, of which Londoners get a glimpse when the streets are "up."

Electricity is generated in the Metropolis at scores of points. The oldest company distributing the energy is the London Electric Supply Corporation, whose station at Deptford was long the largest in the world. Whether it is now or not, its capacity is enormous. To obtain even a superficial knowledge of the lighting of London these works must be visited. Here we are, then. A bewildering maze of engines and machinery fills the large engine house. To the right is the older plant — powerful engines connected to dynamos by rope pulleys. To the left are some of the newer engines, coupled direct to huge dynamos which are revolving so rapidly and noiselessly that but for the little sparks that come and go they would seem to be motionless. At present — it is 11 a.m., with a bright sky overhead — there is a light load on, not much electricity is being consumed. Hence there are only two engines running. As the demand in-

etc., of the mysterious current that is passing through the cables below, and the handles enable them to regulate it. Though they seem to have it completely in harness, this is the most dangerous part of the works.

Among the municipal corporations which supply electricity St. Pancras and Shoreditch occupy important positions. Of the London authorities St. Pancras led the way in opening a station, while Shoreditch was the first borough in the country to combine on a

IN THE LONDON ELECTRIC SUPPLY CORPORATION'S WORKS.

creases others will be started to keep pace with it. There is no drawing on reserves when the rush comes about dusk, as at a gas works. As electricity is wanted so it must be generated and supplied, because storing it, while possible, is not commercially practicable. And, as a consequence, some engines are always running.

On a gallery to the left the switch-board is situated. It has as many rows of dials as a clockmaker's shop, and underneath are ranged levers like those in the signal cabin on the iron road. The quivering hands on the gauges show the attendants the pressure,

large scale the destruction of dust and refuse with the production of electricity. The two things often go hand in hand now. Still, to Shoreditch is due the credit which should always be given to the pioneer.

Let us take a peep at its station. Begin at the yard, into which the refuse—household, trade, and street—is brought. Little mountains of clinkers from the furnaces are here a feature of the scenery. The economic disposal of this waste is one of the most important problems connected with the undertaking—which is not creditable to us as a commercial nation. Among it, for one

DRAWING RETORTS BY HAND (SOUTH METROPOLITAN GAS COMPANY).

thing, are some articles which would pass as relics from Pompeii.

Cross the yard, and we are at the lift which raises the rubbish to the top of the furnaces (already described in the article on "London's Toilet"). Through the engine house, along the gallery in front of an elaborate switch-board, and into another room containing a switch-board for public lighting. If you pulled down one of those levers projecting from it, all the arc lamps on one side of a street would go out. The lights are, except when fog envelops the borough, switched on and off according to a time table. And that points to the coming doom of the man with the stick as well as of the lamp cleaner with his light, portable ladder. Electric lamps, of course, do not need their attention. Both will be superseded by the now familiar figure who supplies the arc lamps with carbon, which is consumed in the production of the light.

Electricity is coming more and more into use in London for lighting. Hundreds of miles of streets are laid with cables, and yet it is impossible to walk very far without seeing more being put down. The road is up. In the gutter stands a huge reel of leaden cable. Presently this is rolled nearer the hole, and then the passers-by stop and gaze expectantly. At last they are going to behold that famous little dog which rushes through the earthenware pipe with a string tied to its tail and thus makes a connection between two lengths. But, alas! this sagacious animal is purely mythical. No dog is used, no member of the brute creation, though there is a tradition that a rat was once pressed into service, and that to ensure all possible speed a ferret was sent after it to tell it to hurry up. Instead of resorting to any device of this kind, the men put an ordinary drain rod through the pipe. To the end of this very prosaic tool a string is attached, and to the end of the string a rope, and to the end of the rope the beginning of the cable. It is all very simple. Londoners, however, are likely to see much of it in the near future.

Gas is supplied to the great city mostly by two corporations. One, the Gas Light and Coke Company, has more than sixty square miles of territory north of the Thames

and makes, in round figures, 22,211,000,000 cubic feet of gas per annum. Its works are scattered all over London, though the output at Beckton is as large as at all the others combined. The other great company is the South Metropolitan, which supplies an enormous area on the south side of the river with 11,272,916,000 cubic feet per annum. These companies, with the Commercial Company, supply most of the gas used for street lighting, as well as that consumed by the "flares" on theatres and other public buildings. There are, however, a number of minor companies—the Crystal Palace, the Tottenham, the West Ham, the Wandsworth and District, and others.

To see one of the sources of the old-fashioned light we cannot do better than journey up the Old Kent Road to the headquarters of the South Metropolitan Gas Company. Through the gateway past towers, stacks of pipes, heaps of coke, shops in which lamp-repairing and other work is being carried on, and enormous gas-holders, and, behold! the egg stage of gas-making—taking in the coal. Below, the Surrey Canal, to our side of which three barges are moored. High above, a number of cranes. With a rattle as the chain runs over the wheel at the end of the arm, an iron tub descends, lights on a heap of slack in the hold of one of the craft, opens like a pair of scissors, and closes on the top of the mass. Then a signal, and away the big bucket swings aloft. It is as if a giant's arm had reached down and seized a handful. The illustration on page 280 shows the coal being taken in at the Vauxhall works of the South Metropolitan Gas Company.

Next, the retorts—the old type of retorts, fed by hand, and not the modern gas-extracting chambers that are stoked by machinery, though there are some of these in the works. And now it is not scorchingly hot. Mounted on a platform that runs on rails, a half-naked stoker, black, shiny, arms and face so beaded with perspiration that they catch and hold every speck of dust, stands in front of one of a whole series of doors something like those of an ordinary steam boiler, from the top of each of which a pipe runs upwards. Mopping his brow with one hand, he takes

LAMP CLEANER.

thrown the door open. One glance, with his hands shading his eyes, and, having cleared the opening of the pipe of the tar which has been deposited in it, he plunges a rake into the retort, and draws out the carbonised contents, from which smoke ascends in clouds as they fall down between the platform and the retorts on to sloping iron shelves below where we stand, there to have water played on them and assume the appearance of the coke of commerce. Soon the retort is empty, an incandescent tube, whose sides are white with the intensity of the heat.

Perspiration pours from the silhouetted figure of the stoker. You can see it oozing out of him in great beads. But on! on! there is no time to lose. The retort must be charged speedily, else the cold air will bring about a certain loss of efficiency. So he wheels round to a long scoop like an enormous cheese taster that has been filled with coal from a heap in the rear. By the help of his assistants, he raises the end of this implement to the mouth of the retort, runs it in and turns it over, thus discharging the contents. Again and again does he repeat this operation till the retort is charged.

a light from a jet close by, and applies it to the door. Pop! A flame bursts out all round it, burns for a few moments, and then dies out. That gets rid of the gas in the retort.

And now there is a blinding, searing glare of light that casts the muscular worker into vivid relief. He has

PAYING OUT A LEADEN CABLE.

works on Greenwich Marshes One of these is actually double the size of "Jumbo"!

From the huge holders the gas passes, at a pressure regulated just inside the gates, into the mains, to be distributed among hundreds of thousands of customers. Within recent years these have increased

There! the work is done—done for six hours. Remember, however, that only one-half of the process has been visible to us. An exact duplicate of the scene we have witnessed has taken place on the other side, for the retorts are drawn and filled from both ends. And, of course, some of the retorts are emptied and fed without using the movable platform, as shown in the illustration on page 276.

We cannot follow the gas from the retorts to the mains. That were too long a journey. Enough that it is drawn off by engines, known as "exhausters," which send it through the works—through plant where it is cooled, washed, etc.; through the meters, which are of the size that the harassed householder sometimes sees in his dreams at the end of the Christmas quarter (they are as big as a railway carriage and register up to hundreds of millions of cubic feet on seven dials); and, lastly, into the huge, towering gasholders, the largest of which—the famous telescopic "Jumbo"—has a capacity of 5,500,000 feet. Vast as this monster is, however, there are two larger at the South Metropolitan Company's

SUPPLYING ARC LAMP
WITH CARBON.

enormously. Thanks to that beneficial invention, the coin-freed meter, gas companies have tapped a new public—a public which purchases gas by the pennyworth; and now consumers of this class are numbered by the million and are being added to daily. The South Metropolitan Company alone has more than 120,000 slot meters in use, and is installing others at the rate of 250 or 300 per week.

Not that these figures represent so many

Round that special instrument tragedy and comedy centre. It gives the gas industry a human interest which it did not possess in the old days. Let us take a short walk with one of the officials who collect the coppers from meters of this class. Before we reach his round—and matters are so arranged that every person who buys gas by the pennyworth is visited once every five weeks—he tells of a Mrs. Jones who sent a message post-haste to the works the other day. That

LAMP REPAIRING SHOP (SOUTH METROPOLITAN GAS COMPANY).

new customers. No; some people who feel the pinch of poverty acutely clear out their ordinary meter and get a slot one in its place. The advantage is obvious. They pay as they go on. There is no bill running up, no looking forward with anxiety to the end of the quarter, no risk of receiving the company's terrible ultimatum, "Pay up, or your gas will be cut off." It is true that this threat is not often carried out, even when an unfortunate consumer cannot scrape together enough to wipe off the debt; but how many thousands there are in this great city who expect to hear it four times a year! In general, however, the installing of a slot meter means the gaining of a new customer.

message, as delivered accurately enough by her daughter, was this:—

"Mother wants you to send a man to open our meter at once. She's put some money in, and she can't get father's dinner."

Now the collector begins to make his calls. For a while he proceeds without incident; but presently he picks out a two-shilling piece from among a lot of coppers. What is it doing in that galley? Accident? Ignorance of the principle of the meter? No; the occupier of the house deliberately put it there to prevent herself from spending it. So she is not surprised when the collector hands her 1s. 11d. Slot meters, that official observes afterwards, are very popular as money boxes.

COLLECTING PENNIES FROM A SLOT METER.

And so we go on till we come to an unoccupied house, the late tenant of which has not given the gas company notice of removal. Perhaps the collector will find that he has been anticipated—that one of those ingenious and enterprising gentry who make a speciality of entering empty dwellings and breaking open slot meters has been here before him. But no; the money is safe.

By this time the collector is burdened with copper. We will satisfy our curiosity as to how he gets rid of his load, and then will leave him. There proves to be no great mystery about the matter, after all. He has shopkeepers who take the bronze from him in small quantities, and such as he cannot dispose of in this way he leaves at a branch of the company's bank.

But the mass of coin he and his fellow collectors—nearly a hundred in all—handle in the course of a year is enormous. Conceive, if you can, £320,000, the takings per annum from the slot meters, in pennies. Seven hundred and fifteen tons of bronze! What mind can grasp the vastness and the infinite ramifications of the lighting system of London? None. The subject is too large, too complicated, and is yearly becoming larger and more complicated.

TAKING IN COAL AT VAUXHALL (SOUTH METROPOLITAN GAS COMPANY).

PUNCH AND JUDY.

SIDESHOW LONDON.

By A. ST. JOHN ADCOCK.

TO repeat a highly respectable platitude— London is one vast Vanity Fair. You can walk about and see most of its shows and sideshows for nothing, but there are proprietorial sideshows in it that you cannot see without first paying a penny at the door or putting at least a halfpenny into the slot.

This "slot" variety is a recent development, and managers of the older sideshows find it such a formidable competitor that they adopt it now as a supplement to their customary exhibits; hence the pleasure-seeker is tempted in some busy London thoroughfare by a display of automatic picture machines ranged round an open-fronted shop, at the rear of which a shooting range yawns like a gigantic baker's oven, with gas jets shining in the depths of it; while for a penny paid to a vociferous showman he can go upstairs and admire a bearded lady seated in an otherwise empty drawing-room, and look into the unfurnished dining-room where, for his delight, three reputed Africans lick red-hot pokers that sizzle on their tongues, and quaff boiling lead out of rusty ladles with manifestations of keen enjoyment.

These upstairs exhibitions do not commence,

as a rule, until evening, so if you are bent on a round of visits to Sideshow London you begin with the automatic shows, the shooting galleries, and the penny waxworks, which are open all day.

Shops devoted wholly to automatic shows have multiplied rapidly, and are as popular in Blackwall, Kentish Town, and Lambeth, as in Oxford Street and the more select ways of the West. Some drape their doors with crimson hangings and are ornately decorated inside, others are unadorned to very bleakness; but it is a rare thing to see any of them without visitors, and of an evening they are all crowded.

The public enter gratis and, sooner or later, succumb to the fascinations of one or other of the machines, and drop in a penny or a halfpenny as the case may be, to set little leaden figures under glass playing cricket or football, or peer down a glazed opening and turn a handle to witness, in a series of biograph views, a scene from a familiar melodrama, the changing of the guard at Buckingham Palace, or some ludicrous episode of domestic life.

Suppose, however, you make Piccadilly Circus your starting point, and, pacing one of the most fashionable streets thereabouts, drop into a typical West-End sideshow of more catholic pretensions.

It is a frontless shop in which well-dressed people stroll among groves of automatic machines; at intervals a coin rattles into a slot and the whirr of the handle turning breaks the quiet of the place, or the sharp crack of a rifle sounds from the select shooting gallery at the end, where a marksman is disbursing a penny on two shots at the target.

Near the shooting gallery is a curtained

appears on a cramped stage to astonish all beholders with tricks of parlour magic.

On your way to this sideshow, if in your north-west passage you navigated the sombre old backwaters of Bloomsbury, it is more than likely that, as you turned into Russell Square, you were greeted by reedy tootlings and that quavering nasal clatter that is the birthright of Punch, and there you beheld his striped theatre erected against the railings and a semi-circle of auditors, mostly juvenile, spreading out before it.

A WEST-END SIDESHOW (PICCADILLY).

doorway, with " Pay here " on a label pinned to the curtain, and if you hand sixpence to the lecturer waiting there he will usher you into a small lobby and call your attention to the beauties of a huge painting that is less patronised by daylight critics than by young and elderly connoisseurs who swagger in and out in evening dress after the gas is lighted.

Across London, in the north-west, is a similar sideshow, larger but less aristocratic, noisy with the jolly ripple and rumble of a piano playing popular airs by machinery, and possessing, instead of the shooting gallery, a dapper juggler who periodically

Of course, you have known his preposterous drama by heart since childhood, yet you were constrained to linger shamefacedly and laugh at it again, looking over the children's heads, and when the solemn showman, piping and thumping his drum, shook his little bag insinuatingly under your chin, your hand went involuntarily to your pocket for old remembrance sake.

Perhaps, if you are a well-to-do father or grandfather, when the performance ended and the other showman was walking off with the theatre, you stopped the man with the drum and retained Mr. Punch and his company as a sideshow for an imminent children's party ;

in which event there will be work to do in the way of rehabilitating the puppets to-night when the show gets home.

There are peripatetic waxworks that wander about London restlessly and, conscious of their own artistic deficiencies, occasionally acquire alien attractions by leaguing themselves with a cheap palmist or phrenologist and keeping him on tap, as it were, in a bower among the effigies. But our half-dozen permanent penny waxworks are superior to this, and you cannot do better than patronise the largest. The window tempting you with a waxwork nurse soothing a wounded waxwork soldier by showing him a bottle of physic, you pay at the turnstile in the doorway, the lady

A RIFLE RANGE (ISLINGTON).

attendant discontinuing a fantasia on the barrel organ to take your penny.

The shop and the floors above are rich in waxen allegories symbolising the might of the British Empire; also in wax models of statesmen, warriors, thinkers, with here and there distributed among them renowned ruffians who have been crowded out of the Chamber of Horrors, which galaxy of great criminals is on the third floor here, though in some of the other waxworks it is down in the basement, and gains an additional horror from its situation.

The chief object in the principal room is a waxwork Cabinet Meeting, obviously called together at a supreme crisis, for three Ministers have risen to speak simultaneously, and a choice collection of British generals is crowded into a tight corner in the immediate background ready for any emergency. You may not recognise everybody, but that is immaterial, as each gentleman has his name written on a scrap of paper pinned to his chest.

As for the shooting galleries, like the automatic shows they are everywhere. A few are attached to cutlers' shops; a few to barbers' shops, where customers improve their marksmanship while they wait to be shaved; most of them, however, are independent

THE LION-JAWED MAN.

A TATTOOED COUPLE AT TEA.

showmen sometimes hire untenanted shops at low rentals till they are re-let, and run shows on their own account; oftener they are glad to get engagements for successive weeks at regular show places, such as the two at Islington, those in Whitechapel, in Kilburn, in Deptford, or in Canning Town.

Wherefore, while the Cattle Show and later the World's Fair are in progress at the Agricultural Hall, you may pay your penny and be entertained over the shooting gallery at Islington by a pair of Oriental jugglers in one room, and in the other by a gentleman and his wife who are tattooed from necks to heels with ingenious designs in half the colours of the rainbow.

Going again next week you find the front room appropriated to an elegant "electric lady," who communicates electric shocks to those who touch her; while the back room is the happy hunting ground of a noble savage. Good living and little exercise incline him to obesity, but he exerts himself in a war dance when enough spectators are present, and performs the feat that has won for him the proud title of "The Lion-jawed Man." Having crammed four bones as large as human fingers crosswise in between his teeth, he inserts the

of such trade connections. The primitive type with rows of bottles for targets still survives, but the better equipped, thoroughly modernised gallery is more generally favoured, and not infrequently flourishes under the special patronage of local rifle associations.

There is one of this latter class at Islington; it is a fixture there all the year round, and at the right time of year the proprietor enlarges his enterprise by engaging travelling showmen to set up their shows in his first-floor apartments.

The right time of year is in the winter. Throughout the summer living skeletons, midget families, and such like celebrities tour about in caravans and are to be viewed in tents at country fairs; but winter drives them into London and the big provincial cities.

Here their

A WAXWORK SHOW (EDGWARE ROAD).

mouth of a tankard into his own, closes his thick lips all round it like a sucker, and thus holding it defies mankind at large to pull it out.

During this same period the Whitechapel establishment is graced by the presence of a fat woman of stupendous girth and weight. Here the shows are held in the shop itself, the rearward half of it being temporarily curtained off just now and transformed into a living-room for the stout lady, she taking no pleasure in going up and down stairs.

Her showman shouts at the door, while one of his subordinates manipulates the barrel organ with masterly skill; and as soon as a satisfactory percent-

A FAT LADY.

Next week she is bewitching Islington; the tattooed people have transferred themselves to Canning Town; and the noble savage is earning fresh laurels with his tankard in the wilds of Kilburn.

One of the regular show shops has a weird predilection for dead skeletons. Two or three of them have a touching belief in the attractiveness of freaks preserved in spirits; and these are plentiful, whereas the living article is by way of becoming scarce in London, for good live freaks gravitate to Barnum's nowadays unless a minor showman is lucky enough to hear of them in time and intercept them. It is true you may even yet be

age of the crowd outside has come in and paid its pennies, the organist stops to breathe, and the showman, posing by the drapery that conceals his treasure, cries impressively, "Ladies and gentlemen, the young lady will now appear!"

She is always a "young lady," whatever her age may be, and she dawns on our expectant eyes from between the curtains, gliding with a solid and queenly dignity that is only slightly marred by the fact that she carries an oyster shell in which she will presently take a collection for her private exchequer, the taking of private collections being a weakness inherent in all freaks and living sideshows from time immemorial.

startled by seeing in a shop window a presentment of an elephant-headed man larger than life, with one leg elephantine and the other human, and a writing trunk of the first water; but inside you discover that he dwindles to a leathery-looking object pickled in a glass jar, and having the appearance of a fossilised small boy playing a flageolet.

Nevertheless there was once a real elephant-headed man about town; likewise an elastic-skinned man, and other personages equally gifted, and you may go and see them immortalised in wax to this day in one of the permanent penny waxworks; but in the flesh Sideshow London knows them no more.

SERVED THROUGH THE WINDOW (WHITECHAPEL ROAD).

BAR AND SALOON LONDON.

By GRAHAM HILL.

WITH the exception of one particularly privileged house in Covent Garden —which is permitted to be opened on three days of the week for twenty-one and a-half hours out of the twenty-four—the licensed hours within the Metropolitan area are twenty and a-half a day. The public-house is the first to open its doors in the morning; it is the last to close them in the early morning following. Mid-day and midnight are both embraced in the working hours of the London licensed victualler. There are suburbs in which the closure is applied at 11 p.m., and bars in the West-End where the presence of a customer before eleven o'clock in the day would be regarded as an intrusion. London has been styled the city of great contrasts, and the truth of this remark is emphasised to the visitor who regards the Metropolis from the "licensed to be drunk on the premises" point of view. Luxury and squalor, gilded affluence and shame-faced dinginess, the marble entrance-hall and the swing doors, stand shoulder to shoulder through the heart of the town.

If we would obtain a comprehensive impression of Bar and Saloon London we must be astir with the dawn. All through the night the market carts have been jogging into town, and although it is not yet three

o'clock Covent Garden Market has been long awake. Already a small crowd is gathered around the portals of the market house. With the first stroke of three the doors are unbolted, and the business of the day commences. For the next four or five hours the smart-looking, alert barmen will, literally and figuratively, have their hands full.

The buffets at the terminal railway stations are among the earliest saloons to open, and as we make our way to Piccadilly through the smaller thoroughfares signs of activity are everywhere observable in the licensed world. Tubs of bar refuse, which repose on the kerbs against the coming of the dustmen, attract the scrutiny of the early prowler, potmen are polishing the huge swinging lamps and plate-glass windows, and barrels of beer are being lowered into dark yawning cellars. The four thousand licensed houses and beer shops of the Metropolis are being put in order for the daily round.

Let us pause for a moment in the security of the island pavement in Piccadilly Circus. Half a dozen well-known bars are in sight, while behind the solid blockade of buildings that hedge about the Circus half a hundred licensed houses are within a few minutes' walk of our halting place. The Piccadilly, the Leicester Lounge, and the wine shops of Soho

INSIDE A PUBLIC-HOUSE ON SATURDAY NIGHT.

are behind us, the St. James's Restaurant is hidden from view by the curve of the noble Quadrant, the Café Royal catches our eye from the opposite side of Regent Street, while the Criterion occupies nearly one whole side of the Circus. We enter the long marble saloon of the Criterion, and pass into the American bar. It is still early, the sun is barely over the yardarm, and only some half-dozen men are assembled. We

of the other sex. If we retrace our steps across the Circus, and pass through Leicester Square to Maiden Lane—we have no time to look into the handsome bar of the Queen's Hotel, or dive into the beer saloon of the adjacent Brasserie on our way— we shall find at Rule's a similar scene on a smaller scale. There is a distinctly theatrical flavour about the company, and the theatrical traditions of the house are

THE CRITERION BAR.

must return to the Criterion in the late evening if we would see this popular resort at its brightest. Here are men in evening dress and men in mufti, guardsmen and garrulous music-hall artists, City men, well-known racing men, and popular jockeys—all sorts and conditions of men—composing a human panorama in a state of perpetual motion.

At the neighbouring St. James's we shall encounter a similar crowd, but interspersed with the male element we notice a sprinkling

recalled by the pictures and playbills which cover the walls. Stage-land in the more exalted form of leading actors and theatrical capitalists is to the fore again at Romano's, which rears its striking yellow frontage in the Strand. We have dropped the feminine element at Rule's, and shall pick it up again later at Short's, "the oldest wine-house in London." The Garrick is a newer theatrical rendezvous, and facing it, hard by St. Martin's Church, is yet another, the Chandos, the morning house of call for ladies who have paid their diurnal visit to one or other of the dramatic and musical agencies that flourish in the locality.

In the wine houses a different class of customer is usually encountered. At Short's, whose chief branch is just east of the Gaiety Restaurant in the Strand, port is the favourite beverage. A few wine shops are conducted by a privileged class called "free

A STRAND WINE-BAR (SHORT'S).

vintners"—men who have completed service under indentures with a free vintner—who require no licence, and who have the consolation of knowing that, on dying, their businesses can be carried on by their widows with the same immunity from restrictions.

The Cheshire Cheese, rich in tradition of

A CITY WINE-BAR
(THE BODEGA,
BUCKLERSBURY).

Dr. Johnson and his contemporaries, still retains its ancient form. We approach the sanded bar through a narrow court, and warm ourselves before the old shell-shaped iron grate in a company that is representative of journalism rather than literature, the journalism of sport predominating. The Rainbow Tavern, which for scores of years did one of the most serious, select, and conservative businesses in London, is now a Bodega. The Bodegas adapt themselves to circumstances. They cater for men and women or for men only, according to locality and environment. Let us drop into the commodious branch in Bucklersbury, sometimes known as the "Free Exchange." The heavy swing doorway is flanked on either side by a sandwich counter and a cigar stall. The circular bar occupies the centre of the shop, and on an adjacent stand reposes a whole Cheddar cheese of noble proportions; while baskets of plain but wholesome lunch biscuits are within reach. Besides the above, mention may be made of Henekey's wine house in High Holborn, which was established as far back as 1695.

The Stock Exchange has for years resorted to Mabey's, in Throgmorton

Street, for both meat and drink. It is a rat-less and bustling crowd that one encounters in this famous establishment, a note-book and pencil-carrying crowd, that converses in figures and argues in vulgar fractions. Mabey's from the outside has the appearance of a City sale room ; some of the other bars of the neighbourhood are small and dimly lighted offices, fitted up with a counter and stocked with good liquor. There are half a dozen such within hail of Shorter's Court.

Going further east into Bishopsgate Street Without we come to "Dirty Dick's," so named after its original proprietor, who found a grubby consolation for blighted matrimonial projects — his intended bride died on the morning appointed for the wedding—in a protracted abstinence from soap and water. Dirty Dick is also known to history on account of the rule, that was rigorously enforced at this house during his lifetime, which denied a customer more than one drink at each visit. At an adjacent hostelry in Artillery Lane this "one call, one cup" system still obtains, and a printed copy of the rules of the house is presented to each new customer. Another curious house is the Vine Tavern, in the Mile End Road, a wooden building which stands detached and apart, like an island, in the middle of the broad thoroughfare. Near by, in the Whitechapel Road, is to be seen an open bar — the only one of its kind in

London—where, as shown in our photographic illustration on page 286, customers stand on the pavement about the pewter-topped window-ledge, and imbibe their refreshments in sight of the passers by.

Discussion halls, which constituted a popular feature of public-house life some fifty years ago, are now almost extinct, and the time-honoured practice of formally celebrating a change of ownership of licensed property is fast falling into disuse. The Cogers' Hall, near Fleet Street, still holds discussions ; but the custom of inviting some of the nobility and gentry of the neighbourhood to spend a long damp day at the joint expense of an outgoing and an incoming tenant is now seldom observed. A modified form of "a change" is still occasionally to be witnessed, but the proceedings are marked by their brevity and orderliness. The gaugers employed by the two contracting parties having completed their duties of checking the stock, the legal deeds are signed, the money is paid over, and an adjournment is then made to the bar. A fund is started by the new and the old landlords, the other interested parties also contribute, and the proceeds are devoted to the disbursement of champagne and other liquors among the assembled well-wishers of the new management.

Sunday closing in London, though rigorously paraded, is rarely strictly observed.

AT A "CHANGE" IN THE EAST-END.

Many houses in the City proper and the West-End are held on the six days' licence, which precludes a Sunday trade, but by far the greater number of publicans are entitled to open on Sundays between the hours of one and three in the afternoon and from six to eleven in the evening. The licensing law permits a traveller, who has journeyed a distance of three miles, to obtain refreshment during closed hours, provided that

he has not travelled for the express purpose of obtaining the drink to which he is legally entitled. But this provision is seldom enforced.

For example, on Sundays during the summer months the Bull and Bush at Hampstead is a very popular resort with pedestrians, cyclists, horsemen, motorists, and travellers in every description of conveyance. All the morning there is a continuous stream of visitors, and the broad roadway is filled with a great variety of vehicles, from the neat dogcart to the stately four-in-hand. Stylish gowns mingle with cycling suits and immaculate frock coats, the outer walls present a network of spokes and handle-bars, and the snorting motor is oftentimes the centre of an interested group apart.

In the poorer parts of the Metropolis the authorities assume a more precautionary attitude towards travellers who demand to be served with liquid refreshment out of licensed hours on Sunday morning. The same law applies to both Hampstead and Whitechapel, but in the latter neighbourhood it is dispensed with rigid formality. In the Clothing Exchange, locally known as "Rag Fair," which lies off Middlesex Street (née Petticoat Lane), thousands of people assemble on the Sabbath to sell and purchase ready-made and re-made clothes. The doors of the local hostelry are open for *bonâ fide* travellers, but they are zealously guarded. The proprietor, with note-book in hand, interrogates every aspiring customer. If he is without a railway ticket, his name and address are duly entered upon the landlord's tablet; if he produces his "return half," it is subjected to close scrutiny. Should the date be obliterated—by accident or otherwise—the policeman on point duty is consulted. The precaution is adopted at all the houses in the neighbourhood.

It was an observant Frenchman who, arguing from insufficient information, was deluded by the obvious into the reflection that the omnibus system of London was arranged for the purpose, when it was not taking travellers from a public-house to a railway station, or from a railway station to a public-house, of conveying passengers from one public-house to another. It is, of course, a fact that the termini of the majority of 'bus routes are made at public-houses, and that the average Londoner, in pointing out the way to a stranger, will punctuate his directions with references to well-known taverns. Tell the most puzzled cabman the name of the nearest hostelry, and you give him his bearings in a word. Wonderful structures are these establishments that give individuality to neighbourhoods. Islington has its "Angel," Cricklewood its "Crown," Kilburn its "Lord Palmerston," Newington its "Elephant and Castle," Camden Town its "Mother Red Cap," Hendon its "Welsh Harp," Finsbury Park its "Manor House," Finchley its "Bald-

DURING PROHIBITED HOURS (WHITECHAPEL) : I. SATISFYING THE LANDLORD. II. WAITING TO ENTER.

Faced Stag," Kentish Town its "Mother Shipton," and Pimlico its "Monster," while "Swiss Cottage" is named after its distinguishing hostelry. No Londoner could associate any of these houses with any other neighbourhood. Structurally they may be widely different, but in their general plan and their working arrangements they are so much alike that a description of one will stand as a description of all.

Let us glance into this palatial building that runs like a headland into the sea of traffic and divides the current of it into two streams. Omnibuses are drawn up against the kerb on both sides of the house, and a dozen huge lamps throw a flood of light far across the roadways. The interior is divided into some half-dozen compartments, which are duly labelled, and the printed announcement, "Parlour prices charged in this department," or "Glasses only," signifies that a practical purpose is served by these partitions. There is a great deal of noise, but no technical disorder, in the "four-ale" bar, where a small crowd of omnibus drivers and conductors are making full use of their short respite. In the corresponding bar opposite the "horny-handed sons of toil" are interspersed with lady customers; and in the bottle and jug department more women are to be descried,

who while their vessels are being filled are fortifying themselves against the return journey. Of children there are none to be seen. This is a flourishing house, and, rather than be bothered with the labour of "corking and sealing" the vessels and interrogating the deceptively ancient-looking youngsters as to their age, Mr. Publican will not serve any children under the age of fourteen years. The distinction between the "private" bar and the "saloon" bar is subtle. The same prices are charged in both. The customer whose desire is to escape the "mutable many" will patronise the former; the latter is affected by the "lads of the village" and their ladies. The saloon bar is the ante-chamber of the billiard-room, its *habitués* are mostly known to the landlord, and often address the barmaids by their Christian names.

As the hour of twelve-thirty approaches, preparations for closing are ostentatiously paraded; the potmen look to the fastenings of doors, lights are lowered, and cries of "Time, gentlemen, please!" grow more peremptory as the minute hand creeps towards its nadir. With the clock strike the customers are outside, the doors are bolted, and the policeman on duty disperses the reluctant groups and clears his beat of dawdlers against the visit of the inspector.

OUTSIDE THE "BULL AND BUSH," HAMPSTEAD, ON SUNDAY MORNING.

A CHRISTENING AT A WEST-END CHURCH.

CHRISTENING LONDON.

By SHEILA E. BRAINE

BABIES may be all alike—to quote a piece of masculine heterodoxy—but anyone who looks into the subject will speedily discover that christenings differ. The tiny pilgrims just starting on life's strange and perilous journey have their feet set for them in this path or that. The Church, broadly speaking, receives them : but there are more creeds and churches than one, and, in consequence, varying modes of reception. London, city of the world, furnishes us with many examples in kind and in degree.

Let us begin at the top of the social scale, and find ourselves for the nonce among the highest in the land. Here comes a white-robed nurse, tall and elegant, with trailing skirts ; she carries in her arms a royal infant, and a powdered footman precedes her. Arrived at the drawing-room, where an august party is already assembled, a lady-in-waiting takes the precious baby from her, and the christening service begins. She then presents him to the Queen, the chief sponsor, and her Majesty,

at the prescribed moment, hands him to the Archbishop of Canterbury. The princeling is baptised with consecrated water brought from the Jordan, while the "font" is represented by a golden bowl of exquisite design, which, by the way, is used for all infant "royalties" born within the limits of the United Kingdom. Around it the sponsors are grouped, according to their rank. An ordinary baby contents himself with three, but the heir to a throne may have as many as a dozen, all told.

Needless to say, the hero of the day is always clothed in the daintiest and most costly of garments : nothing is too beautiful for him, He wears pure white, naturally, as we think ; but less than half a century back another royal baby went through a similar ceremony in all the bravery of a silver cloth dress tied with pink bows, and an enormously long train. Any sum, say the authorities on such matters, may be paid for a christening robe trimmed with real lace.

Fifteen guineas is an ordinary price : one from the Paris Exhibition was sold by a Knightsbridge tradesman for fifty! Some families possess historic christening suits, which are

A NURSE : NEW STYLE.

preserved with the greatest care. A London-Scottish young lady was baptised in her grandmother's wedding veil and the robe worn successively by her father and two aunts.

The Chapel Royal, St. James's, sees many a christening in "high life"; so does All Saints' Church, Knightsbridge. A favourite time is shortly after luncheon. The guests then return to the house for tea, at which popular and informal gathering a splendid cake is sure to figure, with Baby's name and the date of his birth writ large upon it. Sometimes a Mamma of sentiment will save a slice for her darling to taste in after-years.

The ceremony at the church is neither long nor elaborate. The family and friends group themselves near the font. The godmother, when the time arrives, gives the baby to the officiating clergyman—a terrible moment for the young, unpractised curate—and the chief godfather replies to the question "Name this child." The clergyman either sprinkles the baby or pours a few drops of water on its face from a carved, silver-mounted shell.

The carriages convey the christening party back to the house, or, if the guests separate, they probably meet again at a grand dinner given in honour of the son and heir. Baby in full array and Baby's presents are on view,

while Nurse, all smiles, does not disdain any occasional offerings slipped discreetly into her palm. Very different is she from the "Sarah Gamp" portrayed by Dickens. As to the christening gifts, a simple silver mug is no longer the only article that suggests itself to the mind. Wealthy godfathers and "fairy godmothers" bestow a handsome sum of money, from £100 to £1,000, or arrange that the child shall have a certain amount of "pocket money," paid regularly on each birthday until his twenty-first. Here is a list of presents given to some lucky babies of both sexes : A clock, Irish loving-cup, gold bowl (from the King), perambulator, carriage rug, gold bangle, Louis XV. spoons, silver porringer of antique pattern, clasped Bible, prayer book and hymn book, any number of lovely embroidered robes, and real lace handkerchiefs and veils. A popular present is a tiny gold charm representing the sign of the Zodiac under which the child was born ; this the little angel wears, hung round his neck for luck, by a fine gold chain.

No flourish of trumpets heralds the recep-

A NURSE : OLD STYLE.

tion of a "slum" baby into the bosom of the Church. No cake, no presents, no lace furbelows are for him! He arrives rolled up in an old shawl, and wearing a hood borrowed from a neighbour. In some parishes—at Poplar and Westminster, for example—there are evening christenings once a week, to fit in with the hard-working parents' daily engagements. Wander in some Wednesday night about half-past eight, and you may chance upon a curate, two women, and a baby standing round the font, in a silent, dimly-lighted church. Sponsors? Well, "Albert Edward" has a godmother, at any rate, although his godfathers are conspicuously absent; and, being a wise child, he sleeps placidly through the entire ceremony.

Sunday afternoon is a grand time for christenings in populous neighbourhoods. The officiating clergyman may find as many as half a dozen babies awaiting him, decked out as finely as their proud mothers can manage. One, disliking the whole proceeding, starts crying; the rest follow suit: and the parson's voice is drowned by a chorus of wails. Poor little souls, they already find life too hard for them!

Not unfrequently the clergy are called upon to bestow rather singular names in holy baptism. The parents have a leaning towards something flowery, as, for instance, "Dahlia Lorella"; or they desire to "date" their offspring, and so label them "Corona-

A SCOTTISH CHRISTENING IN LONDON.

tion," "Mafeking," "Magersfontein," or something equally terrible. Royal appellations are popular; hence we get the certainly startling "Queen Victoria" Jones, also "Princess Alice Maud Mary," shortened for common use into "Princess Mogg," and the less ambitious "Princess." The last mentioned was selected by a harassed father, because the relatives fought pitched battles about

A BATCH OF CHRISTENINGS.

the baby's name, and he decided that "Princess" could give offence to no one. In the register of St. Martin's-in-the-Fields we find "Alice Centurion." One small scrap of humanity had to be "Bill," for the reason that William and Willy were already there; while a certain wee Jack owned an elder brother John and a father also John.

The tall Scottish minister entering yonder house is about to christen a "bonny bairn," and the family and sundry friends are already seated round the drawing-room. They rise as he enters, in his ordinary attire, and the brief and simple ceremony commences. A white cloth is spread upon a small table, and the family punch-bowl, an old relic, serves for a more sacred purpose than the one for which it was originally designed. A trying moment soon arrives for the father: he has to stand, the rest being seated, while the minister solemnly and pointedly addresses him on behalf of the child, indicating his duties and responsibilities towards it. Then the mother places the baby in her husband's arms, and it is he who presents it to the minister.

Dark eyes, olive complexions, the murmur of a Southern tongue—signs are these that we have reached the Italian quarter of our all-embracing Metropolis. Entering the Italian church, Hatton Garden, one presently discovers, by the dim light of a dull afternoon, a couple of tiny *bambini*, probably from Saffron Hill, with their attendant guardians. Italians, be it remarked, choose their children's godparents most carefully, for the latter will henceforth rank almost as members of the family.

An old nurse, with strongly marked features, dressed in her native costume, carries Annunziata, aged five days, who is wrapped in a voluminous white shawl, tied round the middle, rather like a Christmas cracker, with a broad, red ribbon. Baby number two, small Agostino, wears a mantle, a much be-ribboned hood, and a cap with a blue bow. As he is to be christened first, these adornments are removed with speed.

The baptismal service used in the Roman Catholic Church is a highly symbolic one: we can but glance briefly at its most salient details. The priest asks, meeting the baptismal group, "Agostino, what dost thou demand of the Church?" and the sponsors

reply, "Eternal life." The evil spirit is exorcised that it may come out of the child, the sign of the cross made upon the little one's forehead and breast, prayers are offered, and the "salt of wisdom" is put into its mouth. Arrived at the font, the priest touches the child's ears and nose; a burning taper is also placed for a second in the tiny hand, in token that it must keep its light shining before the world. The sponsors holding it over the font, due east and west, the priest anoints it with oil between the shoulders in the form of a cross. He next pours the holy water three times upon the little head; and, with a brief exhortation, the service is ended.

Wesleyans have no sponsors for their children, neither have the Congregationalists; with the latter baptism, although generally practised, is optional. Quakers do not christen at all, and the Salvation Army "dedicates."

A "dedication" is naturally of a military character. We are passing the barracks; let us enter the hall where an evening prayer-meeting has begun. Yonder stands the Captain of the corps, and the Adjutant and his wife, parents of the child about to be "dedicated." Behind them are rows of earnest faces, many framed in the dark blue bonnet we know so well. The little girl smiles in her mother's arms, recking not of future warfare, while her parents promise to train her up as a "faithful soldier" and to keep her from "intoxicating drink, finery, wealth, hurtful reading, worldly acquaintance." The Captain takes the child, the corps stand, and solemnly "Mary Greenwood" is dedicated to the service of God and the Salvation Army. He calls out, energetically: "Those who will pray for these parents and this child, and in every way they can help them to carry out the promises made this day—Bayonets—fix!"

"God bless these parents!"

"Amen!"

"God bless this child!"

"Amen!"

"God bless the Army!"

"Amen!"

The "volleys" rattle through the hall; the new recruit cries.

Does not this touch of nature make all our babies kin? And so, having brought them to this first stage on their earthly pilgrimage, let us take our leave of them.

I. A CHRISTENING AT THE ITALIAN CHURCH, HATTON GARDEN.   II. A SALVATION ARMY
"DEDICATION."

COUNTY COUNCIL LONDON.

By FREDERICK DOLMAN, L.C.C.

THE London County Council has nothing like the Lord Mayor's Show with which to impress the Londoner in the street, and the annual dinner of its Chairman cannot yet pretend to the prestige of the Guildhall banquet. Yet during its existence it has acquired for London's millions a human interest and a living significance such as no other public body has ever possessed. In the civic activity it calls forth the Council's election every three years is comparable only with London's share in Parliamentary general elections.

On the other hand, it would be hard to find a provincial town which knows so little of its municipal rulers and the actual method of their daily work as does London of its County Council. At election time the Council and its work are the subject of hundreds of meetings, of thousands of newspaper columns, and millions of leaflets and pamphlets. At all times Londoners are constantly confronted with the letters "L.C.C."—at street improvement works, in the parks and on the bridges, on fire-engines and tramcars, and so on. But you might ask a dozen men in the street to direct you to the Council's meeting place without obtaining the desired information. London has not yet its Hôtel de Ville, like Paris or Brussels, to be regarded not only as one of the sights of the capital for its strangers, but also as the head-centre of municipal activity for its citizens. Perhaps this is largely the reason why Londoners, now well acquainted with the civic energy which is transforming the face of their great city, are at present apt to know so little of its source.

Of the hundreds who are crossing Trafalgar Square at this moment, I wonder what small fraction are aware that within a stone's throw —up a side street—are the headquarters of the largest municipality in the world, with a revenue exceeding that possessed by several of the European states. It would require some enterprise for any one of them to discover the "Entrance to Public Gallery" between the shops in Cockspur Street, although to a few earnest students of municipal affairs this is a place of weekly pilgrimage. As it is nearly three o'clock on Tuesday afternoon, the County Hall's front door round the corner in Spring Gardens might be identified, after a few moments' observation, by the intermittent stream of members making their way to it for the usual weekly meeting.

It is a formidable programme of business which each member finds ready for him on his seat in the unpretentious but comfortable council chamber. There are sixty or seventy large pages in the "agenda," to be disposed of in the four hours which, except on unusual occasions, represent the limit of the sitting! Nothing surprises the stranger in the gallery so much as the speed with which, at times, page after page of this agenda is turned over by the Chairman, amidst the silent acquiescence of the members. The stranger afterwards learns that practically the whole business of the Council is put before it in the shape of reports from its committees, which the members of the Council generally have already carefully read in the privacy of their homes, the agenda invariably reaching them by Saturday night's post in readiness for Sunday's leisure. Furthermore, the committees work so well that, as a rule, it is only on important matters of policy that their decisions are ever challenged in the open Council.

Nor is debate on these matters ever unduly prolonged. A fifteen minutes rule prevails at Spring Gardens, and the member who would speak longer than this time must receive the consent of the Council, whilst with the approval of the Chairman the debate can be "closured" at any time. Notwithstanding these time-saving expedients, the Chairman finds it necessary to travel through the agenda-

AT THE L.C.C. LICENSING SESSIONS (CLERKENWELL): EXAMINING A WITNESS.

MONDAY, May 6th.	
Industrial and Reformatry. Schools Com. (Feltham)	10.45
Horton Asylum Building and Estate) Sub-Committee (at Asylum)	11.0
Manor Asylum : Epsom) Sub-Committee, *at rising of above*	
Building Act Committee	2.0
General Purposes Sub-Committee (Contracts)	2.30
General Purposes Committee	3.0
Parks Sub-Committee (S.W.)	4.0
Fire Brigade Sub-Com. (Stores) at Chief Station.	4.30
Technical Education Board	5.0

TUESDAY, 7th.	
Housing of the Working Classes Committee (Lordship-lane estate), meet at King's-cross station	10.0
Finance Sub-Committee (Works Dept.)	11.0
Asylums General Purposes Sub-Committee at County Hall	11.0
Finance Committee (Special)	2.15
Claybury Asylum (Special) Sub-Committee at County Hall	2.15
Parks Sub-Committee (S.E.)	2.30
Highways Sub-Committee (Tramways)	2.30
COUNCIL	3.0

WEDNESDAY. 8th.	
Housing of the Working Classes Committee	11.0
Parks Sub-Committee (N.W.)	12.0
Asylums Special Sub-Committee (Pathologist) at County Hall	2.30
Bridges Committee (Audit 2.15), Committee meet at Spring-gardens and proceed to Vauxhall-bridge	2.30
Theatres and Music Halls Committee	2.30
Tech. Educ. Board (Secondary Schools Sub-Com.)	3.0
Finance Committee (Exam. of Accounts, 2.30)	3.30
Parks Sub-Committee (N.E.)	4.0

WEDNESDAY, 8th—*cont.*	
Tech. Ed. Board (Science, Art & Sub-Com.)	4.0
Tech. Educ. board (Higher Education Sub-Com.)	4.30

THURSDAY, 9th.	
Main Drainage Committee (Meet at Charing Cross Pier)	10.0
Cane Hill Asylum Sub-Com. (at Asylum)	10.20
Establishment Committee	2.15
Highways Committee	2.30
Public Health Sub-Committee (Inspectors)	3.0
Fire Brigade Committee	3.30
Public Health Committee	3.30
Parliamentary Committee	4.0

FRIDAY, 10th.	
Joint Sub-Committee (Main Drainage and Finance Committees) on allocations made by G. Bull	11.0
Housing of the Working Classes Sub-Committee (Amendment of Housing Acts)	11.0
Colney Hatch Asylum Sub-Committee (at Asylum)	11.0
Public Control Sub-Committee	2.30
Public Control Committee	3.0
Housing of the Working Classes (Statistical) Sub-Committee	3.0
Parks Sub-Committee (General)	3.30
Joint Committee on Fire Brigade Expenditure	3.30
Local Gov. Sub-Com. (London Government Act)	3.30
Inebriates Acts Committee	4.0
Local Government and Taxation Committee	4.0

SATURDAY, 11th.	
Parks Sub-Committee (N.W.), View Meet at Spring-gardens	2.0
Hampstead-heath railway station	2.45

A WEEK'S WORK : PAGES FROM A MEMBER'S DIARY.

paper at a high rate of speed, and as he proceeds it may be observed that first one member, then another, shows an anxious alertness, ready to strike in at the proper moment with his question or his challenge.

"Report of the —— Committee," calls out the Chairman of the Council. "I move the reception of the report," responds a voice from the front row of the semi-circular benches on which seats are allotted to the chairmen of the committees. "That the report be received," says the Chairman of the Council. If it is the report of a committee, such as the "Highways" or the "Theatres," dealing with some subject of great current interest, there will be a bunch of questions for its chairman "on the reception of the report," and possibly a general debate.

The report having been received, its recommendations are enumerated. To any of these recommendations an amendment may be moved, the usual form of which is to refer it back to the committee "for further consideration," with sometimes a statement of the reason for this course. A show of hands, as a rule, decides the fate of such amendments, the decisions mostly confirming that of the committee. On the rare occasions when ten members rise in their places to claim a division, the division is taken by passing through an "aye" and "no" lobby as in the House of Commons.

Although the benches are always fairly well filled, the stranger in the gallery will notice much coming and going on the part of members. There is a constituent or a friend to be seen in the lobby, a book to be consulted in the library, or even a cigarette to be enjoyed in the smoking-room. After four o'clock the desire for tea begins to manifest itself. The Council's tea-room is an important feature in what may be termed the inner life of the L.C.C. Tea, with the kindred beverages that cheer without inebriating, bread-and-butter, and a dainty assortment of cakes form the only refreshments obtainable at Spring Gardens, and they are provided, together with the service of waitresses, at the councillors' own cost. Now and again the Council's sittings have been unduly prolonged, and on such occasions these edibles have, of course, proved wofully inadequate. The minority, it is said, once nearly starved the majority into surrender on an important question by

L.C.C. OPEN SPACE NOTICE BOARD.

keeping the Council sitting till long past midnight, sustaining themselves in the meantime on a pre-organised supply of provender from one of the political clubs.

But if the tea-room is deficient in its resources in such an emergency, it has at normal times an important influence on the good-fellowship of the members of the Council, and therefore on the easy working of the great administrative machine which is in their hands. Apart from exceptional occasions, such as the Chairman's garden party in the summer and dinner party in the winter, it affords the general body of members their best opportunities of becoming personally acquainted with each other. Over the teacups sit together in amity Moderate and Progressive who would otherwise remain strangers unless they happened to belong to the same committee. Over the teacups they learn to respect and even esteem each other without compromising their differences of opinion. In the tea-room, too, members entertain the visitors they have introduced to the Chairman's daïs, and it is often graced by the presence of ladies, whose animated talk is prone to sudden arrest on their catching sight of the awe-inspiring maps or plans with which the walls are usually adorned, the room being devoted to the labours of committees on other days of the week.

Yes, if you could see this room on the morrow you would begin to realise the vast amount of the Council's varied work, of which this weekly meeting is only a sort of synopsis, a synopsis which is again reduced to the smallest proportion in the newspaper reports, from which alone Londoners generally learn of their Council's doings. Probably ten or a dozen members of a committee of fifteen are seated round a long table, their chairman at the head, with a clerk and one or two other officials by his side. They are steadily going

through a paper of business which may contain over a hundred items, listening to official reports, examining maps and plans, perhaps interviewing small deputations representing affected interests; then quietly discussing in an easy conversational style matters on which difference of opinion shows itself. The committee has been sitting for two hours, and may sit for two hours more. It is the Council in miniature, with the differences which privacy creates. On some matters, for example, speech is freer from the absence of reporters, and a useful part is taken in the

FIRE BRIGADE COMMITTEE STARTING ON AN INSPECTION.

deliberations of the committee by members who never have the courage to rise from their seats in the Council chamber.

If we leave this room and pass along the lobby, we shall probably find four or five rooms in succession similarly occupied. There are twenty-four standing committees, and only six rooms at Spring Gardens available for their meetings. Some meet weekly, others fortnightly, and, including sub-committees, it is a common thing for fifty engagements to figure on the Council's printed diary for the week. Although, as we shall see, some of these are not at the County Hall, it is obvious that each of the six committee-rooms sees a great deal of service, whilst occasionally even the library and the smoking-room have to be invaded for purposes of joint deliberation. The largest of the committee-rooms, for instance, is this afternoon tenanted by the Theatres Committee, which is just now in consultation with a distinguished actor-manager respecting alterations in his theatre required by public safety. To-morrow it may be occupied by the Parliamentary or the Public Health Committee, the one busy with the preparation of the Council's legislation for the coming session, the other immersed in important details concerning the regulation of

11, Regent Street; if you then desire to interview some member of the Chemist's staff, you must retrace your steps to Craven Street, only to find that you have passed on the way in Pall Mall the office of a gentleman whom it is necessary to consult on some architectural matter. There is no estimating the loss of time and temper which during a single week of County Council London is thus occasioned to officials and business men generally. Let us hope that with their

L.C.C. STONEMASONS AT WORK.

cowsheds, slaughter-houses, common lodging-houses, and the sanitary supervision of London generally. On another afternoon it will be taken possession of by the General Purposes Committee—the Cabinet at Spring Gardens, consisting mainly of the chairmen of all the other committees, and advising the Council on all matters of policy—or the scarcely less influential Finance Committee, which regulates its purse-strings.

In the County Hall itself there is room for only a small portion of the professional and clerical staff employed by the Council. This is scattered about in eighteen different buildings, some of them nearly a third of a mile away. If you have business with the Parks Department, for instance, you must go to

expletives they mingle prayers for the time which the whole central staff shall be concentrated in a County Hall which shall be worthy of the Imperial capital.

This central staff, which maintains an excellent *esprit de corps* with the help of their own monthly journal and several recreative clubs, forms, of course, but a small proportion of the army of workers employed by the L.C.C.—an army now about 13,000 strong, whose operations extend all over the 118 square miles of County Council London, and in some directions a good distance beyond them. In the illustrations on this and the opposite pages are to be seen a few of the two or three thousand men—masons, bricklayers, navvies, and others — in the regular employment of the Works Department of the Council.

As I have said, members of the Council themselves have to travel far and wide in fulfilment of their duties. Let us accompany some of them on their journeyings.

It is about half-past nine on Monday morning when a little group of L.C.C.'s meet on the platform of Waterloo Station. They are the members of the Industrial Schools Committee, bound for Feltham, where is situated one of the L.C.C. schools for reclaiming boys from an evil life. It is an hour's journey in train and waggonette, followed by a tour of inspection and two or three hours' work round the committee-table, with an interval for luncheon provided from the school stores at the individual cost of each member. Once a month this visit is made; and every summer, at the annual sports,

I. C.C. WHARF.

the whole Council has an opportunity of becoming acquainted with the school, while the best cricketers among them will probably engage in a match with the school team. The care of these boys takes members of the committee further afield than Feltham and Mayford, inasmuch as the Council has a home at Lowestoft for apprentices to the fishing smacks, whilst other boys are given their start in life on farms to which one of their legal guardians, out of regard for their welfare, occasionally pays surprise visits.

Most of the work of the Asylums Com-

mittee similarly involves its thirty or forty members in journeys out of London, the main body dividing themselves into sub-committees for regularly visiting the seven L.C.C. asylums in the country around the Metropolis. It is one of the largest committees, and at the same time the one for which there is least competition among the general body of the Council's 137 members. This is not simply because of the exceptional demand it makes upon the members' time — several of them often spend about half the week, I believe, in visiting asylums — but because of the nervous strain imposed by constant intercourse with hundreds of painfully afflicted people.

Every autumn the members of the Theatres Committee hold sittings at the Clerkenwell and Newington Sessions Houses, sitting one day to license places of entertainment north of the Thames, and another day to license those situated south of the Thames.

Nearly all the other committees have occasional "views" to undertake. During the summer the members of the Parks Committee spend some of their Saturday afternoons driving round to the Council's many open spaces, in order that improvements may be considered and difficulties grappled with on the spot. Once a year the Fire Brigade Committee inspects every fire station in London, driving through each district in its turn on one of the Brigade vans, and making one or two trips up and down the Thames in a Brigade tug.

Now and again the members of the Main Drainage Committee are conveyed from Charing Cross Pier in the Council's launch *Beatrice* to see the progress of work at Barking and Crossness, where the sewage of London is so dealt with before reaching the river that whitebait can now be caught as well as eaten at Greenwich, and there are rumours of salmon at Staines. Then the Bridges Committee may have to visit one of the ten Thames bridges which are under the control of the L.C.C. Then, again, the Housing Committee must occasionally make an expedition to Tottenham and Edmonton, in furtherance of its scheme for the establishment of a County Council town there with some 40,000 inhabitants; or possibly to some such place south or west of London, with a view to the purchase of another estate for the accommodation of overcrowded Londoners.

As for the officials of the Council, they are ubiquitous, although it is practically only the firemen that the general public ever recognise at their work. In one street surveyors will be examining an infringement of what is known as the "building line"—securing uniform width of road and pavement—for report to the Building Act Committee. In another representatives of the Public Control Department have stopped an itinerant coal-vendor and are testing his weights. This shop is visited on a complaint that the young women employed there are worked excessive hours or are unprovided with seats; that factory is being surveyed to ascertain whether it has adequate means of exit for its hundreds of workers in the event of fire. And so on through the whole range of social and industrial life in the Metropolis. There are important features of the L.C.C.'s administration, such as the parks and others, to which I have only incidentally alluded, for they are dealt with elsewhere in this work. But in numberless relatively small matters, lost in the crowd of its larger activities, the County Council day by day has its part in Living London.

A SITTING OF THE LONDON COUNTY COUNCIL.

DYNAMO CLASS AT THE CITY AND GUILDS INSTITUTE (SOUTH KENSINGTON).

THE LONDON CITY COMPANIES.

By CHARLES WELCH, F.S.A

OF London it may be truly said that the past lives in the present. Turn whither we will, we find sturdy modern institutions, fully up-to-date and foremost in the ranks of progress, whose origin dates back to a venerable antiquity. Especially is this the case with those great public bodies, known to most Londoners in little more than name—the City Livery Companies. Some of their functions have become closely identified with our national life. Take, for instance, the term "hall-marked." How many of us realise that we owe this expression to the stamping by the Companies of the approved wares of craftsmen? What was once a practice with most of the guilds now survives almost solely with the Goldsmiths' Company, which carries out these duties by virtue of ancient charters and modern statutes, and without cost, either direct or indirect, to the trade or to the public. The ancient ceremony known as the "Trial of the Pyx," for testing the coinage of the realm, also takes place at Goldsmiths' Hall, under the joint direction of the officers of his Majesty's Mint and those of the Goldsmiths' Company.

87

Little is generally known of the inner life of these great corporate bodies. Let us take a peep behind the scenes. The Companies follow an ancient order of precedence which includes eighty-nine crafts. Of these seventy-seven only survive, but the gaps caused by the extinct corporations have not been filled up, each Company still retaining its ancient rank. At the head of the list are the twelve Great Companies, distinguished from the remainder by their greater wealth and importance. The relative importance of the Minor Companies, as the rest are called, is fairly well indicated by their position on the list, with but one or two exceptions. The Mercers are the premier Company, and an old dispute as to seniority between the Skinners (the sixth) and the Merchant Taylors (the seventh) is now only remembered by the wise decision of the Lord Mayor of the time, who ordered that each Company should every year invite the other to dinner.

The governing body varies in the different guilds, but usually consists of a Master, Bailiff, or Prime Warden, two or more other wardens, and a Court of Assistants the latter being elected from the general body of the Company who are known as Liverymen. Another class, that of the Freemen, have no share in the government, but possess a claim upon the charity of the Company. Substantial fees are payable to qualify for each of these grades, the first step being to "take up the Freedom." Those who enter by "patrimony," as sons of Freemen, or by "servitude" as apprentices of Freemen, are received at a lower scale than "redemptioners," who, as outsiders, have no claim upon the Company for admission, which they can obtain only by special consent.

The Master and Wardens wear gowns deeply trimmed with fur, and in certain Com-

OUTSIDE A CELL, BRIDEWELL HOSPITAL.

panies a hood is also worn. Some Companies provide silver medals for their Liverymen, and a gold badge for each of the Assistants; others present a badge to every Past-Master. These insignia become the personal property of the recipients, but the official badge of the Master, a jewel of far higher value, is solely for official use.

The election day, held on the feast of the Company's patron saint, is the red-letter day of the year, and very quaint are the ceremonies observed on the occasion. These vary, of course, in the different guilds. With some, the new Master and Wardens are crowned at table by the outgoing officials with the ancient election garlands. In other Companies the new officials are pledged by their outgoing brethren in the

loving cup during the course of the banquet. Many of the Companies attend a neighbouring church in procession to hear a sermon before or after the election. The Mercers' Company has a chapel of its own at its Hall in Cheapside, where divine service is performed every Sunday throughout the year.

Each of the Halls has a court-room, where the meetings of the governing body are held, the Master and Wardens being clothed in their robes, attended by the Clerk and other officers in their official dress. Our photographic illustration opposite represents a sitting of the Court of the Cutlers' Company, at which the Company's apprentices attend to show specimens of their work.

Some of the Companies possess estates in Ireland which form part of the original Plantation of Ulster in the reign of James I. Two of the Companies, the Vintners and the Dyers, have important privileges on the river Thames, enjoying with the Crown the right of keeping a "game of swans." The Fishmongers perform a very useful public office in seizing all unsound fish brought for sale to Billingsgate.

Perhaps the greatest work which the Companies perform is in the cause of education. Their public schools have a world-wide reputation. To the Mercers Dean Colet entrusted his great foundation, St. Paul's School, which is now housed in a splendid building at Hammersmith. This Company has also its own school at Barnard's Inn. Merchant Taylors' School, which long stood in Suffolk Lane, is now more pleasantly accommodated at the Charterhouse. The Haberdashers are trustees of the Aske Schools at Hoxton and Hatcham, the Skinners have their famous school at Tonbridge, and the Drapers, Stationers, Brewers, Coopers, and other Companies have well-known and flourishing schools under their charge. The Ironmongers' and Haberdashers' Companies, though possessed of small corporate incomes, administer most extensive and varied educational endowments.

The University scholarships and exhibitions which so many of the Companies have in

COURT OF THE CUTLERS' COMPANY : EXAMINING THE WORK OF THEIR APPRENTICES.

their gift are the means of launching many an earnest student of slender means upon a successful career in life. But apart from their trust income the Companies liberally support the claims of national education; a noteworthy instance being that of the Drapers' Company, which has bestowed upon each of the Universities of Oxford and London munificent grants of several thousands of pounds.

The City Companies were the pioneers in technical education, and jointly with the City Corporation, founded in 1880 the City and Guilds of London Institute. Here, at the Institute's City and West-End colleges, young students receive at moderate fees practical as well as theoretical instruction in various arts and handicrafts. The Goldsmiths' Company have established an Institute of their own at New Cross, and the Drapers' support the People's Palace in East London. Both of these institutions —already referred to in "Institute London"— combine general with technical instruction, and each has a recreative side.

Many of the Companies also make independent provision for technical instruction in their particular crafts. The Carpenters hold lectures and classes at their Hall,

A PLAYING CARD DESIGN (PLAYING CARD MAKERS' COMPANY).

and other Companies hold periodical exhibitions, at which prizes are awarded for excellent workmanship. The Clothworkers' Company follows its industry to its principal seat in Yorkshire, where it has established and support successful technical colleges. Another useful work is that of registering, after examination, duly qualified workmen, who receive certificates of competency, and in some cases the freedom of the Company. The Plumbers took the lead in this direction, and have sought legislative authority for compulsory registration. The Spectacle Makers' and Gardeners' Companies have also taken action on these useful lines.

Great as are the educational trusts committed to the care of the City guilds, their charitable endowments are even more numerous, and comprise almost every form of practical benevolence. The oldest form of provision for the aged and decayed guildsman was the almshouse. In many a quiet corner of the City until recently were to be seen the almshouses of the various Companies.

Later on, the value of City land and the need of less confined quarters led to the removal of these retreats to more open sites.

Of the grants and subscriptions made by the Companies to our great national charities it is unnecessary

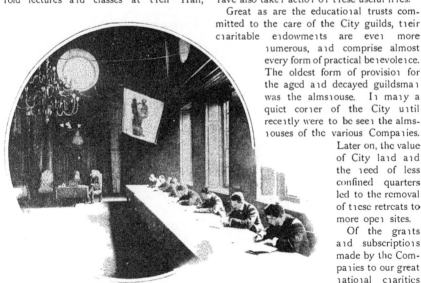

AN EXAMINATION AT APOTHECARIES' HALL.

to speak: the donation lists of these institutions show how greatly they are indebted to such munificence. An entire wing of the London Hospital was built by the Grocers' Company at an expense of £25,000. Some Companies administer trusts for special classes of sufferers—the Clothworkers and others have in their gift important charities for the blind. The Home for Convalescents, established by the Merchant Taylors' Company at Bognor, is free, excellently managed, and replete with every comfort.

Each Company has a marked individuality, which comes upon the visitor as a pleasant surprise. At the election feast of the Broderers there is a Master's song, which the newly - elected Master is required to sing. The Fruiterers present every new Lord Mayor with a magnificent trophy of fruit, and are in return invited to a banquet at the Mansion House. The Makers of Playing Cards present each guest at their annual Livery banquet with a pack of cards, the back of which is embellished with an elaborate artistic design. (On the opposite page is a facsimile of one of the designs.) The Clockmakers have a library and museum, both of which are in the Guildhall Library. At Apothecaries' Hall the aspiring medical student can, after duly satisfying the examiners, obtain a qualification to practise medicine and surgery; here, too, the profession and the public can obtain pure drugs. The Gunmakers have a proof-house at Whitechapel, where they examine and stamp firearms.

The Stationers are strictly a trade company, and, like the Society of Apothecaries, have a trading stock, shares in which are allotted to

their members in rotation. Their chief publications are almanacs, and among these is the authorised edition of the celebrated "Old Moore." Of much greater importance are the duties devolving on the Stationers under the Copyright Act. To secure the exclusive right of publication of any work it must be " entered at Stationers' Hall."

.DRESS-MAKING CLASS AT THE GOLDSMITHS' INSTITUTE.

This process, which is effected in the Registry, is illustrated on page 310.

The Halls of the Companies are among the chief public ornaments of the City. Some of the minor Companies do not possess Halls, many others, whose Halls were destroyed in the Great Fire of London, or subsequently, have not rebuilt them, and the number of existing buildings of this kind is thus reduced to thirty-seven. In most cases these sumptuous structures have to be sought for, their street frontage being insignificant. This is especially the case with the Mercers', Drapers', Merchant Taylors', and Clothworkers' Halls, where one enters through a narrow doorway into a veritable palace. The gardens have almost all disappeared, but that of the Drapers', in Throgmorton Avenue, and the famous mulberry tree of the Girdlers, in Basinghall Street, still afford a refreshing sight in summer.

These stately homes of the Companies have the highest interest for the connoisseur, on account of their many historic and art treasures, some of which are of great antiquity, while others are masterpieces of modern art. To the former belong the ancient plate, illuminated records, tapestries, early paintings, and ancient armour. The latter include modern paintings, sculpture, porcelain, etc., found chiefly in the Halls of the more wealthy Companies.

The privilege of the Honorary Freedom and Livery is granted at rare intervals by many of the guilds to eminent statesmen, warriors, travellers, philanthropists, and others.

Part of one of the cells in this Hospital is shown in our illustration on page 306.

The hospitality of the Companies is extended to all the most notable in our land and to distinguished visitors from our colonies and from foreign countries. The Salters' present each guest with a pair of little bone spoons, a survival, possibly, of the old practice which required all who came to dinner to bring with them their knife and spoon. At

THE COPYRIGHT REGISTRY, STATIONERS' HALL.

Even ladies have been thus honoured by the Turners' and Gardeners' Companies, whilst some of the guilds permit women to take up their freedom by patrimony. Twice in the year the whole of the Livery are summoned to the Guildhall—on Midsummer Day to elect the Sheriffs, and on Michaelmas Day to elect the Lord Mayor and other officers. They have also a vote in the election of members of Parliament for the City. Apprentices are bound at the Halls and encouraged by gifts and good advice, receiving also in some cases help to start in business. The disobedient and incorrigible are brought before the City Chamberlain, who, in his court at Guildhall, has power to commit them to a short term of imprisonment at Bridewell.

many of the Halls the guest is presented, on leaving, with a box of cakes or candied fruits, technically known as "service."

The position of the City Companies of to-day is unique, not only in the history of our own country, but in that of the world. Their existence, in the case of the most ancient guilds, for a period of from 700 to possibly 1,000 years; their past and present services to the country; the immense trusts of which they have been the chosen and faithful almoners; the independence and admirable fitness of their present condition; and the distinguished men who have adorned and still adorn their roll of members—in all these respects they present a combination of age, excellence, and modern vigour absolutely without parallel. Well may we join in the sentiment of the toast so often heard in their halls, "May they flourish, root and branch, for ever."

LONDON GETS UP IN THE MORNING.

By GEORGE R. SIMS.

LONDON is a city that never sleeps, but a very large proportion of its inhabitants take a night's rest, and consequently have to get up in the morning. The process, simple enough in itself, has many attendant variations. There are lazy people who sometimes envy the domestic dog, who wakes, stretches himself, shakes himself, wags his tail, and is ready for another day of life; there are others to whom the morning ablutions and toilet are a delight, not to be hurried over or mechanically performed.

It is a wonderfully human picture — this rising of the people of a great city for the labours and pleasures of the day — that would greet our eyes could we, like Asmodeus, lift the roofs and gaze within the houses. Let us glance at a few of its details.

In the hospitals, the great palaces of pain, certain nurses and officers remain on night duty till the waking hour. Between five and half-past the sufferers who are asleep are gently roused by a nurse, and those who are able to get up begin to wash and dress. Then the stronger patients, those who are getting better, make their tea and boil their eggs and help to prepare breakfast for the cases who are too weak to

MARY JANE DESCENDS.

help themselves. By seven o'clock the wards are all awake, the day nurses have come on, and everything is being prepared for the visit of the matron, to be followed by that of the house surgeon.

After the hospital is up, the patients who can get about pay little visits of sympathy to the bedsides of their weaker fellow sufferers. Pale faces appear at the windows, sunken eyes look out upon the daily life of the streets, and, in fancy, see far away to the home where dear ones are waking and whispering, maybe, a little prayer for the absent one fighting the battle of life and death.

But there are men, labouring men, whose waking hour is earlier than that of the hospitals. By four o'clock in the morning certain workers must be summoned, for the day's toil will begin at five— at the dock gate and in the great markets you must be afoot betimes. In the common lodging-houses there is frequently a "caller," who goes round and wakes the heavy sleepers. The man who lives in lodgings and has no wife is occasionally roused by a passing policeman, who performs the friendly act from the street.

The rising of the domestic servant is frequently one of the little worries of the good housewife. She has generally a quick ear, and, tread Mary Jane never so softly, should she descend the stairs at a later hour than usual the mistress will hear her, and there will be "words" later in the morning.

Cook, in the ordinary household in which there is no kitchenmaid, is the first to rise, for she has to light the kitchen fire and prepare the kitchen breakfast. One by one the girls come down, as a rule listlessly, for domestic service lends itself to heavy sleep, and the household work of the day begins.

In houses where there is a nursery it is there that the first *joyous* sounds of a new day of life are heard. Young children, like the birds, have a habit of saluting the morning either with song or its equivalent. Romps are frequently indulged in before nightgowns are off and baths are ready. There is an urgent enquiry for toys directly the little eyes are open. Baby girls betray the maternal instinct in a demand for dolls, while little boys have been known to introduce, not only woolly rabbits and baa-lambs on wheels into the nursery bed, but have frequently emptied the entire contents of a huge Noah's Ark on the counterpane pell-mell with Shem, Ham, and Japhet, who have passed an open-eyed night in close quarters, their necks entangled in the hind legs of the greater carnivora. If, in a weak moment, Papa has bought the baby boy a trumpet or a drum, music will sometimes assault the parental ear at an hour when it is least soothing.

It is not infrequently Baby's gentle task to wake Mamma, especially if it is a first baby. When Baby has grown to the age of four or five he—if it is a he—occasionally toddles out of his bed and

rouses Papa, bringing a new and favourite toy with him. The fond father, who wakes up with a terrified start to find a black kitten sitting on his neck, easily checks his wrath when he finds that it is his little son who has placed it there, and is eagerly waiting for Daddy to have a game of romps with him.

The family getting up in the morning where the children have to start for school before nine o'clock is to many a mother a daily anxiety. There is so much to be done in a short time; and when it happens also that Papa is a City man, who goes early to business, there is a double strain. Between her husband's comfort and the punctual despatch of the children with the maid, who sees them safely to the seminary, her time is fully occupied. Sometimes everything goes wrong. The servants begin it by over-sleeping themselves. There is trouble among the children—sometimes a quarrel and tears. Boots at the last moment are found not to be ready; a school-book has been mislaid. Papa has found his razors have been used by Master Tom for wood-carving, and the shaving process has involved loss of time and temper.

But at last the children have been hastily despatched, with injunctions to hurry, for they are ten minutes late. At last Papa,

THE CHILDREN AWAKE.

W R

with a piece of black sticking-plaster on his chin, has gone grumbling down the garden path on his way to the suburban railway station. Then the sorely tried wife and mother returns to the empty breakfast table, and has a strong cup of tea to soothe her nerves, and for a few minutes forgets her family cares, until the housemaid comes in to clear away. Then she takes the opportunity of expressing her views upon early rising.

In the getting up of the idle classes the variety is endless, for the riser has, as a rule, but himself or herself to please. The society belle may continue to take her beauty sleep long after the ordinary world is astir, and then enjoy the extra luxury of breakfast in bed ; or she may be one of the bright, healthy English girls who are up betimes, and taking their morning canter in the Row between eight and nine a.m. The young gentleman who, living in bachelor chambers, is studying life from its late side, is not an early riser. His valet looks in occasionally as the morning advances, and finding him still sleeping retires discreetly. Such a young gentleman, when he wakes to the consciousness that another day has arrived to be killed, occasionally feels "nipped," and requires a slight stimulant before he rises and performs his toilet, and in dressing-gown and slippers lounges into his sitting-room and toys with a carefully prepared breakfast. His earlier toilet is not an elaborate process. He postpones the artistic touches until he is ready to saunter out and allow the fashionable streets of the West to become aware of his presence.

But the waking up is not all comedy even to the well-to-do and well dressed. The night is merciful to most of us in that it brings a little space of forgetfulness, but with the morning the knowledge of life returns. Many a beautiful English girl opens her eyes to the morning sunshine and finds

A LATE RISER.

no joy in it, or in the song of the glad birds that fill the air with melody.

For her the course of true love has justified the proverb. There are jealous pangs gnawing at her heart, perhaps despair is in her soul. The scene of last night's ball comes back to her as the flood-gates of memory are opened. It may have been only a lovers' tiff, it may have been the parting of the ways ; but it makes the waking hour a sad one, and the doubting maiden sighs with Mariana that she is weary, and she rises with a pale face and dresses listlessly.

The morning postman plays an important part in the domestic drama of "The Awakening." The envelope pushed into the little box with the familiar rat-tat, now in many districts supplemented by the vigorous ring —for knockers are somewhat out of fashion— may contain the best or the worst of news. Brought to the bedside of the late sleeper it may make his waking hour one of tragedy or flood the room with sunlight on the foggiest November day.

88

The letter may be eagerly expected, or anticipated with dread. It comes at last, and nearly always by the first post. If you are in doubt as to the view which the Fates have taken of the situation, you either tear the envelope open hastily with trembling fingers or you turn it over and over and then put it aside for a while, postponing the verdict as long as possible.

In many a little home the morning letter may mean ruin or salvation. The young clerk out of a berth, with a wife and child to keep, has sent in his application for a situation that has been advertised. He has mentioned his references; he has spent his last sixpence in postage stamps. When he

WELCOME NEWS.

wakes in the morning—lying late, as he has no work to do—his anxious wife stands by his bedside with a letter.

He takes it, but dreads to open it. Is it a message of hope bidding him call at a City office, or is it the stereotyped reply which some firms are courteous enough to send to applicants if they are not too numerous?

The wife waits; the man sits up, and, nerving himself for his fate, tears the envelope open. Tremblingly he unfolds the letter and scans the contents. "Thank God!" he cries, "Thank God!" There is no need to say more. The loving little wife's eyes fill with grateful tears as she falls on her knees and puts her arms round her husband's neck. The letter lies open on the counterpane; she can read the glad news. "Mr. —— is requested to call at the City office. If his references are satisfactory," etc., etc

There are certain days in our lives when most of us wake with eager anticipation of the postman's burden. The birthday means loving greetings from relatives and friends long after it has ceased to mean presents, and, because it is still customary to consider the knocking off of another year of our allotted span as a feat to rejoice at, most men and women who have retained the "joy of living" wake smilingly upon their birthday morn and ask for their letters.

The waking of the dramatist on the morning after the production of his new play, of the actors and actresses who have taken part in it, is largely influenced by the previous night's reception; but all are anxious 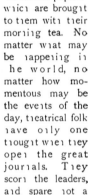 "to see the papers" which are brought to them with their morning tea. No matter what may be happening in the world, no matter how momentous may be the events of the day, theatrical folk have only one thought when they open the great journals. They scorn the leaders, and spare not a glance for the latest news. The criticism of the new play is the printed matter in which their interest is centred. They read notice after notice, sometimes with a smile, sometimes with a frown. On the nature of the notices, so far as they are individually concerned, depends the humour in which the player folk will get up in the morning.

There are times when the "paper in bed" makes half the country rise gloomily from slumber. The news of a disaster to England's arms, of a terrible accident at sea, of the death of a popular member of the Royal Family, affects the spirits of the whole thinking community. There have been days when all London has risen with an aching heart, and gone sadly and wearily forth to the day's work.

And there are days when the greater part of London rises gaily. These are the days

READING THE
PRESS NOTICES.

quently. But these promises are rarely kept.

On Sunday morning the majority of Londoners take "an extra hour" in bed. There are good folk who go to early service, and many Roman Catholics who go to early mass. There are people bound for distant country trips who are up and about before the life of the day begins; but as a rule the servants have a little indulgence, and breakfast is later. The workers, enjoying the relief from labour, and accepting Sunday as a "day of rest," interpret the phrase literally, and take a portion of it in bed. The "getting up" is a slower and more elaborate process. The creeping hands of the clock inspire no terror of lost trains, the warning horn of the express 'bus will not sound to-day, and church, which is generally

of national rejoicing, of street pageantry, of general holiday-making. The spirit of the gala day is infectious; even those who can take no part in it have a kindly sympathy with it, and get up with a sense of pleasure which has no part in the ordinary working day.

So vast is London, and so small the area usually covered by a public pageant, that early rising is the order of the day on most of these occasions. The police regulations compel the crowd to concentrate on the given points long before the hour of procession. Then the knuckles of the housemaid knock at the bedroom door at an unaccustomed hour, and there is no turning of the sluggard for the "slumber again." Habitual late risers are invariably the first to get up on these occasions. They make elaborate over-night preparations for not being late down, and are among the earliest in the streets. If the morning is fine and warm, they descant loudly on its beauty, and announce their intention of turning over a new leaf and enjoying the early hours of London's sunshine more fre-

THE BRIDE OF
THE DAY.

close at hand, does not begin till eleven. In humble homes Mother is up and about long before Father; for the children must be dressed neatly and sent to Sunday school, with credit to themselves and their parents.

All the hopes and fears of life come home to London in its waking hour. Some of its children rise with their hearts elate and their nerves braced for high endeavour; others wake with a sigh for the days that are no more, and with grim forebodings for the future.

The bride of the day, her heart full of love for the man whose life she is to share, wakes for the last time in the old, familiar home. Some little mist may gather in her eyes as she thinks of the parting from those who have been beside her always until now, and she is filled with vague wonder as to how the new tie may mould and fashion the life that is to be.

But she has given her heart long ago, and to-day she is to give her hand. And so love overcomes all the pain of parting, and hope is in her heart, though the tears may be in her eyes as she looks round the little room for the last time, and begins the elaborate preparations that lead up to the bridal dress and veil and the little family circle of admiration, before she timidly goes down the steps to the carriage leaning on her father's arm,

and is driven away to change her name and be linked by a golden fetter to the man of her heart.

And there is one waking hour on which all thoughts are concentrated now and again as the days go by.

When the hour of doom is to sound for a fellow creature, the hour known and fixed beforehand, many a man and many a woman wakes with a feeling of intense pity—not so much, perhaps, for the condemned criminal as for those who love him.

When a hanging morning dawns on London our thoughts go out to the condemned cell in which a fellow creature is waking from his last sleep on earth.

It is said that most of these unhappy ones sleep soundly until the warder approaches and, gently touching them, bids them rise and prepare for the awful moment that has come.

It is not good to dwell upon this waking scene. But, with all its horror, the mental torture for the victim is a question of an hour or two at most.

But for the mother, the wife, of such a man. Ah! God help them in their waking upon that fatal day. The pity of every human heart is theirs when the hour of doom strikes upon their listening ears, and they know that, far away from them, to son or to husband the awful end has come.

IN THE CONDEMNED CELL.

NET MAKING.

LONDON'S STREET INDUSTRIES.

By P. F. WILLIAM RYAN.

TRADE followed the flag! Trade was a chubby fellow about the height of an umbrella, with an empty bottle clutched tightly under his arm. With his left hand he helped along a tiny mite who was as yet but a novice in the art of walking. The mite's left fist, about the size of a small tomato, was clenched desperately. It was an exciting moment; the eyes of the children proclaimed it. Fifty or sixty yards away was the man selling flags and windmills, his handcart surrounded by an eager crowd of juveniles. What a calamity it would be if the two arrived on the scene only to find his stock sold out! Their troubles were not quite over when, breathless, they reached the spot; for, though there were plenty of flags, there was still some danger that they might have to wait for their proper turn amongst a dozen customers. In the Borough you never wait for your turn. You make it, and take it. The elder boy was a staunch Imperialist. He handed over his bottle and accepted a miniature Union Jack reverently. The babe

"SWEEP!"

solemnly opened his fist and looked at his halfpenny. What would it be—flag or windmill, windmill or flag? His small soul was torn with doubt, yet they cruelly hurried him. Then he took a windmill, just because he wanted a flag, and toddled away brokenhearted to cry his big blue eyes out for his folly and his halfpenny.

The toffee-man enjoys beyond all his peers the admiration of the juniors amongst the rising generation. They would make him a Minister of the Crown if only in his flight to Downing Street he would forget to leave a deputy-warden of his stock-in-trade. The toffee-man manufactures his sweetstuff under

CRUMPETS.

SWEETSTUFF MAKING.

the eyes of his patrons. In this respect he differs from all his rivals. In Farringdon Street, Fleet Street, the Strand, Ludgate Hill, and many other tho-roughfares pedestrians

FLAGS AND WINDMILLS.

are tempted with nougat and American caramels, Turkish delight, and other mysterious compounds set out on handcarts with some pretence at artistic effect.

Besides the street confectioners and fruiterers, who pander, of course, to mere luxury, there is a legion of men and women who make a living out of the sale of homely delicacies. Some of these are nearly as well known as though their names figured in beautiful gilt letters over a shop in Piccadilly or Oxford Street. Watercress is much favoured by Londoners, and the numberless hawkers who trade in it find a ready sale for their stock. The shrimp - sellers hardly command such extensive patronage, but they nevertheless cater largely for the metropolitan tea-table. In many quarters there is a brisk demand for muffins and crumpets; nor is there any lack of customers for fritters. The fish hawker is a regular feature of street life. In the eastern districts especially his hand-cart is a great aid to the humble housekeeper in varying the daily menu.

The baker, the milkman, and

the saltman may not be popular idols, but from a commercial point of view their position is impregnable. The milkman labours under the imputation of slavishly imitating the early rising habits of the lark. A sleepy age might forgive him the plagiarism; what excites its wrath is the spirited reveille he performs with his tin cans on the area railings.

Most of those who cultivate a street industry adhere absolutely to one line of business. Take the men who hawk hats — and there are many of them — they never think of bartering any other article of dress. Almost any day one can buy a brand new silk hat for five or six shillings in certain streets. The seller is usually also the maker, which accounts for its cheapness. Its pattern might not be the theme of universal laudation at a church parade; but hats are worn at other places. Then there is the vendor of hats that have seen their zenith, and in the autumn of their days are glad to find a resting place on anybody's head.

SALT.

They are at the best second-hand; and at the worst, goodness knows how many hands they have passed through. But the best as well as the worst go for

BREAD.

a song. Needles and thread and similar trifles for women's

SHRIMPS.

WINDOW-CLEANING.

use are hawked from house to house in the poorer neighbourhoods, while many an honest penny is turned by the sale of plants suitable for suburban gardens.

To one man, at all events, London never metes out hard times. It is always the harvest of the chimney-sweep, whose familiar cry brings his calling within the category of Street Industries. One sees him everywhere, and the richness of his workaday complexion serves as well as an auditors' report to demonstrate his prosperity. On Sundays he often drives out with his family, happy in the consciousness that neither war nor pestilence can eliminate soot from this beautiful world. The window-cleaner is almost equally happy so far as business is concerned, for the climate is his faithful ally. Sometimes he is a permanent servant of one

of the limited liability companies which exist for purposes of

WATERCRESS.

this trade. There is, however quite an army of window-cleaners who work for themselves. These are often Jacks-of-all-trades, ready to put in a pane of glass as well as to polish it.

The coal man is known by his cry. As he leads his horse through the streets he occasionally curves his hand round his mouth and indulges in a demoniacal yell, which is doubtless his professional rendering of "Coal! Coal!" Nobody understands him; everybody hears him! Another familiar street trader is the greengrocer, who carts his stock from door to door, and whose brisk business many a shopkeeper might envy. The china-mender is a less striking figure in the streets than the chair-mender. When the latter is at work a contingent of children belonging to the neighbourhood generally act as his overseers.

FISH.

OLD HATS.

MILK.

" SCISSORS TO GRIND."

Sometimes he is assisted by his wife, sometimes he labours in single blessedness. Occasionally the chair-mender is a woman—the widow, very likely, of one of the trade. The broken chair is usually taken to a quiet square or to a retired quarter of the pavement, and there operated upon. The industry is far from being as good as it once was.

The periodical visits of the scissors-grinder, with his impressive machinery, is an event in the more gloomy streets of the Metropolis. It could not well be otherwise seeing the fuss his wheel makes, not to speak of the sparks he sends flying when

a knife bearing signs of long and arduous service is submitted to his tender mercies. Judging by appearances, the scissors-grinder is often one who has acquired a hankering after " cold steel " in the ranks of the King's army. Saw sharpening is much less showy, much less exciting. There are no sparks, and but a poor substitute in the form of a diabolical noise that might well set even artificial teeth on edge. To the butcher, however, it is a delicate operation, to be watched with the same solicitude as a Paderewski might bestow upon his piano when in the tuner's hands.

Street manufacturers are not numerous. Amongst them, however, must be reckoned

CHAIR-MENDING.

the old ladies who make holders for kettles and irons. The tinker is never at a loss for opportunities to practise his calling ; and his wife, with the most praiseworthy industry, adds to the family income by making wire stands for flower-pots and similar trifles, which she hawks from house to house. That fishing nets should still be made by hand at a seaside village seems only natural ; but to see them in process of manufacture in a London thoroughfare lends an unexpected suggestion of poetry to a prosaic scene. Greater dignity, however, belongs to the woolwork-picture maker, for he is an artist. With his needle and thread he launches coquettish yachts on frolicsome waves, and dots the horizon with armadas. The photographer is an

I. KETTLE-HOLDER MAKING.　　II. SAW SHARPENING.

aristocrat amongst those who make a living in the streets. The engraver on glass finds his patrons mainly amongst publicans, though glass ware has now become so cheap that his services are little needed.

One's sympathies go out to the shoeblack

more than to any other class of street industrialist, except perhaps the flower - girl. Little wonder; for his life is a hard one, his earnings are sometimes precarious, and yet he is always civil, and apparently content with a small payment. The shoeblacks, following the example of more important crafts, have trade societies. Of these the oldest and most important belongs to the City. Its members, like those of the Borough organisation, wear red jackets. Blue is the colour of the fraternity in East London. In Marylebone they affect white, and at King's Cross brown. Some of the more well-to-do members of the trade provide chairs for their patients, with convenient pedestals for the feet. To the average customer five minutes in one of these imposing chairs must be rather trying. It is probably for the purpose of assisting modest patrons to bear with equanimity the "splendid isolation" of the position that the proprietors sometimes keep on hand a supply of periodical literature. One remarkable member of the corps has a partner in the business—a cat. Since the days of her kittenhood she has been

89

in the trade. A most worthy cat she is in all respects, her one fault being a pronounced spice of vanity. At a word of praise, such as one might let drop as a matter of course without any thought of flattering a reprehensible weakness, she arches her back and rubs against your ankles, purring in an ecstasy of delight.

Step-cleaners in the Metropolis—"step-girls" they are usually called—are legion. It is a curious calling, but those who follow it no doubt prefer it, with all its drawbacks, to employment which would impose restrictions on their liberty. As a class they are in a sense alien to the hard-driven sisterhood of more mature years who offer their services as charwomen. The vendor of fly-paper is more than a business man, he is a humanitarian. He displays samples of his goods on his hat, a mode of advertisement that is frequently productive of painful surprises to the unthinking fly. Many humble workers eke out an existence by preparing firewood. The pulling down of an old building comes as a godsend to these people. The rotten timber is bought for next to nothing, and cut into small pieces. It is then hawked through the poorer quarters in a barrow, and sold by measure.

I. COALS.   II. FLY-PAPERS.
III. WOOLWORK PICTURE
MAKING.   IV. SHOEBLACK.

The parts that are too tough to be sawn up are called "crump wood." There is firewood and firewood! It is a prosaic trade till

OLD IRON.

Christmas comes. Think of the logs flaming and crackling in the grate on a December night—*the* Night — when the blinds are drawn, and the light shines on the faces of loved ones, and transmutes to gold the mistletoe berries, and to globules of glistening crimson the ripe holly fruit. The Yule-log man is not there, he is out in the shadows; but he has thrown the glamour of poetry over that English hearth.

Perhaps the day is wet. Here is a salesman offering sacks to keep out the rain. This one is old and blind, and in other days was a miller. He is useful still ; for, though some people are above facing the weather in a closely woven sack, there are carters and scavengers and errand boys who think little of fashion and much of a dry skin. A parcel has to be sent post-haste ; you can purchase the services of a licensed messenger at the nearest corner. You drive up to your door in a four-wheeler. Before you have stepped on to the pavement a couple of rivals for the privilege of helping with your luggage have appeared as if by magic. The clock-mender

is now a pathetic figure amongst the army of street dealers ; his trade is no longer what it was. The man who buys old iron is one of the few who make a living on the streets by paying out money rather than taking it in.

What cannot you buy in London's highways? Here is a hawker with feather dusters on cane handles, and another with brushes of all sorts and sizes. There are artificial flowers of tints to make a botanist green with envy, and artificial butterflies of tropical brilliancy. A man with "counter cloths"—used for mopping up the liquor which overflows from customers' glasses—is disappearing into a public-house. At your heels is a locksmith rattling a hundred keys on a huge ring. The traffic in old leather bags and portmanteaux is limited. On Saturday nights you may see a barrow laden with them in the neighbourhood of a cheap restaurant or a big public-house. On Sunday afternoons in summer choice fruits are hawked noisily through the residential streets of the west. But in summer and winter, through

STEP-CLEANING.

GREENGROCER.

every night of the year, there is a delicacy on sale which shames the language of eulogy —the baked potato. There it is, big as a melon, and piping hot, its jacket of brown crisped in parts to big, shiny, coal-black blisters.

The children of Little Italy supply a fair proportion of those who trade in chestnuts and ice-cream. Often the Italian cannot speak a word of English. What does it matter! The coppers of his customers are sufficiently explanatory. In the City and the

BRUSHES.

leading arteries of the town business is good, but one can only marvel how the chestnut man in the quieter districts wards off starvation—sometimes, indeed, famine must press close upon his heels. There is a young Sicilian who rolls his barrow to one of the sleepiest of the central London squares. Why he should select such a pitch is a mystery. For hours the nuts on his fire crisp, and crisp, and burn; yet, except on Sundays, hardly a coin comes his way. In

CLOCK-MENDER.

the deepening gloom of a winter's evening, when the tide of life sets homewards, one sometimes sees a group of children gathered round him. They are not buying. They are gaping at him in silence, hypnotised by his pinched face, his great haggard eyes, his air of patient, abject poverty. The tattered dreamer, the wondering children, the battered furnace, form a strangely unreal picture, half buried in the shadows that swathe the square. The man is a helpless, hapless, stricken lotus-eater; the melancholy antithesis of the eager, alert, strenuous army—the tireless, dauntless army, of all ages and all nations —who wring a livelihood, copper by copper, in the fair way of trade from the countless simple needs of the World's Emporium.

OLD SACKS.   YULE LOGS.   LICENSED MESSENGER.

BIRD-LAND AND PET-LAND IN LONDON.

By HENRY SCHERREN.

A PET PYTHON.

LONDON is a paradise of birds. Here you may see, between January and December, a wealth of bird life which can scarcely be paralleled in any equal area in the British Isles. The Metropolis is one vast preserve; and there is no other city where such interest is taken by the people in the birds.

All have watched the gulls on the Thames, with their outlying flocks that spread into St. James's Park, making the sky white with their pinions, or flecking the river with silver-grey patches as they settle on its bosom. At the working man's dinner-hour there will be few among the crowds that line the Embankment who have forgotten their feathered friends. The gulls swoop down to the parapet to seize the food thrown to them in the air, the bolder ones coming so near as to be within hand's reach, but all fearless from past experience of their treatment. Here is, then, the link between man and the gulls. The birds have learnt that it is pleasanter to spend the winter on a sheltered river, where people provide them with food, than to forage on the sea-shore, when close-time is over, and the plume-hunter is on the lookout for "wings."

London has its share—its full share—of sparrows. They swarm everywhere; they nest under the eaves, in trees, bushes, in ivy and other climbing plants, and the predatory cat takes heavy toll of their young. They come to the window-sill for breadcrumbs, squabble in the streets for the corn dropped from the nosebags of the cab horses, and carry off dainty morsels from beneath the bills of larger birds. They soon learn to know their friends. A gentleman feeds those in Hyde Park and St. James's Park. The birds fly to meet him, circle round him, and have grown so tame that they will take food from his hand.

The London pigeons are as familiar as those of Venice, from which they differ in being the pets of the people, not of visitors. Illustrations on the opposite page show how they are fed outside the Guildhall and in Hyde Park. Similar scenes may be witnessed any day round St. Paul's Cathedral, where there are two colonies — one frequenting the east and the other the west end of the building—that do not intermix. At the British Museum many of the regular visitors to the Reading Room make a practice of bringing food for the pigeons that come flying down from their resting places among the statuary of the pediment. Let me describe a pretty incident of which I was an eye-witness. The children of a boarding school were feeding some birds which were enjoying the feast, and hard by was a group of poorly-clad girls and boys, looking on with wistful eyes. A dainty little miss, after consulting her governess, left her companions, and pressed her bag of food into the hands of one of the astonished children. East and west were immediately united in the pleasant task of feeding the birds.

Among the strangest facts of London bird-life are the numbers and the tameness of the wood-pigeons which began to settle here about 1880. In St. James's Park, in many of the squares, and on the Embankment, they may be seen strutting about quite fearlessly heedless of the presence of man. This is in strong contrast to their wildness in the country. They are summer visitors—leaving

I. FEEDING PIGEONS OUTSIDE THE GUILDHALL.   II. GULLS NEAR THE THAMES EMBANKMENT.
III. FEEDING PIGEONS IN HYDE PARK.   IV. FEEDING SPARROWS FROM HIS HAND (HYDE PARK).
V. FEEDING THE DUCKS IN ST. JAMES'S PARK.

A BIRD SHOP ON WHEELS.

us in the autumn to return again in spring, and many nest here. Birds, and of course other animals, have means of communication of which man knows nothing, beyond the fact that it exists. A naturalist, passing through a West-End square, saw a solitary wood-pigeon. He scattered some corn on the ground, of which the bird picked up a few grains, and then flew off in the direction of St. James's Park. It returned in a few minutes accompanied by its mate. It had evidently imparted the good news that there were free rations for wood-pigeons within easy distance.

London is a great centre for homing pigeons, which so many people miscall "carriers." As one comes into town, especially on the east side, one must notice the dormer windows leading into the lofts of the pigeon-flyers. Not that pigeon-racing is confined to the East-End. The King and the Prince of Wales are among its patrons. At a race of the London North Road Federation thirty birds from the royal lofts were tossed with the rest; and at a show at the Royal Aquarium birds from the Sandringham lofts have been exhibited. The London homers fly *to*, not *from*, the Metropolis. Their power of finding their way back is due to training for condition and for knowledge of the route, over which they are tossed at constantly increasing distances. Even with this training a considerable percentage of birds is lost in

long-distance races. Some of the London newspapers still employ homing pigeons to bring "copy" and sketches from Epsom and the 'Varsity Boat Race.

"Fancy" pigeons are largely kept, bred, and exhibited. At the Crystal Palace and the Royal Aquarium shows are penned the finest specimens of the numberless varieties. Here are heavily wattled carriers, snaky magpies, pouters swelling with the sense of their dignity, snowy fantails that emulate the peacock in display, and a host of other breeds, nearly every one of which has its special club, all governed by the rules of the Pigeon Club, which takes cognisance of matters relating to the "fancy" generally.

Rookeries, with the exception of the colony in Gray's Inn, are confined to the suburbs. Interference with the trees, as in Kensington Gardens, has driven the birds away. But one may be pretty sure of seeing a magpie in Regent's Park, the jay in some of the outlying districts, and an occasional jackdaw.

In all the parks the ornamental waterfowl are a great feature; and feeding the birds constitutes one of the chief pleasures of the children. The stately swan is conspicuous among the ducks and geese. The dabchick and moorhen have nested on some of the lakes; the kingfisher and mallard have been noted on the Regent's Canal; and the ringplover has been photographed on her nest within the postal district. From time to time the surplus stock of waterfowl belonging to the County Council is sold in Battersea Park.

The parks have become the home of a number of species of smaller birds that there find sheltered nesting places. In the County Council parks miniature aviaries have been erected, in which many brightplumaged species are kept, to the delight of the visitors.

Bird-lovers are social. In one of the large rooms at a famous West-End restaurant, after a modest dinner, the members of the British Ornithologists' Club discuss matters relating to birds, and exhibit rare specimens. The East-End, too, has its social evenings, devoted not so much to exhibition as to singing contests, in which the birds seem to take as much interest as their owners.

Pet-Land is an extensive region, with boundaries that cannot be strictly defined. Just as "one man's meat is another man's poison," so one man's pet may be, and often is, the abhorrence of his next-door neighbour. The man whom Shylock quoted as unable to abide the "harmless, necessary cat" was neither the first nor the last of his kind. Nevertheless, he may have had a Pet-Land of his own, though its limits were too strait to admit of Puss dwelling therein. To feline as well as to canine pets, however, I need merely refer, for they have been already dealt with in the article on "Cat and Dog London."

The providing of pets is a distinct calling. In many of the places where costermongers have their "pitches" may be seen a bird stall, usually with a pretty good stock. Here, at a reasonable price—perhaps from a perambulating dealer—one may buy a grey parrot, with an unimpeachable character as to language, a gaily-plumaged parrakeet, or a cockatoo. Java sparrows and other East Indian finches are here in plenty. The buyer who wants a British bird can be supplied, for the stock includes a jackdaw, a magpie, a jay, larks, starlings, blackbirds, thrushes, linnets, bull-finches, and a goldfinch or two. These dealers will also supply cages —gorgeous affairs, re-splendent with brass and gilding—for their permanent residence, or small wooden structures in which to take the new pets home. When the purchaser declines to pay the few pence asked for a small wooden

cage, the bird is deftly put into a paper bag, with the corners twisted up, and so carried off by its new owner.

From the street-dealers other pets may be procured—gold-fish for the aquarium; pond-tortoises, as surely carnivorous as the land-tortoises (mendaciously warranted to clear the garden of slugs) are vegetarians; green lizards imported from the Continent; the smaller lizards of our own country and their legless relation, the slow-worm; newts, brilliant in nuptial attire, with a waving crest all down the back; black-and-yellow sala-manders from Central Europe; and tree-frogs, scarcely to be distinguished from the leaves on which they have taken up their position.

Larger and rarer pets are to be obtained from the shops where such things are made a speciality. Does the purchaser want a monkey? The dealer will show him a macaque from India, a green monkey from Africa, or a capuchin from South America, and might guarantee to deliver a gorilla within a reasonable time. Are lemurs more to his taste? Here are all sorts and sizes, from the tiny "mouse" he can carry away in his pocket, to the ruffed lemur, as big and as fluffy as a Persian cat. Would he like a suricate, or meerkat, as the C.I.V.'s learnt to call this funny little beast in South Africa? There are half a dozen sitting bolt-upright, like tiny mungooses, and

IN A BIRD AND ANIMAL SHOP (GREAT PORTLAND STREET).

CAGED.

scratching away at the wire-netting in vain efforts to get out. A few armadilloes are pretty sure to be in stock; and, if something specially "creepy" is wanted, there is no lack of snakes, or a few baby crocodiles may be produced for inspection.

In such a shop there is sure to be plenty of birds—Indian mynas that "talk," the rarer parrots and parrakeets, the monstrous-billed toucans, and a host of others to be seen year after year at the Cage Bird Shows. There are special shops where the stock consists of canaries of various breeds—Norwich, Hartz Mountain Rollers, Lizards, etc. — fancy pigeons, poultry, and waterfowl.

Children affect guinea-pigs, rabbits, white mice and rats. Birds require too much attention for them, and will not bear the vigorous display of interest the average child takes in its pets. Guinea-pigs may be handled and rabbits carried about by the ears without ill-consequences; while mice and rats will thrive under conditions that would soon kill any cage-bird. A little girl of my acquaintance has a pretty pet rat, which is tame and affectionate. Immediately its cage door is opened it runs to her, climbs on her shoulder, and waits to be fed.

The goat is the pet of the children of the poor, and may be said to be, in some degree, their playmate. It has also another character—it is their draught animal; and some

of them show considerable ingenuity in utilising an old box for a carriage and scraps of rope for harness.

There are not very many London dwellings in which a pet of some kind is not kept. Among the labouring classes who have migrated to town from rural districts larks and blackbirds are in high .favour, and the song brings back memories of green fields far away. The poor are always· considerate towards their pets, and many instances are known in which they have denied themselves necessaries that their favourites should be fed.

Everyone will recognise the first illustration on this page as characteristic of not a few London homes, especially in the suburbs. Some rail at the cruelty of keeping caged birds; but even in the case of those that have been deprived of their freedom there is another side to the question—the brightness these petted little prisoners bring into dull, grey human lives. That all caged birds are not unhappy is shown by the fact that some, when released, have returned of their own accord. They are well fed and cared for, and the loss of liberty is not too high a price to pay for such advantages, to which

FEEDING PET LEMURS.

must be added security from their natural enemies.

The fowls and ducks of suburban gardens are on the confines of Pet-Land rather than true denizens; but many fanciers make pets of their poultry, especially of stock birds whose progeny have won honours in the show-pen.

The monkey, from its intelligence and affection, is a king of pets, when its propensity for mischief can be kept within due bounds. If a census could be taken of the pet monkeys in London, the number would come as a surprise to most people. The temper of these animals is, however, somewhat uncertain; and some which are on their best behaviour with the master will scratch and bite the children or the maids. The Monkey-House at the Zoological Gardens is a sort of penitentiary for such naughty pets.

The second illustration on the opposite page represents a collection of pet lemurs and squirrel monkeys probably unequalled in this country. The animals are kept in roomy cages, with space for exercise; the house is just warm enough, with a current of pure air flowing through. They are well cared for by the man in charge, but their owner and friend would feel he had missed a pleasure if he omitted to visit them at least once a day

The lady to whom the 10-foot python shown on page 324 belongs is exceedingly proud of it, as she may well be, for it is a fine reptile, quite tame, and seemingly delighted to be handled by its mistress, and showing no sign of resentment when taken up by others. Every Friday it is treated to a swim in a large bath, and the next day it gets its weekly meal.

The care shown for wild birds and for pets of all kinds is repaid a thousand-fold by the pleasure derived from the consequent fearlessness in the one case and the affection in the other. A bond of sympathy is thus established between Man and the lower animals over which he has dominion. But the care of pets imposes obligations, and these will be best discharged if we resolve—

" Never to blend our pleasure or our pride
With sorrow of the meanest thing that feels."

A STREET BIRD STALL.

MATCHBOX FILLING (MESSRS. R. BELL AND CO., LTD.).

SCENES FROM FACTORY LONDON.

By C. DUNCAN LUCAS.

WE are early astir to-day. The residential west is like a city of the dead: not a blind is up; save for a few stragglers—a weary-eyed policeman or two, a white-faced night-bird in evening dress tramping to his rooms, and a sprinkling of loafers—the streets are deserted. The only sound that breaks the stillness is the clatter of our cab-horse's hoofs. *En route* to the east we pass the great City workrooms, affording employment to thousands of men, women, and girls — tailors, dressmakers, shirt-makers, milliners, tie-makers, makers of artificial flowers—too many, in fact, to name. Little by little the scene changes. As each mile is covered it becomes more animated. The drama of the day is beginning. London's toilers are turning out, multiplying minute by minute, and as the tall chimneys come

into view we are plunged into a stream of hurrying humanity that carries everything before it. The humble homes are sending forth their wage-earners. A kiss on the doorstep, a wave of the hand, and the father or mother has joined the great throng.

It is a many-sided crowd, a crowd representing almost every nationality in Europe, and every kind of man, woman, and child. A picture of more violent contrasts you could not imagine. Extreme age walks side by side with adolescent youth, and rude health brings out in sharp relief the pallid features of the consumptive. Every turning helps to swell the tide, which sweeps on fast and furious until at length there is a diversion. We are now in a factory quarter of London, and the crowd suddenly scatters. A thousand eager souls race for this building, another thousand for that. The rest disappear through big gates as if by magic. There are factories for the preparation of almost everything that mortal man can desire — for tinned meats, jams, biscuits, pickles, cheap clothing, hats, babies' food, mineral waters, sweets, cakes, soap, matches, tobacco, pipes, jewellery, upholstery, leather, pottery—indeed it is difficult to call to mind a single article in everyday use in the manufacture of which the Metropolis is not concerned.

The average person has little idea of the

arrayed in many colours have just trooped in. They are match-makers, and the factory belongs to Messrs. R. Bell and Co., of Bromley-by-Bow. Picture to yourself a gigantic room, clean and airy. To the right a couple of drums in charge of women are revolving, and on these drums are strands of cotton— a hundred of them, and each one 2,500 yards in length. On its way from one drum to the other the cotton is drawn through a pan of hot stearin until its coating of wax is of the required thickness. It is then put aside,

CREAM FONDANT MOULDING ROOM (MESSRS. CLARKE, NICKOLLS AND COOMBS, LTD.).

immensity of London's Factory-land or of the vast number of people who find employment there. In its busy lives hundreds of thousands of workers are engaged day by day in performing some essential service to the British race ; and it is not too much to say that if its factories were to disappear this big, ever-growing city would be bereft of half its strength.

Let us visit that huge place opposite, the yard of which is stacked with timber. A regiment of bright-looking women and girls

and when it is sufficiently firm it is given over to the young woman on our left.

She is a fine-looking girl. Quietly dressed and with an air of responsibility about her, she is a young mother. Her husband is employed at the soap works hard by, and though some one has to tend the babies during the day she is happy—happy because there are two incomes to maintain the bairns in plenty. Her daily output is 2,500,000 match stems. Watch her. She has a cutting machine all to herself, and as the strands of wax flow into the frame she presses her thumbs at a certain spot, and behold a hundred stems are cut. Her thumbs never weary. The stems ready, up they go to the roof to be dipped. A man stands at a slab on which is spread the composition—a thick paste. He takes a frame and presses it on to the slab, and in ten seconds you have 10,000 finished matches. If any one should suffer from the deadly "phossy jaw" this man should, for he has been dipping matches for a quarter of a century, but he breathes the air of Heaven—the kindly proprietors, who do not look upon their employés merely as so many machines, lay stress on this—and as a further precaution fans are kept going throughout the day to drive away the fumes.

No one is idle here. Big strapping girls are making wooden boxes at the rate of 120 gross a day: others are filling the boxes with matches at a speed that beggars description; while over the way men are cutting timber for wooden "lights" with knives as sharp as razors.

If time did not press there would be much more to see, but we are due at Hackney Wick to witness 2,000 men and women making sweets.

The factory of Messrs. Clarke, Nickolls & Coombs supplies the sweet - toothed brigade of Great Britain with 2,000 varieties of sweets, and so agreeable is the stuff that in the course of twelve months from fifteen to twenty tons of it are consumed by the employés themselves. Step into this building by the railway where the workers are a hundred strong. Some are boiling sugar in great pans; some are kneading a thick, jelly-like, transparent substance that we have never seen before. It is sugar and water. One woman is especially vigorous, and we admire her biceps. Presently she flings her jelly on to an iron peg and proceeds to pull it about with the strength of a Sandow. In two or three minutes it resembles a beautiful skein of silk. Later on it will go through a rolling machine, from which it will emerge a delicious sweetmeat.

There are few more curious sights than those that are presented at a sweet factory. On our tour of inspection we drop into the fondant room. It is full of grey-headed women. But they are not aged. Their greyness is merely starch. Wash away the starch and you have pretty young English-women. These grey-faced damsels make the starch moulds into which the fondant material in its liquid state is dropped to be properly shaped. Walk upstairs and you have a contrast. An apartment is reserved for the exertions of half a dozen girls whose complexions are of a rich coffee colour. Brown as a berry, we put them down as thorough-bred Africans. But they are Cockneys, and brown only because they dabble in coffee and cocoa beans. They are experts in chocolate.

What an industry this is! Men and women, old and young, scrupulously clean, 2,000 of them, are working ·for dear life. Literally tons of sweets are in the process of making. Suddenly a bell clangs. It is the dinner hour. Labour ceases on the instant, and 700 women troop into the great dining-hall, where penny, twopenny, and threepenny meals are in readiness. There is some chaffing going on to-day, and on inquiry we learn that a chocolate specialist is about to be married. As she has been making sweets for five years the good-natured firm will present her with a five-pound note on her wedding day.

We will now introduce ourselves to the soap-worker. Stand on tip-toe—we are in the factory of Messrs. Edward Cook and Co., of Bow—and peer into that colossal pan. The perspiring individual by our side is the soap-boiler, and the tumbling yellow liquid that we see is soap in its first stage. There are a hundred tons of it, and the men are pumping it into an iron vessel. Passing through iron pipes into an adjoining room it flows into frames, where it remains for forty-eight hours until it has cooled. They are extra busy to-day. One lot of frames is already cold, and the men are attacking the soap—great solid blocks over half a ton in weight. These blocks are carried away, and busy hands will presently cut them up into bars.

Women, girls, and boys, as well as men, find employment here. It is a case of soap in every nook and cranny. One woman is engaged on toilet soap. As the slabs are pushed into the mill she adds the colouring

ONE OF THE CIGAR MANUFACTURING DEPARTMENTS AT MESSRS. SALMON AND GLUCKSTEIN'S, LTD.

matter and pours in the sweet-smelling scent.
Round and round goes the mill, and presently
the soap is thrown out in beautiful long
ribbons. These ribbons are subsequently
put into a machine which binds them. Tons

and they make cigars all day long, from two
to three hundred per day apiece. There is
no busier spot in the universe than a tobacco
factory. Scrutinise these men; read their
faces. Doggedness is written all over them;

MARKING SOAP FOR HOTELS, CLUBS, ETC. (MESSRS. EDWARD COOK AND CO., LTD.).

upon tons of soap are in preparation. One
group of workers is marking soap for hotels,
clubs, shipping companies, etc. Not a
moment is wasted. Study the face of that
young bread-winner in the blue blouse. It
is as clear as noonday that she is thinking
of her home. One of a little group, she packs
up soap from early morning till dewy eve.
And observe that lad over there. He is the
sole support of a widowed mother. As
a shop boy he might be worth five or six
shillings a week, but here as a soap-wrapper
he earns double that sum.

Glance now at our photographic picture
of a corner of a department in the great
tobacco factory belonging to Messrs. Salmon
and Gluckstein, Clarence Works, City Road.
In this room are employed some 250 persons
—Englishmen, Scotsmen, Welshmen, Irishmen, Frenchmen, Germans, Scandinavians,
Dutchmen, Belgians, Poles, and others—

their fingers are never idle; their backs never
ache. As soon as a man has finished his
hundred cigars away he rushes to get enough
leaf to produce another hundred. He earns
on an average from £2 10s. to £3 a week.
In the next room women are just as busy.
These are stripping the stalks from the
leaves; those are sorting the leaves for
quality; to the right, men are employed in
preparing the leaf for the cigar maker. In
other rooms you find girls busily engaged in
banding, bundling, and boxing cigars, which
are then passed on for maturing. In an adjoining department cigarette making is in
progress on a colossal scale, and many
machines are here running at a high rate of
speed, producing huge quantities of cigarettes
hourly. Apart from these machines, very
large numbers of men and women are engaged in making cigarettes by hand.

The whole factory is a beehive of activity

Yet despite the feverish movements, which form the chief characteristic of this splendidly equipped establishment, there is a pleasant sense of comfort about the place. Of stuffiness there is none; every room is well lighted and ventilated, and both men and women are not only interested but happy in their work. Perfection of organisation and consideration for the welfare and health of the employés are apparent throughout this huge and up-to-date tobacco factory.

Down at Lambeth, at Messrs. Doulton's, we have the artistic factory hand—the potter. The clay is brought by ship and barge from the pits, and when it has been crushed, washed, and mixed is passed on to the potter. Come into the potter's room. There he is at his wheel spinning round a piece of clay that is soon to be a tea-pot. He is a genius this fellow, and has innumerable differently-shaped articles to his credit. Close by a muscular little fellow is committing a violent assault and battery on a lump of clay. Dashing it down on a slab, he punches it for all he is worth. There is humour in his bright young eye; he belongs to a boxing club. He is not playing, however. He is "knocking the wind out of it," so to speak, so that when he hands it to the potter the latter will have no difficulty in dealing with it. From the potter's room we go to the turners' room. Here a dozen men are giving our potter's vessels—they have been put aside for a while to get stiff—the finish necessary for decorative purposes. Each man is working his hardest. The big fellow to our right is putting on handles and spouts; the small boys who look so chirpy carry the vessels away—on their heads—when they are complete and ready for ornamentation.

Downstairs are the studios. The one we stop at is tenanted entirely by ladies. Twenty of them are seated at a table. They are colouring and decorating the ware prior to its despatch to the kilns. The colours are all very quiet in effect, but will ultimately be developed by the firing. Now to the kilns below. One of them is as big as a house. It is choke-full of ware. Stokers are here, there, and everywhere, and the fires are at white heat. The kilns are unapproachable, so fierce are the flames; yet the jugs and the candlesticks and the teapots and every other sort of ware must remain in that fiery furnace for nine days. Such is the work of the potter.

By way of a change we will visit a babies' and invalids' food factory at Peckham. To-day at Messrs. Mellin's they are making enough food-stuff to fill a hundred thousand little stomachs for a month. The factory is a mass of food. British babies must be fed, and men and women are scurrying hither and thither intent on one purpose only—the nourishing of the young. Yet there is absolute cleanliness and, strange to say, scarcely any noise. The food is non-farinaceous, or starch free, and in the process of manufacture the wheaten flour and malt after saturation are transformed at a certain temperature and then strained through the finest of sieves and taken into vacuum pans

THE POTTER AT WORK (MESSRS. DOULTON AND CO., LTD.).

WRAPPING INFANTS' FOOD (MESSRS.
MELLIN'S FOOD, LTD.).

of great capacity—five in number—in which the liquid is evaporated until the result is a fine powder. A great point of interest in connection with the food is that it is untouched by hand.

The next process is the most interesting of all; but we must see this for ourselves, so we will look into the bottling department. A number of men are standing at a narrow table. At the far end is the bottling machine. At the top is a hopper, and a conveyer feeds the machine which rotates and fills the bottles—four thousand in an hour. And the men? They are working like mad, for the bottles are being carried along the table by an endless chain, and each man has something to do and something that must be done in a second. One is putting a strip of cork into the mouths of the bottles as they travel by, another is dropping in the stoppers, a third is pressing the stoppers down, and so on. It is a kind of magic. Upstairs women are wrapping the food as fast as they can go. Baby is clamouring, and his appetite must, of course, be appeased, and at a break-neck pace too.

And now before quitting Factory Land let us glance at those who produce "Living

London." The vast printing works of La Belle Sauvage are teeming with life. We will not wait to count the men, because their name is legion, but we will count the machines. There are forty of them in the basement, besides others in different parts of the immense buildings, and mostly magazines and weekly periodicals, presently to be scattered over the face of the globe, are being reeled off at the most furious rate. So great are the bustle and the din that it is impossible to hear one's self speak. Those machines over yonder are printing "Living London." The boys at the top, as agile as young monkeys, are slipping in the paper, one sheet at a time. Away it goes, round rolls the sheet over the type, and out it comes at the other end. It falls into a tray, and a clean shaven man, very wide-awake, having satisfied himself that it is perfect, it is left where it is until the tray is full. Before anything further can be done the ink must be allowed to dry, so the hillock of sheets is put into a lift and sent up to the next floor to the drying room. In this chamber "Living London" remains for a couple of days, when, the ink being dry, it goes away to a machine to be cut up into sheets of eight pages.

Ascend now to the fourth storey, to a

airy room which is full of women. Several thousands of sheets have just come up. This young woman with the jet-black hair is looking after a machine which is folding the sheets into four; her colleagues at the tables are folding them by hand. Further on we introduce ourselves to a battalion of British maidens armed with long needles. They are sewing the folded sheets together.

From the sewing department "Living London" proceeds to an adjoining room, where it is bound into parts. Observe that big man with the enormous glue pot. A pile of stitched parts of "Living London" is by his side, and he is smearing the backs with glue. As fast as each pile is finished it is passed on to another regiment of women, who fix on the outside covers: and then the copies are trimmed and tied up in parcels. How many hundreds of parcels lie before us one is unable to say, but presently an attack is made on them. A number of broad-shouldered men appear and pack them away in the lift, which conveys them to the ground floor, from

which they are transferred to the publishing department, where for the time being we leave them. Returning early on publishing day we witness one of the busiest and most interesting scenes in the world of print. La Belle Sauvage Yard is crammed with vehicles. Newsagents' carts, carriers' carts, railway vans block up the entire space; while from the publishing office perspiring men and boys are hurrying out with stacks of "Living London" and other publications on their backs. One by one the carts and vans pass out with their loads, and "Living London" has started on its journey across the English-speaking globe.

Such is the useful life of some scores of thousands of dwellers in the great city. When the hands of the clock—how anxiously they are watched!—point to six, seven, or eight, as the case may be, comes the hour of release. The bells begin to sound, the streets are once more full, and the factory worker heads for home, happy in the consciousness that a good day's work has been accomplished.

PRINTING "LIVING LONDON" (MESSRS. CASSELL AND CO., LTD.).

LUNATIC LONDON.

By T. W. WILKINSON.

Under the Dome.

THE QUARTERLY MAGAZINE OF
BETHLEM ROYAL HOSPITAL.

THE BETHLEM MAGAZINE.

FROM Whitehall the roads of Lunatic London radiate in all directions—to the "mental" wards in workhouses, to Bethlem and St. Luke's Hospitals, to private asylums and the more distant county institutions, to remote suburban solitudes where doctors, unknown to most of their *clientèle*, have charge of "single patients."

Whitehall is the hub, because there is situated the office of the Commissioners in Lunacy, under whose care the law places all who are certified to be mentally deranged. But a number of those found insane by inquisition — "Chancery lunatics" — are detained in private houses and chartered hospitals, and, being frequently seen by the Lord Chancellor's visitors, they are, as a result, most carefully looked after.

For those lowest in the social scale—pauper lunatics—the workhouse is usually the first place of custody. Bright, well-fitted rooms are here their quarters unless they become violent, when they are placed in a padded room. Padded room! The sound conjures up all sorts of unpleasant

visions. But the newest type of such prisons is as comfortable as maniacal fury warrants. It is about three feet wide and seven feet high, and lined throughout—top, bottom, sides, and door—with perfectly smooth padded rubber, more yielding than a pneumatic tyre inflated for a lady's weight.

Lunatics not suitable for treatment in the workhouse are transferred sooner or later to the county asylum. They are sent away singly or in batches, and then London may see them no more, may never hear of them again. Sometimes a man is lost to the outer world for ever when he leaves the poorhouse gate, and never in more pathetic circumstances than when he is absolutely unknown.

This is of a truth one of life's tragedies. A poor creature, found wandering, is brought to the workhouse by a policeman. "What's your name?" A stare or a guttural noise: no intelligible reply. "What's—your—name?" Still silence. Further questioning, then searching, then attempting to induce him to write are alike futile to discover his identity. Not a word does he utter, not a letter does he form on the slate. At the asylum renewed efforts are made to find out his name. It is all in vain. Who he is, whence he comes, to what circumstances his mental condition is due—these things are mysteries, and mysteries they remain to the end of the chapter. He continues to be a nameless lunatic as long as life lasts, and ultimately descends to the grave unknown.

Patients whose condition appears to admit of amelioration, and who, while belonging to a superior class to that confined in public madhouses, are yet unable to pay the cost of maintenance in a private asylum, are eligible for admission to Bethlem and St. Luke's Hospitals. Of the two charities the former is the older and more important, and, if no longer one of the fashionable sights of London, is nevertheless deeply interesting.

Enter it, marking as you cross its portals the notice prohibiting visitors from posting patients' letters without showing them to the medical superintendent—a rule made, of course, solely in the interests of the general public. At once you are struck by the blending of the old and new. The building itself, the third Bethlem, belongs to the first decade of the nineteenth century; its fittings and appointments are only of yesterday. In the board-room, you discover presently, there is a collection of shields bearing the names, crests, and mottoes of an unbroken line of presidents and treasurers

of the hospital extending far back into the sixteenth century; in the wards the most modern methods in the care and treatment of the insane can be studied. Ancient as Bethlem is, it is the centre whence the latest knowledge pertaining to the medical aspects of lunacy are diffused all over the world.

It is now eleven a.m. The wards are nearly deserted, most of the inmates being in the extensive grounds at the back. Let us pause here for a moment. Down below, spread like a panorama, there is a slice of the gardens, with a maze of trees and shrubs and flower beds, among which females are

A CHRISTMAS ENTERTAINMENT AT ST. LUKE'S.

PADDED ROOM IN A LONDON WORKHOUSE.

winding in the sun. Nearer the building more are pacing to and fro; and over there others are resting on seats. With these male figures are mingled—figures of doctors, who are making their morning round.

A few steps, and we gaze on a companion picture, which includes men only. And now there is more life and movement, and the babble of voices and the sound of joyous laughter rise on the fresh morning air. Yonder the tennis courts—seven or eight in number—with their light-hearted players, and there the rackets courts. Not at all like prisoners are those men. And, indeed, some of them are not such in any sense whatever. Several could walk into Lambeth Road this minute, for they are voluntary boarders—patients, that is to say, who have come here of their own free will and without being certified.

In the background is another remedial agent, which looks from here like the apparatus of a lark-catching combine, but which is really an all-the-year-round cricket ground. The pitch is of asphalt covered with cocoa-nut matting, while the ball—which is an ordinary composition one—cannot travel far before it is pulled up short by a net. Play takes place on this pocket ground two or

three times a week, summer and winter alike, and it has been the scene of a distinct novelty in English sports—a cricket week at Christmas.

To one of the female wards now. It is a long, narrow apartment, with a bright and cheerful air and a dominating note of comfort. Some of the female patients are occupied with needlework; in the middle distance a young lady is seated at one of the many excellent pianos that are scattered about the building; and beyond her another female guest is working and curing herself simultaneously by painting flowers on the panels of the door leading to the adjoining ward. The pursuit of art, as well as of music and literature, is encouraged to the utmost. Neither here nor at St. Luke's is it possible to carry out the rule in county asylums of finding most patients bodily work —though at the latter institution some of the inmates are employed at gardening, etc. —because the guests generally belong to the educated and professional classes. So the policy followed at Bethlem is the cultivation of music, painting, and literary composition. This practice, unlike that in operation in large institutions for the insane, does not effect a financial saving on the one hand, and, on the other, it necessarily affords no physical exercise. But the other reasons for which lunatics are employed—occupying the mind and restoring confidence—are fully attained.

To see the Bethlem system in operation let us take a peep into a male ward after dinner. Why, the place is a regular academy of fine arts. All the pianos are engaged; easels are scattered over the floor, with an inmate working away in front of each; and here and there a guest is bent over a table, pen in hand, and committing his thoughts to paper—writing, perhaps, for the quarterly magazine of the hospital, *Under the Dome*. He may be on the staff of that entertaining little periodical, which has its own art critic— who, of course, "does" the picture exhibitions —or one of the regular gentlemen who attend concerts and confer immortality on instrumentalists and vocalists. Or he may be (this is a frightful drop, but no matter) only an outside contributor, bent on submitting a poem or an essay to the editor in spite of that gentleman's notice that he cannot undertake to return rejected communications. Altogether, the ward is the very antithesis of that conjured up by the popular imagination.

Pass now to the recreation room, noticing on the way the many pictures with which the walls are hung. Some are from the brushes of inmates, and are consequently interesting apart from their artistic merit, which in some cases is considerable. The most curious example is not in the wards, but near the main staircase. The subject is Father Christmas, but Father Christmas as he was never yet conceived by a sound mind. Scarcely recognisable is our old friend in the character presented—as a man of sorrows, with long-drawn face and tear-laden eyes.

But to the recreation room. Night is the time to see this delightful side of the hospital. Viewed from the back when a play is presented, it is like a West-End theatre on a small scale. From the orchestra—which is occupied by a band composed of doctors, attendants, and inmates under treatment—come the strains of the overture. Then there is a lull, broken only by the usual chatter, which presently ceases abruptly. Another burst from the orchestra, the curtain which has hidden the fine stage ascends, the characters in the "opening" are "discovered," and then all settle down with a buzz of expectancy. The play has begun.

Such is the scene on one night. On another there is a dance, on a third a "social" or concert, and so on. Entertainments follow one another in quick succession. And Bethlem was once a show place, where the morbid flocked to see its inmates in chains! Nowadays it merits the name by which it is known to many of its guests — Liberty Hall.

Grimy, forbidding St. Luke's is essentially the twin-sister of Bethlem; not so comfortable, perhaps, not with such fine grounds, but broadly a replica of the famous cure house. It receives the same class of patients,

has pretty much the same rules, and has the same system of wards.

Though it is not seen at its best and brightest soon after lunch time, we will stroll through it when the inmates are indoors, resting after their mid-day meal. Into a long room, windows overlooking Old Street on one side, doors leading into sleeping chambers on the other. Silence, absolute silence. The taciturnity of the insane, coupled with their self-absorption and their love of solitude, makes the patients seem more like lay figures than living, breathing men. Through one of the windows a man appears to gaze on the kaleidoscopic bustle and movement below—appears, because his eye is fixed as if he saw nothing and his face is marble in its impassivity. Near him a younger man, his gaze fixed on the ceiling with the same stoniness. To right and left men asleep or looking fixedly at nothing

CRICKET (BETHLEM).

GARDENING (ST. LUKE'S).

course—so many forward, so many back—muttering unintelligibly and raising her arms aloft with machine-like regularity.

How truly painful it is to study the faces of the patients in this and other rooms! The knitted brow of acute melancholia, the grotesque indications of delusion — here per-plexity, misery, and fear, there dignity and exaltation — the fixed look of weariness indicative of the reaction that follows acute mania, are all present, with many other characteristic expressions. The rage depicted on some faces might make a thoughtful man apprehensive. What chance would the attendants have if a number of the patients banded together and attacked them? Yes, but by a blessed dispensation of Providence lunatics never combine; they have lost the faculty of com-. bination.

Very different from the ordinary routine aspect we have seen is that which the hospital wears on St. Luke's Day. For then its little chapel is filled with inmates and officials, and a sacred concert is given, as well as an address, which is generally delivered by an eminent divine. Christmas also is a great festival at St. Luke's, having for many years been celebrated with much seasonable fare and fun.

With these and other red-letter days, frequent dramatic and musical entertain-ments, occasional dances, billiards and other games, and ample reading facilities, life in the hospital is not so dull and monotonous as thousands who pass along Old Street may imagine. Everything possible is done to rouse and amuse patients, and that in this the officials succeed is attested by the high percentage of cures—a percentage which, happily, increases every year.

Another part of Lunatic London remains to be noticed briefly. It is composed of a large number of ordinary dwelling-houses interspersed with private asylums, and inhabited by the general body of that section of the insane who can afford to pay for care and treatment. The tenants of the common-

but a chair, the legs of a couch, or the floor. Over all an air of unreality. With one exception, the patients are automata. That exception, the only natural and life-like personality in the room, sits at a table—a greybeard, engaged in his favourite pastime of making copies, in water colour, of pictures from the illustrated papers.

Another room, where the worst female cases are associated. More movement and noise here, but not much. Yonder is a group of patients, with two attendants of neat, nurse-like appearance. In one corner a woman is to be seen standing like a pillar; in another a lunatic is in the atti-tude of prayer—outwardly, a rapt devotee; and close by a poor deluded creature is kneeling before a box of paints, some of which she has been sucking.

And here is a striking contrast. While a middle-aged woman is sitting in listless vacuity, her head drooping, her hands clasped in her lap, fit model for Melancholia, in the middle of the room there is another striding to and fro with regular steps over a fixed

place residences are mostly doctors, who receive "single patients"—harmless, chronic cases, as a rule—for about two guineas per week, for the same reason that "paying guests" are received. Whether they all give adequate value for the money is a point which, interesting though it may be, need not be entered into here.

The other establishments, which are euphemistically known as "licensed houses," because they are licensed annually by the Commissioners in Lunacy, who have power to grant, renew, or withhold such licences in their absolute discretion, vary as much in comfort and charges as in size. Some have all the appointments of a good private house, and a patient may, if he or his friends choose to pay accordingly, have his own private suite of rooms and his own special attendant. And no doubt these proprietary asylums are, as a whole, well conducted.

NEEDLEWORK (BETHLEM).

PREPARING MODELS (MADAME TUSSAUD'S).

A COUNTRY COUSIN'S DAY IN TOWN.

By GEORGE R. SIMS.

MOST of us have country cousins. Sometimes they come to town. When they come in a family party they have, as a rule, a definite programme, and can be relied upon to "do" many of the sights of the Metropolis without your personal guidance. But the male country cousin occasionally comes alone—comes for a day—"runs up to London," having previously sent you a letter to say that he shall take it kindly if you will meet him and show him round.

In my mind's eye I have a typical country cousin. He is of frugal mind and not given to jauntings. But there is an excursion from the Lancashire town in which he lives—one of the so-called pleasure trips which take you from your home in the dead of night and deposit you in London shortly after breakfast time, giving you a long day in the capital, and picking you up again on platform 12 about midnight for reconveyance to the town in which you have a vote and a bed.

It is a country cousin of that kind I am waiting for this autumn morning at St. Pancras. Punctually at nine o'clock the long "excursion" by which he is travelling steams into the station. I grasp his hand, hurry him into a hansom, take him to my house, where he "smartens himself up" and has a hasty breakfast; and then we sally forth to put an amount of hard work into the fourteen hours' holiday that lie before us that would justify the charge of "slave-driving" against any employer who compelled us to do it for money.

First, because I live in Regent's Park, near Baker Street, I take my country cousin to the famous waxworks of Madame Tussaud.

At the great waxwork show, after we have made the acquaintance of kings and emperors, rulers and statesmen, literary and historic and scientific celebrities, and that great gallery of criminal notorieties who remain permanently underground, I have the good fortune to meet Mr. John Tussaud, the modeller to the world-famed exhibition. Here is a chance of taking my companion behind the scenes, and showing him something that the ordinary visitor would never see.

Following Mr. Tussaud into his atelier, we find several celebrities rapidly approaching completion. The figures have been built up, the features have been modelled—in many instances from sittings given by the originals—and now they are ready to have their hair on and their eyes put in.

In the wig department there is a stock of every shade of hair. Directly the correct nuance has been ascertained, the hitherto bald head is carefully covered. The parting is scientifically made, and the curling or waving, if any, is performed by an experienced *coiffeur*. Mr. Tussaud, as we enter his atelier, points to a reigning sovereign whose hair is at present much in the condition it would be after his morning bath.

"We can't do his hair yet," says the artist, "be-

woman who has just been tried and found guilty at the Old Bailey of poisoning her husband, is without eyes. The sockets are empty. Presently the eye specialist enters, in a blouse such as sculptors wear at their work. In his hand is a box containing eyes of all possible colours. Pinned to the figure is a memorandum on which are all the details of identification that used to be given on certain foreign passports. The eyes, according to this memorandum, are light blue. The specialist picks out a couple of eyes, and Mr. Tussaud steps back and criticises the effect. "Too dark," he says; "try a lighter pair." The eyes are removed, and a fresh pair tried. This time the effect is considered satisfactory. The eyes are passed. For years to come the visitors to

A HIGH DIVE AT THE ROYAL AQUARIUM.

cause we don't know whether he parts it in the middle or at the side."

At that moment the assistant enters with a telegram.

"The Emperor of —— parts his hair at the side, sir," he says, holding up the opened "wire."

Tussaud's have telegraphed to the Court Chamberlain asking for the information, and thus the parting of his Imperial Majesty's hair has been settled beyond dispute.

We notice that another figure, that of a

Tussaud's will gaze into them, and perhaps wonder how a woman with such gentle eyes could have been guilty of so cruel a crime.

We should like to stay longer at Tussaud's, for my country cousin is intensely interested in this private view, but time is on the wing and so must we be.

We hurry off to the Baker Street station of the Metropolitan Railway, jump into a train just as it is starting, the doors are closed one after the other by an acrobatic porter, and we plunge into the dark tunnel with "Bang! bang!! bang!!!" ringing in our ears. In a short time we alight at Mark Lane, and steering our way through the busy throngs of business men and workers we enter the charmed precincts of the Tower.

Every country visitor looks upon the Tower as one of the sights of London that must on no account be missed, though there are thousands of Londoners living within a mile or two of it who have never entered it. In "Living London" it has a special article to itself

After an hour at the Tower we make our way out, and joining the great stream of dull drab humanity hurry to Cheapside; where, to show my friend a phase of City life, I take him into Pimm's, and let him elbow bankers and stockjobbers and City merchants and clerks at the famous luncheon counter. Here he eats with appetite

THE ARTISTS' ROOM, PAGANI'S.

a magnificent slice of game pie, and when he has drained the foaming goblet of ebony stout asks for another, and fills me with envy of his digestive powers. He would have taken his time, amid the rush of hasty snacksmen, but I have to tear him away, for the items on the programme are not few, though far between.

We now go to Westminster, and stroll into the pleasure halls of the Royal Aquarium. We see a performance to commence with on the stage, and are conducted into many side-shows. We see a tattooed gentleman and a fasting lady, inspect a gold mine and an exhibition of pictorial posters, witness a marvellous exhibition of swimming, and see a young lady dive from the roof into a water

tank; and then, hailing a hansom, we make our way to Piccadilly.

Arrived at St. James's Hall, I take him for half an hour to see a performance ever dear to the provincial heart, the Mohawk Moore and Burgess combination. These famous coloured singers and comedians have charmed many generations of Londoners. Their business is peculiar, the songs and the music have the negro strain of sadness. Tears and laughter jostle each other, as it were, in this unique entertainment. Hardly have sympathetic female eyes grown moist over the closing of the shutters for the death of Little Willie, or the bereaved lover's request to the departed Belle Mahone to wait for him at Heaven's gate, before the comic man is diverting them with his quaint replies to the staid "interlocutor," who is always addressed by his surname with the prefix of "Mr.," and never smiles at the humorous answers he receives to his many inquiries. Then there is a general banging of heads and knees with tambourines, and all is joy—until suddenly the "interlocutor" announces "Climbing up the Golden Stairs" or an old-world plantation song of the camp meeting days. Then angels and burnt cork meet in quaint conjunction, and the tenors and the boy altos come in by themselves with sympathetic effect, and the audience sits solemnly as if in chapel or church.

The first part, or concert, is followed by a Darky drama and sketches. I think my visitor would have liked to stay, but I have another famous show to introduce him to, and so I conduct him across the road to a house of mystery, the Egyptian Hall,

MOHAWK MOORE AND BURGESS MINSTRELS AT ST JAMES'S HALL.

IN THE BRASSERIE, HÔTEL DE L'EUROPE, LEICESTER SQUARE.

where for many a long year Mr. Maskelyne and his company of magicians, conjurers, illusionists, and scientific investigators of the phenomena produced by "mediums," have held sway.

When we get out into the busy street again, it is filled with the crowd coming away from a matinée at the St. James's Theatre. My friend feels that he would like to sit still for a bit, and "think things out." So I take him home, and let him rest until it is time to start out for dinner and "an evening's amusement."

Your country cousin up for the day, while fully conscious of the hospitality you offer him in your home, likes to dine "somewhere." It is part of the programme. He likes to go back and say that he saw one of the restaurants that folk talk about.

So when he is rested I take him to Pagani's, because I want to show him something that everybody who dines at a restaurant does not see.

By the courtesy of Signor Meschini, one of the proprietors, the world-famous little "artists' room" is reserved for us, and there we dine *à deux*.

A wonderful room this, and renowned over Europe; for here the most artistic of London's visitors and London's celebrities have written their names on the wall. Here in lead pencil are autographs that the collector would give gold for. Here are drawings

made on the spot at the hour of coffee **and** cigars. The Italian prima donna, the world-famous pianist, the fashionable artist, the great humourist, the queen of tragedy, the king of comedy, have all contributed to the wall of celebrities. One day not long since **a new** waiter, eager to show his usefulness, began to scrub out what he called "the scribbling on the wall." Messrs. Pagani have in consequence protected the signatures of their world-famed patrons with thick sheets of glass. These have been obligingly removed for our photographer.

From Pagani's soon after eight o'clock **we** set out on foot. We pass down Regent Street, where, thanks to the sensible habit of some of the tradespeople of leaving the shutters down and the shops lighted up, the gloom of the desert no longer prevails after closing hours; and so across Piccadilly Circus, gay with illuminated devices, into the ever gorgeous Leicester Square.

First I take my friend into the Alhambra. Here we see one of the poetic and beautifully draped ballets for which the house is famous, and my friend, who has music in his soul, is loud in his praise of the magnificent orchestra.

There is many a tempting item upon the programme, but the hours are hastening on. Leaving by the Leicester Square exit, we stroll across to the brightly

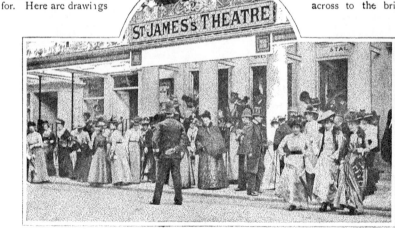

AFTER A MATINÉE

THE EMPIRE PROMENADE.

glittering brasserie of the Hôtel de l'Europe, where at comfortable tables, amid jewelled lights, one can drink the long glass of lager in the most approved Continental manner, and listen to the strains of an admirable band.

Here are the citizens dark and fair of many capitals, little family parties, husbands and wives, lovers and their lasses, folk from the country slightly overawed by the surrounding splendour, and young Londoners complacently accepting the new advance towards the comfort and roominess of the Continental bier halle and café. My country cousin would gladly linger over his lager. But the hour of the Biograph is approaching at the Palace, and thither we wend our way.

The Palace is peculiar among the great theatres of variety. It has no promenade, and its stall audiences are frequently as fashionable as that of the opera, with here and there a tourist not in evening dress, who only heightens the effect of the surrounding toilettes.

The Biograph is the distinguishing feature of the Palace. It followed the living pictures, and has not disappeared; it looks like becoming a permanent feature of the programme. There are a truthfulness and a

reality about the Palace pictures. They are always original, up to date. You can see the Derby run over again on the evening of the race; a Royal reception repeated within a few hours of its happening. The journey on a railway engine through Swiss valleys or Canadian snows gives one the feeling of travelling. When my friend has travelled by the express train of the Palace Biograph over the Rocky Mountains, and finds himself as the lights go up still sitting in his stall, he jumps up and exclaims, "Do we get out here?"

I reply in the affirmative, for still before us lies another palace of pleasure, the famous Empire. At the Empire we stroll about, for I want the man from the North to see something of Living London as it takes its evening pleasure in grand array.

To point out to him the famous men about town, the great financiers, the eminent counsel, the "club men," the racing men, and the literary and artistic celebrities who promenade in the grand lounge and chatter in the famous foyer, amid the rustle of silks and the flashing of diamonds, is exhausting, so I suggest that we should take two seats, for which we have already paid, and see the performance. We are in time for the finish of the grand ballet. All that lavish outlay and artistic taste can accomplish in the matter of adorning the female form divine is accomplished at the Empire. Nowhere in the world is the grand finale of a ballet presented with more costly and at the same time refined magnificence. The three great variety theatres of London—the Alhambra, the Palace, and the Empire—are unique; no other capital has anything like them. As a consequence, and also to a certain extent because the entertainment does not demand a great knowledge of the language, they always include among their audience a very large proportion of foreign as well as provincial visitors.

Soon after eleven the audience in most places of entertainment in London begins to make a decided move. At the variety theatres the stalls for some reason empty first, although one would have thought that the train and tram and 'bus catchers to the suburbs would have been the earliest to go.

But at ten minutes past eleven the house empties rapidly from all parts, and by half-past eleven most of the lights of the theatres and halls in the West-End of London have paled their highly effectual fires.

At a quarter past eleven, having given my country cousin a hurried peep into the luxurious Criterion bar and American café, and allowed him to feast his eyes upon the tempting display of lobsters and crabs in the famous front windows of Scott's, I assure him it is time to take a hansom. But we are outside the entrance to the Café Royal, and he suggests that, as he has a long journey before him, he shall be allowed to take his final refreshment seated comfortably on a luxurious lounge at this, one of the oldest and also one of the best-known café restaurants of London.

And so it is twenty minutes to twelve when at last I succeed in putting him into a hansom, which bears us swiftly to St. Pancras, where we find platform number 12 rapidly filling with the excursionists who have had a day in London, and are now going to have a night on the railway.

The clock points to ten minutes past midnight, the porters begin to shut doors, the rear guard waves the green lantern, and with a hearty " Good-bye" my country cousin is whirled away into the darkness.

And, having seen more of the amusements of London in one day than I generally see in six months, I go home to bed, and dream that all the shows of London are performing round me, and that I am vainly endeavouring to fight my way through the crowd of wild performers and seek refuge in a hermit's cell beside a silent pool.

A country cousin can accomplish an amount of sight-seeing in twelve hours without fatigue which would leave the ordinary Londoner a hopeless wreck.

" GOOD-BYE."

IN A REGISTRY OFFICE (MRS. HUNT'S, DUKE STREET, W.): SERVANTS SEEKING SITUATIONS.

SERVANT LONDON.

By N. MURRELL MARRIS.

MAID-OF-ALL-WORK.

"THERE are no servants to be had!"

The cry begins with the mistresses, it is taken up by the registry offices, it is repeated in the Press. Yet in London alone we have a great army of servants, who spend their lives waiting upon a still larger army of their fellow men and upon each other.

There are always servants for the rich. Money will buy service, if it will not buy faithfulness; it will buy plausibility, if it cannot secure honesty. In the humbler household, where the servant is truly one of the family, character becomes a matter of the utmost importance; and amid this great army the friendly, faithful domestic is still to be

found. Servant London is an integral part of all London life, and the class which employs no servants most often supplies them. So huge is the panorama now unfolded, that only a few of its scenes can be given, only a few of its figures can be sketched in.

When the great city wakes, the servants wake with it. Peep through the grey and curtainless windows of Westminster Hospital. In the servants' quarters the drowsy wardmaids and kitchen staff are dressing. It is only half-past five, and a raw winter morning; yet within an hour the great building will be cleaned down from top to bottom, and the

HOUSEMAID.

long procession of meals will have begun. No clattering over work, no exchange of amenities at the area steps; housemaid, wardmaid, kitchen-maid, cook — all are subject to rigid discipline.

Eastward the sun is rising, and the river glows a fitful red; eastward still, past the Tower, where the officials' households are waking and the

OUTSIDE A REGISTRY OFFICE (TOTTENHAM COURT ROAD): READING THE NOTICES.

soldier servants begin their day's work; east, and further east to the furthest edge of the city, where Greater London is now wide awake. Follow the river till you reach a desolate region lying below high-water mark, not very far from the Victoria Docks—a region where still the pools on the waste land are salt when the tide is high, and where thousands of grey-faced houses, built squat upon the reeking earth, lean towards each other for mutual support.

This is the servantless land.

These endless rows of expressionless grey houses, with their specious air of comfort and gentility, their bay window and antimacassar-covered table, are tenanted by two, it may even be by three, families housed in the four rooms. These are the people who "do for themselves." And here many of our servants get such guidance in housework as serves them for a training. Here are born and

CLUB PAGE.

object, she creeps out of her dingy pallet bed at the back of the underground kitchen which is her home. A grated window shows the filthy pavement, the yellow fog, and the boots of the passers-by.

bred the sisters of the little "Marchioness," true "slaveys" in all but spirit, who recount the last battle with the "missus" with that dramatic instinct which never fails the child of the street. "And I give 'er as good as 'er give me, I did; and well she knows I won't stand 'er lip!"

Louisarann is fortunate; she left school in the seventh standard (says her mother proudly), and now the "Mabys Ladies" (Metropolitan Association for Befriending Young Servants) have been able to find her "a place—£8 a year all found, and no washin'." Lucky girl! Alice Mary, her sister, left school as ignorant as she entered it, but she too has found work. She has gone as "'general' to the public-house round the corner—father bein' an old customer, and the 'Pig and Whistle' mos' respectable." She minds the "biby" during the day, and perhaps takes a turn at "mindin' the bar" during the evenings.

Let us follow Louisarann to her first place. A lodging-house is "genteel," but life there is not very amusing. It is about six when, on a winter morning, a small shivering

CLUB WAITER.

Hastily gathering her meagre wardrobe from the bed where she has piled it for warmth, she dresses herself, gives her face a shudder-ing smudge of ice-cold water, and draws on a pair of old gloves given to her by "one of the gents upstairs," to keep the soot out of her broken chilblains while she cleans her flues. Poor Louisarann is neither quick nor skilful, and she gets blacker and blacker as she works.

She has only time to wipe off a few of the worst smuts before she is carrying hot water when she has a chance, and she gives an extra "shine" to the "drorin'-room gent's." He is a "real swell, and mos' considerut, the dinin'-room bein' a commercial gent," good-natured, but stingy as to tips. The gents are all right, "but it's the top floor widdy and me as falls out!"

To be rung up three pair of stairs just to be sent all the way down and up again for "an extry knife, as though hanyone couldn't wipe the bacon fat off on a bit o' bread, is one of the widdy's narsty ways." Louisarann has

IN A SERVANTS' HALL : AT DINNER.

up to the top of the house. Down she clatters, and snatching her brushes climbs up again to do the grates in the three sitting-rooms ; then up and down she toils, carrying coal and removing ashes. Her mistress, half awake and proportionately cross, comes into the now warm kitchen to make herself a cup of tea and get the breakfast for husband and household. Upstairs Louisarann removes the dirty glasses and cigarette ends, gives a hasty "sweep up," and then, amid the appetising smell of frizzling bacon, toils again up and down stairs, staggering under the heavy breakfast trays. While all the hungry souls but herself are breakfasting, she cleans the rows of boots. She likes to do things well

93

to snatch her breakfast—as she does all her meals—standing.

But the girl has pluck ; she refrains from "langwidge," when "missus" is worse than usual, being determined to stay long enough to get a character. Behind all is the great consolation — the day out! To-day she makes her way through the thick and filthy fog to a great house in Berkeley Square, where her cousin Jane is housemaid, "second of four." Carefully the "slavey" feels her way down the area steps, and is admitted.

Jane is a little ashamed of her cousin's shabby appearance, so she takes Louisarann upstairs and "tidies her up a bit." The "slavey" looks round the neat room, and thinks of her bed in the back kitchen, and then and there makes up her mind to "better herself, for she wouldn't stay no longer, not if she was rose every month, she wouldn't." And Jane, sympathising, offers to step round with her to the registry office, if she can get off by-and-by, and speak for her. As they go downstairs, the "slavey" sees a young lady sitting by a fire in a pretty room, sewing, while a housemaid "takes up the bits." Jane gives an expressive shrug, but as the lady looks up says sweetly, "Good morning, mademoiselle." Jane wants to buy her next best dress from her ladyship's maid, who has all the "wardrobe," and who knows how to put on the price if one is not over civil. All day long the panorama of life below stairs unfolds itself before Louisarann's astonished gaze; and she reads with awe the printed rules

COACHMAN.

ably, and in some great state is observed. Then the upper servants, among whom the groom of the chambers is numbered, do not take their meals with the "hall" servants. They are served in the steward's room, and supper at nine o'clock is really a dinner in miniature. Each course which appears up-

GROOM.

stairs is repeated below for the "room" servants, even to the "second" ices, prepared by the still-room maids, and dessert of every kind. A glass of claret replaces the homely beer—occasionally something costlier than claret. The ladies are in demi-toilette, with evening blouses, and not seldom with gloves and fan; on great occasions the lady's maid appears in full dress, with ornaments and even jewels, a complete copy of her ladyship. Precedence is strictly observed, and the servants sit according to their master's rank. The valets and ladies' maids staying in the house join the party in the steward's room. When there are a number coming and going, the presiding butler and housekeeper do not trouble about the individual names, but use those of the master for convenience. Thus the inquiry may be heard, "What can I pass your ladyship?" "Duke, what will you take?"

Where do these servants all come from—

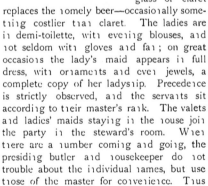

FOOTMAN.

regulating the work of the huge household. During dinner the butler takes the lead, the cook the foot of the table; men sit one side, women the other. As the meat is cleared away, the butler and cook, lady's maid and valet, rise and sweep from the servants' hall. They have gone to the housekeeper's room for dessert and their after-dinner chat. The distinction between "room" servants and "hall" servants is rigidly maintained.

Customs in the big houses vary consider-

who supplies them? There are formal and informal registry offices. One coachman carries the news of Jones leaving to another; there are inquiries at the china shop, or the mistress "just mentions it" to her butcher, a most respectable man, who has served her since her marriage. There are also Servants' Homes, to each of which a registry is attached, and which may be termed, in fact, if not in name, Protection Societies, as the officials fight the servants' battles for them, recovering wages due and giving them that "character" without which they can never get a respectable situation. The difficulties of securing true characters are enormous— about one-half the mistresses are employed in obtaining servants' characters from the other half— and when obtained they are not always to be relied upon, for a mistress "does not like to have unpleasantness."

deemed sufficient. What can there be to prevent the accomplice from impersonating the complaisant mistress who is losing a "treasure"? The Associated Guild of Registries does much to separate the sheep from the goats, but it cannot prevent the risk to servants who answer specious advertisements There are "situations," with "good wages for suitable young women," which are not "places" within the accepted meaning of the word, and if the lights in Servant London are bright the shadows are black indeed.

A much-dressed lady is deep in conversation with the head of the registry office. She is the wife of a rich tradesman at Clapham. She keeps a cook-general, house-parlourmaid, and nurse. They are all very trim and neat, and the house-parlourmaid wears the latest thing in cap streamers. The nurse's white dress in summer

SERVANTS' FIRE BRIGADE AT THE HOTEL CECIL.

The law of master and servant also is sufficiently rigid, and prevents a mistress from recording suspicions which she cannot prove. Certain registries — among them the one depicted in our illustration on page 351, which "suits" over 50,000 customers yearly—have a black list, which is carefully posted up and which records the history of the black sheep, male and female. Even as there is a trade in the writing of begging letters, so there is one in the manufacturing of servants' characters, and such a calling will prosper, in spite of all risks of detection and punishment, so long as a written character is

and her grey uniform in winter mark her separation from the common nurse in coloured clothes. These servants have good places, and they know it, although the rule of "No followers allowed" is strictly adhered to. They serve their mistress fairly, though they do not care about her. The children are the bond between them; and "cook" is always sure of a kiss if she asks for one, for the children—as yet—are no respecters of persons. Next door to them lives Selina, grim and grey, who serves her old-maid mistress with a faithfulness proof against all temptations, but who rules her with a

SERVANTS' RECREATION ROOM AT THE ARMY AND NAVY CLUB.

combination of obstinate humility and rampant remonstrances. Yet her mistress, who sometimes sheds a tear in secret because "Selina is so cross," would not change her for all the streamer-bedecked parlourmaids in the world.

Across the road a young housemaid sings as she does her work. She has joined the Girls' Friendly Society, and a portrait of her "G.F.S. lady" is on the mantelpiece in her pretty attic bedroom looking over the Common. On Sundays she gets out to service regularly. She lifts her dress high to show the starched white petticoat beneath it, and as she carries her new prayer-book in the other hand she feels sure that soon there will be a desirable young man only too ready to walk out with her, and then she would not change places with anyone in the world.

Let us now enter one of the fashionable squares on a summer afternoon. Servant life is manifest on every hand. In the garden nurses are sitting under the trees; from the doors the children and nursery maids are driving off to the park, with the schoolroom footman on the box. A newsboy comes leisurely across the square, making it ring with his cry, "Hall the winners!" He knows his customers. The door of a great house opens. A powdered footman stands on the steps and signals to the boy; his face is

anxious as he takes the paper. He is gone in a moment, and the house is impassive and undisturbed once more. A little later the butler comes out, and makes his way along Piccadilly towards Charing Cross. He drops in, say, at the Hotel Cecil for a moment, and hears news of the latest interesting arrival. He has several friends there, one a *chef* in the servants' kitchen, which provides for the wants of the staff of 500 persons; another a waiter in the banqueting-room. The latter is one of the hotel fire brigade, and the butler stays to witness a drill and practice. His master is a naval officer, so he next visits a friend, a waiter at the Army and Navy Club, who gives him the latest gossip; for in the recreation room set apart for the club servants the day's news is discussed with vigour over a game of billiards.

In connection with St. Paul's, Knightsbridge, is a Servants' Club which offers a variety of attractions. The Chesterfield Union, a benefit society for gentlemen's

LADY'S MAID LEARNING HAIR-DRESSING.

servants, meets on the ground-floor. Above are a couple of billiard tables and one for bagatelle, while in the basement are a skittle alley and a fine ping-pong table. The top floor contains a reading and dining room, where a chop and tea may be obtained at one end, and light literature at the other; here, too, smoking concerts such as are depicted in our illustration below are organised by the members.

A coachmen's club is to be found in the immediate neighbourhood of Berkeley Square, and the Duke of Westminster gave land for the Grosvenor Club in Buckingham Palace Road; but here, though there are a number of members who are servants, men engaged in other occupations are also admitted.

Hyde Park is the real recreation ground of West-End servants. Before the dew is off the grass the grooms are exercising the horses. Here is a grey-haired man, grown old in the service of "the family," now proudly superintending the baby horsemanship of the young heir on his diminutive pony. Behind him flies a young girl at full canter, her long hair streaming in the wind, as the groom thunders along after his delightful little mistress. As the sun grows hotter the "generals" bring their "bibies" to sprawl and sleep on the grass. The neat maid returning from a hairdressing lesson in Bond Street has an interesting chat with a gentleman's gentleman who has just turned his master out in first-class style, and is himself as near a copy of him as possible. In the late afternoon the magnificent coachman surveys with stolid pride his equally magnificent horses, as they sweep round into the Drive—"my horses," which even "her ladyship" cannot have out at will. As dusk falls sweethearts crowd the shady alleys of the Park or while away an hour upon the Serpentine; and more than one of the cyclists enjoying the cool of the evening is a domestic servant.

"What!" exclaimed a visitor to her friend, "another new bicycle, and such a beauty?" as she looked at two machines side by side in the narrow hall.

"Oh, no! That is not mine; that is cook's—she says she can't keep in condition unless she has her ride every day."

The great wheel of life in London is for ever turning, and the hands which turn it are those of the servants.

SMOKING CONCERT AT A SERVANTS' CLUB (ST. PAUL'S, KNIGHTSBRIDGE).

THE PESTERING ACQUAINTANCE.

LONDON'S LITTLE WORRIES.

By GEORGE R. SIMS.

SOME one has said that a succession of little worries has a worse effect on the nervous system than one great big worry. Whether that be true or not, there is no doubt that the Londoner's life is beset with little worries, and that he manages to bear up against them with commendable fortitude.

The business man has a hundred little worries beside the ordinary and legitimate cares of his business. Let him be guarded in his office never so effectually the worriers will manage to get at him. They will waylay him in the street as he goes to his lunch, stop him on the steps of the Metropolitan Railway as he is about to dive down below for his evening train, seize his arm as he is stepping into his hansom or his brougham. As a rule these people have some slight claim of acquaintanceship or introduction, or the City man would make short work of them. The worrier generally succeeds in capturing his prey just when

every second is valuable. There are heads of great business houses who face a commercial crisis with iron nerves, but are haunted day and night by the dread of being held up by one of the worrying fraternity.

While the business man is suffering in the City, his wife has frequently her little worries at home. In this catalogue the great servant question does not enter, for when a worry comes in that direction it is almost always a big one. The next-door neighbours are a fruitful source of a wife's little worries. The family on one side have dear little children who play at ball in the garden. If they would keep the ball on their own ground all would be well, but it is constantly coming over into some one else's. If you are the some one else and amiable, you don't object to your servant answering the pitiful little cry, "Please will you give me my ball?" say three or four times a day. But if the youthful pleaders cannot make anyone hear they will come to the front door and ring and ask permission to go into the garden themselves and hunt for the missing property. If it has hidden itself among the flower beds the search is not always conducted with dexterity of tread. When it dawns upon you that your neighbour's children are making your garden their daily hunting ground for lost balls, you lose your temper. One day you pronounce an ultimatum. You will preserve your flowers though a hundred balls be lost. Then you are looked upon as unneighbourly by the children's parents. They scowl at you when you meet in the street. Occasionally on fine summer evenings they make audible remarks to your disparagement.

A small vendetta grows sometimes out of this lost ball business. You find a dead cat in your garden path, and you credit it at once to the big brother next door. Occasionally you look up from your garden chair and discover the small children at an upper window making rude faces at you. A letter for you, left by mistake at your neighbour's house, is kept for two days and then given back to the postman. Unneighbourly messages are sent in when you have a musical evening.

Music enters largely into the catalogue of London's little worries. The piano next door is a fertile source of annoyance. In a flat it occasionally embitters existence. In most London houses there is a piano, and it must occasionally be played. But the hours of practice are, as a rule, ill chosen. A piano against a wall in terraces or semi-detached villas invariably plays into two houses at once. The next-door piano sometimes leads to the Law Courts.

There are three animals who contribute largely to London's little worries—the dog that barks, the cat that trespasses, and the cock that crows. The parrot is a rarer source of annoyance, but he makes up for it by being more persistent. To live next door to a screaming parrot would tax the patience of Job. People who have suffered under the infliction have often wondered why it was not included in the lengthy list of that good man's visitations.

The dog does not matter so much in the daytime; such noise as he makes mingles with and is lost in the general *brouhaha*. But when in the dead of night —the hour of sleep—he begins to howl, or to bark savagely at imaginary burglars, or to bay the moon, he is a source of discomfort to an entire neighbourhood. Many a father of a family forgets that his wife is awake too, when out of the fulness of his heart his mouth speaketh.

The cat worry leads to a retaliation of a more practical kind. It has been known to cause threats of murder to poor pussy. "If she comes into my garden again, madam," cries the indignant householder proud of his floriculture, "I'll shoot that cat!" There is a more terrible end than being shot. It is one to which poor Tom often comes through playing Romeo under the balcony of a feline Juliet. The Capulets in their wrath with the Montagus seek the Apothe-

"LOST BALL."

cary, and the dose proves fatal to Romeo, who, finding a tempting supper in Juliet's garden, partakes of it and crawls home to die. You may see at any time in London handbills offering a reward for information which will lead to the detection of the poisoner of a favourite cat. In the Dogs' Cemetery in Hyde Park a heartbroken mistress has buried her murdered tabby. Over its grave originally was an inscription which consigned to dreadful torture hereafter the heartless assassin. The inscription was considered out of order in a cemetery, and the lady was compelled to remove it. So she went to a Chaldean student and had the inscription translated into that language. There it now figures on Pussy's headstone. As no one can read it, it gives no offence. But the curse remains.

The parrot up to a certain point, when his language has been carefully selected for him, is amusing. But he begins to be the reverse when he is placed in the balcony to enjoy the sunshine of a summer's day. In his joy he becomes incoherent, and shrieks. When a jubilating parrot shrieks for a couple of hours at a stretch he is the little worry of an entire neighbourhood.

The begging letter impostor who knocks at your door and leaves a catalogue of

" I'LL SHOOT THAT CAT ! "

his miseries, stating that he will call for an answer later on, is an infliction so widespread that he deserves an article to himself. He often works in connection with a gang.

The rush for the omnibus is a little worry which the fair sex appreciate more than the mere man. You can see a crowd of ladies at certain hours of the day standing at well-known street corners, and every face is anxious. For 'bus after 'bus comes up full inside and out. On wet days the anxiety is increased, for then "inside" is a necessity. To make sure of securing a seat in the 'bus is always an anxiety to a woman, when her time is limited, or she has to be at a certain place at a certain hour. When it is a case of the "last 'bus," the anxiety becomes tearful, almost hysterical. For to many a cab is a consideration; the difference between half-a-crown and two-pence is sufficient to worry the careful house-wife who has a limited income, the young professional lady, the governess, or the shop assistant.

In the winter time there are little worries with the domestic interior which disturb the whole family. The chimney that *will* fill the sitting room with a choking smoke is one of them. In the summer the chim-

" I WILL CALL FOR AN ANSWER. "

ney, always a fertile source of anxiety, varies the performance by emptying its soot suddenly over the hearthrug and carpet, and reducing antimacassars and chair covers to a pitiful plight indeed. In the winter, when the frost sets in, comes the worry of the frozen cistern and the waterless home. When the frost is followed by a sudden thaw comes the worst worry of all —the bursting pipe. Then the household assembles hurriedly with cries of terror, as through the ceiling descends a sudden mountain torrent. The servants rush hither and thither with basins and buckets to collect the cataract, and a male member is despatched in hot haste for the plumber. In most cases the plumber is wanted in half a dozen houses at once and arrives when the last possible pound's worth of mischief has been done.

The chimney on fire, in addition to the mess and anxiety and the damage, means a summons and a fine. "Only a chim." is the official report at the fire station when the message for help comes through, but "only a chim." is very expensive to the London householder.

One of the worries to which all Londoners are subjected is that of having their pockets picked. There is not a day passes but a lady finds that while shopping, or travelling by 'bus or tram or by train, she has been relieved of her purse, which she invariably carries in a manner to facilitate its extraction by the expert London thief. When she returns to her home pale, tearful and excited, and gasps out, "I've had my pocket picked—my purse is gone!" the worry is shared by her family. Then there is frequently much anxious calculation as to what was in it. People who lose their purses are rarely quite sure what was in them. Sometimes there is intense relief to find that a five-pound note or a trinket had been left at home. Papa does not carry his money so recklessly as Mamma, but he occasionally loses his watch, or a pin, and be he

ever so well-to-do the loss is a worry to him. He regrets that watch and refers to it for many a month afterwards. If it is a gold one he registers a vow never again to wear anything but a Waterbury.

The lost umbrella is a little worry familiar to all of us. The umbrella stands at the head of the articles that Londoners have a habit of losing. It is left in cabs and trams and railway trains and on counters. It occasionally happens that you are utterly unable to say where you left it.

BEHIND THE SMOKERS.

The umbrella acquires a new value in the Londoner's eyes when he comes home without it. In the first hour of his bereavement he discovers that his umbrella was very dear to him. Few of us lose an umbrella with equanimity. It is always a passing cloud across the everyday skies of life.

In humble homes washing day is a little worry—especially to father. Mother's mind is occupied, and the feminine nose is not so delicate in the matter of the steamy odour which washing diffuses through the house. In the humble home, scrubbing day is also a trial to the male members. For this reason many respectable

94

"MY PURSE IS GONE!"

working-class fathers do not immediately return to the domestic roof when released from toil on Saturday afternoon.

Spring cleaning and house painting are little worries with which all Londoners are familiar. I hesitate to put spring cleaning in the catalogue. It extends over a period of time, and runs into so many "new" things in the carpet and curtain line which "we really must have" when the house has been done up, that it strikes the major rather than the minor note in one's "troubled lot below."

The latchkey occasionally leads to a little worry. Sometimes we go out without it when we are supposed to have it with us. This always happens when its possession is most sorely needed. Paterfamilias is going to a City banquet, or to dine at his club, and won't be home till late. The household retires at its usual time. About one o'clock the head of the family returns from the festivity in a hansom. He pays the driver and dismisses him, then puffing calmly at his cigar puts his hand in his pocket for his latchkey. It isn't there. There is nothing for it but to knock. It is no good ringing, because the bells ring below, and everyone is upstairs. So he knocks, gently at first, then, seeing no light moving about, he knocks again and presently

loses his temper and bangs furiously. The whole neighbourhood probably hears him before his own people. But eventually he sees a light, and inside the door he can hear a nervous hand manipulating the chain.

The forgotten latchkey is a little worry that wise men have decided to avoid. They now carry the useful and convenient article on a chain attached to their braces.

There are Londoners who suffer systematic annoyance from the unfortunate peculiarities of the locality in which they have made a home. Brown is in a constant state of fever owing to the proximity of certain church bells, which he declares ring without ceasing. Jones is the victim of a steam whistle, which at some large works hard by his happy home makes hideous disturbance at an unearthly hour in the morning and at intervals during the day. Robinson is the victim of "vibration," a railway passing near his residence, his windows are perpetually rattling, his house occasionally "shudders," and when a limited mail passes in the night his bed (the expression is his) "rocks him" not to sleep but out of it.

Street noises have become such maddening minor worries to Londoners of late years that the law has been invoked. The old London cries are no longer prized for their quaintness. The street hawker is ordered to moderate his methods by the passing policeman, and the newspaper boy gets fourteen days for announcing another "great railway accident" or a "shocking murder" to the homestaying householder.

There are little worries of the outdoor walk with which all Londoners are familiar. Orange peel and banana skins on the pavement are so worrying to pedestrians that special police notices are issued with regard to them.

The Londoner who doesn't smoke is constantly finding a worry in the Londoner who does. Since the fair sex and the "pale young curate" have socially elevated the top of the 'bus and the roof of the tram there has been continual outcry against the outside smoker, who puffs his tobacco into an eye that looks upon it unsympathetically. On some 'buses and trams in the back seats only may pipe, cigar, or cigarette be indulged in. The tobacco smoke worry has been relieved to this extent.

There is another little worry which many Londoners have endured for years almost uncomplainingly, that is the worry of trying to buy a postage stamp after 8 p.m. in a suburban neighbourhood. It occasionally leads to another little worry, namely, a letter of no particular interest, for which you have to pay the postman twopence.

That the area merchant—the gentleman with a bag on a barrow—who calls at your area door to barter with your cook is a worry is proved by the large number of London houses which now exhibit in bold display the printed legend "No Bottles," sometimes in conjunction with the warning hint "Beware of the Dog."

Against this worry one can always barricade one's doors, but there is a worrier from whom there is little protection. The whining beggar who follows nervous women in the lonely street after nightfall is not easily disposed of. If the beggar is a man he has only to look villainous and to talk gruffly to levy his blackmail. If the beggar is a woman she sometimes obtains her object by pleasantly referring to the fact that she has left the bedside of a child who is suffering from scarlet fever, small-pox, or some other infectious disease. There are nervous ladies who, after being accompanied for a few minutes by such a woman, not only bestow alms in their alarm, but rush home and disrobe and subject their clothes to a disinfecting process before they wear them again. For the worrying beggar with the scarlatina child always takes care to rub shoulders with her prey.

These are but a few of London's little worries, but they are a sample of the mass. They are inevitable in the complex life of a great city. On the whole they are borne philosophically by everyone—except the people personally affected by them.

A WHINING APPEAL.

LONDON'S WASH-HOUSES AND BATHS.

By I. BROOKE-ALDER.

GREAT as have been the improvements to London, and numerous the benefits bestowed upon its inhabitants during recent years, there is probably no item of advancement more noticeable than that which concerns provision for cleanliness. Time was when to find a fitted bath-room in an otherwise elegant private house was the exception, and when a swimming bath was a well-nigh unknown luxury to dwellers in the Metropolis; but nowadays quite modest houses boast their hot-water furnished bath, rendering the all-over wash an easily acquired feature of the daily programme; and almost every district owns its public bathing establishment, comprising under one roof several grades of baths—private and swimming.

But besides these noteworthy signs of grace, immense progress has been made in regard to wash-houses, or laundries, where, under the new order of things, the public is provided with accommodation and every time-saving appliance for the washing of clothes and household belongings. For the rapid increase in the facilities for cleanliness thanks are due to the various Borough Councils and to the liberality of certain philanthropists, who, in conjunction with the (ordinarily) grumbling ratepayers, have provided the means to this satisfactory end. The modern public baths and their adjacent wash-houses are the natural result of the gradual adoption of an Act of Parliament relating to this subject. The comprehensive scale of their enterprise can be gauged by realising the extent to which they have been adopted in the Metropolis and its suburbs. Their far-reaching influence for good can,

IN A PUBLIC WASH-HOUSE (MARYLEBONE ROAD): WASHING.

MEN'S PRIVATE BATHS (HORNSEY ROAD BATHS AND WASH-HOUSES).

various kinds of comparatively expensive baths, such as medicated, electric, vapour, spray, and Turkish.

The first visit to a public wash-house is an experience that is not easily banished from the memory, especially if it take place in a poor locality and on a popular day. Shoreditch, Hackney, Bermondsey, Westminster, Soho (Marshall Street, Golden Square), are fruitful examples, and Friday and Saturday notable days. Marylebone runs them close. It is remarkable that as the week progresses the class of person who brings her possessions to the wash-houses deteriorates. By some unwritten law or unpublished code of manners the orderly members of the local community almost entirely monopolise the first half of the week, whilst the last three days belong to a gradually descending scale. The exceptions to this almost invariable rule are furnished by those whose wage-earning employment leaves them free only during the "early closing" hours of Saturday. On Monday come demure dames, primly precise of bearing, arrayed with an almost awe-inspiring neatness, even to the full complement of buttons on boots and gloves, and the exact adjustment of the chenille spotted veil. Behind these worthy matrons is borne by an attendant the brown paper

however, only be adequately judged by those who are familiar with the daily life of Living London, in its many phases, from the lowest upwards.

To such a well-informed Cockney the consideration of "how London washes" would provide a fairly exhaustive review of Metropolitan existence. He would see in his mind's eye the various representatives of hard-working poverty washing their meagre scraps of clothing; the moderately prosperous members of the tradesman class enjoying frequent hot baths; the vast numbers that stand for energetic youth taking lessons in swimming, or joining in aquatic sports; and the smaller detachment which impersonates leisurely wealth indulging in the

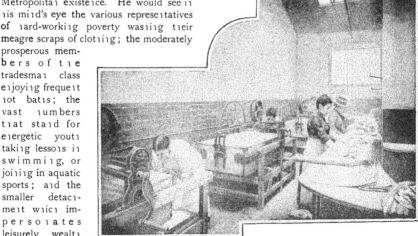

IN A PUBLIC WASH-HOUSE (MARSHALL STREET, W.): FOLDING AND MANGLING.

enclosed consignment of linen destined for the soapsuds. Tuesday sees a reproduction of such dignified processions, with, perhaps, less dignity as the afternoon advances. By Wednesday all pomp and vanity have disappeared. Washing is frankly carried, tied up in a sheet by the laundress herself, the great bundle protruding from the shawl that serves her as hat and mantle combined, or it shares a crippled perambulator with two small children. To Tom and Sallie the weekly sojourn in the wash-house ante-room, "'long er Mrs. O'Hagan's Pat and Noran," while their mothers do the washing, is the most delightful of outings!

On entering such a laundry from the street, or a cool stone staircase, the immediate impression is of overwhelming heat and discomforting clouds of steam ; but that soon passes, and one is conscious of a lofty, well-ventilated room, divided from end to end by rows of troughs, separated into couples by six-feet high partitions. In each division stands a woman washing ; at her feet a pile of dirty clothes, and behind her a basket of clean ones. Her arms are plunged elbow-deep into one of the two troughs of which she is temporary proprietress. Water in plenty, hot and cold, is hers for the turning of overhanging taps, whilst the conversion of the rinsing trough into a copper is as easily accomplished—by opening a steam-containing valve. Her "wash" completed, she carries her basket to one of the men in charge of the row of wringers situated in an adjoining room. A few moments of rapid water-expelling whirling whilst the laundress "stands at ease," and the clothes are returned to her almost dry. She folds them on long tables near at hand, and puts them into a mangle, many of which machines are, it should be stated, now worked automatically. Should she wish to iron her finer items, she has but to take ready-heated irons from the stove hard by. Would she air her clothes she hangs them on a "horse" and pushes it into a hot-air compartment.

And for all this luxury as laundress the authorities charge but three-halfpence an hour! Soap and soda they do not provide, nor do they limit her to any given number of hours ; so she may stay from 8 a.m. to 8 p.m. should she feel disposed. The average attend-ance at each wash-house of the Metropolis is from two to three hundred persons every weekday.

It is curious to notice in the most crowded districts how many nationalities are represented by these people—a blonde Swedish girl helping a dusky daughter of the South to get through a heap of ironing, or a broad-nosed Russian grudgingly lending a piece of soap to a sharp-featured Polish Jewess. Strange peeps into some tragedies can sometimes be gained, as when the overworked looking eldest child comes clattering up the stone staircase bringing to its mother for a little while, the few-weeks-old baby ; or when the half-sober husband lounges in to bully the price of another drink out of her. She is the breadwinner, it seems.

The price charged for hot baths and use of towels is twopence, fourpence, and sixpence, according to class and locality, and half each of these sums for children. All such private baths are kept scrupulously clean, and the cabins in which they are fixed are furnished with a seat, hooks for clothing, and, in the case of the best, a strip of carpet, mirror, and brush and comb. That these liberal conditions are appreciated is testified by the fact that they are used by between fifty and seventy thousand persons at each institution annually. At Westminster they tell a tale of a certain flower-seller which is well worth quoting : Every Saturday evening, week in, week out, comes this girl, clad just as she would be when crying "Penny er bunch" on the kerb-stone. She enters from the street by the "wash-house" door, and proceeds to a private room, where she takes off all her clothes but her skirt and jacket, and puts her front locks into curlers. Then she hires a trough, mangle, etc., for an hour, submits her underwear to the cleansing process, finally hanging it up to air ; that done, she buys a ticket for a twopenny hot bath, bathes herself, puts on her clean clothes, combs her fringe, and for the expenditure of threepence-halfpenny emerges as good an imitation of "new woman" as anybody else could compass at any price !

For those who can afford a "first-class" bath a comfortable waiting-room is provided, with fire and a goodly supply of newspapers. It often serves as a sort of House of Assembly to a certain set of local worthies, who

TURKISH BATH (JERMYN STREET): SHAMPOOING ROOM.

WATER POLO MATCH (WESTMINSTER BATHS).

TEACHING SCHOOLBOYS TO SWIM (KENSINGTON BATHS).

count on the opportunity thus afforded to meet neighbours and discuss the affairs of the nation.

That swimming should at last have come to be regarded by the School Board as a necessary item of education is a fact on which we should heartily congratulate ourselves. Thanks in the matter are undoubtedly due to the persistent efforts of a few private enthusiasts as well as to the energy of such philanthropic bodies as the Life-saving Society, the Swimming Association of England, and the London Schools Swimming Association.

Practical testimony is given to the seriousness of the modern views of the situation by the provision of free lessons in swimming at the public elementary schools. All the summer large detachments from the various Board schools, in charge of masters or mistresses, present themselves daily for lessons at several of the baths. Funny scenes occur when the children take their first plunge into so large an expanse of water! Some of them decline to leave the steps at the shallow end, or cling desperately to the rail that runs round, only gaining courage by very slow degrees and after having been carried about by the patient instructor. But such alarms are gradually conquered, and the children become as much at home as ducks in the water, and willingly take part in various sports and life-saving instruction, their competency as swimmers and life-savers often being the means of rescuing playmates from drowning in the course of holiday expe-

ditions. It has even happened that a child has rescued his father.

In order to bring the benefits afforded by the swimming bath within the reach of most young folk the ordinary twopenny entrance-fee is reduced to a penny for schools; and that the art of natation may be more generally acquired many University men and others generously give their services as instructors and also pay for the bath. There are, for instance, associations formed amongst the Post Office *employés*, telegraph boys, shop assistants, poor boys and girls in Homes, and others, all of which are encouraged by well-known enthusiastic experts, and meet for practice and instruction.

The swimming clubs of London number about two hundred, and are composed of members of every class—boys and girls, young men and maidens, representing all the various grades of well-being. In several instances their formation resulted from the initiative of some of the large employers, such as Messrs. Cook, Son and Co., of St. Paul's Churchyard, whose care for the physical development of their clerks and others has had the happiest effect both mentally and physically. The "Ravensbourne" is the designation by which Messrs. Cook's club is known; and, thanks to the excellent work done at its weekly meetings, its annual display at Westminster Baths draws great crowds of spectators—friends of the competitors and members of similar associations.

Another popular meeting is the free public display held every summer at the Highgate

Ponds by the Life-saving Society, at which as many as 30,000 spectators assemble.

A curious lack of knowledge of self-preservation is disclosed by our soldiers, it having been found necessary to teach swimming to thousands of the Guards. They learned the art at St. George's Baths, Buckingham Palace Road, and it was amusing to note that some of the stalwart fellows, absolutely dauntless in other circumstances, showed an almost childlike timidity in facing so unaccustomed an experience. How well their quickly acquired courage and ability in dealing with water have served them has since been remarkably demonstrated.

Although the feminine portion of the community is making undeniable progress towards the popularising of swimming, it is found somewhat difficult to interest the poorer classes of girls in this art. Broadly speaking, they do not care for gymnastics of whatever sort in anything like the degree that their brothers do. This they prove by their disregard of the opportunity for exercise provided all the winter by the covering in and fitting with gymnastic appliances of some of the swimming baths. But the same remarks do not hold good in connection with the sisters of our public school boys, University men, and so on ; they are veritable mermaids! Ambitious mermaids, too, with a very decided intention to rival all comers in proficiency and grace. Thanks to their comprehensive love of frame-developing sports, their achievements in the water are of no mean order. To see them at their best one should belong to the Bath Club, a luxurious institution in Dover Street, Piccadilly, once the town mansion of Lord Abergavenny, where, whilst enjoying all the

95

advantages of an ordinary social club, one has the run of every variety of bath—Turkish, shower, douche, swimming, etc.—provided on the premises. This popular and well-managed establishment is frequented by both ladies and gentlemen, who claim the use of the baths on alternate days. There are 2,000 members, of whom 500 are of the gentler sex.

The swimming bath at this club is unique in its accessories, having suspended over the water, besides several diving boards and Newman's water-chute, not a few gymnastic appliances, such as trapeze and travelling rings. The contests at the Bath Club, either for the men members or their feminine relatives, always attract a large attendance —spectators filling the gallery and thickly surrounding the bath edge. The variety of costumes worn by the ladies — some of mermaid-imitating scales, others of gaily striped materials—and the floral decorations of the place provide a very attractive spectacle.

The height of luxury in the way of taking a bath is attained by the Turkish variety. It is practised in perfection at the Hammam (or Turkish bath) in Jermyn Street, St. James's. It costs four shillings, and it takes two hours; but nothing yet invented by Londoners, or annexed from abroad, has ever come near

TURKISH BATH (JERMYN STREET) : COOLING ROOM.

the delicious experience or the restorative quality of the Turkish bath. One enters, a world-weary wreck, tired from travelling, working, pleasuring, maybe, rheumatic; one sits, or reclines, in a succession of hot-air rooms, each of the eight hotter than the last —varying from 112° F. to 280° F.—until a sufficient perspiration has been attained. Then one is conducted to the shampooing room, and, whilst reposing on a marble slab, one is massaged by light-handed attendants. That process is followed by a series of brushes and different soaps; and, after a variety of shower douches and a plunge into cold water, the bath is complete. A sojourn in a lofty cooling room, a quiet smoke, or a light meal, and one sallies forth a new being. A visit to the gallery of the attendant hairdressers makes perfection more perfect.

This bath is patronised by gentlemen only, but many districts now boast their Hammam, open to both sexes—among others, Charing Cross, Earl's Court, Islington, Camden Town, Brixton—at all of which the price is extremely moderate, some even descending to one shilling.

The vapour bath (obtainable at the Marylebone and a few other public baths) is an excellent substitute for the Turkish should limited time be a consideration. Various medicated baths are also used by a section of Londoners—such as pine, bran, sulphur—to cure certain ailments, as alternative to foreign springs, etc., whilst electricity is impelled through the water at the request of some others. This sort of bath is occasionally used in conjunction with the Swedish system of treatment (massage and exercises by means of mechanical appliances), now much practised in the Metropolis.

Given the desire to wash, the means are certainly not lacking in Living London.

LADIES USING THE CHUTE (BATH CLUB).

AWAITING THE ARRIVAL OF MINISTERS TO ATTEND A CABINET COUNCIL.

SCENES FROM OFFICIAL LIFE IN LONDON.

By L. BRINDLE.

IT has been said, and with very good reason, that the things that impress one most in London are the things that one does not see, which one cannot see, but of which one has a tolerably accurate knowledge if a student of such matters, derived and assimilated from a hundred sources in the course of many years.

Royalty, Parliament, the City, all these are in truth wonderfully impressive, and we see them, or something pertaining to them, almost every day of our lives in London. But all the time there is something else which we feel among us, but which we never see unless we are more than usually favoured mortals. In London, especially when some country visitor is with us, we often feel a sense of pride and importance which may be partly accounted for by the ostensible wonders of the capital and partly by the common instinct to which Dr. Johnson gave utterance when he remarked to Boswell, "I will venture to say there is more learning and science within the circumference of ten miles from where we now sit than in all the rest of the kingdom." Yet even with all this there is a balance still to be accounted for, and I think that if most of my readers will examine their own minds on the subject they will agree that it is made up of that other instinct which consists mainly of one's appreciation of the fact that here in London we are pulling every day the strings of the Empire, the greatest empire which has ever existed. We do not see these strings, nor do we see anybody pulling them—seldom indeed do we catch a glimpse of the dignitaries who perform this awe-inspiring task. But we know that it is done, and we know furthermore that there is not a nation of the world but has just as much appreciation—it may be admiring appreciation or it may be bitter appreciation —of this great and all-important fact as we and our country visitor have. We walk with him along the western side of Whitehall, and we point out to him the solid and stately structures which make this such a noble thoroughfare. And it is here, within an area of but a few acres after all, that these strings are for the most part pulled. To-day a Minister in one of

A RECEPTION AT THE FOREIGN OFFICE

these buildings dictates an instruction to one of his private secretaries; an hour later the message which is the result of it is speeding its way along thousands of miles of the ocean bed. To-morrow our great pro-consul acts upon the order which he has received, and the news of the significant departure in policy is cabled back to every newspaper in London, to every newspaper in the world—more than that, to the chancellery of every Power; and the foreign Ministers knit their foreheads and bite their pens and scowl when they read this news, and understand that Downing Street has advanced another point. One of the big strings has been pulled again.

And, again, there is a crisis in some home affair which is of urgent importance to the well-being of a very large number of people. It may pertain to the care of an industry, or to the soundness of the people's education, or to any other of the thousand questions which ever and again are troubling the public mind. Interested persons hurry now to Whitehall, and there are long conversations in the rooms of Ministers, after which the interested persons, with their minds all in a state of doubt and trepidation, go their way. A few hours later an order is promulgated from the seat of authority, and, as likely as not, the trouble at that moment is at an end. One of the smaller strings has been pulled. We never see the pulling of these strings, but we feel each and every day that it is being done here in London as it can be nowhere else, and somehow this grand, this exalted official life that is being lived in the Metropolis permeates the atmosphere which we breathe and gives us a quickening sense of pride and importance.

But now, though we have said that none of these things are visible, we will avail ourselves of a more than usually special permit—which we will say at once would be granted to no person alive, save the King and his Ministers—and will take brief glimpses at some of the scenes which are enacted in Downing Street and other places curtained off from the public gaze. When we come down to a cold analysis there is much that is quite ordinary in these scenes; but they inspire a vast amount of awe not-

withstanding. To all outward appearances a meeting of company directors is much the same as a meeting of kings, but they are very different meetings after all. So it is with these scenes.

What meeting, for instance, would one regard with greater interest and curiosity than a meeting of the Cabinet, fraught as it often is with the destiny of the nation? This is so well realised that, especially on a cold damp afternoon in the middle of winter when the Ministers gather themselves together from the four points of the compass in Downing Street for the first time since the beginning of the autumn recess, there is quite a big crowd to see them going in, one by one, to their solemn deliberations which have regard to the programme of the forthcoming session of Parliament. Some come on foot, some in hansom cabs, others drive up in their own well-appointed carriages, and Ministers have even been known upon occasion to ride up to a Cabinet Council upon their cycles. It is the same with other Cabinet Councils, which are held in frequent succession after the first one, but it is in this that the public interest is keenest, because it marks the awakening of official life after the autumn siesta. The people see the Ministers come and see them disappear under the archway that leads to the great quadrangle, and then as far as they are concerned, the Cabinet Council is at an end, for they witness no more of it, and only the most meagre paragraph report of its doings, and that usually mere speculation, ever finds its way into the papers.

A wonderful secrecy is preserved with regard to all that pertains to these meetings. They are usually held in a room on the ground floor at the Foreign Office, and in white letters there is painted on the door of it "Private." The furniture of the room is not elaborate, and there is little to distract the attention of Ministers from the business in hand. The Prime Minister takes his seat at the head of the table, and the other Ministers place themselves round the board as best suits their convenience, but in no set order. Then the door is closed, and upon no pretence whatever may any outsider gain admission

374   LIVING LONDON.

to the chamber until all is over. The
Prime Minister has an electric bell at his
elbow, and if need arises he summons
a departmental official or a servant to the
room, but he does so as seldom as possible,
and when the outsider is present the deliberations are suspended. Ministers may
bring with them the private Government
papers which have been addressed to them,
and of which they have need, and there are
also upon the table documents that have
been printed in the private Government
printing office, and which are endorsed
"Most Secret. For the use of the Cabinet"; but they may produce no paper
for the making of notes for their own
use as to the proceedings of the day. It
is a strict rule that no minutes of any
kind whatsoever shall be made of the
business which is discussed, each Minister
having perforce to content himself with
his mental impression of what takes place.
This is all for the sake of secrecy. The
business may be comparatively trivial, and
may last but half an hour; or there may be
laid before this meeting of the executive
Government a threat of war or a proposal
for peace from some foreign country, and
for hours and hours the Cabinet may sit
with anxious faces and minds which hesitate
between two courses upon which depend the
future of our Empire. Ministers have even
been known to be summoned to a meeting
of the Cabinet when Big Ben hard by has
been striking the midnight hour, and have
remained in conference until the daylight
has streamed through the windows upon
their ashen, worn-out countenances.

But there is another great Council of
the State, about which we are privileged to
learn even less. The only report which we
are ever allowed to read is the simple
one contained in the Court announcements,
which may run thus:—

"His Majesty The King held a Council at Buckingham Palace to-day at 12 o'clock. There were
present:—The Archbishop of Canterbury, the Duke
of Devonshire, K.G. (Lord President), the Duke of
Norfolk, K.G., and the Marquess of Cholmondeley."

That is all. It is a Privy Council which
has been held in this case, and it usually
assembles in one of the royal residences, the
King, of course, presiding. There are many
members of the Privy Council; but as a
rule only Ministers, certain great officers of
the Household, and sometimes the Archbishop of Canterbury, are summoned to the
meetings.

A COUNCIL AT BUCKINGHAM PALACE.

A summons to the whole
Council is sent out only upon
the most extraordinary occasion. What the functions of
the Privy Council precisely are
it is hard to say; a Privy
Councillor himself would
have difficulty in answering
such a question. But in
theory it is what the Cabinet
is in practice. Its real practical value is as a necessary
medium between the throne
and the executive Govern-
ment, and so we may imagine
at these meetings the King
and his Ministers chatting
over points in matters of
State, or perchance discussing
details of some ceremony
which is soon to take place.
The Privy Council is thus
of service; but perhaps the
general sentiment concerning
it as a whole, as apart from
its divisions, is that it is a
very good reserve council,
which might conceivably
upon occasion be of the
greatest utility. The Privy
Councillor, whom we see in

A DEPUTATION TO THE COLONIAL SECRETARY.

our fancy with the King, has taken an oath
that he will "advise his Majesty to the best
of his cunning and discretion," that he will
keep the King's council secret, that he will
help and strengthen the execution of what
shall be resolved, and, amongst other things,
that he will observe, keep, and do all that
a good and true Councillor ought to do
to his Sovereign Lord. Besides the King
and his Councillors there is admitted to
the apartment the Clerk of the Council,
who has also to take a most solemn oath
that he will reveal nothing of what is discussed.

These are the Councils of the chiefs;
consider the latter now in their own departments where they are certainly not less
interesting, and only a trifle less private.
There are two of the ministerial offices that
help to make up the great quadrangle to
the left of Downing Street, which possess
deeper interest for the curious outsider than

most of the others, and these are the
Foreign Office and the Colonial Office, the
work of each of which is of vast and en-
during importance.

Observe the Secretary of State for
Foreign Affairs at work in his own room.
As befits the apartment which is reserved
for the man who deals direct with the
heads of all other Governments, it is luxuriously furnished. There are beautiful,
morocco leather-covered chairs, and there
is a particular one of them upon which
scores of ambassadors have in turn been
wont to sit when they have called upon
the Minister to discuss some matter of
urgent international importance. There is
a writing table in the room with a number
of pigeon-holes attached to it, labelled
"Home Secretary," "Minister of the
Colonies," and so forth. It is not too
much to say that here are contained the
secrets of an empire. At the Foreign Office

AFTER A NAVAL DISASTER: ENQUIRERS AT THE ADMIRALTY.

room suggests work, hard work, and heavy responsibility.

In another department there is the Home Secretary on duty. He, too, is a very busy man, controlling as he does most of those insular matters which more closely affect the comfort and prosperity of people at home. Ordinary folk understand the functions of the Home Secretary better than they do those of the Foreign Minister. Some of them may have heard that he has in a little room hard by his own a telephone by means of which he may speak direct to New Scotland Yard at any time without a moment's delay upon a matter of life or death. It is really so.

upon occasion his Lordship will hold a great reception, and there will come to it the Corps Diplomatique, and many other persons of high degree, presenting an imposing and even showy spectacle.

There are perhaps fewer displays of magnificence in connection with other great departments, but they are scarcely less interesting. The Foreign Office may deal with the world; but at least the Colonial Office, on the other side of the great archway, concerns itself with all that part of the world which we have the pleasure to call our own. Wending our way up the wide and handsome staircase, having some business with the Colonial Secretary or one of his subordinates, we are ushered by an attendant into a waiting-room overlooking the quadrangle, which is pleasant enough in its way, but which is principally decorated with maps with big blotches of red upon them. This is indicative of the business of the office. Probably there are many other persons waiting in this room, even some with dark skins who form a deputation to the Minister from one of those far-off lands which are under the British sway. Within, the Colonial Secretary is hard at work with more maps around him. Everything in the

A little further down Whitehall there is a building, one of the Government group, at the sight of which all but millionaires are often apt to experience a curious creepy feeling. This is the Treasury, which is presided over by the Chancellor of the Exchequer, and whence the income tax and all other taxes come. It is the headquarters of the national finance, and when folk want to grumble whilst there is yet time — as they invariably do—at the taxes they have to pay, they repair to the Treasury in deputation form, and talk the matter over with the Chancellor. But whoever he be, the Chancellor is invariably a shrewd man with a cold heart, and the deputation in departing is not often a merry one. Elsewhere there are the Education Office, the Board of Trade, the India Office, and others, the precise characters of which are indicated in their titles. There is an office for everything and everywhere.

There are still two which have not yet been mentioned, but in regard to which public interest is always keen; at special times exceptionally so. The War Office and the Admiralty, controlling as they do the mighty forces of the Empire on land and sea, have in due season news to give which will make London throb with pride, and which will at the same time cast a perpetual shadow over many homes that were once the happiest in the land. There may be a report that a British warship has foundered, and there are groups of terror-stricken mothers and wives and sisters— perhaps male relatives also—in the comfortless corridors of the enormous building which lies between Spring Gardens and the Horse Guards. Looking from one of the windows the King, with a brilliant staff of War Office officials, may perhaps be seen distributing the medals of victory to his soldiers upon the Horse Guards Parade, but these poor

creatures in the Admiralty can hardly think at such a time of the glory of arms. A soothing word may be spoken by one of the officials attired in a blue uniform with an anchor on his cap, but what consolation is that?

In the War Office itself the Commander-in-Chief is assisted in his multifarious duties by men who themselves have been the heroes of many engagements. In imagination one may see a line of red and khaki spreading from the War Office to the uttermost ends of the Empire, and with our preliminary reflection in mind the War Office then is a convenient spot to terminate a tour through secret places which have told such a tale of the great imperial body of which London is the mighty throbbing heart.

Photo: Russell & Sons, Baker St., W

PRESENTATION OF WAR MEDALS ON THE HORSE GUARDS PARADE : ARRIVAL OF THE KING.

SATURDAY NIGHT IN LONDON.

By A. ST. JOHN ADCOCK.

FOR persons who live above a certain social level Saturday night has no particular features to distinguish it from any other night of the week; but for the vast majority of those who live below that serene altitude it is the most important night of the secular six: it means to them pretty much what a coming into port means to the seaman or a harvest-home to the farmer.

The City emptying itself much earlier than usual on Saturday, outgoing trains, 'buses, and trams are crammed to excess between one o'clock and five; then, from six to eight, incoming trams, 'buses, and trains are equally burdened, for many who went out early are returning now with friends, sweethearts, wives, or, at pantomime time, with small excited members of their families, in a hurry to add themselves to the extra long Saturday-night queues stretching away from the pit and gallery doors of the principal theatres.

Now, too, when there is a chance of escaping observation in the darkness, the pawn-shops are at their busiest: shrinking figures, mostly of women, flit in and out by obscure side-doors, some on a regular Saturday night errand to redeem Sunday wearing apparel that is as regularly put away again on Tuesday or Wednesday when the domestic treasury is again exhausted; others carrying household articles sufficiently mortgageable to raise the price of to-morrow's dinner, a husband being out of work, or delayed on the way home exhaustively refreshing himself, and not expected to arrive with any considerable salvage of his week's wages.

There are insignificant, comfortable people who sent a servant out to do their shopping this morning or ordered their Sunday requirements of tradesmen who call at the door, and this evening they will go, perhaps, to some little party at the house of a friend, or give a little party of their own; or, during the summer and autumn, they may make an afternoon excursion up the river to Hampton Court or down to Greenwich, and come back

SATURDAY NIGHT IN KING STREET, HAMMERSMITH.

BRACES.

pleasantly tired, just in time to share a 'bus or a railway carriage with jovial amateur cricketers or footballers coming from a Saturday's match.

In the main, however, Saturday night is given over to the great weekly shopping carnival of the poor, and of all such as live carefully on limited incomes. They do their marketing, from custom or necessity or for sheer preference, in the very last hours of the last day of the week, and they do most of it in those boisterous, cheerful, plenteous, cornucopia-like thoroughfares where costermongers are still allowed to congregate and compete with the shopkeepers.

Of course, the genteel business ways of the west know nothing whatever of that carnival. In that region shutters are up early, and when Berwick Street and other arteries of Soho are congested with stalls and buyers and sellers, and doing a roaring trade in every sense of the phrase, the select shops of Oxford Street, Regent Street, and Piccadilly are, nearly all of them, closed and enjoying a foretaste of their Sunday sleep.

Broadly speaking, Saturday night's trade follows the costers, and finds them all over London: it finds them south under the arches and littering the streets around Brixton Station, in the Old Kent Road, on Deptford Broadway; up north in Phœnix Street, in Chapel Street, Islington, in Queen's Crescent,

Kentish Town; away west straggling for a mile or more along Harrow Road, or in King Street, Hammersmith; eastward in Crisp Street by the docks, and nowhere in greater variety, more breezily good-humoured, or attended by a more cosmopolitan crowd than in Whitechapel Road.

On the way thither, through Aldgate, we pass Butchers' Row and the uncommonly miscellaneous line of stalls facing it, where business has been steadily increasing ever since 1901. Some of the butchers have put up intimations that they make a speciality of "kosher" meat, and other signs are not wanting that we are in the neighbourhood of the Ghetto: round the side-streets are Jewish hotels and restaurants; in the High Street there are bakers, printers, all manner of traders who have announcements in Hebrew characters painted on their windows; a Hebrew theatrical poster appeals to us from a hoarding; dusky foreign Jews pass in the crowd chattering in a barbarous Yiddish.

As we push farther east the crowd becomes denser and livelier: an incongruously blended multitude in which abject squalor elbows coquettish elegance, and sickly misery and robust good-humour, and frank poverty and poverty decently disguised, and lean knavery and leaner honesty, drunkenness and sobriety, care and frivolity, shabby home-bred loafers and picturesque, quaintly-garbed loafers from over sea, all hustle or loiter side by side, in one vast, motley, ever-moving panorama

BOOTS AND SHOES: TRYING ON.

By this we are past the Pavilion Theatre and on the broad pavement that sweeps down to Mile End Gate. Up between flags of the pavement sprout stunted trees that drip dirty tears in the foggy weeks of winter and with the coming of spring break into a pleasant laughter of dusty green leaves. They are girdled with iron railings, and betwixt and before and behind them costermongers' stands and barrows are scattered in great plenty.

There are fruit and vegetable stalls, there are fish stalls, haberdashers', stationers', tailors', toy, jewellery, butchers', cutlery, boot, hat and cap, and unmistakably second-hand ironmongery stalls, all along to Mile End Gate; and, to add to the crush and the tumult, enterprising shopkeepers have rushed selections of their goods out of doors and ranged them among the stalls and set assistants bawling in wildernesses of furniture and crockery, or chaunting incessantly amidst clustered pillars of linoleum and carpet like lay priests in ruined temples.

The stalls and these overflowings of the shops are intersected by stands where weary marketers may solace themselves with light refreshments in the way of whelks liberally seasoned with vinegar and pepper, cheap but indigestible pastry, toffee, or fried soles; and there are ice-cream barrows that dispense ices and ginger-beer in summer, and in winter supply baked potatoes and hot drinks.

Intersecting other stalls are a cripple in a wheeled-chair manipulating a concertina; a man with a tray suspended round his neck selling "electric" pens; an enormous brass weighing machine that soars up glittering and catching light from all the surrounding naphtha lamps till it seems itself a thing of fire; a galvanic battery and a "lung-tester," both popular with boys, who take shocks from the one and blow into the long tube of the other with a joy in the results that is worth at least twice what they pay for it; and, with a naphtha lamp all to himself, a sombre, wooden-legged man presides over a seedy collection of umbrellas stuck in a ricketty home-made stand and holds a specimen umbrella open over his own head as if he lived at the best of times in an invisible shower.

And buyers are stopping to haggle with the sellers; loafers and lurchers go by continuously; passing by also are rough artisans in their working clothes out shopping with their wives, and dainty fascinating young Jewesses dressed in ornate imitation of the latest West-End fashions and escorted by dapper young Jews in tall hats, resplendent linen, and suits reminiscent of Piccadilly.

Stand aside and see them passing; and here, passing with them, a couple of jovial sailors, arm-in-arm, flourishing their pipes and singing lustily; a wan woman in rusty widow's weeds leading a child in one hand and carrying her frugal marketings in the other; a young man wheeling a perambulator with a baby and some beef and a cabbage in it, while his wife, a keen, brisk little woman, chaffers at the fish stall for something toothsome to take home for supper; dowdy women, Jew and Gentile, in faded bonnets, or bright-coloured shawls, or with no other head-covering than their own plenteous hair; three dandy soldiers making a splash of red where the throng is drabbest; a sleek Oriental, astray from the docks, in his white linen costume and white turban or crimson fez; a lank, long-bearded Hebrew in an ample frock coat and ancient tall hat, moving in profound meditation, with a certain air of aloofness separating him from the surging, restless mob, as if the sanctities of the Synagogue and his newly-ended Sabbath still wrapped him about in an atmosphere of unworldly calm.

A few paces farther on, and here is a weedy youth swathed in a white apron shrilly inviting attention to a pyramid of pigs'-trotters on a board on trestles against the front of a public-house, in the saloon doorway of which a pair of musicians are manufacturing music with a diminutive harmonium and a tin-whistle, while outside the smaller public-house near by gossiping men and women with no taste for either music or pig's-trotters lounge drinking in the open air.

Across in the New Cut, and Lower Marsh, Lambeth, there is the same crush and uproar, the same smoky flare of innumerable naphtha lamps, the same bewildering miscellany of stalls, but the customers and idlers are, on the whole, more poverty-stricken, more depressed, more common-place. There are

SATURDAY NIGHT IN WHITECHAPEL ROAD.

flower-stalls and second-hand book stalls here, as there are in Farringdon Street and Shoreditch High Street; there is a sedate optician's stall with wilted old ladies and gentlemen pottering about it at intervals testing their sights at different-sized letters printed on a card and sparing a trifle from their week's addlings to treat themselves to new pairs of spectacles; there is a misanthropic-looking man sitting on a stool in the gutter with piles of muffins on a small table beside him; and there are the

the road is blocked by an eager concourse of girls and young and elderly women, and peering over their agitated shoulders we focus with difficulty a low, improvised counter buried under stacks of ladies' jackets, blouses, dresses, shawls, while four feminine hucksters, one at each corner of the counter, hold up articles of such wearing apparel for inspection and cackle persuasively in chorus. They do the thing better in such a place as Hoxton Street, for there the roadway is left to every other description of stall, and the

INSIDE A BIG PROVISION STORES (HAMMERSMITH).

usual hawkers wandering up and down with toasting forks, boot-laces, braces, song-sheets, and meat-jacks with wooden legs of mutton turning on them to illustrate their uses.

In nearly every market street to-night there are cheap-jacks selling crockery, and quacks vending corn-cures and ointment, and in some, notably in Stratford High Street and Deptford Broadway, there is occasionally a male quack, or one of the gentler sex, who, to create a sensation and gather an audience, will plant a chair in the public eye and extract the teeth of penurious sufferers gratis.

Half way through one Saturday market

trade in women's clothing is carried on in skeleton shops, the fronts of which have been knocked out so that passing ladies may stray in without hindrance and wallow in second-hand garments that hang thickly round the walls and are strewn and heaped prodigally about the floors.

In other streets we have side-glimpses of brilliantly-lighted interiors opulently festooned and garlanded and hung with cheap boots and shoes, and, thus environed, men and women, affluent with Saturday's wages, examining and selecting from the stock, or a small child on a high chair having a pair of shoes tried on under the critical gaze of

CHINA.

its father and mother and the shopman; or, especially in such localities as Leather Lane and Whitecross Street, where boot-stalls abound, a similar scene is frequently enacting in the open air, with the diminutive customer perched, for "fitting" purposes, close to the stall.

In all the tumultuous market streets, and in broad, centre thoroughfares where there are few or no costermongers, big drapers have a passion for Saturday clearance sales that no woman who loves a bargain is stoical enough to ignore; and provision shops and mammoth general stores, in a cheery glamour of gas or electric light, are simmering and humming like exaggerated hives. Smart servant-maids in some districts, and in all practical housewives, domesticated husbands, children, singly or in pairs, and furnished with baskets and pencilled lists of their requirements, flow in and out of these emporiums in apparently endless streams.

While the Saturday saturnalia is thus at its fiercest and gayest and noisiest throughout the main roads and market streets, in grimy, quiet byways of Whitechapel there are snug Hebrew coffee rooms and restaurants, re-awakened after a Sabbath snooze, wherein Jews of divers nationalities are gossiping over coffee and wine and cigarettes, or beguiling the hours with dominoes and card-playing. In other dim, sinister byways there is, here and there, in an obscure room behind some retiring hostelry, a boxing match going forward for the delectation of an audience of flashy, rowdy sportsmen and

their down-at-heel hangers-on; likewise, about Whitechapel and Bermondsey, Southwark and Soho, in shyer, furtive dens that are overshadowed always by fear of a police raid, there are feverish, secret gamesters gathered round the green tables. In the neighbourhood of Soho — much favoured by exiles from all countries —they are more numerous and of superior quality, and in some exclusive, elegant, equally secret clubs you may gamble with bejewelled gentry whose losses on the turn of the wheel or the cards are far from being limited by the size of a week's salary.

Meanwhile, theatres are full, and music-halls; and Saturday dances, sing-songs, and smoking concerts in assembly rooms and over public-houses are liberally encouraged. When people begin to come out from these entertainments, the crowd that is still abroad marketing is of a poorer, hungrier stamp than that which enlivened the streets an hour or two ago. Stalls are beginning to disappear, and those that remain are mostly refreshment stalls, or fruit and meat stalls that are trying to sell off their surplus stock by auction.

Fruit stalls in Whitechapel Road have a special weakness for finishing up in this way—a way which is common to the meat shops and stalls in all the market streets

OUTSIDE A PUBLIC-HOUSE.

everywhere. The large cheap butchers' shops in Bermondsey and elsewhere make a practice of "selling off" by auction all the evening, but elsewhere it is the custom to adopt this course only after ten o'clock.

Then, after ten o'clock, you may see feminine butchers hammering on their stalls with the blunt ends of their choppers, and shouting and cheapening their primest beef and mutton as frantically and as successfully as any butcher of the sterner sex who, goaded to frenzy by the approach of midnight, is pedestalled on his stall, or on the block in his doorway or the sloping flap outside his window, and is lifting meat boastfully in both hands, offering it at absurdly high prices, and yet selling it for ever so little a pound to whomsoever will buy.

Rain or snow will thin the streets by keeping folk at home or driving them to the nearest shops, or to such roofed paradises for the small trader as the Portman Market off Edgware Road. But to-night has been fine, and everything at its best.

And now 'buses and trams begin to fill with laughing, chattering myriads returning from the theatres, and with shop assistants just emancipated. Laundry vans are coming back from delivering the last of their washing; in thousands of lowly, decent households busy mothers are ironing the last of to-morrow's linen on a corner of the supper table, or the whole family are seated to a rare but inexpensive feast at the latter end of a hard week.

Twelve strikes, and the public-houses close, not without brawling and a drunken fight or two; but the last stragglers will soon be making for home; the last stall will soon have packed up and gone away; the latest shop will be putting up its shutters, and all the flare and fever and flurry and wrangling and business and merriment of Saturday night will be quieting down at last under the touch of Sunday morning.

SELLING MEAT BY AUCTION.

PRINTED BY CASSELL AND COMPANY, LIMITED, LA BELLE SAUVAGE, LUDGATE HILL, LONDON, E.C.

SELECTIONS FROM
CASSELL & COMPANY'S PUBLICATIONS.

ILLUSTRATED AND FINE ART WORKS.

The Coronation Book of Edward VII., King of All the Britains and Emperor of India. By W. J. LOFTIE, B.A., F.S.A. With 24 Coloured Plates and numerous Illustrations. Sumptuously Illuminated in Gold and Colours. 10s. 6d.

The National Gallery. Edited by Sir EDWARD J. POYNTER, P.R.A. Illustrating every Picture in the National Gallery. In Three Volumes. The price has now been raised to £14 14s. the set, net.

The National Portrait Gallery. Edited by LIONEL CUST, M.A., F.S.A. *An Edition de Luxe.* Limited to 750 copies, numbered. Containing reproductions of every Picture in the Gallery. In Two Volumes, paper covers, 6 guineas the set net; half morocco, 8 guineas net; full morocco, 10 guineas net.

The Life and Paintings of Vicat Cole, R.A. Illustrated with 59 Full Plates, and numerous smaller Plates of Pictures and Studies, reproduced from Photographs by Collotype and other Processes. In Three Volumes, £3 3s. the set.

Sights and Scenes in Oxford City and University. With upwards of 100 Plates after Original Photographs. In One Volume, 21s. net.

Rivers of Great Britain. Descriptive, Historical, Pictorial.
Rivers of the East Coast. With numerous highly finished Engravings. Royal 4to, with Etching as Frontispiece, 42s. *Popular Edition,* 16s.
Rivers of the South and West Coasts. With Etching as Frontispiece and numerous Illustrations in Text. Royal 4to, 42s. *Popular Edition,* 16s.

The Works of Charles Burton Barber. Illustrated with 41 Plates and Portrait, and containing an Introduction by HARRY FURNISS. Royal 4to, cloth, gilt top, 7s. 6d.

Annals of Westminster Abbey. By E. T. BRADLEY (Mrs. A. MURRAY SMITH). Illustrated by H. M. PAGET, W. HATHERELL, R.I., and F. WALKER, F.S.A. With a Preface by the Dean of Westminster. Royal 4to. *Cheap Edition,* 21s.

The History of "Punch." By M. H. SPIELMANN. With about 170 Illustrations, Portraits, and Facsimiles. Cloth, 16s.; *Large Paper Edition,* £2 2s, net.

Horses and Dogs. By O. EERELMAN. With Descriptive Text. Translated from the Dutch by CLARA BELL. With Photogravure Frontispiece, 12 Exquisite Collotypes, and Several Full-page and other Engravings in the Text. 25s, net.

The Magazine of Art. Yearly Volume. With a Series of Exquisite Plates, and about 800 Illustrations from Original Drawings by the First Artists of the Day and from Famous Paintings. Cloth gilt, gilt edges, 21s.

British Sculpture and Sculptors of To-day. By M. H. SPIELMANN. Illustrated. Paper, 5s. net; Cloth, 7s. 6d. net.

Chinese Porcelain. By COSMO MONKHOUSE. Preface and Notes by Dr. S. W. BUSHELL. With Coloured Plates. 30s. net.

English Porcelain. By W. BURTON. With 83 Plates, including 35 in Colours. *Limited Edition.* 30s. net.

The Tidal Thames. By GRANT ALLEN. With India-proof impressions of 20 magnificent Full-page Photogravure Plates, and with many other Illustrations in the text, after original drawings by W. L. WYLLIE, A.R.A. 42s. net.

Landscape Painting in Water Colours. By J. MACWHIRTER, R.A. With 23 Coloured Plates, 5s.

Marine Painting in Water Colour. By W. L. WYLLIE, A.R.A. With 23 Coloured Plates, 5s.

Cathedrals, Abbeys, and Churches of England and Wales: Descriptive, Historical, Pictorial. With nearly 500 Illustrations. *Popular Edition,* in Two Vols., cloth, 12s. the set.

Familiar Garden Flowers. By F. E. HULME. Cheap Edition. Complete in Five Vols. With 40 Full-page Original Coloured Plates in each. 3s. 6d. each.

Familiar Wild Flowers. By F. E. HULME, F.L.S., &c. Cheap Edition. Complete in Six Vols. With 40 Full-page Original Coloured Plates in each. 3s. 6d. each. In Paste Grain, Six Volumes, In box to match, 25s, net.

A Masque of Days. From the Last Essays of Elia. By WALTER CRANE. With 40 Designs in Colour. 6s.

The Wallace Collection at Hertford House. Being Notes on the Pictures and other Works of Art, with special reference to the history of their acquisition. By M. H. SPIELMANN. With numerous illustrations. Paper covers, 1s.

Ballads and Songs. By WILLIAM MAKEPEACE THACKERAY. With Original Illustrations by H. M. BROCK. 6s.

British Ballads. With 300 Original Illustrations. *Cheap Edition.* Two Vols. in One, cloth, 7s. 6d.

The Nation's Pictures. A Selection from the most modern Paintings in the Public Picture Galleries of Great Britain, Vols. I. and II. (each complete in itself), containing 48 Pictures reproduced in Colour by the latest and most perfect process of Chromo-photography. Cloth, 12s.; half leather, 15s.

The Queen's London. Containing about 450 Exquisite Views of London and its Environs, together with a fine series of Pictures of Queen Victoria's Diamond Jubilee and Funeral Processions. *New and Enlarged Edition,* 10s. 6d.

The Queen's Empire. In Two Volumes, containing nearly 700 splendid full-page illustrations, reproduced from photographs, a large number of which have been made specially for this work, and printed on Plate Paper. Cloth, 9s. each.

Pictorial England and Wales. With upwards of 320 beautiful Illustrations prepared from copyright photographs. Cloth gilt, 9s. Superior paper, half persian, in box, 15s. net.

Pictorial Scotland and Ireland. With 320 Copyright Illustrations. 9s.

Pictorial Scotland. With 225 Copyright Illustrations, 7s. 6d.

Sacred Art. The Bible Story Pictured by Eminent Modern Painters. Edited by A. G. TEMPLE, F.S.A. With nearly 200 Full-page Illustrations, beautifully printed on plate paper, and descriptive text. Large 4to, 9s.

Peril and Patriotism: True Tales of Heroic Deeds and Startling Adventures. Profusely Illustrated. 5s.

Picturesque Mediterranean, The. With a Series of Magnificent Illustrations from Original Designs by leading Artists of the day. In 2 Vols. £3 2s. each.

Picturesque Europe. Complete in Five Volumes. 6s. each. Containing 13 Exquisite Steel Plates, and about 200 Original Engravings, 18s. each. THE BRITISH ISLES. *Cheap Edition.* Containing 13 exquisite Litho Plates, and about 400 Original Engravings. (Two Vols. in One), 10s. 6d.

Picturesque America. In Four Vols. With 12 Exquisite Steel Plates and about 200 Original Wood Engravings in each. £12 12s. the Set. *Popular Edition.* 18s. each.

Picturesque Canada. With about Six Hundred Original Illustrations. Complete in Two Volumes. £9 9s. the set.

Egypt: Descriptive, Historical, and Picturesque. By Prof. G. EBERS. Translated by CLARA BELL. With about 800 Magnificent Original Illustrations. *Popular Edition,* in Two Volumes, cloth, gilt edges, 42s.

Our Own Country. With about 1,200 Original Illustrations and Steel Frontispieces. *Cheap Edition.* Three Double Vols., 5s. each.

London Afternoons. By W. J. LOFTIE, F.S.A. Illustrated. 10s. 6d. net.

Old and New London. Complete in Six Vols., with about 1,200 Engravings. *Cheap Edition,* 4s. 6d. each. Vols. I. and II. are by WALTER THORNBURY, the other Vols. are by EDWARD WALFORD.

Greater London. By EDWARD WALFORD. With about 400 Original Illustrations. Two Vols. *Cheap Edition,* 4s. 6d. each.

The Countries of the World. By Dr. ROBERT BROWN. Illustrated. *Cheap Edition.* Complete in Six Vols. 6s. each.

The Royal Shakspere. *People's Edition.* With over 50 Full-page Illustrations. In Three Volumes. 15s. the set.

Universal History, Cassell's Illustrated. Profusely Illustrated. *Cheap Edition.* Complete in Four Vols. 5s. each.

Wars of the 'Nineties, The. A History of the Warfare of the Last Ten Years of the Nineteenth Century. By A. HILLIARD ATTERIDGE. Profusely Illustrated. In One Vol., 7s. 6d.

The Doré Fine-Art Volumes:—
The Doré Bible. *Popular Edition,* 15s. Also in leather binding, price on application.
Milton's Paradise Lost. *Cheap Edition,* 12s. 6d.; *Popular Edition,* 7s. 6d.
Doré Gallery, The. *Popular Edition,* 42s.
Dante's Inferno. *Large 4to Edition,* 21s.
Dante's Purgatory and Paradise. *Cheap Edition,* 7s. 6d.
The Doré Don Quixote. *Cheap Edition,* 10s. 6d.

The Story of the Sea. Edited by "Q." Illustrated. *Cheap Edition.* In Two Vols. 5s. each.

The World of Adventure. Profusely Illustrated with stirring Pictures and Eighteen Coloured Plates. In Three Vols. 5s. each.

CASSELL & COMPANY, LIMITED: LONDON, PARIS, NEW YORK & MELBOURNE.

BIOGRAPHY, TRAVELS, HISTORY, LITERATURE, CYCLOPÆDIAS, &c.

Aconcágua and Tierra del Fuego. By Sir MARTIN CONWAY. Illustrated. 12s. 6d. net.

British Nigeria. By Lieut.-Col. MOCKLER FERRY-MAN. With 16 Illustrations. 12s. 6d. net.

The Dominion of the Air: The Story of Aerial Navigation. By the Rev. J. M. BACON. With numerous Illustrations from Photographs. 6s.

The Land of the Dons. By LEONARD WILLIAMS. With about 42 Illustrations. 15s. net.

Pictures of Many Wars. By FREDERIC VIL-LIERS. A Thrilling Narrative of Experiences on the Battlefield and Reminiscences of a world-famous War Correspondent in many parts of the Globe. Illustrated. 6s.

Britain at Work. A Pictorial Description of our National Industries. Written by popular authors, and containing nearly 500 Illustrations. 12s.

Madrid: Her Records and Romances. By LEONARD WILLIAMS. With 20 Illustrations. 10s. net.

The Life of the Rev. Joseph Parker, D.D. By the Rev. WM. ADAMSON, D.D. With Portraits and Illustrations. Cloth, 6s. net.

The Real Siberia. By J. FOSTER FRASER. Illustrated. 6s.

Her Majesty's Tower. By HEPWORTH DIXON. With an Introduction by W. J. LOFTIE, B.A., F.S.A., and containing 16 Coloured Plates specially prepared by H. E. TIDMARSH. *Popular Edition.* Two Vols. 12s. the Set.

Behind the Scenes in the Transvaal. By D. M. WILSON. 7s. 6d.

With the "Ophir" Round the Empire. By WILLIAM MAXWELL. Illustrated. 6s.

An Eton Boy's Letters. By NUGENT BANKES. 5s.

Memoirs and Correspondence of Lyon Playfair. First Lord Playfair of St. Andrews. By Sir WEMYSS REID. *Cheap Edition,* 7s. 6d.

The Life of William Ewart Gladstone. Edited by Sir WEMYSS REID. Profusely Illustrated. In One Vol., cloth, 7s. 6d. ; or, in Two Vols., cloth, gilt top, 9s.

Houghton, Lord. The Life, Letters, and Friendships of Richard Monckton Milnes, First Lord Houghton. By Sir T. WEMYSS REID. Two Vols., 32s.

William Landels, D.D. By the Rev. THOMAS D. LANDELS, M.A. Cloth, 6s.

Britain's Roll of Glory; or, The Victoria Cross, its Heroes, and their Valour. By D. H. PARRY. With 8 Full-page Illustrations. *New and Enlarged Edition.* Cloth, gilt edges, 5s. This volume contains a description of the deeds which won the V.C. during the recent South African War.

The Black Watch. The Record of an Historic Regiment. By ARCHIBALD FORBES, LL.D. *Popular Edition.* With 8 Illustrations. 3s. 6d.

The Tale of a Field Hospital. By Sir FREDERICK TREVES, Bart., K.C.V.O., C.B., F.R.C.S. *Popular Edition* With 14 Full-page Illustrations from Photographs. 3s. 6d.

Social England. A Record of the Progress of the People in Religion, Laws, Learning, Arts, Science, Literature, and Manners, from the Earliest Times to the Present Day. By various Writers. Edited by H. D. TRAILL, D.C.L., and J. S. MANN, M.A. *Illustrated Edition.* Vol. I., 12s. net; Vols. II. and III., 14s. net. each. To be completed in Six Vols.

The Automobile. From the French of Gerard Lavergne. Revised and Edited by PAUL N. HASLUCK. With 536 Illustrations. 10s. 6d. net.

Cassell's New French Dictionary. Edited by JAMES BOÏELLE, B.A., late Examiner in the University of London. 7s. 6d.

Living London. Edited by GEORGE R. SIMS. Vols. I. and II., each containing upwards of 450 Illustrations from Photographs and Drawings by leading Artists. Cloth, 12s. each ; half leather, 16s. each.

Cassell's Dictionary of Practical Garden-ing. Edited by WALTER P. WRIGHT. With 20 Coloured Plates, and upwards of 1,000 Illustrations from Photographs taken direct from Nature. Complete in Two Vols., half leather, gilt top, 30s. net.

Cassell's Family Doctor. By A MEDICAL MAN. Illustrated. *Cheap Edition,* 6s.

Cassell's Family Lawyer. A Popular Exposition of the Civil Law of England and Scotland. 10s. 6d.

The Law and History of Copyright in Books. By AUGUSTINE BIRRELL, M.P. 3s. 6d. net.

The Dictionary of English History. Edited by SIDNEY J. LOW, B.A., and Prof. F. S. PULLING, M.A. *New and Revised Edition.* 7s. 6d.

Memories and Studies of War and Peace. By ARCHIBALD FORBES, LL.D. *Cheap Edition,* 6s.

The Encyclopædic Dictionary. *New Edition* brought up to date with thousands of words added. 7s. 6d.

Cassell's Biographical Dictionary, containing Memoirs of the Most Eminent Men and Women of all Ages and Countries. *Cheap Edition,* 3s. 6d.

Cassell's Cyclopædia of Mechanics. Edited by PAUL N. HASLUCK. With upwards of 2,400 Illustrations. Series I., 7s. 6d. Series II., 7s. 6d.

Cassell's Miniature Cyclopædia. Containing 30,000 Subjects. *Cheap Edition,* 1s. ; cloth, 1s. 6d.

Cassell's Concise Cyclopædia. With about 600 Illustrations. *Cheap Edition.* 5s.

English Writers. By HENRY MORLEY, LL.D. In 11 Vols., 5s. each.

SCIENCE AND NATURAL HISTORY.

Works by Richard Kearton, F.Z.S. Illustrated from Photographs taken direct from Nature by C. Kearton.

White's Natural History of Selborne. With Notes by R. KEARTON, F.Z.S. Author of "With Nature and a Camera," &c. Containing over 100 Illustrations from Photographs by CHERRY and RICHARD KEARTON. 6s.

Strange Adventures in Dicky-Bird Land. Cloth, 3s. 6d. ; cloth gilt, gilt edges, 5s.

Our Bird Friends. A Book for all Boys and Girls. With 100 Illustrations. Cloth gilt, 5s.

Birds, Our Rarer British Breeding: Their Nests, Eggs, and Summer Haunts. With about 70 Illustrations. 7s. 6d.

Wild Life at Home: How to Study and Photograph It. With about 100 Illustrations from Photographs. 6s.

With Nature and a Camera. With 180 Pictures of Birds, Animals, &c., from Photographs. *Cheap Edition,* 7s. 6d.

British Birds' Nests: How, Where, and When to Find and Identify Them. With nearly 150 Illustrations of Nests, Eggs, Young, etc., from Photographs by C. KEARTON. 21s.

The Century Science Series. Edited by Sir HENRY ROSCOE, D.C.L., F.R.S. *Cheap Edition,* 2s. 6d. each. (*A List sent post free on application.*)

Practical Electricity. Completely rewritten by Prof. W. E. AYRTON, F.R.S. With 247 Illustrations. 9s.

The Story of Our Planet. By Prof. BONNEY, F.R.S. With Six Coloured Plates and Maps, and about 100 Illustrations. *Cheap Edition,* 7s. 6d.

The Earth's Beginning. By Sir ROBERT BALL, LL.D., etc. Illustrated. 7s. 6d.

The Story of the Sun. By Sir ROBERT BALL, LL.D., &c. *Cheap Edition.* Illustrated. 10s. 6d.

The Story of the Heavens. By Sir ROBERT BALL, LL.D., &c. Illustrated. *Cheap Edition,* 10s. 6d.

Star-Land. By Sir ROBERT BALL, LL.D., &c. Illustrated. *Revised Edition.* 7s. 6d.

Popular History of Animals for Young People. By HENRY SCHERREN, F.Z.S. With 13 Coloured Plates and Numerous Illustrations in the Text. 6s.

Natural History, Cassell's. With about 2,000 Illustrations. *Cheap Edition.* Three Double Vols., 6s. each.

Figuier's Popular Scientific Works. Six Volumes. Fully Illustrated. *Cheap Edition,* 3s. 6d. each.

Science for All. *Revised Edition.* Edited by Dr. ROBERT BROWN, F.R.G.S., &c. Complete in Five Vols., with over 1,700 Illustrations. 3s. 6d. each.

Our Earth and its Story. Edited by Dr. ROBERT BROWN. Illustrated. *Cheap Edition.* Three Volumes. 5s. each.

Familiar Butterflies and Moths. By W. KIRBY, F.S.A. With 18 Coloured Plates. Price 6s.

Illustrated Book of the Dog. By VERO SHAW, B.A. With Coloured Plates. Cloth, 35s. ; half morocco, 45s.

Canaries and Cage-Birds, The Illustrated Book of. With 56 Facsimile Coloured Plates. Cloth, 35s. ; half morocco, 45s.

The New Book of Poultry. By L. WRIGHT. With 30 Coloured Plates. *New Edition.* 21s.

The Practical Poultry Keeper. By LEWIS WRIGHT. With Eight Coloured Plates and numerous Illustrations in Text. *New and Enlarged Edition.* 3s. 6d.

The Practical Rabbit-Keeper. By "CUNI-CULUS," assisted by Eminent Fanciers. With Illustrations.

CASSELL & COMPANY, LIMITED: LONDON, PARIS, NEW YORK & MELBOURNE.

BIBLES, RELIGIOUS WORKS, &c.

Works by the Very Rev. Dean Farrar, D.D., F.R.S.

The Life of Lives: Further Studies in the Life of Christ. 15s.

The Life of Christ.
Illustrated Edition. Large type, 4to, cloth, 7s. 6d.; cloth, full gilt, gilt edges, 10s. 6d.
Popular Edition. Cloth gilt, gilt edges, 7s. 6d.
Cheap Edition, with 16 Full-page Plates, cloth gilt, 3s. 6d.

The Life and Work of St. Paul.
Library Edition (20th Thousand). Two Vols., 24s.; morocco, £2 2s.
Illustrated Edition, 4to, cloth, £1 1s.; morocco, £2 2s.
Illustrated Edition, large type, 4to, 7s. 6d.
Cheap Edition, with 16 Full-page Plates, 3s. 6d.
Popular Edition. Cloth, gilt edges, 7s. 6d.

The Early Days of Christianity.
Library Edition (Ninth Thousand). Two Vols., demy 8vo, 24s. Morocco, £2 2s.
Popular Edition, complete in One Volume, cloth, gilt edges, 7s. 6d.
Cheap Edition, cloth gilt, 3s. 6d.

The Three Homes. Illustrated. *New Edition*, 3s. 6d.

Early Christianity and Paganism. By the Very Rev. H. D. M. SPENCE, D.D. Illustrated. 18s. net.

Side-Lights on the Conflicts of Methodism. During the Second Quarter of the Nineteenth Century, 1827-1852. *Cheap Edition.* Unabridged. Cloth, 3s. 6d.

The Family Prayer Book. Edited by CANON GARBETT, M.A., and Rev. S. MARTIN. Illustrated. 7s. 6d.

The Old Testament Commentary for English Readers. Edited by BISHOP ELLICOTT. *Popular Edition*, unabridged. Five Vols., 6s. each.

The New Testament Commentary for English Readers. Edited by BISHOP ELLICOTT. *Popular Edition*, unabridged. Three Vols., 6s. each.

Special Pocket Editions of Ellicott's Commentaries. ST. MATTHEW, ST. MARK, ST. LUKE, ST. JOHN. On Thin Paper. Foolscap 8vo, 2s. each.

Cassell's Guinea Bible. With 900 Illustrations and Coloured Maps. Royal 4to, leather, 21s. net. Persian antique, with corners and clasps, 25s. net.

Life and Work of Our Redeemer. By Eminent Divines. Illustrated. 6s.

The Doré Bible. *Popular Edition*, with 200 Full-page Illustrations by GUSTAVE DORÉ. In One Vol., cloth gilt, gilt edges, 15s. Also in leather binding, price on application.

Holy Land and the Bible, The. A Book of Scripture Illustrations gathered in Palestine. By the Rev. CUNNINGHAM GEIKIE, D.D. *Cheap Edition*, 7s. 6d. *Superior Edition*, with 24 Collotype Plates, 10s. 6d.

The History of Protestantism. By the Rev. J. A. WYLIE, LL.D. Containing upwards of 600 Original Illustrations. *Cheap Edition.* Complete in Three Vols., 5s. each.

Matin and Vesper Bells. Earlier and Later Collected Poems (Chiefly Sacred). By J. R. MACDUFF, D.D. With Frontispiece. Two Vols., cloth, 7s. 6d. the set.

The Church of England. A History for the People. By the Very Rev. H. D. M. SPENCE, D.D., Dean of Gloucester. Illustrated. Complete in Four Vols., 6s. each. *Popular Edition.* 3s. 6d.

Cassell's Illustrated Bunyan. With 200 Original Illustrations. *Popular Edition.* 3s. 6d.

Quiver, The. For Sunday and General Reading. With about 900 Original Illustrations and Coloured Picture for Frontispiece. Yearly Volume, 7s. 6d.; Monthly Parts, 6d.

Bible Dictionary, Cassell's Concise. By the Rev. ROBERT HUNTER, LL.D., F.G.S. With 12 Coloured Page Maps, and large Map of Palestine in Pocket. 6s.

The Child's Life of Christ. With about 200 Original Illustrations. 7s. 6d. Superior Edition, 10s. 6d.

BIBLE BIOGRAPHIES.
Extra foolscap 8vo. Illustrated. 1s. 6d. each.

The Story of Moses and Joshua. By the Rev. J. TELFORD.

The Story of the Judges. By the Rev. J. WYCLIFFE GEDGE.

The Story of Samuel and Saul. By the Rev. D. C. TOVEY.

The Story of David. By the Rev. J. WILD.

The Story of Joseph. Its Lessons for To-day. By the Rev. GEORGE BAINTON.

The Story of Jesus. In Verse. By J. R. MACDUFF, D.D. Illustrated.

FICTION AND MISCELLANEOUS WORKS.

Under the Iron Flail. By JOHN OXENHAM. 6s.

Nebo the Nailer. By the Rev. S. BARING-GOULD. 6s.

A Fair Freebooter. By BASIL MARNAN. 6s.

The Cloistering of Ursula. By CLINTON SCOLLARD. 6s.

The Dictator's Daughter. By EDGAR JEPSON. 6s.

The Lord Protector. By S. LEVETT-YEATS. 6s.

Under the White Cockade. By HALLIWELL SUTCLIFFE. 6s.

Bakshish. By ROMA WHITE. 6s.

Tommy and Grizel. 6s.
Sentimental Tommy. 6s.
The Little Minister. Illus. 6s.
} By J. M. BARRIE.

The Giant's Gate. 6s.
The Garden of Swords. Illus. 6s.
Kronstadt. 6s.
The Impregnable City. 3s. 6d. 6s.
Sea Wolves, The. 3s. 6d.
The Iron Pirate. 3s. 6d.
} By MAX PEMBERTON.

Kate Bonnet. 6s.
Afield and Afloat. 6s.
The Vizier of the Two-Horned Alexander. 3s. 6d.
The Girl at Cobhurst. 3s. 6d.
Mrs. Cliff's Yacht. 3s. 6d.
The Adventures of Captain Horn. 3s. 6d.
} By FRANK STOCKTON.

A Bitter Heritage. 6s.
A Vanished Rival. 6s.
} By J. BLOUNDELLE BURTON.

Alice of Old Vincennes. By MAURICE THOMPSON. 6s.

The Princess Cynthia. By MARGUERITE BRYANT. 6s.

Lepidus the Centurion. By EDWIN LESTER ARNOLD. 6s.

Spectre Gold: A Romance of Klondyke. By HEADON HILL. 6s.

A Soldier of the King. By DORA M. JONES. 6s.

Volumes by R. L. Stevenson :—
Treasure Island.
Kidnapped.
Catriona.
The Wrecker.
The Master of Ballantrae.
Island Nights' Entertainments. 3s. 6d. only.
The Black Arrow.
} Library Edition, 6s. each. Popular Edition, 3s. 6d. each.

People's Editions at 6d. are issued of these Books.

Cupid's Garden. By ELLEN THORNEYCROFT FOWLER. *Cheap Edition*, 3s. 6d.
The Laird's Luck. 6s.
Old Fires and Profitable Ghosts. 6s.
The Ship of Stars. 6s.
Dead Man's Rock. 5s.
The Delectable Duchy. 5s.
"I Saw Three Ships." 5s.
Noughts and Crosses. 5s.
The Splendid Spur. *Cheap Edition*, 3s. 6d.
The Astonishing History of Troy Town. 5s.
Wandering Heath. 5s.
Ia. A Love Story. 3s. 6d.
} Volumes by Q. (A. T. QUILLER COUCH).

King Solomon's Mines. By RIDER HAGGARD. Illustrated. 3s. 6d. *People's Edition*, 6d.

Ill-Gotten Gold. By W. G. TARBET. 6s.

Cassell's Magazine. With upwards of 1,000 Original Illustrations. Yearly Vol., 8s. Half yearly Vol., 5s.

The New Penny Magazine. With 650 Illustrations. Quarterly Volumes, 2s. 6d. each.

Cassell's Saturday Journal. Yearly Volume. New and Enlarged Series. Illustrated throughout. 8s.

Chums. The Illustrated Paper for Boys. Yearly Vol. 8s.

The Gardener. Yearly Volume, 7s. 6d.

Work: The Handy Man's Paper. Half-Yearly Volume, 4s. 6d.

Building World. Half-Yearly Volume, 4s. 6d.

CASSELL & COMPANY, LIMITED: LONDON, PARIS, NEW YORK & MELBOURNE.

EDUCATIONAL WORKS.

Cassell's Brush Work Series; the Colour-Box Superseded. Series I.—WILD FLOWERS. Series II.—PICTURES WANTING WORDS. Series III.—ENTERTAINING PICTURES. 3d. per Set, each containing 12 Sheets. Each Sheet includes a Set of Six Water Colours.

Things New and Old, Scholars' Companion to. Five Books. 2d. each.

Eyes and No Eyes Series, Cassell's. By ARABELLA BUCKLEY. In Six Books. Books 1 and 2, 4d. each; Books 3 to 6, 6d. each: or in One Volume, complete, 3s. 6d.

The Coming of The Kilogram; or, The Battle of the Standards. By H. O. ARNOLD-FORSTER, M.A. Illustrated. *Cheap Edition*, 6d.

A History of England. From the Landing of Julius Cæsar to the Present Day. By H. O. ARNOLD-FORSTER, M.A. Illustrated. 5s.

Founders of the Empire. By PHILIP GIBBS. Illustrated. Cloth, 1s. 8d.

English Literature, A First Sketch of. By Professor HENRY MORLEY. *New and Cheap Edition.* 7s. 6d.

Cassell's New Geographical Readers. Illustrated. Seven Books, from 9d. to 1s. 9d. each.

Geography: A Practical Method of Teaching. Two Vols. 6d. each.

In Danger's Hour; or, Stout Hearts and Stirring Deeds. A Book of Adventures for School and Home. With Coloured Plates and other Illustrations. 1s. 8d. Bevelled boards, gilt, gilt edges, 2s. 6d.

This World of Ours. By H. O. ARNOLD-FORSTER, M.A. Illustrated. *Cheap Edition*, 2s. 6d.

Things New and Old; or, Stories from English History. By H. O. ARNOLD-FORSTER, M.A. Fully Illustrated and strongly bound in cloth. Books for the Seven Standards, 9d. to 1s. 8d. each.

Object Lessons from Nature. By Prof. L. C. MIALL, F.L.S. Illustrated. Two Vols., 1s. 6d. each.

Gaudeamus. A Selection of 100 Songs for Colleges and Schools. Edited by JOHN FARMER. Words and Music, cloth gilt, 5s. Words of the Songs, paper covers, 6d.; cloth, 9d.

Dulce Domum. Rhymes and Songs for Children. Edited by JOHN FARMER. 4to edition, 5s. Two Parts, 6d. each.

Little Folks' History of England. By ISA CRAIG-KNOX. With Thirty Illustrations. Cloth, 1s. 6d.

Hand and Eye Training. By GEORGE RICKS, B.Sc., and JOSEPH VAUGHAN. Five Vols., varying in price from 2s. to 6s. each.

The Young Citizen; or, Lessons in Our Laws. By H. F. LESTER, B.A. Illustrated, 2s. 6d. (Also in Two Parts under the title of "Lessons in Our Laws." 1s. 6d. each.)

A Complete Manual of Spelling. On the Principles of Contrast and Comparison. By J. D. MORELL, LL.D. Cloth, 1s. *Cheap Edition*, 6d.

Geographical Readers, Modern School.

Modern School Readers, Cassell's.

Modern School Copy Books, Cassell's.

** *For particulars of the above Series of Elementary School Books see Cassell & Company's Educational Catalogue.*

Cassell's NEW French Dictionary. Edited by JAMES BOIELLE, B.A. Cloth, 7s. 6d.; half leather, 10s. 6d.

Cassell's German-English, English-German Dictionary. *Cheap Edition.* Cloth, 3s. 6d.

Cassell's Latin Dictionary (LATIN-ENGLISH AND ENGLISH-LATIN). Cloth, 3s. 6d.

Popular Educator, Cassell's. With Illustrations, Coloured Plates, and Maps in Colours. Complete in Eight Vols., 5s. each.

Cassell's Technical Educator. An Entirely New Work, with Coloured Plates and Engravings. Complete in Six Vols., 3s. 6d. each.

The Marlborough German Grammar. Arranged and Compiled by the Rev. J. F. BRIGHT, M.A. 3s. 6d.

The Marlborough French Grammar. *New and Revised Edition.* Cloth, 2s. 6d.

The Marlborough French Exercises. *New and Revised Edition.* Cloth, 3s. 6d.

Marlborough Arithmetic Examples. 3s.

Cassell's Lessons in French. With Supplement on French Syntax. *New and Revised Edition.* In Two Parts, cloth, 1s. 6d. each. Complete in One Vol., 2s. 6d.

China Painting. By Miss FLORENCE LEWIS. With 16 Original Coloured Plates. 5s.

Neutral Tint, A Course of Painting in. With 24 Plates from Designs by R. P. LEITCH. 4to, cloth, 5s.

BOOKS FOR CHILDREN AND YOUNG PEOPLE.

Little Folks. Half-yearly Volumes. With Six Full-page Coloured Plates and numerous Illustrations printed in Colour. Boards, 3s. 6d.; cloth, 5s.

Bo-Peep. A Treasury for the Little Ones. With Eight Coloured Plates, and numerous Illustrations in Colour. Boards, 2s. 6d.; cloth, 3s. 6d.

Tiny Tots. Yearly Volume. 1s. 4d.; cloth, 1s. 6d.

The Ten Travellers. By S. H. HAMER. With Four Coloured Plates and numerous Illustrations by HARRY B. NEILSON. 1s. 6d.

Birds, Beasts, and Fishes. By S. H. HAMER. With Four Coloured Plates and numerous Illustrations. 1s. 6d.

Topsy Turvy Tales. By S. H. HAMER. With Four Coloured Plates and Illustrations by HARRY B. NEILSON. 1s. 6d.

The Jungle School: or, Dr. Jibber-Jabber Burchall's Academy. By S. H. HAMER. With Four Coloured Plates and other Illustrations by HARRY B. NEILSON. 1s. 6d.

Peter Piper's Peepshow; or, All the Fun of the Fair. By S. H. HAMER. With Four Coloured Plates and other Illustrations by LEWIS BAUMER. 1s. 6d.

Animal Land for Little People. By S. H. HAMER. Illustrated from Photographs and Original Drawings, and containing Four Coloured Plates. 1s. 6d.

Beneath the Banner. Being Narratives of Noble Lives and Brave Deeds. By F. J. CROSS. *Revised and Enlarged Edition.* Illustrated. Limp cloth, 1s.; cloth boards, gilt edges, 2s.

Notable Shipwrecks. *Cheap Edition. Revised and Enlarged.* Limp Cloth, 1s. *Illustrated Edition.* Cloth gilt, bevelled boards, 2s.

The Master of the Strong Hearts. A Story of Custer's Last Rally. By E. S. BROOKS. Illustrated. 2s. 6d.

Sisters Three. By JESSIE MANSERGH. With Eight Plates. 3s. 6d.

Tom and Some Other Girls. By JESSIE MANSERGH. With Eight Plates. 3s. 6d.

New Edition of Works by Mrs. L. T. Meade:—

A World of Girls.
Red Rose and Tiger Lily.
Bashful Fifteen.
A Sweet Girl Graduate.
The Rebellion of Lil Carrington.
Merry Girls of England.
Polly: A New-Fashioned Girl.
The Palace Beautiful.

Each containing 8 Coloured Plates 288 pp., Ex. Crown 8vo. 3s. 6d.

Blazing Arrow.
Chieftain and Scout. } By EDWARD S. ELLIS. Illustrated. 2s. 6d. each.

Bear Cavern. By EDWARD S. ELLIS. Illustrated. 1s. 6d. (*For Titles of other Volumes by E. S. Ellis, see Cassell & Company's Catalogue.*)

Five Stars in a Little Pool. By EDITH CARRINGTON. Illustrated. 3s. 6d.

A Girl Without Ambition. By ISABEL SUART ROBSON. With Eight Plates. 3s. 6d.

Mrs. Pederson's Niece. By ISABEL SUART ROBSON. With Eight Plates. 3s. 6d.

The White House at Inch Gow. By Mrs. PITT. Illustrated. *Cheap Edition*, 2s. 6d.

Little Mother Bunch. By Mrs. MOLESWORTH. Illustrated. Cloth, 2s. 6d.

Magic at Home. By Prof. HOFFMAN. Fully Illustrated. 3s. 6d.

With Redskins on the Warpath. By S. WALKEY. 2s. 6d.

CASSELL & COMPANY'S COMPLETE CATALOGUE, containing a List of upwards of ONE THOUSAND VOLUMES, including Bibles and Religious Works, Fine Art Volumes, Children's Books, Dictionaries, Educational Works, History, Natural History, Household and Domestic Treatises, Handbooks and Guides, Science, Travels, &c. &c., together with a Synopsis of their numerous Illustrated Serial Publications, sent post free on application to CASSELL & COMPANY, LIMITED, Ludgate Hill, London.

CASSELL & COMPANY, LIMITED: LONDON, PARIS, NEW YORK & MELBOURNE.